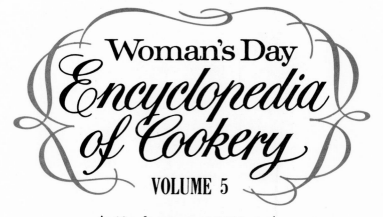

Woman's Day
Encyclopedia of Cookery
VOLUME 5

in 12 volumes—over 2,000 pages—
with more than 1,500 illustrations in color,
1,000 entries and 8,500 recipes
1,200 menus, 50 specialty cook books
and a host of delightful features by distinguished food writers.

ॐ

Prepared and edited by the Editors of Woman's Day
Editor: EILEEN TIGHE
Managing Editor: EVELYN GRANT   *Food Editor:* GLENNA MCGINNIS
Art Consultant: HAROLD SITTERLE   *Photographic Editor:* BEN CALVO
Associates: OLIVIA RISBERG, CHARLOTTE SCRIPTURE,
CAROLYN STORM, JOHANNA BAFARO

ॐ

SPECIAL PROJECT STAFF
Editor: NIKA STANDEN HAZELTON   *Art Director:* LEONARD A. ROMAGNA
Associates: L. GERALDINE MARSTELLER, HELEN FEINGOLD,
SUSAN J. KNOX, INEZ M. KRECH

ॐ

FAWCETT PUBLICATIONS, INC.   NEW YORK

PRINTED AND BOUND BY
FAWCETT-HAYNES PRINTING CORPORATION
ROCKVILLE, MARYLAND

Table of Contents

VOLUME 5

FINNISH COOKERY TO GUMDROP

Definitions and 700 Recipes
How to buy, store, prepare, cook, and serve ·
Nutritive Food Values · Caloric Values

To help you plan more varied meals
with the recipes in this volume

Foreword

To the best of our knowledge, no work of this magnitude ever has been undertaken by any author, editor, or publisher in America. The editors of Woman's Day, with a special staff of experts, present to you this Encyclopedia of Cookery, a comprehensive and colorful library on all culinary matters. The twelve-volume encyclopedia contains in its 2,000 pages over 8,500 recipes from all over the world, 1,500 food illustrations in color, 1,200 menus, 50 special cook books and over 1,000 food definitions. In addition, there are full details about all foods, their nutritive and caloric values, how to buy, serve, prepare, and cook them. There is a history of food and cooking, articles on nutrition, diet, entertaining, menu planning, herbs and spices. Every topic of culinary interest is covered. Five years of intensive work have gone into its preparation, backed by twenty-five years of food and cookery experience in the publication of Woman's Day.

We think you will find this Encyclopedia of Cookery the most complete and authoritative work ever published on the subject. It is a library for everyone who cares about good food and the fine art of preparing it.

The Editors

FINNISH COOKERY

by Nika Hazelton

ERIK BLEGVAD · 64

Finland is a land where the seasons and seasonal foods are savored. The winter is long, dark, and quiet, and people stay at home, with good music, and good books: The largest bookstore in Europe is in Finland's capital, Helsinki. When the days lengthen in the early spring, the skiers flock to impress their tracks upon virgin snow in the deep, quiet forests. Spring is like the released waters of a dam: flowers, bushes. and trees burst into bud and bloom almost overnight. The fruit and grains ripen in a few weeks.

During the summer the nights are brief, twilight nights. The Finnish people worship the sun in this all too brief season in which it shines almost without stopping; whole families rush to the forests to pick the succulent berries of the north and to gather the wild mushrooms that are unbelievably delicious. The foliage of autumn is brilliant, like that of our own northern American states; and then, the winter snows fall to protect the earth.

Finnish cookery is Scandinavian, but simpler and more austere. The foods of Finland as basic foods. Salmon is most plentiful in the rivers of northern Finland. The center cuts are fried or broiled, the end pieces are used for fish puddings, and the scraps for soup. Herring is another popular fish, imported salted or smoked. A small kind of fish called *silakka,* or Baltic herring, is eaten fresh.

The Finns are great meat eaters, especially of fresh and cured pork, an effective buttress against the cold. Game abounds in the forests, from ptarmigan, the arctic snowbird which resembles a small grouse, to venison and the prized reindeer.

In the old days, the Finns lived largely on cereal grains and root vegetables in winter. In some of the rural districts they still do, but the revolution brought by canned and frozen foods, and by the

FINNISH

rapid transportation that whisks food from Europe's southern countries to the frozen north, are changing the food habits of the Finns. Today, the gruels, porridges, dumplings, cereal puddings, and the pancakes made from wheat, rye, barley, and oats, are gradually giving way to a lighter diet; and carrots, turnips, and dried peas are used more imaginatively. Dried fruits are eaten very frequently and potatoes remain king of the table as in all of Scandinavia. The Finns eat them daily, perhaps with a little pork gravy or with fish. The high vitamin content of potatoes is a safeguard of the nation's health.

The Finns are a nation of coffee drinkers at all times of the day and night. The coffee is made by brewing the grounds and allowing them to settle. With the coffee they serve breads and pastries, cakes and cookies.

APPETIZERS

SILLISALAATTI
(Herring Salad)

1 medium-size salt herring
1½ cups diced cooked beets
1 cup diced cooked carrots
1 cup diced boiled potatoes
1 cup diced cooked beef
2 dill pickles, diced
2 unpeeled tart apples, diced
2 hard-cooked eggs, chopped
Dressing
Lettuce leaves

Wash herring, drain, cover with cold water, and let soak overnight. Drain, cut off head and tail, and remove bones. Cut fillets into small pieces. Combine with next 7 ingredients. Cover and chill. Prepare Dressing and mix with salad; press into mold or round glass bowl and chill thoroughly. Turn out on cold platter, garnished with crisp lettuce leaves. Makes 8 servings.

Dressing

1 cup heavy cream
1½ tablespoons sugar
2 tablespoons vinegar
1 teaspoon prepared mustard
½ teaspoon salt
¼ teaspoon white pepper

Whip cream stiff; combine with remaining ingredients.

KARJALANPIIRAAT
(Karelian Pasties)

3⅔ cups rye flour
1 cup water (about)
2 teaspoons salt
1 cup uncooked rice
Milk
3 tablespoons melted butter
1 tablespoon heavy cream
Egg Butter

Mix flour, water, and 2 teaspoons salt to form a stiff dough. Knead well; work

Sillisalaatti ▲

Appelsiinikeitto ▼

Tayetty Uunikauki ▲   Viipurin Rinkeli ▼

into a long 18-inch roll and cut into 20 equal pieces. Shape these into balls and flatten them on a floured board. Roll into paper-thin rounds. Place one on top of the other, with a sprinkling of flour in between. Meanwhile cook the rice in the milk until soft. Drain. Place a heaping tablespoon of rice down the center of each pastry round. Fold the sides of the rounds toward the center, leaving a narrow gap down the middle, but bringing dough together at the ends. Pinch, using thumb and forefinger. Fold edges back. Bake in preheated hot oven (400° F.) for about 15 minutes, until browned. Brush with combined melted butter and cream. Serve with Egg Butter. Makes 20.

Egg Butter
2 hard-cooked eggs, chopped
1 cup butter, slightly softened

Cream ingredients together well.

SOUPS

KESÄKEITTO
(Summer Vegetable Soup)
1 tablespoon salt
½ tablespoon sugar
4 cups boiling water
2 medium carrots, sliced
1 small cauliflower, broken into flowerets
1 cup sliced potatoes
1 cup (fresh or frozen) cut green beans
1 cup (fresh or frozen) shelled peas
1 cup (fresh or frozen) chopped spinach
6 tablespoons all-purpose flour
6 cups milk
2 tablespoons butter
¼ cup chopped parsley

Add salt and sugar to water. Bring to a boil in deep kettle. Add carrots, cauliflower, potatoes, and beans. Cook over low heat until half done. Add peas and spinach. Cook until vegetables are almost but not quite tender. Stir flour and milk to a smooth paste. Pour over vegetables. Cook until soup is hot and thickened, about 8 minutes. Remove from heat and stir in butter. Sprinkle with parsley. Makes 8 large servings.

APPELSIINIKEITTO
(Orange Soup)
5 oranges
4 cups water
½ cup sugar
   Few drops of red liquid food coloring
1 tablespoon cornstarch
2 tablespoons water
   Whipped cream

Squeeze 3 of the oranges. Combine water, sugar, and food coloring. Heat to just below boiling stage. Mix cornstarch and water to a smooth paste. Gradually stir into hot liquid. Cook until slightly thickened and clear. Add orange juice. Chill soup. Peel and slice remaining 2 oranges. Add to soup before serving. Serve with whipped cream. Makes 4 servings.

FISH

TÄYTETTY UUNIHAUKI
(Baked Stuffed Pike)
1 pike (3 pounds)
 Salt
½ cup uncooked rice
½ pound spinach
2 eggs, lightly beaten
2 tablespoons butter or margarine
½ cup soft bread crumbs
 Water

Clean the fish and rub with 1 tablespoon salt. Cook rice and spinach separately. Drain and chop spinach and mix with drained rice. Add eggs and 1 teaspoon salt. Put this stuffing into the fish and sew up. Brown butter in a casserole. Put in fish and baste with butter. Sprinkle with bread crumbs and bake in preheated moderate oven (350°F.). After 10 minutes add a little water to bottom of casserole. Cook for 40 minutes, basting frequently. Makes 4 to 6 servings.

KALA-RIISIVUOKA
(Fish and Rice Casserole)
⅔ cup uncooked rice
5 tablespoons tomato sauce
1 egg
1 pound fish fillets, fresh or frozen, thawed
½ teaspoon salt
¼ teaspoon pepper
⅔ cup milk or half milk and half cream
1 tablespoon dry bread crumbs
3 tablespoons butter or margarine
1 tablespoon chopped parsley or watercress

Rinse the rice and cook in boiling salted water until soft but not mushy. Rinse and drain. Mix tomato sauce with the rice. Beat egg slightly. Sprinkle fish fillets with salt and pepper and dip fillets into egg. Butter 1-quart baking dish and place a layer of half of the rice on the bottom of the dish. Top with the fish fillets and cover with remaining rice. Pour milk over the top of the casserole. Sprinkle with bread crumbs and dot with butter. Bake in preheated hot oven (400°F.) for 30 to 45 minutes. Before serving, sprinkle top with chopped parsley. Serve with spinach and pickled beets. Makes 4 to 5 servings.

KALAKUKKO
(Fish Loaf)
Filling
2 pounds fish fillets (sole, cod, flounder, or other)
½ pound fat fresh pork
 Salt
 Fat pork trimmings or lard

Rinse fillets, drain, and cut into small pieces. Slice pork thin, dice fine, and cook slowly for 10 minutes. Set aside.

Dough
2 cups sifted all-purpose flour
2 cups sifted rye flour
1 teaspoon salt
1 tablespoon sugar
½ cup water
½ to ¾ cup milk
 Flour
5 tablespoons cold butter

Sift dry ingredients together twice. Combine water and milk and stir into the flour. Then beat in butter thoroughly, adding a tablespoon or more of milk if needed to make dough stiff enough to knead. Knead thoroughly until tough and elastic. Roll it out to ½ inch thick and cut into an oval shape. On half of the oval sprinkle a little flour. Cover flour with a layer of fish, scatter the cooked pork mixture over the fish, and cover with another layer of fish. Season with a little salt. Fold the other half of the pastry over the filled half, brush edges of pastry with the water, and press together. Place on greased cookie sheet and bake in very slow oven (225°F. to 250°F.) for about 3 hours. Brush top of loaf with fat pork trimmings after first 15 minutes; repeat every 30 minutes. When done, remove from oven and wrap the hot roll in a folded clean cloth to soften crust. To serve, cut into generous slices and serve with additional melted butter. Makes 4 to 6 servings.

MEAT

LIHA JA PERUNAMUREKE
(Sliced Beef and Potato Loaf)
2 pounds ground cooked beef
3 large beets, cooked
4 potatoes, boiled
3 eggs, beaten
1 tablespoon minced pickled onions
2 tablespoons drained capers
1 tablespoon salt
1 teaspoon pepper
¼ cup butter or margarine
2 large onions, peeled and sliced
 Sauce

Put ground meat, beets, and potatoes through coarse grinder together. Add eggs, pickled onions, and capers, and mix. Add seasonings. Mix and shape into a loaf. Press firmly with hands to make a good loaf shape. Dip sharp knife into hot water and slice loaf into thick slices; brown slices on both sides in butter in large frying pan. Remove to warm serving platter and keep hot. When all slices are browned, brown onion slices in the same pan. Skim cooked onions out and scatter over meat slices. Pour sauce over meat. Makes 6 or more servings.

Sauce
1½ tablespoons all-purpose flour
1 tablespoon tomato juice
1 teaspoon prepared mustard
½ teaspoon salt
¼ teaspoon pepper
¾ cup light cream

In the same pan in which the meat and onions were cooked, stir flour smoothly into remaining fat. Slowly stir in tomato juice and mustard, mixing well. Add salt, pepper, and cream. Stir constantly over low heat until slightly thickened.

LINDSTRÖMIN PIHVI
(Beef a la Lindstrom)
1 pound ground beef
1 egg, slightly beaten
1 beet, cooked and finely diced
1 medium potato, boiled and finely diced
2 tablespoons minced pickled onions
1 tablespoon chopped drained capers
¾ teaspoon salt
⅛ teaspoon pepper
 Butter or margarine for frying

Gravy
2 tablespoons all-purpose flour
½ cup water
1 teaspoon prepared mustard
½ cup light cream
 Salt and pepper

Combine all ingredients except butter and blend well. Shape mixture into medium-size patties. Brown patties on both sides in butter in a heavy skillet. When meat patties are cooked and well browned, remove and keep warm on a serving dish.
■ **To prepare gravy,** stir flour into the drippings in the skillet. Cook until golden brown, stirring well to loosen all particles. Slowly stir in water. Add mustard. Stir in cream; reheat but do not boil. Season with salt and pepper to taste. Serve with fried potatoes and vegetables. Makes about 4 servings.

LIHAKOHOKAS
(Meat Soufflé)
¼ cup butter or margarine
¼ cup all-purpose flour
2 cups milk
3 eggs
2 cups ground meat, cooked or raw
1½ teaspoons salt
¼ teaspoon pepper
4 anchovy fillets, diced

In a saucepan melt butter. Stir in flour. Gradually stir in milk. Cook over low heat, stirring constantly, until smooth and thickened. Beat egg yolks. Gradually add hot sauce to the egg yolks. Stir in meat, seasonings, and anchovies. Cool. Beat egg whites until stiff but not dry. Fold egg whites into sauce. Pour mixture into a buttered 2-quart baking dish and bake in preheated moderate oven (350°F.) for 30 to 45 minutes, or until firm. Serve at once with green salad. Makes 6 servings.

MAKSALAATIKKO
(Liver Pudding)
2 cups water
1 teaspoon salt
1 cup uncooked rice
1 small onion, chopped
 Butter or margarine
1½ cups milk
1 pound raw liver, minced

¼ cup molasses
1 teaspoon ground ginger
½ cup raisins
¼ teaspoon white pepper
1 teaspoon crumbled dried marjoram
1 egg, beaten
½ cup dry bread crumbs
Lingonberry jam

Bring water to boil. Add salt and gradually pour in the rice. Cook, covered, over low heat for 15 to 20 minutes, until water is absorbed. Cool slightly. Brown the onion in 1 tablespoon butter. Add milk, liver, onion, molasses, spices and raisins to the rice. Mix in egg. Pour into a well-greased casserole. Sprinkle with bread crumbs and dot with butter. Bake in preheated moderate oven (350°F.) for 45 minutes. Reduce temperature to very slow (250°F.) and cook for 20 minutes longer. Serve with lingonberry or cranberry jam and melted butter to pour over. Makes 4 to 6 servings.

SIANLIHAKASTIKE
(Pork Stew)

¼ pound boneless pork
1 onion, sliced
1 tablespoon all-purpose flour
1⅓ cups milk or water, heated
Salt and pepper

Cut pork into ¼-inch slices. Cut slices into 1-inch pieces. Brown pork and onion in skillet. Remove pork and onion to serving dish and keep hot. Stir flour into pan juices. Cook until slightly browned, stirring constantly. Gradually stir in milk. Cook until thick and smooth. Season with salt and pepper to taste. Pour sauce over pork and onion. Makes 4 servings.

PERUNA JA PEKONI LAATIKKO
(Potato and Bacon Pudding)

½ pound bacon, diced
2 pounds potatoes, cooked and diced (about 4 cups)
1 cup milk
3 eggs
1 teaspoon salt
⅛ teaspoon white pepper

Fry bacon in skillet until half done; drain off fat. Combine potatoes and bacon. Place in greased 2-quart baking dish. Beat milk, eggs, salt, and pepper. Pour mixture over potatoes and bacon. Bake in preheated moderate oven (350°F.) for about 30 minutes, or until set. Makes 6 servings.

TILLIKASTIKE
(Dill Sauce)

¾ cup heavy cream
1¼ cups mayonnaise
2 tablespoons chopped fresh dill

Whip cream until stiff. Combine with mayonnaise. Just before serving add dill. Makes about 2½ cups.
Note: This sauce is served with baked fish or eel, boiled fish, pickled salmon, and cold meats.

VEGETABLES

PORKKANAKOHOKAS
(Carrot Soufflé)

1½ pounds carrots
1 cup soft stale bread crumbs
1 cup milk
Melted butter or margarine
3 egg yolks
1 teaspoon salt
4 egg whites

Wash carrots, scrape, and cut into pieces. Cover with lightly salted boiling water and cook for 20 minutes, or until tender. Drain. Whirl in blender. Combine crumbs and milk; beat in 3 tablespoons melted butter. Beat egg yolks and beat into crumb mixture. Add salt. Combine with carrots. Beat egg whites until stiff but not dry. Fold egg whites into carrot mixture. Grease a 2-quart baking dish. Set in shallow pan of hot water. Bake in preheated moderate oven (350°F.) for 30 to 45 minutes, until risen, set, and lightly browned. Serve at once with ½ cup melted butter poured over top. Makes 6 servings.

PAISTETUT SIENET
(Fried Mushrooms)

1 pound mushrooms
3 tablespoons butter
1 medium onion, chopped
2 tablespoons fine dry bread crumbs
1 cup boiling milk
Salt and white pepper
½ cup dairy sour cream

Slice mushrooms. Melt butter and sauté mushrooms in it until lightly brown, stirring constantly. Add onion, bread crumbs, and milk. Season to taste, and add sour cream. Heat through but do not boil. Makes 4 servings.

DESSERTS, CAKES, AND COOKIES

PAISTETUT MANTELIOMENAT
(Baked Almond Apples)

4 medium baking apples
⅓ cup blanched almonds
½ cup sugar
2 eggs
½ cup all-purpose flour
1 cup fine dry bread crumbs
¼ cup butter
Custard sauce
Jam

Peel and core apples. Chop almonds and mix with ¼ cup sugar. Stuff apples with mixture. Lightly beat eggs with remaining sugar. Dip apples into flour, egg, and bread crumbs. Melt butter in skillet. Brown apples in it on all sides. Put apples in baking dish and bake in preheated moderate oven (350°F.) for 35 minutes to 1 hour, depending on type and size of apples, or until apples are tender. Serve with custard sauce and jam. Makes 4 servings.

OMENAPUURO
(Apple Porridge)

⅓ cup uncooked rice
4 cups water
1 pound fresh apples or ½ pound dried apples, softened
¼ cup sugar
1 cinnamon stick
Rind of 1 lemon, thinly peeled
Cream

Cook rice in 4 cups water until half done. Peel and chop apples. Add apples, sugar, cinnamon, and lemon rind to rice. Cook, covered, over lowest possible heat, stirring frequently, until rice is tender. Time depends on kind of rice used. Chill and serve cold with additional sugar and cream. Makes 4 servings.

VESI-SOKERIKAKKU
(Finnish Cake)

2 eggs
¾ cup sugar
6 tablespoons boiling water
¾ cup all-purpose flour
1 tablespoon potato flour
2 teaspoons baking powder

Beat the eggs until thick and lemon-colored. Gradually beat in sugar. Slowly beat in boiling water. Beat for an additional 15 minutes. Sift flour with remaining ingredients. Stir dry ingredients into egg mixture. Pour mixture into two buttered and floured 8-inch layer-cake pans. Bake in preheated moderate oven (350°F.) for 30 minutes. Unmold, cool layers on a rack, and frost or fill as desired. Makes two 8-inch layers.

HIRVENSARVET
(Antler Cookies)

¼ cup butter
½ cup sugar
2 egg yolks
1 egg, beaten
2 teaspoons ground cardamom
¼ cup heavy cream or undiluted evaporated milk
2 cups sifted all-purpose flour
1 cup cornstarch
1 teaspoon baking soda

Cream butter and beat in sugar, beating until sugar crystals have disappeared. Beat in egg yolks, egg, and cardamom. Beat in cream. Sift together flour, cornstarch, and baking soda. Add to batter and mix thoroughly. On lightly floured board roll dough to ¼-inch thickness. Cut dough into pieces 1 x 2 inches. In each piece, about ¾ from each end, make a crosswise cut about the width of the dough. Pull both ends to make a curve, so that the cuts open a little. Bake on a greased cookie sheet in moderate oven (350°F.) for 15 minutes, or until golden brown. Makes about 3 dozen.

VIIPURIN RINKELI
(Viipuri Twists)

- 1 egg
- 7 tablespoons sugar
- ¾ cup milk
- 1 package active dry yeast or 1 cake compressed yeast
- ¼ cup lukewarm water*
- ¼ teaspoon salt
- ½ teaspoon ground cardamom
- ¼ teaspoon ground nutmeg
- 2 tablespoons softened butter
- 3 cups sifted all-purpose flour (about)

Beat egg and gradually beat in sugar. Heat milk to lukewarm and beat into egg mixture. Dissolve yeast in lukewarm water. *Use very warm water (105°F. to 115°F.) for dry yeast; use lukewarm water (80°F. to 90°F.) for compressed. Let stand for a few minutes, then stir until dissolved. Add yeast to egg mixture. Stir in salt, spices, and butter. Gradually beat in flour and knead mixture on a lightly floured board until smooth and elastic. Cover and let rise until doubled in bulk. Punch down dough and shape into a long thin roll about 36 inches long. Shape the long roll of dough into a large pretzel shape on a lightly greased cookie sheet. Pretzel will just about cover the cookie sheet. Brush twist with boiling water. Let rise until doubled in bulk. Brush with boiling water again. Bake in preheated moderate oven (375°F.) for 20 to 25 minutes, or until twist is golden brown. Brush with boiling water once during baking. Brush twist again after it has been removed from the oven. Makes 8 to 10 servings.

FISH ***by James A. Beard***—Fish are cold-blooded aquatic animals and, broadly speaking, include shellfish as well as the tapered, scaly animal with backbone, gills, and fins. Gastronomy is, of course, concerned only with edible types of fish, which are usually divided into three groups: salt-water fish such as sea bass, pompano, cod, haddock, halibut, herring, mackerel, salmon, shad, sole, sturgeon, swordfish, tuna; fresh-water fish such as bass, catfish, trout, perch; and shellfish such as abalone, clams, crabs, crayfish, lobsters, mussels, oysters, scallops, and shrimps.

Fish constitute a major part of the world's diet, yet in the United States its popularity is weak compared with its abundant use in French, Italian, Russian, and Oriental cuisines. This is all the more remarkable considering the importance of the fishing industry in the history of this country. Our early settlers might not have survived without the bounty of cod in the waters off Massachusetts. The native Indians, before them, were excellent fishermen. Tribes in the West fished migrating salmon with baskets, a forerunner of the nets which are still used. They also fished the candlefish or smelt in quantity, for the high oil content made the fish useful as tapers when they were dried and set alight. It was a fishing boat that rescued Washington after the battle of Long Island and fishing boats that ferried him across the Delaware. In the 19th century American sailing was made famous by whalers plying their way to all points of the globe.

Processing and marketing advances have made fish available to Americans in all parts of the country. Whereas in the past, people were limited to local fish in season or to salted or cured fish from distant waters, nowadays inland as well as coastal areas can have their pick of dozens of varieties of fresh and frozen fish the year round. The housewife need no longer worry about cleaning and scaling fish. This is done for her by the fishmonger or the food store; and she may also buy fish filleted and even breaded, ready for the pan.

Nevertheless, few American families get acquainted with more than two or three types of fish in their lifetimes. This is a pity. Culinary delights await anyone who is willing to sample everything from the tiniest whitebait to the lovely trout and pike, the lordly sturgeon and salmon, the whole gamut of shellfish, and the lesser-known fish, such as skate, sunfish, and salmon trout.

Fish lends itself to a wide range of preparations. It can be sautéed, panned, broiled, baked, braised, poached, or steamed. Some fish, such as trout, are perhaps at their best done simply—sautéed in butter—and others, particularly sole, can take elaborate saucing. Most shellfish are delicious cold as well as hot, and cold salmon is a superb spring and summer treat. Fish is also used to great advantage when combined with other ingredients to make fishballs or cakes, mousses, and stews, such as the renowned bouillabaisse. Great care should be taken to avoid overcooking fish. Prolonged heat dries out the delicate flesh and makes it uninteresting if not unpalatable, which is the way one encounters it in many restaurants. Overcooking has probably been more responsible for the poor reputation of fish than any other reason.

Fish can be eaten raw. The Japanese prize it highly thus. In fact, there are many *sushi* bars in Japan where only raw fish is dispensed, perfectly cut and attractively served. Naturally, fish used in this way must be as fresh as tomorrow. Also, in the South Pacific, and in Mexico, and some of the other Latin American countries, sliced raw fish marinated in lime or lemon juice forms the basis for a wonderfully good, cooling dish. In Mexico it is called *seviche,* and is served in a delicious sauce made with onion, green chilies, fresh tomato, olive oil, and herbs.

Cold and hot smoked fish, as well as salted fish, are found in almost every cuisine around the world. One dried fish, used by Indians with their curries, is curiously named 'Bombay duck."

Fish roe is among the most sought-after food from the sea. Shad roe is a seasonal delicacy in America; salmon, herring, and sole roe are fancied in other countries, notably England, Greece, and the Scandinavian countries. Of course, one of the most expensive, elegant, and fabled foods to be found anywhere in the world is the roe of sturgeon, caviar.

Availability—Fresh fish are available year round, marketed in the following forms:

Whole or Round—As they come out of the water, with skin, bones, and organs intact

Drawn—The whole fish with only the entrails removed

Dressed and Pan-Dressed—Scaled, with entrails, head, tail, and fins removed. This form is ready-to-cook as purchased. Fish weighing less than one pound are referred to as pan-dressed, and fish of more than 1 pound as dressed

Steaks—A cross-section slice from large dressed fish. Ready-to-cook as purchased

Fillets—The sides of the fish, cut lengthwise away from the backbone. Fillets are practically boneless, with all or most of the skin removed. Butterfly fillets are the two fillets, one from each side of the fish, held together by uncut flesh. Ready-to-cook as purchased

Frozen fish are sometimes packaged whole, but are available mostly in the form of steaks, fillets, portions, and complete fish dinners. Portions are cut from blocks of frozen fish fillets. They may be cut in rectangles, squares, or sticks. Fillets and portions are sold breaded, precooked, or ready-to-cook.

Bonito, caviar, salt codfish, codfish cakes, smoked eels, fish balls, haddock, mackerel, salmon, sardines, shad, trout, and tuna fish are available canned.

Cured fish is available salted, smoked, and pickled, and is sold by the pound, in small packages, or in jars or cans.

Available dry-salted are: Anchovies, bass, bloater, caviar, cod, cusk, drum, haddock, hake, halibut, herring, mackerel, pollack, shark, and whiting.

Available brine-salted are: Alewife, herring, mackerel, mullet, salmon, shad, sprats, and whiting.

Available smoked or kippered are: Alewife, anchovies, bloater, bowfin, butterfish, carp, finnan haddie, garfish, hake, halibut, herring, mackerel, mullet, pollack, salmon, sardines, shad, sturgeon, trout, and whitefish.

Eels and herring are available pickled.

Purchasing Guide—To select the freshest fish in your market, look for those with bright, clear, bulging eyes; gills that look and smell clean; scales that are shiny and lie close to the skin; and firm flesh with some spring to it when pressed with a finger. Of course, there should be no strong, unpleasant odor.

☐ Whole and drawn fish: allow 1 pound per serving

☐ Dressed fish: allow ½ pound per serving

☐ Fillets and steaks: allow ⅓ pound per serving

Storage—Fresh fish is very perishable. Wrap fish in moisture-proof paper or place in a tightly covered container in the coldest part of the refrigerator.

Keep frozen fish solidly frozen until ready to use. Once thawed, do not refreeze, use immediately.

Keep canned fish in a cool dry place. Once opened, refrigerate.

Wrap smoked fish and refrigerate. Pickled fish should be refrigerated. Dried fish should be kept in a cool dry place.

☐ Dried, kitchen shelf: 3 to 4 weeks

☐ Canned, kitchen shelf: 1 year

☐ Fresh, raw, refrigerator shelf: 1 or 2 days

☐ Fresh, cooked, or Frozen, or Canned and opened, refrigerator shelf: 3 or 4 days

☐ Smoked, refrigerator shelf: 1 to 2 weeks

☐ Pickled and Dried, refrigerator shelf: 2 to 3 months

☐ Fresh, raw, and Smoked, refrigerator frozen-food compartment, prepared for freezing: 2 to 3 weeks

☐ Fresh, refrigerator frozen-food compartment, cooked, prepared for freezing: 3 to 4 weeks

☐ Frozen, refrigerator frozen-food compartment: 2 months

☐ Dried and Pickled, refrigerator frozen-food compartment, prepared for freezing: 4 to 5 months

☐ Frozen, Fresh, prepared for freezing, raw or cooked, Dried, Pickled, or Smoked, freezer: 1 year

Nutritive Food Values—Depending on the type, fish is a very good to excellent source of easily digested protein. Fish contains varying amounts of fluorine, iron, calcium, and B vitamins. Salt-water fish provides iodine. Fish-liver oils are rich in vitamins A and D. Roe and livers are rich in riboflavin and thiamine.

The food value of canned fish is similar to the fresh fish, except when oil is added. Curing destroys much of the vitamin content of the fish and sometimes increases the caloric value.

Basic Preparation

☐ **To Clean and Dress**—Most fish we find in the food stores are already cleaned and dressed. Your fish dealer will fillet a fish, cut it into steaks, and bone it for you. However, if you are an angler or are married to one, you will be faced with scaling and cleaning your own catch, unless you have a friendly fishman who will do it for you. Here is the method:

Scaling—Wet fish can be scaled more easily than dry, so soak the fish in water for a few minutes. Place the fish on a table, holding it firmly by the head with one hand. In the other hand hold a sharp knife and, starting at the tail, scrape toward the head, taking off the scales. Be sure to remove all scales around the fins and the base of the head.

Cleaning—With a sharp knife slit the belly of the fish the full length from the vent (anal opening) to the head. Remove the intestines. Next, cut around the pelvic fins (those on the underside toward the head); pull fins off, being careful not to tear fish. Take off the head by cutting above the collarbone, and also remove the pectoral fins (on either side just back of the gills). If the backbone is large, just cut through to it on each side of the fish; then place the fish on the edge of the table so the head hangs over, and snap the backbone by bending the head down. Then cut any remaining flesh that holds the head to the body.

Cut off the tail. Next remove the dorsal fin (the large one on the back of the fish). Cut along each side of it and give a quick pull forward toward the head to remove the fin and its root bones. Take out the anal fins (at the back on the underside) in the same way. Do not take fins off with shears, because simply trimming them will not remove the little bones at the base.

Next wash the fish in cold running water, being sure it is free of any membranes and viscera. It is now dressed and ready for cooking. Large fish may, of course, be cut crosswise into steaks.

Filleting—With a sharp knife cut along the back of the fish from the tail to the head. Next, cut down to the backbone just back of the head on one side of the fish. Then, laying the knife flat, cut the flesh down one whole side, slicing it away from the ribs and backbone. Lift the whole side off in one piece. Turn fish over and repeat on the other side.

☐ **To Freeze**—Freeze as soon as possible. Clean and dress fish. Wash thoroughly in running cold water. Small fish may be frozen whole, large fish may be cut into steaks, chunks, and fillets.

Fish should be wrapped in moisture-vapor-proof wrapping, excluding all air from package. Seal and freeze.

Lean fish, such as scrod, cod, flounder, haddock, halibut, ocean perch, pollack, sole, swordfish, and whiting, should be dipped before freezing into a solution of 4 cups cold water to ¼ cup salt for 20 to 30 seconds. This helps to retain the flavor and firmness of the fish.

Fatty fish, such as salmon, smelts, mackerel, trout, tuna, carp, and whitefish, should be dipped into a solution of 4 cups water to 1 tablespoon ascorbic acid for 20 seconds, to prevent off flavors and yellowing of the skin.

☐ **To Thaw Frozen Fish**—Thaw fish in the refrigerator until just able to handle; allow about 8 hours for 1 pound. Or thaw at room temperature, allowing 4 hours for 1 pound. Fish may be cooked in the frozen state; however, cook at a lower temperature and for a longer period of time.

Follow the same basic methods of preparation as used for fresh fish, and use thawed frozen fish interchangeably with fresh fish in recipes.

☐ **To Use Canned Fish**—It may be used for sandwich fillings, in chowders, casseroles, salads, dips and spreads.

☐ **To Use Cured Fish**—Pickled fish may be eaten as is. Whitefish, chub, and salmon are hot-smoked and may be eaten without further cooking. Haddock and herring are cold-smoked and should be cooked. Most dried and smoked fish may be cooked without soaking except for salt cod and herring in brine; these require the removal of some of the salt for palatability.

COOKING METHODS

Since fish resemble each other, cooking methods and recipes can very often be interchanged.

Wash fish quickly in cold, salted water. Cut fish into portions of the desired size.

Fish is tender and may be cooked by either dry- or moist-heat methods. Fish should be handled carefully during cooking to retain its form. Use low or moderately high temperatures for cooking fish. Cook fish only until it flakes easily with a fork. Avoid overcooking as it tends to make fish dry and tough. Fat fish are most desirable for baking and broiling. Lean fish may be broiled or baked if basted frequently with fat. Both fat and lean fish may be fried in small portions. Poaching, panfrying, deep frying, and steaming are other methods of fish cookery.

Red Snapper
Perch Porgy
Mackerel

Mullet
Striped Bass

Whiting
Trout

Haddock
Bluefish
Flounder
Pike

☐ **To Broil**—Many varieties of fish are suitable for broiling. Among them are split whole mackerel, whitefish, sea and brook trout; fillets such as sole, flounder, and whiting; steaks of salmon, tuna, cod, haddock, halibut, and swordfish.

1. Wash split whole fish quickly in cold water. Wipe fillets or steaks with a damp cloth or paper towel. Thaw frozen fish just before using.

2. Place on greased broiler rack and brush with melted fat. Sprinkle with salt and pepper.

3. Broil split fish or fillets on one side only, placing fish about 3 inches from unit and avoiding too high heat. (Steaks may be turned once.)

4. Broil for 8 to 12 minutes, or until fish flakes easily when tested with a fork. Brush again with fat during broiling.

Serve very hot on hot plates. Good plain or with lemon butter, parsley butter, or other sauce.

☐ **To Charcoal Broil**—Certainly no other method of cooking fish gives it such a distinctive flavor as charcoal broiling. If possible, cook the fish in a separate hinged grill; it will be easier to turn.

Rub the grill well with oil and bacon fat. Broil over glowing coals, brushing the fish with oil or fat once or twice as it cooks. Turn once or twice to cook on both sides. Test with a fork or toothpick. The fish is done when it flakes easily. *Do not overcook.* A fairly large whole fish should take about 6 minutes per side. A small fish or a fillet should take about 5 minutes altogether.

☐ **To Oven Broil**—Oil the broiling pan or lay a sheet of foil on it. Brush the fish well with oil or butter. Remember that fillets need more lubrication than whole fish. Preheat your broiler for 10 minutes. Broil the fish 3 to 4 inches below the heat. Steak cuts and whole fish should be turned during the cooking process, but most fillets do not need turning. Baste or brush with butter or a mixture of butter and oil several times during the cooking. Season to taste and add a squeeze of lemon juice.

Filleted fish will take from 5 to 10 minutes to broil, depending upon the thickness of the fillets.

Steaks will take from 6 to 12 minutes.

Split or boned fish or split fish with the backbone intact will take 6 to 15 minutes, depending on the size. Whole fish will take from 6 to 20 minutes.

Fish with the skin on should be dusted with flour and brushed with butter or oil.

Thin fillets of fluke, flounder, and sole need not be turned during broiling.

☐ **To Panfry or Sauté**—Fillets, steaks, and small whole fish may be panfried.

Good varieties to use are perch, rockfish, catfish, cod, haddock, butterfish, flounder, sole, sunfish, bream, porgies, trout, mullet, and smelts.

1. Wipe fish with a damp cloth or paper towel. Thaw frozen fish just before using.

2. Cut fillets or steaks into serving pieces. Leave small fish whole. Dip fish into undiluted evaporated milk or beaten egg.

3. Roll in mixture of equal parts of all-purpose flour and cornmeal, well seasoned with salt and pepper. Or roll in flour, dip in egg, then roll in bread crumbs or cracker crumbs.

4. Use a large deep skillet and slow to medium heat to avoid spattering. Heat enough fat in skillet to cover bottom and fry fish for 3 to 5 minutes on each side, turning carefully with fork or flat turner. Add more fat as needed. *Do not overcook.*

Serve very hot on hot plates with tartare sauce, lemon or parsley butter, chili sauce, or ketchup.

☐ **To Deep Fry**—Best fish for deep frying are fillets such as sole, flounder, cod, haddock, whitefish, ocean perch, and whiting. Whole small butterfish, porgies, smelts, or perch may also be deep fried.

1. Wipe fish with a damp cloth or paper towel. Thaw frozen fish just before using.

2. Cut fillets or steaks into serving pieces. Leave small fish whole.

3. Roll in seasoned flour and dip into mixture of slightly beaten egg and water, allowing 2 tablespoons cold water to each egg.

4. Roll in fine dry bread crumbs or cracker meal. For a thicker crust, coat twice with egg and crumbs.

5. Arrange a few pieces of fish in frying basket just to cover the bottom. Do not overlap pieces.

6. Fry in hot deep fat, such as hydrogenated fat, vegetable oil, or lard (370° F. on a frying thermometer) until golden brown. Drain and serve very hot.

☐ **To Bake**—Good varieties of fish to bake are red snapper, bass, haddock, shad, bluefish, weakfish, cod, and salmon.

1. Have whole fish cleaned and dressed but not split. Head and tail may be left on. Wash fish and wipe dry.

2. If desired, stuff fish lightly with well-seasoned bread stuffing; close opening with toothpicks or needle and thread.

3. Cut 3 or 4 gashes about ¼ inch deep into skin and insert thin slices of salt pork or bacon.

4. Place a pinch of ground thyme or marjoram, 1 minced onion, 3 tablespoons minced parsley, and 2 tablespoons fat in pan. Or add chopped tomatoes.

5. Put fish in pan and bake in preheated moderate oven (350°F.) until fish flakes easily when tested with a fork. Allow 10 to 15 minutes per pound, depending on thickness of fish.

☐ **To Steam**—Use a trivet or rack or even a small colander in a covered pan. Don't let the water touch the fish. Large chunks of nonoily fish are usually steamed, but steaks, fillets, or whole small fish may also be cooked this way. Most often steamed are cod, bluefish, bass, scrod, red snapper, carp, and flounder.

1. Wipe fish with a damp cloth or paper towel. Thaw frozen fish just before using.

2. Place on a greased small rack in a large saucepan. Steaks or fillets may be sprinkled with salt and pepper. Seasoning does not penetrate larger chunks with skin. Large chunks of fish may be tied in a piece of cheesecloth for easy handling.

3. Add just enough boiling water to come up to top of rack. Cover tightly.

4. Bring to boil, reduce heat, and steam for about 10 minutes to the pound, depending on thickness. Fish is done when it flakes easily from bone when tested with a fork. *Do not overcook.*

5. Remove skin. Serve fish hot with melted butter or Cheese-Mustard Sauce, Curry Sauce, or Creole Sauce (page 694).

☐ **To Poach**—This is a quick and easy way to cook fish for salads, casserole dishes, fish cakes, or for creamed fish or chowder. Thick fish steaks or large chunks of fish are ideal for poaching, although fillets may also be used. Varieties suitable for poaching are halibut, cod, carp, haddock, red snapper, salmon, pickerel, trout, pike, and sole.

1. Wipe fish with a damp cloth or paper towel. Thaw frozen fish just before using.

2. Pour about 2 cups water into a large skillet. Add 1½ teaspoons salt, 1 slice of lemon or 1 tablespoon vinegar, 1 slice of onion separated into rings, few parsley sprigs, or celery leaves, ¼ teaspoon peppercorns, and 1 bay leaf. Boil for 5 minutes; reduce heat.

3. Add fish, cover, and simmer gently for about 10 minutes, or just until fish flakes easily when tested with a fork. If fish is very thick, turn once during cooking. Do not overcook.

Serve hot immediately with drawn-butter sauce, Shrimp or Lobster Sauce (page 695), wine sauce, or other preferred sauce, using the fish stock to make the sauce.

Or cool in the broth, chill, and serve with mayonnaise, Thousand Island dressing, or fresh lemon juice.

FISH COOK BOOK

A collection of recipes
for fillets, steaks, and whole fish,
plus a special group
of forty fine fish sauces

EARL THOLLANDER

DEEP-FRIED BUTTERFISH WITH SOUR-CREAM SAUCE

2 pounds butterfish
Salt and pepper
¾ cup sifted all-purpose flour
1 egg, slightly beaten
½ cup milk
1 tablespoon melted margarine
Fat for deep frying
1 cup dairy sour cream
1 tablespoon each of minced parsley and scallions
Juice of ½ lemon
Dash of cayenne

Wipe fish with damp cloth or paper towel. Sprinkle with salt and pepper. Combine flour, egg, milk, and margarine; add ½ teaspoon salt and beat until smooth. Dip fish into batter and fry in hot deep fat (370°F. to 375°F. on a frying thermometer) until golden brown. Meanwhile, combine sour cream, ½ teaspoon salt, and remaining ingredients. Heat slightly and serve over hot fish. Makes 4 servings.

Note: Also good with porgies, sea herring, perch, trout.

BROILED COD FILLETS WITH CHEESE SAUCE

1½ pounds fresh or frozen cod fillets
Salt and pepper
½ cup mayonnaise
Few grains of cayenne
1 tablespoon chopped capers
1 tablespoon chopped chives
Few sprigs of parsley, chopped
½ cup grated sharp Cheddar cheese
1 egg white
Pimientos

Wipe fresh or thawed frozen fillets with damp cloth and place on greased broiler rack. Broil under medium heat for 8 to 12 minutes. Sprinkle with salt and pepper. Combine mayonnaise, cayenne, capers, chives, parsley, and cheese. Beat egg white until stiff and fold into dressing. Spread on fish and broil for 5 minutes, or until sauce is puffed. Garnish with strips of pimiento. Makes 4 servings.

Note: Also good with pike, mackerel, perch, whitefish, flounder, hake.

BAKED COD, PIQUANT

1½ pounds fresh or thawed frozen cod fillets
1 teaspoon salt
⅛ teaspoon white pepper
¼ cup melted butter or margarine
Juice of 1 lemon
1 teaspoon grated onion
Paprika
Minced parsley

Wipe fish with damp cloth or paper towel. Cut into serving pieces and arrange in greased shallow baking dish. Sprinkle with salt and pepper. Combine butter, lemon juice, and onion and pour over fish. Sprinkle with paprika. Bake in preheated slow oven (325°F.) for about 30 minutes. Sprinkle with parsley. Makes 4 servings.

Note: Also good with flounder, sole, scrod, haddock, mackerel, halibut.

SMOKED COD EN CASSEROLE

1½ pounds boneless smoked codfish
¾ cup milk
¼ cup butter or margarine
¼ cup diced celery
1 small onion, minced
¼ cup diced green pepper
½ cup all-purpose flour
⅛ teaspoon salt
Dash of pepper
⅛ teaspoon paprika
2¾ cups milk
4 or 5 stuffed olives, chopped
2 tablespoons grated cheese
Chopped chives or parsley

Break fish into small pieces with fork. Place in saucepan over very low heat; pour ¾ cup milk over fish. Allow to stand over low heat for 10 minutes to poach, but do not boil. Melt butter in saucepan; add celery, onion, and pepper. Cook until tender; gradually add flour and seasonings and mix well. Add remaining milk plus milk from soaking fish and cook until thickened. Place fish in greased 1½-quart casserole. Add olives to sauce and pour over fish. Top with cheese. Place under broiler until cheese is melted and browned. Sprinkle with chopped chives or parsley and serve at once. Makes 4 to 6 servings.

Note: Also good with smoked haddock, whitefish, whiting, hake.

FINNAN HADDIE IN CREAM SAUCE

1½ pounds boneless finnan haddie
2 cups milk
1 bay leaf
Pinch of crumbled dried thyme
10 peppercorns
1 onion slice
¼ cup butter or margarine
¼ cup all-purpose flour
¼ cup light cream
Dash of cayenne
1 tablespoon chopped pimiento
2 hard-cooked eggs, chopped

Soak finnan haddie in milk for 1 hour with bay leaf, thyme, peppercorns, and onion. Then place over very low heat and simmer gently for 10 minutes. Flake fish. Melt butter and blend in flour. Add strained milk and cream slowly; cook until thickened, stirring constantly. Add fish and remaining ingredients. Serve on hot toast, hot cooked rice, or baked potatoes. Makes 4 servings.

Note: Also good with smoked whitefish, cod, whiting, haddock, hake.

POACHED FLOUNDER AND MUSHROOMS IN CREAM SAUCE

1½ pounds fresh or thawed frozen flounder fillets
1½ cups fish liquid
1 can (4 ounces) sliced mushrooms
¼ cup butter or margarine
3 tablespoons all-purpose flour
¾ tablespoon salt
⅛ teaspoon white pepper
½ teaspoon Worcestershire
½ cup light cream
4 slices of hot toast

Poach fish as directed on page 686. Drain, reserving 1½ cups fish liquid. Separate fish into large flakes. Cook drained mushrooms in butter for 5 minutes; blend in flour, salt, pepper, and Worcestershire. Add fish liquid and cream slowly, then cook until thickened, stirring constantly. Add fish and serve over hot toast. Sprinkle with paprika or minced chives or parsley, if desired. Makes 4 servings.

Note: Also good with sole, hake, cod, haddock, pompano, pollack, weakfish, pike.

SEVICHE

2 pounds flounder fillets
½ cup fresh lime or lemon juice
⅔ cup chopped peeled tomatoes
½ cup minced green pepper
1 pimiento, chopped fine
1 onion, minced
1 garlic clove, minced
Few sprigs of parsley, chopped
1 teaspoon salt
⅛ teaspoon sugar
¼ cup cider vinegar

Cut fish fillets in finger-length pieces and put in bowl. Add lime juice and stir to coat fish completely. Chill in refrigerator for 8 hours. Drain well. Mix remaining ingredients and spread on fish. Makes 6 to 8 servings.

Note: Also good with red snapper or pompano fillets.

HADDOCK MORNAY

1½ pounds fresh or thawed frozen haddock fillets
1 cup fish liquid
3 tablespoons butter or margarine
3 tablespoons all-purpose flour
1 teaspoon salt
⅛ teaspoon pepper
1 cup milk
½ cup heavy cream
1 teaspoon fresh lemon juice
¼ cup grated process cheese
Minced parsley or paprika

Poach fish as directed on page 686. Drain, reserving 1 cup liquid. Melt butter; blend in flour, salt, and pepper. Add milk, cream, and fish liquid slowly and cook until thickened, stirring constantly. Add lemon juice and cheese and cook over low heat until cheese is melted. Arrange fish on a hot platter and pour sauce over it. Sprinkle with minced parsley or paprika and serve at once. Makes 4 servings.

Note: Also good with hake, pollack, rockfish, weakfish, grouper, drumfish, sheepshead.

BAKED NORWEGIAN HADDOCK LOAF

2½ pounds fresh or 2 pounds thawed frozen haddock fillets
1 tablespoon all-purpose flour
1 tablespoon salt
¼ teaspoon ground nutmeg
2 cups milk, scalded
1 cup heavy cream, scalded

Wash fish and scrape flesh from skin with a sharp knife. Discard dark part, skin, and bones. Force fish through food chopper, using fine blade. Then pound fish for 10 minutes with mallet or edge of saucer. Add flour and seasonings and knead for 5 minutes. Add cooled milk and cream, 1 tablespoon at a time, kneading well after each addition. Turn into pan (8 x 4 x 2 inches), lined with wax paper, or into well-greased 1-quart ring mold. Place in pan of boiling water and bake in preheated slow oven (325°F.) for about 1 hour, or until firm. Turn out, remove paper, and cut into slices. Serve hot with creamed eggs, peas and capers, or creamed lobster. Delicious cold. Makes 6 servings.

Note: Also good with sole, flounder, scrod, cod, whitefish.

MOCK LOBSTER SALAD

2 pounds fresh or thawed frozen haddock
Juice of ½ lemon
1 cup sliced celery
1 teaspoon salt
2 tablespoons paprika
Lettuce cups
¾ cup mayonnaise

Steam fish as directed on page 686. Remove bones and skin and flake fish. Chill. Add lemon juice, celery, salt, and paprika and toss lightly. Arrange in lettuce cups; top with mayonnaise. Makes 4 servings.

Note: Also good with red snapper, bluefish, bass, ocean perch, sole, flounder.

CREAMED HALIBUT, NEW ENGLAND STYLE

1½ pounds fresh or thawed frozen halibut steaks
1 teaspoon salt
¼ teaspoon white pepper
2 tablespoons margarine
1½ tablespoons all-purpose flour
1 cup milk
1 tablespoon chopped parsley

Wipe fish with damp cloth or paper towel. Place in top part of double boiler and sprinkle with salt and pepper. Cover and cook over boiling water for 30 minutes, turning once or twice. Remove fish, reserving liquid, and discard skin and bones. Put fish on a hot platter. Melt margarine; blend in flour. Add milk and fish liquid remaining in double boiler. Cook until thickened, stirring constantly. Add parsley and pour over fish. Sprinkle with paprika if desired. Makes 4 servings.

Note: Also good with ocean perch, whiting, scrod, haddock, bluefish, red snapper.

BAKED STUFFED HAKE FILLETS

1½ pounds fresh or thawed frozen hake fillets
4 bacon strips
1 small onion, chopped
2 tablespoons chopped parsley
2 cups soft bread crumbs
Salt and pepper

Wipe fish with damp cloth or paper towel and cut into serving pieces. Cut half of bacon into small pieces and cook until crisp. Remove bacon. Cook onion in remaining fat until yellowed. Combine cooked bacon and onion with the fat, parsley, and crumbs. Season with salt and pepper. Spread on half of fish pieces; top with remaining fish. Arrange in a greased shallow baking dish and top with remaining bacon strips. Bake in preheated slow oven (325°F.) for 40 to 45 minutes. Makes 4 servings.

Note: Also good with whitefish, sole, ocean perch, haddock, scrod, pollack.

HALIBUT STEAK HASH

2½ cups flaked steamed fresh or frozen halibut, about 1½ pounds raw (directions for steaming, page 686)
3 cups chopped peeled boiled potatoes
Salt and pepper
Bacon or salt-pork drippings

Combine fish and potatoes and season to taste with salt and pepper. Heat enough fat to cover bottom of skillet. Add fish mixture and stir until heated through. Then cook slowly until well browned on bottom. Serve with ketchup or chili sauce. Makes 4 servings.

Note: Also good with red snapper, haddock, cod, weakfish.

DEVILED HALIBUT STEAKS

1½ pounds fresh or frozen halibut steaks
2 tablespoons prepared mustard
1 tablespoon cooking oil
2 tablespoons each of chili sauce and prepared horseradish
1 teaspoon salt

Wipe fresh or thawed frozen steaks with damp cloth or paper towel. Mix remain-ing ingredients together and spread half of mixture on fish. Put on greased broiler rack and broil for about 6 minutes under medium heat. Turn fish, spread with remaining sauce, and broil for 5 or 6 minutes longer. Makes 4 servings.

Note: Also good with cod, pollack, red snapper, carp, scrod.

HALIBUT WITH WINE SAUCE

1½ pounds fresh or thawed frozen halibut steaks
¼ cup butter or margarine
¼ cup all-purpose flour
¼ teaspoon powdered mustard
½ teaspoon Worcestershire
1 teaspoon salt
⅛ teaspoon white pepper
2 cups milk
2 hard-cooked eggs, chopped
¼ cup white wine
1 tablespoon minced parsley
Paprika

Steam fish as directed on page 686. Meanwhile, melt butter; blend in flour and seasonings. Add milk slowly and cook until thickened, stirring constantly. Add eggs and wine. Place fish on hot platter; pour sauce over fish. Sprinkle with parsley and paprika. Makes 4 servings.

Note: Also good with swordfish, tuna, bluefish, red snapper, sea bass.

BROILED MACKEREL WITH MUSTARD SAUCE

2 large or 4 small mackerel (total about 3 pounds)
¼ cup melted butter or margarine
½ teaspoon paprika
2 teaspoons prepared mustard
Juice of ½ lemon
½ teaspoon salt
⅛ teaspoon white pepper

Wash fish quickly in cold water and place on greased broiler rack. Combine remaining ingredients and brush on fish. Broil under medium heat for 8 to 12 minutes, brushing with sauce several times during the broiling. Makes 4 servings.

Note: Also good with bluefish, croaker, bonito, mullet, pike, weakfish.

SAVORY BAKED MACKEREL WITH MUSHROOM STUFFING

Split mackerel (about 4 pounds)
Salt and pepper
1 small onion, chopped
1 tablespoon chopped parsley
¼ pound fresh mushrooms or 1 can (4 ounces) sliced mushrooms
6 tablespoons fat
1 cup soft bread crumbs
1 teaspoon chopped fresh or dried mint

Wash mackerel. Dry with cloth or paper towel and sprinkle inside and out with

Porgies en Papillote

salt and pepper. Cook onion, parsley, and mushrooms in 3 tablespoons hot fat until onion is yellowed. Add to crumbs and mint; season to taste with salt and pepper. Stuff fish with the mixture and close openings with toothpicks or needle and thread. Cut several gashes into skin. Place remaining 3 tablespoons fat in baking pan and put fish in pan. Bake in preheated moderate oven (350°F.) for 45 to 50 minutes, or until fish flakes easily when tested with a fork. Makes 4 servings.

Note: Also good with weakfish, bass, drumfish, mullet, pickerel.

FISH-FRY MULLET AND HUSH PUPPIES
- 10 to 12 pounds mullet
- 2 cups water-ground cornmeal
- 1 cup sifted all-purpose flour
- 2 tablespoons salt
- 1 teaspoon pepper
  Fat for deep frying
  Hush Puppy Batter

If large, cut dressed mullet into serving pieces. Wash but do not dry fish. Roll in mixture of cornmeal, flour, salt, and pepper. Fry in hot deep fat (370° to 375°F. on a frying thermometer) until brown. Remove fish. Drop Hush Puppy Batter by tablespoonfuls into fat; fry until browned. Makes 8 servings.

Note: Also good with catfish, bream, porgies, butterfish, croakers, sunfish.

Hush Puppy Batter
- 4 cups water-ground cornmeal
- 1 tablespoon salt
- 1 tablespoon sugar
- 2 tablespoons baking powder
- 1 cup minced onions
- 6 eggs

Sift dry ingredients. Add onions. Add eggs, one at a time; beat well after each addition. Add 1½ cups hot water.

BAKED PERCH IN TOMATO SAUCE
- 1½ pounds fresh or thawed frozen ocean-perch fillets

2 teaspoons salt
1 small onion, minced
1 garlic clove, minced
3 tablespoons minced parsley
3 tablespoons fat
1 can (6 ounces) tomato paste
⅛ teaspoon crumbled dried thyme
¼ teaspoon white pepper
½ bay leaf
1½ cups water
¼ cup grated Romano or Parmesan
   cheese

Wipe fish with damp cloth or paper towel. Cut into serving pieces, arrange in a greased shallow baking dish, and sprinkle with ½ teaspoon salt. Cook onion, garlic, and parsley in hot fat until onion is yellowed. Add remaining ingredients and heat thoroughly. Pour over fish. Bake in preheated moderate oven (350°F.) for about 30 minutes. Makes 4 servings.

Note: Also good with hake, scrod, whitefish, cod, flounder, sole.

PERCH CASSEROLE

1 pound fresh or thawed frozen
   ocean-perch fillets
1 cup milk, scalded
2 egg yolks, well beaten
1¼ teaspoons salt
⅛ teaspoon white pepper
2 tablespoons sherry
1 can (4 ounces) sliced mushrooms
1 tablespoon butter

Steam fish as directed on page 686. Then lift fillets to shallow baking dish. Add milk to egg yolks, stirring constantly. Add salt, pepper, and sherry, and pour over fish. Cook mushrooms for 2 to 3 minutes in butter; arrange on top of fish. Broil under low heat until golden brown and bubbly. Serve immediately. Makes 4 servings.

Note: Also good with flounder, sole, sea bass, cusk, hake.

PERCH, ITALIAN STYLE

1½ pounds fresh or thawed frozen
   ocean-perch fillets
2 tablespoons minced parsley
1 garlic clove, minced
3 tablespoons olive oil
1 cup hot water
1 teaspoon salt
⅛ teaspoon pepper
   Pinch of oregano or dried mint

Wipe fillets with damp cloth or paper towel. Cut fish into serving pieces. Cook parsley and garlic in hot olive oil in skillet for 3 minutes. Add hot water and bring to a boil. Add fish and seasonings. Cover, bring again to boil, and cook for 5 to 10 minutes, or just until fish flakes easily when tested with a fork. Serve at once with the liquid. Makes 4 servings.

Note: Also good with haddock, pike flounder, sole, rockfish, scrod.

UNCLE ED'S CHOWDER

2 pounds fresh or thawed frozen
   pollack fillets
⅓ cup bacon drippings or margarine
⅓ cup all-purpose flour
1½ cups chopped onions
1 garlic clove, minced
⅔ cup chopped green pepper
1½ cups diced peeled raw potatoes
2 cups tomato purée*
1½ quarts water
1 tablespoon Worcestershire
12 whole cloves
   Dash of hot pepper sauce
1 tablespoon paprika
1 bay leaf, crumbled
1 tablespoon salt
¼ teaspoon pepper
1 lemon, sliced

Wipe fish with damp cloth or paper towel. Cut into 1-inch pieces. Cook drippings and flour together slowly in large heavy kettle until flour is golden brown. Add onions, garlic, and green pepper. Cook for 5 minutes; add potatoes, tomato purée, water, and seasonings. Cover and simmer for 30 minutes. Add fish; cover and poach for 8 minutes; add lemon slices. Makes 4 servings.

*If desired, substitute one 6-ounce can tomato paste and 2 cups water for tomato purée.

Note: Also good with sea bass, mullet, pike, haddock, cod, whitefish, fluke.

PORGIES EN PAPILLOTE

4 porgies (about 1 pound each)
   Salt and pepper
   Unglazed brown paper or foil
¼ cup softened butter or margarine
2 tablespoons minced parsley or green
   onion tops

Wash porgies and remove heads and tails if desired. Dry fish and sprinkle inside and out with salt and pepper. Cut sheets of paper large enough to wrap individual fish. Spread center of each paper with 1 tablespoon butter. Lay fish on spread section and sprinkle with parsley or onion tops. Wrap up and tie with string, if necessary. Place on a cookie sheet and bake in preheated moderate oven (375°F.) for 1 hour, or until done. Serve in paper with potatoes and broiled tomatoes, if desired. Makes 4 servings.

Note: Also good with trout, croakers, sunfish, crappies, pike, rockfish, yellow perch.

PANFRIED PORGIES WITH SHERRY-ALMOND SAUCE

4 porgies (about 1 pound each)
½ cup evaporated milk, undiluted
⅓ cup yellow cornmeal

⅓ cup all-purpose flour
1 tablespoon salt
¼ teaspoon white pepper
   Fat for frying
½ cup slivered blanched almonds
¼ cup melted butter or margarine
¼ cup dry sherry
   Parsley or watercress

Wipe fish with a damp cloth or paper towel. Dip into evaporated milk. Combine cornmeal, flour, salt, and pepper. Roll fish in mixture. Heat enough fat in skillet to cover bottom of pan and panfry fish for about 5 minutes on each side, adding more fat as needed. Meanwhile, cook almonds in butter until lightly browned, add sherry, and heat thoroughly. Remove fish to a hot platter and cover with the sauce. Garnish with parsley. Makes 4 servings.

Note: Also good with butterfish, smelts, perch, bream, trout, mullet.

BROILED SALMON WITH HERBS

1½ pounds fresh or frozen salmon steaks,
   about ¾ inch thick
1 tablespoon grated onion
   Juice of 1 lemon
6 tablespoons melted butter or
   margarine
1 teaspoon salt
¼ teaspoon white pepper
½ teaspoon crumbled dried marjoram
1 tablespoon minced watercress or
   chives
2 tablespoons minced parsley

Wipe fresh or thawed frozen fish with damp cloth or paper towel; arrange on greased broiler rack. Mix remaining ingredients together and pour half over steaks. Broil for about 6 minutes under medium heat; turn and pour remaining sauce over fish. Broil for 5 or 6 minutes longer, or until fish flakes easily when tested with a fork. Remove to hot platter; garnish with additional parsley or watercress. Makes 4 servings.

Note: Also good with swordfish, halibut, striped bass, tuna, cod.

HOT SALMON MOUSSE

1¼ pounds fresh or frozen salmon steaks
¾ teaspoon salt
¼ teaspoon white pepper
1 teaspoon each of Worcestershire and
   onion juice
3 egg whites
1 cup heavy cream
   Sour-Cream Cucumber Sauce (see
   page 695)

Steam salmon steaks as directed on page 686; drain. Force fish through food chopper, using fine blade. Add seasonings and mix well. Add unbeaten egg whites, one at a time, blending thoroughly after each addition. Add cream;

mix well. Pour into well-oiled 1-quart casserole. Place in pan of hot water. Bake in preheated moderate oven (375° F.) for 40 minutes, or until firm. Serve with Cucumber Sauce or lemon or parsley butter. Makes 4 servings.

Note: Also good with swordfish, bonito, halibut, kingfish.

BAKED SCROD PAPRIKA

1½ pounds fresh or thawed frozen scrod fillets or steaks
　Salt and pepper
1 tablespoon vinegar
1 onion, thinly sliced
2 tablespoons margarine
2 tablespoons water
1 tablespoon paprika
1 cup undiluted evaporated milk

Wipe fish with damp cloth or paper towel. Cut into serving pieces and sprinkle with salt and pepper. Arrange in greased 1½-quart baking dish and sprinkle with vinegar. Cook onion in hot margarine until yellowed. Add water, paprika, and evaporated milk; pour over fish. Bake in preheated slow oven (325° F.) for 25 minutes, or until done. Makes 4 servings.

Note: Also good with pollack, carp, bluefish, pike, pompano, mackerel, weakfish.

BROILED SCROD WITH OLIVE SAUCE

1½ pounds fresh or frozen scrod fillets or steaks
　Salt and pepper
¼ cup softened butter or margarine
1 small onion, minced
1 tablespoon vinegar
8 stuffed olives, chopped

Wipe fresh or thawed frozen fish with damp cloth or paper towel and sprinkle with salt and pepper. Place on greased broiler rack. Mix remaining ingredients together and spread on fish. Broil under medium heat until fish flakes easily when tested with a fork, 8 to 12 minutes for fillets, 5 to 6 minutes on each side for steaks. Brush fish with drippings once during cooking. Makes 4 servings.

Note: Also good with flounder, perch, mackerel, halibut, salmon, tuna.

BROILED SHAD ROE

2 pairs medium-size shad roe (use about 1½ pounds of smaller roe)
4 cups boiling water
1½ teaspoons salt
　Juice of 1 lemon
¼ cup melted butter or margarine
　Dash of pepper

Wash roe and place in saucepan. Add boiling water, 1 teaspoon salt, and half of lemon juice. Cover and let stand for 5 minutes. Drain and plunge into cold water for 1 minute. Cut into 4 servings and put on greased broiler rack. Combine the butter, pepper, and the remaining lemon juice and salt. Brush roe with the mixture. Broil under medium heat for 6 to 8 minutes, or until brown and done, turning once. Brush several times with sauce during the cooking. Makes 4 servings.

Note: Also good with mackerel, mullet, flounder, or haddock roe.

FILLETS OF SOLE, SUPREME

1½ pounds fresh or thawed frozen sole fillets
½ cup fish liquid
¼ cup butter or margarine
2 tablespoons all-purpose flour
½ cup milk
¼ cup white wine or sherry
1 egg, slightly beaten
　Salt and pepper

Poach fish as directed on page 686. Lift fish to greased shallow baking dish; reserve ½ cup liquid. Melt butter; blend in flour. Add milk and fish liquid slowly and cook until thickened, stirring constantly. Add wine and bring to a boil. Pour sauce slowly over egg, stirring constantly. Season to taste with salt and pepper. Pour over fish. Brown lightly under broiler unit. Serve at once. Makes 4 servings.

Note: Also good with flounder, whiting, ocean perch, lingcod, grouper, sheepshead, weakfish.

PANFRIED TROUT WITH ANCHOVY FILLETS

4 trout (about 1 pound each)
　Seasoned all-purpose flour
　Olive oil for frying
3 tablespoons butter or margarine
4 anchovy fillets, cut fine
½ cup white wine
1 teaspoon chopped fresh or dried mint
1 tablespoon chopped parsley
　Juice of 1 lemon

Wipe trout with damp cloth or paper towel. Roll in seasoned flour. Heat enough olive oil to cover bottom of skillet. Panfry fish for about 5 minutes on each side. Meanwhile, melt butter in small pan, add anchovy fillets, and heat for 5 minutes. Add wine, mint, and parsley and simmer for 3 minutes; add lemon juice. Put fish on hot platter and pour sauce over all. Serve at once. Makes 4 servings.

Note: Also good with butterfish, croakers, sunfish, fluke, drumfish, porgies.

PANNED TUNA FISH SWEET AND SOUR

2 pounds fresh or frozen tuna fish steaks
　Salt and pepper
　Fat for frying
2 large onions, sliced
⅓ cup wine vinegar
4 sprigs fresh mint or sweet basil, chopped
1 tablespoon sugar

Wipe fresh or thawed frozen tuna with a damp cloth or paper towel. Sprinkle with salt and pepper. Heat enough fat to cover bottom of skillet. Panfry fish for about 5 minutes on each side. Remove fish and set aside. Add onions to fat remaining in skillet and cook for 5 minutes. Then add vinegar, mint, and sugar. Cover and cook for 5 minutes longer; add fish and heat. To serve cold, pour hot sauce over fish and cool. Then chill. Makes 4 servings.

Note: Also good with swordfish, kingfish, salmon.

WHITEFISH CROQUETTES

3 cups flaked steamed whitefish fillets, about 1½ pounds raw (directions for steaming, page 686)
5 tablespoons butter or margarine
5 tablespoons all-purpose flour
¾ teaspoon salt
⅛ teaspoon white pepper
1½ cups milk
1 tablespoon each of minced onion and parsley
1 teaspoon vinegar
1 cup fine dry bread crumbs
1 egg, slightly beaten
2 tablespoons cold water
　Fat for deep frying

Mince fish fine. Melt butter in saucepan; blend in flour, salt, and pepper. Add milk slowly and cook until very thick, stirring constantly. Add onion, parsley, vinegar, and fish and mix well. Chill for several hours. Shape into 12 croquettes. Roll in crumbs and dip into egg mixed with water. Roll again in crumbs. Chill for at least 1 hour. Then fry in hot deep fat (370° to 375°F. on a frying thermometer) until golden brown. Drain on absorbent paper. Serve with Creole Sauce or Creamy Egg Sauce (see page 694). Makes 6 servings.

Note: Also good with haddock, cod, flounder, hake, ocean perch.

WHITEFISH WITH PIQUANT SAUCE

1 pound fresh or thawed frozen whitefish fillets
1 tablespoon cooking oil
1 tablespoon vinegar
2 tablespoons minced onion
1 teaspoon salt
2 teaspoons Worcestershire
⅓ cup ketchup
¼ cup water
1 tablespoon capers
1 cup cooked green peas

Whiting Chowder with Fish Balls

Wipe fish with damp cloth or paper towel. Cut into serving pieces. Bring oil, vinegar, onion, salt, Worcestershire, ketchup, and water to boil in top part of double boiler. Add capers and fish. Cover and cook over boiling water for about 25 minutes, or until fish is done, stirring gently several times. Add peas, heat thoroughly, and serve. Makes 4 servings.

Note: Also good with carp, mackerel, weakfish, sea bass, pike, hake, cod.

WHITING CHOWDER WITH FISH BALLS
- 2½ pounds fresh whiting
- 5 cups cold water
- 1 teaspoon salt
- ½ teaspoon peppercorns
- 1 bay leaf
- 2 parsley sprigs
- 2 celery stalks, cut
- 1 onion, sliced
  Fish Balls
- 4 cups diced peeled raw potatoes
- 3 tablespoons butter or margarine
- 3 tablespoons all-purpose flour
- 4 cups milk
  Dash of cayenne
  Paprika

Put bony section of fish in saucepan with water, seasonings, parsley, celery, and onion. Reserve remaining fish to use in Fish Balls. Heat slowly and simmer for 20 minutes. Strain into large kettle. Bring this fish stock to a boil; add Fish Balls and potatoes; cover, reduce heat, and simmer until potatoes are tender, about 20 minutes. Add hot white sauce made with the butter, flour, and milk. Mix lightly, taking care not to break the Fish Balls. Sprinkle with paprika and chopped parsley, if desired. Makes 6 servings.

Note: Also good with sheepshead, red snapper, carp, catfish.

Fish Balls
  Raw whiting
- 1 egg
- 2 tablespoons cracker crumbs
  Dash of ground mace
- 2 tablespoons minced parsley
- 1 teaspoon salt

Force boned fish through food chopper, using medium blade. Combine with remaining ingredients. Shape into 12 balls.

BROILED MARINATED WHITING
- 1½ pounds fresh or frozen whiting fillets
- ½ cup highly seasoned French dressing
  Paprika

Wipe fresh or thawed frozen fish with damp cloth or paper towel. Cut fish into serving pieces. Let stand in dressing in refrigerator for several hours. Arrange fish on broiler rack; broil under medium heat for about 5 minutes on each side,

or until done. Brush with the dressing used for marinating. Remove to hot platter. Pour drippings from broiler pan over fish. Sprinkle generously with paprika. Makes 4 servings.

Note: Also good with sole, flounder, perch, haddock, whitefish.

SAUCES FOR FISH

*Sauces can add flavor and zest
to plain fish cooked
by any of the basic methods*
Each recipe serves 4 people.

ANCHOVY BUTTER
Heat 3 tablespoons butter or margarine, 1 tablespoon anchovy oil, 2 tablespoons minced anchovy fillets, and 1 tablespoon fresh lemon juice. Good for hot poached, hot steamed, broiled, and baked fish.

BROWN-BUTTER SAUCE
Brown slowly, but do not burn, ¼ cup butter or margarine, stirring constantly. Add 2 teaspoons fresh lemon juice and ¼ teaspoon salt. Good for hot poached, hot steamed, broiled, and baked fish.

CHEESE-MUSTARD SAUCE
Add ⅓ cup shredded cheese (sharp Cheddar, Romano, Parmesan, or process American), ½ teaspoon powdered mustard, and a dash of garlic salt to 1 cup hot seasoned medium white sauce. Good for hot poached, hot steamed, broiled, and baked fish.

CHIFFONADE DRESSING
Combine 1 minced hard-cooked egg, 2 tablespoons minced beets or pimiento, 1 tablespoon minced parsley, 2 tablespoons minced green pepper, and ¾ cup French dressing. Good for cold poached or cold steamed fish.

CHILI-SAUCE BUTTER
Heat ¼ cup butter or margarine. Add 2 tablespoons chili sauce and 1 tablespoon fresh lemon juice. Good for hot poached, hot steamed, broiled, and baked fish.

CREAMED CELERY OR ONION SAUCE
Cook ¼ cup minced celery or onion in 1 tablespoon butter or margarine. Add to 1 cup hot seasoned medium white sauce. Good for hot poached, hot steamed, broiled, and baked fish.

CREAMY EGG SAUCE
Add 2 chopped hard-cooked eggs to 1 cup hot seasoned medium white sauce. Good for hot poached, hot steamed,

broiled, and baked fish.

CREOLE SAUCE
Cook ½ cup chopped onion and 1 minced garlic clove in 3 tablespoons cooking oil until yellowed. Add ½ cup chopped green pepper, 1 bay leaf, 2⅓ cups (one 1-pound, 3-ounce can) tomatoes, 1 teaspoon salt, ⅛ teaspoon pepper, and a dash of cayenne. Simmer for 20 minutes. Good for hot poached, hot steamed, broiled, and baked fish.

CURRY MAYONNAISE
Mix 1 to 3 teaspoons curry powder with 1 cup mayonnaise. Good for cold poached, cold steamed, and fried fish.

CURRY SAUCE
Add 1 to 3 teaspoons curry powder and 1 tablespoon fresh lemon juice to 1 cup hot seasoned medium white sauce. Good for hot poached, hot steamed, broiled, and baked fish.

DILL SAUCE
Add 3 tablespoons minced fresh dill to 1 cup hot seasoned medium white sauce. Good for hot poached, hot steamed, broiled, and baked fish.

EGG AND LEMON SAUCE
Beat 2 egg yolks until lemon-colored. Slowly add 1 cup liquid from poaching fish. Cook over hot water until slightly thickened, stirring constantly. Add 2 tablespoons fresh lemon juice and salt and pepper to taste. Serve at once. Good for hot poached fish.

GARLIC- OR ONION-VINEGAR SAUCE
Rub together 1 minced garlic clove or ½ medium onion, 1 teaspoon sugar, and ½ teaspoon paprika. Add ½ cup hot vinegar. Cool and strain. Good for cold poached, cold steamed, and fried fish.

GOLDENROD SAUCE
Add 2 chopped hard-cooked egg whites to 1 cup hot seasoned medium white sauce. Pour over fish and sprinkle with 2 sieved or riced hard-cooked egg yolks. Good for hot poached, hot steamed, broiled, and baked fish.

GREEN SAUCE
Slowly cook together ½ cup olive oil, 1 minced garlic clove, ⅓ cup minced parsley, 2 tablespoons minced green onion tops, and ½ teaspoon salt for 5 minutes. Add 2 chopped raw spinach leaves. Good for hot poached, hot steamed, broiled, and baked fish.

HERB AND WINE-VINEGAR SAUCE
Heat to boiling ½ cup wine vinegar, 1

onion slice, ½ bay leaf, and ¼ teaspoon each of ground thyme and sage. Cool and strain. Good for cold poached, cold steamed, and fried fish.

HOLLANDAISE SAUCE

Divide ½ cup butter or margarine (1 stick) into 4 pieces. Put 2 eggs, dash of cayenne, 2 tablespoons fresh lemon juice, and 1 piece of butter in top part of double boiler. Cook over ½ inch of boiling water, stirring constantly, until butter melts. Add other pieces of butter, one at a time, stirring until each melts. Then, drop by drop, add 1 tablespoon boiling water, stirring constantly. Serve at once. Good for hot poached and hot steamed fish.

HORSERADISH BUTTER

Heat ¼ cup butter or margarine. Add 1 tablespoon prepared horseradish and 1 teaspoon paprika. Good for hot poached, hot steamed, broiled, and baked fish.

HOT COCKTAIL SAUCE

Combine 1 cup chili sauce, 3 drops of hot pepper sauce, 2 tablespoons fresh lemon juice, 1 teaspoon salt, ¼ teaspoon pepper, 1 teaspoon Worcestershire, 1 tablespoon prepared horseradish, and 2 tablespoons pickle relish. Good for cold poached, cold steamed, and fried fish.

HOT TARTARE SAUCE

Heat together, over boiling water, ¾ cup medium white sauce, ¼ cup mayonnaise, 1 tablespoon fresh lemon juice, 1 teaspoon minced onion, 3 tablespoons minced dill pickle, and 2 tablespoons minced parsley. Add salt and pepper. Good for hot poached, hot steamed, fried, broiled, and baked fish.

LEMON AND CAPER BUTTER

Heat ¼ cup butter or margarine, 2 tablespoons capers, and 1 tablespoon fresh lemon juice. Good for hot poached, hot steamed, broiled, and baked fish.

MIXED HERB MAYONNAISE

Mix 1 cup mayonnaise with 1 teaspoon each of minced chives, dried or fresh marjoram, and fresh basil, mint, or thyme leaves. Good for cold poached, or cold steamed fish.

MUSHROOM SHERRY SAUCE

Cook ½ cup minced fresh mushrooms and 1 tablespoon minced onion in ¼ cup butter or margarine until tender. Add ½ teaspoon salt and 2 tablespoons sherry. Good for hot poached, hot steamed, broiled, and baked fish.

MUSTARD MAYONNAISE

Mix 2 teaspoons powdered mustard, 1 teaspoon sugar, 1 tablespoon malt vinegar, and 1 cup mayonnaise. Chill. Good for cold poached, cold steamed, and fried fish.

ONION OR GARLIC BUTTER

Heat ¼ cup butter or margarine and ½ minced onion or 1 minced garlic clove. Strain. Good for hot poached, hot steamed, broiled, and baked fish.

OYSTER SAUCE

Cook 8 oysters in 1 tablespoon butter or margarine until edges curl. Remove oysters and chop. Add enough light cream to make 1 cup liquid. Use combined cream and oyster liquor to make 1 cup thin cream sauce. Add oysters, salt and pepper to taste, and a dash of ground mace. Good for hot poached, hot steamed, broiled, and baked fish.

PARSLEY, CHERVIL, OR CHIVE BUTTER

Heat ¼ cup butter or margarine and 2 tablespoons minced parsley or chervil, or 1 tablespoon minced chives. Good for hot poached, hot steamed, broiled, and baked fish.

PIMIENTO BUTTER

Heat ¼ cup butter or margarine and 1 minced pimiento. Good for fried, broiled, and baked fish.

PIQUANT SAUCE

Mix ¼ cup thick condiment sauce with ⅔ cup mayonnaise or salad dressing. Good for cold poached, cold steamed, and fried fish.

RAVIGOTE SAUCE

To 1 cup hot thin white sauce add 1 tablespoon tarragon vinegar, juice of 2 lemons, 1 tablespoon each of minced shallot or green onion, fresh or dried chervil, tarragon, and chives. Keep hot for 5 minutes; strain. Beat in 1 tablespoon butter. Served hot it is good for hot poached, hot steamed, broiled, and baked fish. Served cold it is good for cold poached and cold steamed fish.

ROSEMARY MAYONNAISE

Mix 2 teaspoons minced fresh, or 1 teaspoon dried, rosemary leaves and 1 cup mayonnaise. Good for cold poached and cold steamed fish.

SAVORY BUTTER

Cream ⅓ cup butter or margarine until fluffy. Add 1 tablespoon each of minced green onion tops or chives, celery leaves,

and parsley, dash of garlic salt, ½ teaspoon salt, and ½ teaspoon ground sage. Serve cold on hot fish. Good for hot poached, hot steamed, broiled, and baked fish.

SHRIMP OR LOBSTER SAUCE

Add ⅓ cup minced cooked fresh or canned shrimps or lobster and 1 tablespoon fresh lemon juice to 1 cup hot seasoned medium white sauce. Good for hot poached, hot steamed, broiled, and baked fish.

SOUR-CREAM CUCUMBER SAUCE

Combine ¾ cup thick dairy sour cream, 1 tablespoon minced green onion tops, ½ cup grated cucumber, 1 teaspoon salt, 1 tablespoon fresh lemon juice, and a dash of cayenne. Good for cold poached, cold steamed, and fried fish.

SOY BUTTER SAUCE

Heat together 3 tablespoons butter or margarine and 3 tablespoons soy sauce. Good for hot poached, hot steamed, fried, broiled, and baked fish.

TARTARE SAUCE

Combine ⅔ cup mayonnaise, ½ teaspoon minced onion, 1 teaspoon minced parsley, 1 tablespoon each of chopped capers, pickle relish, and stuffed olives, and a dash of cayenne. Good for all fish.

THOUSAND ISLAND DRESSING

Add ¼ cup chili sauce, 2 tablespoons pickle relish, and 1 tablespoon minced green pepper to 1 cup mayonnaise. Good for cold poached and cold steamed fish.

TOMATO MAYONNAISE

Mix ¼ cup chili sauce or ketchup with ¾ cup mayonnaise and 1 teaspoon minced fresh basil. Good for cold poached, cold steamed, and fried fish.

VINAIGRETTE DRESSING

Combine and chill 1 teaspoon salt, ⅛ teaspoon pepper, dash of cayenne, ¼ teaspoon paprika, 3 tablespoons tarragon vinegar, ½ cup salad or olive oil, 1 tablespoon minced green pepper, 1 tablespoon minced parsley, 1 tablespoon chopped sweet pickle, 2 teaspoons chopped chives, and a few drops of onion juice. Good for cold poached, cold steamed, broiled, and baked fish.

WHIPPED-CREAM HORSERADISH SAUCE

Whip ½ cup heavy cream and fold in 1 teaspoon grated onion, 1 tablespoon prepared horseradish, and 1 teaspoon salt. Good for cold poached, cold steamed, and fried fish.

A GOOD MESS OF FISH

by James A. Beard

In answer to the question, "What is your favorite outdoor sport?" probably more Americans would list fishing than any other sort of recreation. My own devotion to the sport began on the banks of the Necanicum River in Oregon, a meandering stream that contained a flourishing colony of crayfish. As a lad in knee pants, I spent many happy hours catching those crayfish with a length of string baited with liver. I had an appreciative mother who delighted in cooking crayfish in spiced wine. We always ate them chilled, and even as a youth I sensed that this was something special.

Many of the world's great gastronomic treats are based on fresh-water fish. Most glamorous of all are freshly caught mountain trout cooked over an outdoor fire. But of course you don't have to be a sportsman to enjoy fish. I'll have to admit that just about the best fish I ever ate was one I didn't catch: poached pike served to me in a little French country inn. And not long ago I had another memorable dish called "A Mess of Lake Perch," served to me at the fabulous Detroit restaurant, The London Chop House, owned by my friend Lester Gruber.

Fortunately for those of us who love fish but who are too busy to catch them, there's bound to be at least one fisherman in the family or the neighborhood. And in recent years food stores have specialized in catering to local preferences. Our lakes and streams abound with fish of many varieties and each region has its favorites. You may choose one of several kinds of trout found in various sections of the country. Some form of fresh-water bass is found in almost every area. The Great Lakes region boasts the elegant whitefish, the fine lake perch and pike, the beloved *brochet* of the French. Crappies, sunfish, and suckers, the vacuum cleaners of the river bottoms, are

A Mess of Brook Trout served with crunchy bread, tomato and onion salad, and fresh fruit.

caught in great numbers. Catfish, which can grow to be as large as 400 pounds, are common and especially popular in the South. Some of the stranger fish, less often encountered, are the sheepshead (a musical fish that sings in the middle of the night), the prehistoric holdover called bowfin (it breathes out of water and burrows into the soil in time of drought), and the buffalo fish (a tasty morsel when smoked).

No matter what your choice in fish, remember this: all fish should be cooked quickly just until it flakes easily when tested with a fork or toothpick.

SAUTÉ MEUNIÈRE

This is the simplest and one of the truly classic ways of preparing fish.

To sauté, dip the fish into milk and roll lightly in flour. Melt plenty of butter in a skillet and let it heat through. Add the fish and cook over brisk heat until it is nicely browned on one side. Turn and brown on the other. Remove to a hot plate. Season and garnish with thin slices of lemon. Add a little more butter to the pan and, when it is melted, pour over the fish. Add an ample quantity of chopped parsley.

Variations

■ **Amandine**—This means the addition of thinly sliced, slivered, chopped, or whole almonds to the sauté. Almonds may be sautéed with the fish or separately with extra butter and added to the hot fish platter.

Chopped hazelnuts or filberts may be used in the same manner as the almonds for a sauté amandine.

■ **Fines Herbes**—Combine equal quantities of chopped parsley, chives, and tarragon and add to the pan just before pouring the sauce over the fish.

■ **Lemon Butter**—Remove fish from the pan, add 3 tablespoons melted butter, and season. Add 1 tablespoon fresh lemon juice and 6 paper-thin slices of peeled lemon; cook for 2 minutes; use to garnish fish.

TRUITE AU BLEU

Many people who eat the trout they catch on the scene feel the only way to cook them is to dip them into flour or cornmeal and sauté them in butter or bacon fat or a mixture of both. I have no argument with this method of preparation; it has my blessing. However, I am perfectly certain that if once you try live trout prepared in the classic manner favored by the Swiss and the French, you will never again use any other method.

Prepare a mixture of 3 parts water to 1 part vinegar. Add 6 peppercorns, part of a bay leaf, and 1 teaspoon salt to each quart of liquid. Bring this to a boil. Plunge in the trout, which have been quickly gutted, and poach them just long enough to cook them through, about 4 minutes for the average fish. Serve them hot with melted butter and boiled potatoes, or chill them and serve cold with mayonnaise.

The vinegar in the water turns the skin of the fish a vivid blue, hence the name *truite au bleu*.

COLD TROUT WITH DILL SAUCE

Poach 6 or 8 trout in Court Bouillon for 5 minutes, or until they are just cooked enough. Chill thoroughly. Remove part of the skin from the top of the trout, leaving the heads and tails intact. Sprinkle with finely chopped dill, parsley, and chives. Arrange alternate slices of cucumber and hard-cooked egg on each fish. Serve them with a sauce made with 1½ cups dairy sour cream, 1 tablespoon chopped fresh dill, 1 teaspoon grated onion, 1 teaspoon powdered mustard, and ½ cup finely chopped hard-cooked egg. Season with salt and pepper. Makes 6 to 8 servings.

Court Bouillon for Poaching Fish

Chop fine 8 to 10 shallots or 12 green onions, 1 garlic clove, 1 leek, 2 or 3 carrots, and plenty of parsley; add 1 teaspoon salt, 1 teaspoon pepper, 1 bay leaf, and a pinch of dried thyme. Cover with 1 cup dry white wine and 4 cups water. Put the Court Bouillon on the stove, bring to boil, and simmer for about 20 minutes. Strain the broth through a fine sieve; add the fish and slowly bring it to a boil. Simmer just long enough to cook the fish.

Court Bouillon Sauce

Reduce the broth quickly to 2 cups. Add 1 cup heavy cream and 4 or 5 egg yolks. Stir well until thickened, taking care that the mixture does not boil. Cream 4 to 5 tablespoons butter with a little flour and add it to the sauce. Stir until smooth, taste for seasoning, and pour over the fish.

COLD TROUT IN JELLY

    6 trout
      Court Bouillon (see above)
      White of egg and egg shells
 1½ envelopes unflavored gelatin
  ⅓ cup water
      Green onion, leek, or chive stems
      Tarragon leaves
      Hard-cooked eggs
      Mayonnaise

Poach the trout in the Court Bouillon and remove to a platter. Reduce the bouillon to 3 cups and clarify with the lightly beaten egg white and shells. Strain. Soften gelatin in the water and stir it into the boiling broth. Chill until it is thick and syrupy.

The fish may be decorated as elaborately as you choose. Or you may prefer to serve them plain, simply masked with the jelly. If you want a spectacular dish, remove about half of the skin from the chilled, cooked trout. Then make a flower design on the flesh: Use the green stems of onions, leeks, or chives, and green tarragon leaves, and make tiny flowers cut out of hard-cooked egg. Pour enough of the jelly over the decorated (or plain) trout to mask it thoroughly. Put the platter with the fish and a bowl of the rest of the jelly in the refrigerator to chill. Just before serving, chop the rest of the jelly very fine and garnish the fish platter with it. Serve with mayonnaise. Makes 6 servings.

FOILED TROUT

    2 carrots
    2 small white onions
    2 shallots or green onions
    2 stalks celery
      Butter or margarine
      Salt and pepper
    6 trout
      Cooking oil

Chop the vegetables fine and sauté them in ¼ cup butter until soft. Add salt and pepper to taste. Split and clean the trout, and stuff each one with a little of the mixture. Dot with butter and place about 3 inches from the broiler unit. Broil for 4 minutes. Season with salt and pepper. Have ready 6 heart-shape pieces of aluminum foil large enough for the trout. Place a fish on each piece of foil near one edge. Fold the rest of the foil *over* the fish and crimp the edges together so that the fish is sealed in. Oil the foil. Place these on a buttered cookie sheet and bake in preheated hot oven (425°F.) for 15 to 18 minutes. Makes 6 servings.

TRUITE FARCIE

    5 onions, chopped
      Butter or margarine
      Salt
  ½ pound raw white-meated fish
      Pepper
    2 egg yolks
    3 egg whites
      Chopped tarragon
      Chopped parsley
   12 good-size trout
    2 cups dry white wine
    1 cup thick white sauce

Sauté about half the chopped onion in 2 tablespoons butter until soft and golden. Season lightly with salt. Grind the white-meated fish several times; salt and pepper it to taste. Add it to the sautéed onion and blend together with a wooden spoon. Add the egg yolks and egg whites, slightly beaten, and season with tarragon and parsley. Stuff the trout with this mixture. Sauté remaining onion in 6 tablespoons of butter until soft. Force it through a sieve or food mill. Cover the bottom of a large shallow baking dish with this onion purée and arrange the trout on top. Dot them with butter, add the wine and bake in preheated very hot oven (450°F.) for 8 to 10 minutes, or until fish are just cooked. Remove to a hot platter. Force the onion-wine mixture through a sieve or food mill and combine it with the white sauce and 1 cup butter. Blend thoroughly and pour over the fish. Sprinkle with chopped parsley. Makes 12 servings.

TROUT IN A CHEMISE
This is the conceit of a very well known Parisian chef, who serves it as a specialty in his own restaurant.

- ½ pound mushrooms
- ¼ cup butter or margarine
  Salt and pepper
- 3 tablespoons all-purpose flour
- ¼ cup heavy cream
- 6 trout, prepared as in Sauté Meunière, page 698
- 6 French Pancakes
  Browned butter
  Lemon juice

Chop the mushrooms very fine. Sauté them in the butter until they are soft and well cooked. Sprinkle with salt, pepper, and the flour. Add the heavy cream and stir until the mixture is thick. Sauté the trout. Spread each French Pancake with the mushroom mixture, place a trout on top of this and roll up the pancake so that the head sticks out one end and the tail the other. Arrange these rolls in a baking dish. Cover with a little browned butter and lemon juice. Heat for just a moment or two in the oven and serve. Delicious with a good green salad and a brittle white wine. Makes 6 servings.

French Pancakes
Beat 1 egg well. Add ¼ cup milk, ¼ cup all-purpose flour, and ¼ teaspoon salt. Beat until smooth and blended. Brush a 7-inch skillet with melted butter or margarine. Put in 1 generous tablespoon of the batter. Working quickly, tip and tilt the pan so that the batter flows evenly over the bottom. Brown quickly on one side. Then turn and brown on the other. Proceed until all of batter is used. Makes 6 pancakes.

OVEN-BRAISED CARP FILLETS
A delightful recipe from the South of France

- 2 medium onions
  Oil
- 4 carp fillets or steaks
  All-purpose flour
- 2 garlic cloves, chopped
- ½ cup chopped parsley
  Dried thyme
- 1 teaspoon salt
- 1 teaspoon pepper
- 1 cup red wine
  Olive oil
  Tomato purée, about 1 cup

- 18 to 20 ripe olives
  Steamed rice

Chop the onions coarsely and place them on a well-oiled baking pan. Dip the fillets into flour and arrange them on the bed of onions. Sprinkle with the garlic, parsley, thyme, salt, and pepper. Add the red wine to the pan and then drizzle olive oil all over the fish. Top each fillet with 3 tablespoons tomato purée. Bake in preheated hot oven (425°F.) for 15 to 18 minutes, basting often with the wine in the pan. Remove fish to a hot serving platter. Blend the sauce in the pan with 3 or 4 more tablespoons tomato purée and add the ripe olives. Pour the sauce around the fish and serve with steamed rice. Makes 4 servings.

ALSATIAN CARP WITH SAUERKRAUT
A most unusual fish recipe.
On your first reading it may not appeal, but you will certainly use it over and over again after the first time.

- 4 pounds sauerkraut
- 4 garlic cloves
- 1 tablespoon coarsely ground pepper
  Beer
- 4 carp fillets
  All-purpose flour
  Butter or bacon fat
  Grated Gruyère or Cheddar cheese
  Dairy sour cream
  Buttered soft bread crumbs

Steam the sauerkraut mixed with the garlic, pepper, and 4 cups beer for 4 to 6 hours in a covered kettle over low heat. Dredge fillets with flour, and sauté in butter or bacon fat until they are nicely browned on both sides. Arrange a layer of the sauerkraut in the bottom of a well-buttered 3-quart baking dish, then add a layer of grated cheese, then a layer of the fish. Cover with sour cream. Repeat these layers and top with a layer of the kraut. Add 2 cups of beer or liquid from the sauerkraut, sprinkle with grated cheese and buttered crumbs. Dot with butter and bake in preheated moderate oven (350°F.) for about 30 minutes. Makes 8 servings.

SWEET-AND-SOUR CARP
Here is a recipe that you have longed to acquire every time you have visited a Chinese restaurant and eaten a steamed fish. If carefully arranged and skewered, it is a fascinating dish to present to your guests.

- 4 to 5 pounds carp
- ¾ cup pineapple juice
- ½ cup wine vinegar
- ½ cup sugar
- ½ cup water
- 3 tablespoons cornstarch
- 1 tablespoon soy sauce
- ½ cup each slivered green onion, green pepper, and pineapple

Clean and scale the fish. Place it on a rack over hot water so that the fish does not touch the water. Cover and steam until it flakes easily, about 25 minutes or

so. Arrange on a serving dish in the form of an S, using a skewer to hold it in place if you need to. Top it with the following sauce: Cook together the pineapple juice, the vinegar, the sugar, and water; thicken with cornstarch, blended with a little cold water. Add soy sauce, green onion, green pepper, and pineapple, and cook just long enough for the onion and pepper to turn bright green. Makes 8 to 10 servings.

WHITEFISH
Whitefish is one of the choicest morsels to come from the Great Lakes, one of the best of all fresh-water fish. Broil or sauté it, or try one of the following methods.

BAKED STUFFED WHITEFISH
Sauté slices of Spanish onion in butter until soft but not colored. Stuff the whitefish with the onion slices alternated with sliced peeled tomato, thinly sliced mushrooms, and chopped parsley. Season with salt and pepper to taste and dot with butter. Sew up the fish and place it in a well-oiled baking dish. Brush fish with oil, sprinkle it with salt and pepper, and bake in preheated hot oven (400°F.) for 25 to 35 minutes. Serve with a tomato sauce.

COLD WHITEFISH
Poach a whole whitefish in Court Bouillon (see page 698). Remove fish from the broth, cool, and chill. Remove the skin and leave head and tail intact. Mask with a mixture of ½ cup each of mayonnaise and dairy sour cream to which add 1 teaspoon prepared mustard, 2 tablespoons finely chopped onion, 2 tablespoons capers, 1 tablespoon finely chopped anchovy fillets, and 2 tablespoons tomato purée or strained chili sauce. Serve with vinegar and salt and pepper to taste.

DEEP-FRIED CATFISH
Use either the whole fish or pieces of fish. Heat fat to 370°F. on a frying thermometer. Beat 2 eggs lightly. Roll out cracker or bread crumbs or use cornmeal. Dip the fish into flour, then into beaten egg, and roll in the crumbs. Fry for 3 to 5 minutes. Drain and season. Serve with tartare sauce.

PIKE AND PICKEREL
Our inland waters are rich with several varieties of pike, pickerel, and muskellunge. Pike is an unpleasant-looking fish and a fierce one. It eats small waterfowl and mammals and puts up a strong fight when hooked. Thus it is one of the most popular sport fish. You may catch a pike which will weigh almost 25 pounds, but those you buy on the market will weigh from 2 to 10 pounds. The French value the delicacy of this fish and prepare it in many delightful ways. Among the most delicious is a braised stuffed pike.

BRAISED STUFFED PIKE

5- pound pike
½ cup chopped onion
½ cup butter
½ pound ground smoked ham
2 cups soft stale bread crumbs
½ cup chopped parsley
½ teaspoon dried thyme
½ teaspoon salt
1 teaspoon pepper
1 egg
  White wine
  Strips of salt pork
  Beurre manié*
2 egg yolks
  Dash of fresh lemon juice
  Chopped parsley

*Make *beurre manié* by kneading 1 table-spoon butter with 2 tablespoons flour. Clean the fish and prepare for stuffing. Sauté the onions in butter until soft. Combine with the next 7 ingredients. Stuff the fish with this mixture and sew it up. Place it in a shallow baking pan with enough white wine to cover the bottom of the pan well. Top the fish with strips of salt pork and bake in preheated moderate oven (350°F.) for about 45 minutes. Baste occasionally and cover the pan after the first 15 minutes of cook-ing. When the fish is done, remove pork and arrange the pike on a platter. Strain the pan juices and thicken with *beurre manié*. Add the slightly beaten egg yolks and stir until well blended. Do not let the sauce boil. Check for seasoning; add lemon juice and some chopped parsley. Pour over fish. Makes 5 or 6 servings.

POACHED PIKE

Poached pike, hot or cold, is a pleasant dish for winter or summer. It may be poached whole or in pieces of 3 to 4 pounds. Wrap the fish in cheesecloth with long ends to serve as handles on either side; use these to lower the fish into and remove it from the pot. Poach the fish in either salted boiling water or in Court Bouillon (page 698) until the fish flakes easily. Serve fish with parsley sauce, hollandaise, or lemon butter. Or try it with a rich cream sauce.

PIKE LOAF

1 pound pike
1 cup thick white sauce
1 whole egg
4 egg yolks
  Salt, pepper, and nutmeg
  Shrimp Sauce
  Cooked cleaned shelled shrimps

Grind the fish very fine. Then pound it in a mortar or give it a second grinding. Beat it with a wooden spoon until it forms a paste. Blend in the white sauce. Gradually work in whole egg and the yolks. Force the mixture through a fine sieve or a food mill. Season to taste with salt, pepper, and nutmeg, and pour into a well-buttered 1½-quart earthenware or glass casserole with straight sides. (A copper or glass oven dish with fairly straight sides will do.) Place the casserole in a pan of hot water and bake in pre-heated moderate oven (375°F.) for 25 or 30 minutes, or until just set. Unmold on a hot platter and surround with Shrimp Sauce. Garnish with cooked shrimp.

Sherry Shrimp Sauce

Heat 1 can frozen cream of shrimp soup with ¼ cup heavy cream. Add 2 table-spoons dry sherry.

COLD PIKE WITH HERBED MAYONNAISE

If you wish to serve a most attractive cold supper dish on a hot summer night, try this cold pike.

Poach the fish in Court Bouillon (see page 698) until it is just tender. Allow about 6 minutes per pound. When it flakes easily when tested with a fork, chill it; and when cool, skin it. If it is a whole fish, leave the head and tail intact. Arrange the cold poached pike on a bed of greens on a platter and cover with Herbed Mayonnaise.

Herbed Mayonnaise

To 2 cups mayonnaise add ¼ cup each of finely chopped parsley and finely chopped chives, ½ cup finely chopped raw spinach, 1 teaspoon chopped tarra-gon, and 1 tablespoon capers. Makes about 3 cups.

PIKE

I think it might be amusing and worthwhile to repeat what is perhaps the most famous recipe for fish in our culinary literature.

IZAAK WALTON'S RECIPE FOR ROASTING A PIKE
from *THE COMPLEAT ANGLER*

"First, open your Pike at the gills, and, if need be, cut also a little slit towards the belly. Out of these take his guts; and keep his liver, which you are to shred very small with thyme, sweet marjoram, and a little winter-savory; to these put some pickled oysters, and some an-chovies, two or three; both these last whole, for the anchovies will melt, and the oysters should not; to these you must add also a pound of sweet butter, which you are to mix with the herbs which are shred, and let them all be well salted. If the Pike be more than a yard long, then you may put into these herbs more than a pound, or if he be less, then less butter will suffice. These being thus mixed, with a blade or two of mace, must be put into the Pike's belly so sewed up as to keep all the butter in his belly if it be possible; if not, then as much of it as you possibly can: but take not off the scales. Then you are to thrust the spit through his mouth, out at his tail; and then take four, or five, or six split sticks, or very thin laths, and a convenient quantity of tape or filleting; these laths are to be tied around about the Pike's body from his head to his tail, and the tape tied somewhat thick to prevent his breaking or falling off from the spit. Let him be roasted very leisurely, and often basted with claret-wine, and an-chovies, and butter, mixed together; and also with what moisture falls from him into the pan. When you have roasted him sufficiently, you are to hold under him, when you unwind or cut the tape that ties him, such a dish as you purpose to eat him out of; and let him fall into it with the sauce that is roasted in his belly; and by this means the Pike will be kept unbroken and complete. Then, to the sauce which was within, and also that sauce in the pan, you are to add a fit quantity of the best butter, and to squeeze the juice of three or four oranges: lastly, you may either put into the Pike, with the oysters, two cloves of garlic, and take it whole out, when the Pike is cut off the spit; or to give the sauce a haut-gout, let the dish into which you let the pike fall be rubbed with it. The using or not using of this garlic is left to your discre-tion."

QUENELLES

Quenelles are delicate fish dumplings, one of the most famous dishes of France. They have always taken a tremendous amount of time to prepare. Ann Seranne has worked out a modern quick method, especially for me, which I give you here:

QUENELLES DE BROCHET

½ pound fillet of pike or snapper
½ teaspoon salt
1 egg white
1 ice cube, cracked
1 cup heavy cream
  Cooked shrimps

Slice the fish into strips ½ inch wide and put into the container of a blender with the salt. Cover and blend for 10 seconds, flicking motor on and off sev-eral times. Add egg white and cracked ice cube, cover, and blend for 10 sec-onds longer. Remove cover and gradually pour in the heavy cream. The mixture will be smooth, thick, and creamy. Drop the mixture from a tablespoon into a large skillet containing about 1 inch of lightly salted simmering water. Poach gently for 8 to 10 minutes. Remove with slotted spoon and place on platter. Makes 12 quenelles to serve 3 or 4. Garnish with cooked shrimps; or to accompany the quenelles, Ann Seranne suggests Brandy Clam Sauce.

Brandy Clam Sauce

½ cup butter
4 egg yolks

2 tablespoons brandy
Pinch of cayenne
⅓ cup hot cream
⅓ cup hot clam juice

In a small saucepan heat the butter to bubbling, but do not let it brown. Into the container of a blender put the egg yolks, brandy, and cayenne. Cover container and flick motor quickly on and off at high speed. Remove cover, turn motor on high, and gradually add the hot butter in a steady stream. Turn motor to low speed and gradually add the combined cream and clam juice. Heat over hot, not boiling, water, stirring. Makes about 2 cups.

FLAGEOLET

FLAGEOLET—A small green haricot bean which looks like a baby Lima bean and is used either fresh or dried. Flageolets are delicious whole or puréed, and are used as a garnish for meat dishes, especially lamb or mutton.

Flageolets are imported from France and Belgium either dried, or packed ready to heat and serve. Dried flageolets are soaked in water and cooked like other beans. To serve cooked flageolets, combine them with a little minced onion cooked in butter, or with crumbled crisp bacon or diced cooked ham.

FLAKE

FLAKE—A flake is a small, flat, thin, loose piece of food which looks like a scale rather than a crumb. Many of the cereal grains are available in flake form.

"To flake" is a term used in fish cookery. When fish flakes easily at the touch of a toothpick or fork, it is cooked.

FLAMBÉ, FLAMED

FLAMBÉ, FLAMED—The French word and the English one are synonymous and describe foods which are served flaming. This can be done by pouring a warmed spirit, such as brandy, over the food and setting it alight. Or sugar cubes may be soaked in spirits and put over the food or combined with it before it is ignited. As the alcohol burns away, a new and different flavor is added to main dishes, desserts, and beverages.

In French cooking, where flaming is much used, the process may also take place before the food is cooked. Meat and chicken dishes are browned in butter, flamed for the special flavor it adds, and then cooked.

The most frequently used spirits for flaming are brandy, rum, and kirsch. Any strongly alcoholic liquid, including flavoring extracts, can be flamed. The alcohol vanishes completely in the burning, leaving only the flavor of the liquid, so

that flamed foods may be eaten by people who do not care for alcohol, or are allergic to it.

The best known flamed foods are desserts, such as Crêpes Suzette, Cherries Jubilee, and English Plum Pudding. Taste is the best guide as to whether to flame a food or not.

Flaming has become a fashionable way to serve since it is a dramatic performance, especially by candlelight or by no other light than its own. The main thing to remember is that the spirit should be heated before setting it on fire. The best way of doing this is to warm a large spoon or a ladle over a flame, candle or kitchen stove, and pour the spirit into the spoon or ladle. You may then pour the warmed spirit over the food which is to be flamed.

A word of caution: Do not carry a flaming dish, but light it at the table. It is safer.

CHICKEN FLAMBÉE

1 frying chicken (about 3 pounds), quartered
¼ cup butter
1 teaspoon salt
Pepper
½ cup white wine
2 shallots, chopped
2 tablespoons chopped parsley
1 can (4 ounces) sliced mushrooms
¼ cup brandy

Brown chicken lightly on all sides in butter. Season with the salt and pepper to taste. Add white wine, cover, and simmer for about 30 minutes. Add shallots, parsley, and mushrooms, and continue cooking for about 15 minutes, or until chicken is tender and sauce is cooked down. Remove to warmed serving platter. Pour brandy over chicken and ignite. Makes 4 servings.

CRÊPES SUZETTE

4 eggs, well beaten
1 cup milk
1 cup sifted all-purpose flour
1 tablespoon brandy
1 teaspoon salt
2 teaspoons sugar
Melted butter
Suzette Sauce

Mix well all ingredients except Suzette Sauce. Let stand in refrigerator for 2 to 3 hours. When thicker than heavy cream, add a little more milk. Heat a 7- or 8-inch skillet and brush with melted butter. Put in 1 generous tablespoon batter. Working quickly, tip and tilt the pan so that the batter flows evenly over the bottom. Cook quickly. As soon as the pancake browns on one side, turn quickly and brown the other side. Proceed until all of batter is used. Reheat the Suzette Sauce. Makes about 32 crêpes.

Suzette Sauce

Cream 1 cup sweet butter until light and fluffy. Add grated rinds of 1 small orange and 1 lemon and ¼ cup sugar. Melt in top pan of chafing dish over direct heat. Add juice of 1 orange and heat to reduce mixture to half. Add 2 ounces (¼ cup) each of brandy and Curaçao or Cointreau and 1 ounce (2 tablespoons) kirsch. Ignite with match flame. Then add the crêpes, one at a time. Bathe each in the sauce, fold in quarters, and put to one side of the pan. When all are ready to serve, sprinkle with a little sugar, pour on about 2 ounces of brandy and ignite.

FLAMING CHERRIES JUBILEE

About 2 cups (1-pound, 1-ounce can) dark sweet cherries
2 tablespoons sugar
Dash of salt
1 tablespoon cornstarch
⅓ cup rum, brandy or kirsch
1 quart ice cream

Drain cherries and pit. Add enough water to syrup to make 1 cup. In top pan of chafing dish mix sugar, salt, and cornstarch. Add syrup. Cook over direct heat until slightly thickened. Add cherries and heat. Add liquor, ignite and spoon over ice cream. Makes 6 servings.

BANANAS AU RHUM

¼ cup butter or margarine
6 ripe bananas, peeled and halved
¼ cup firmly packed brown sugar
Ground cinnamon
½ cup rum or kirsch

Melt butter in top pan of chafing dish over direct heat. Add bananas; sprinkle with half of sugar and a dash of cinnamon. Cook until bananas are lightly browned. Turn, and sprinkle again with sugar and cinnamon. When soft, add rum and ignite. Sprinkle some of the sauce over each portion. Makes 4 servings.

FLAMING PLUM PUDDING

½ cup dried currants
½ cup raisins
⅓ cup brandy
½ cup sugar
3 cups sifted all-purpose flour
1 teaspoon baking soda
1½ teaspoons salt
½ teaspoon each of ground ginger, cloves, and nutmeg
1 teaspoon ground cinnamon

½ cup chopped nuts
¼ cup each of chopped citron and
    candied orange peel
1 apple, grated
1 cup suet, chopped fine
1½ cups milk
½ cup molasses
½ cup brandy
    Brandy Hard Sauce

Soak the currants and raisins overnight in ⅓ cup brandy. Sift dry ingredients together; add the soaked currants and raisins with any liquid remaining, the nuts, citron, orange peel, and apple. Stir in suet, milk, and molasses. Pour into 2 buttered 1-½-quart molds. Cover tightly with a lid or double thickness of wax paper or foil; secure with string. Put on rack in bottom of large kettle; add boiling water to half cover mold. Cover and steam for 3 hours. Unmold on a heat-proof plate. Pour ½ cup brandy, heated and flaming, over the pudding and serve. Serve Brandy Hard Sauce separately. Makes 8 servings.

Brandy Hard Sauce

Cream 1 cup sweet butter and 2 cups sifted confectioners' sugar; beat in 1 teaspoon vanilla and ¼ cup brandy. Makes 2 cups.

NEW ORLEANS CAFÉ BRÛLOT

½ cinnamon stick
6 whole cloves
    Rind of ½ lemon, thinly cut
    Rind of ¼ orange, thinly cut
3 sugar lumps
½ cup brandy
3 cups strong coffee

Place cinnamon, cloves, lemon and orange rinds, and sugar lumps in brûlot bowl or chafing dish. Pour brandy into large heated ladle. Flame brandy and pour over ingredients in bowl. Keep on ladling the brandy until the sugar has completely dissolved. Gradually add coffee, ladling the mixture until the flame has died out. Serve immediately. Makes 4 servings.

Chicken Flambée ▲

New Orleans Café Brûlot ▼

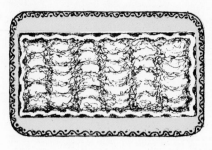

FLAN—A flan can be either of two things: One, a straight-sided, open-faced tart that stands alone in its own pastry shell with any savory or sweet filling. This kind of flan is a feature of French cooking. *Quiche Lorraine* is the best known of the savory flans.

The flan tart is made with flan rings, which can be bought in hardware or household stores. Flan rings are simple metal hoops of varying heights, that are placed on a cookie sheet. The pastry is placed on the cookie sheet inside the ring for the bottom of the tart. The ring is also lined with pastry. The pastry may be baked empty or with a filling. When the flan is done, the ring is removed and the flan slid onto a rack or a serving dish. Flans can also be baked in springform pans, which have removable bottoms. The whole pan is lined with pastry. When ready to be unmolded, the pan is set on a wide-mouthed jar and the upper ring part of the pan is loosened and allowed to slide down to the table. Then, a long thin knife or spatula is run under the flan so that it can be slid off the bottom of the pan onto a dish. A flan ring can be improvised by shaping several layers of heavy-duty aluminum foil into the desired shape.

When baking a flan which will be filled later, it should be treated as a pie shell is: in order to prevent the pastry from puffing up or collapsing, the dough should be covered with a sheet of heavy unwaxed brown paper and weighted with dry beans or rice. These will hold the pastry against the mold during the baking. Paper and beans are then removed.

The second culinary meaning of the word flan is a custard or caramel cream thickened with eggs or with other thickening agents such as Irish moss or gum arabic. This kind of flan is a standard dessert in Spanish-speaking countries.

QUICHE LORRAINE
1½ cups (6 ounces) grated imported
    Swiss cheese
8 slices of crisp bacon, crumbled
    Pastry for 1-crust pie, unbaked

3 eggs
1 cup heavy cream
½ cup milk
½ teaspoon salt
¼ teaspoon pepper
  Dash of cayenne
½ teaspoon powdered mustard

Sprinkle cheese and bacon into pastry-lined pie pan. Beat remaining ingredients together and pour over cheese and bacon. Bake in preheated moderate oven (375°F.) for 45 minutes, or until firm and browned. Makes 6 servings.

APPLE FLAN
¼ cup sugar
⅛ teaspoon salt
  Butter
1 egg yolk
¼ teaspoon vanilla extract
1 cup unsifted all-purpose flour (not
    instant type)
  Grated rind of ½ lemon
1 cup sweetened applesauce
2 cups thinly sliced peeled apples
½ cup honey
½ teaspoon cinnamon

Put sugar, salt, 6 tablespoons butter at room temperature, egg yolk, vanilla, flour, and lemon rind in bowl. Blend with fingers, kneading until mixture holds together. If very soft, refrigerate for 30 minutes. Press dough on bottom and sides of loose-bottomed round layer pan (9 inches). Press with palms or fingers to even dough. Trim edges with dull knife and refrigerate until firm. Or put in freezer for 30 minutes before filling. Spread bottom of shell with applesauce. Mix apples, honey, and 2 tablespoons melted butter, and arrange on applesauce. Sprinkle with cinnamon. Bake in preheated very hot oven (450°F.) for 10 minutes. Reduce heat to moderate (350°F.) and bake for 35 to 40 minutes longer. Cool to room temperature. Remove rim of pan and cut flan in wedges. Makes 6 servings.

FLAN DE PIÑA
(Pineapple Caramel Custard)
2 cups pineapple juice
2 cups sugar
¼ cup water
5 eggs

Heat pineapple juice with 1 cup sugar. Boil over moderate heat until a thin syrup is formed (222°F. on a candy thermometer), or until pineapple syrup spins a thread 2 inches long when dropped from a fork or spoon. Remove from heat and cool. Boil 1 cup sugar with water for 8 minutes. Pour this syrup into a 9-inch layer-cake pan and carmelize to a golden color over low heat. Swirl pan to coat sides and bottom. Beat eggs lightly and combine with cooled pineapple syrup. Strain mixture into caramel-coated pan. Place pan into a pan containing 1 inch of hot water

and bake in preheated moderate oven (350°F.) for 1 hour, or until set. Cool completely before unmolding upside down on a platter. Makes 6 to 8 servings.

FLANK—A cut of beef taken from the side of the animal between ribs and hip. It is available as flank steak and as flank-steak fillets and is most often braised or broiled.

FLANNEL CAKE—A griddle cake. This name, used most frequently in New England or camp cookery, implies a thick pancake made in plate size.

FLANNEL CAKES
2 cups all-purpose flour
3 teaspoons baking powder
2 teaspoons sugar
½ teaspoon salt
2 eggs, separated
1½ cups milk
2 tablespoons melted butter

Sift together flour, baking powder, sugar, and salt. Beat egg yolks well, and add milk and butter. Pour into the flour and mix until just blended. Beat the egg whites until stiff but not dry. Fold into the flour mixture. Pour ½ to ¾ cup onto hot greased griddle. Spread with spoon if necessary. Brown on one side, turn and brown on the other side. Serve hot with syrup and sausages. Makes about 4 to 6 cakes.

FLAPJACK—Call them flapjacks, hot-cakes, wheat cakes, flannel cakes, or pancakes; they are all griddle cakes and their batters resemble each other closely.

LOGGERS' FLAPJACKS
1¾ cups all-purpose flour
1 teaspoon baking powder
½ teaspoon salt
1 teaspoon baking soda
½ cup sour milk or buttermilk
1 cup milk
1 egg, beaten

Sift together flour, baking powder, and salt. Stir soda into sour milk. Add milk and beaten egg. Beat mixture into flour. Cook on hot bacon-greased griddle. Makes about 12 flapjacks.

FLATFISH—Any of a very large group of fish found in seas throughout the world. The best known food fish in the group are flounder, halibut, turbot, and sole.

FLAVOR—The qualities of a substance affecting the senses of smell and taste are called "flavor." When applied to food, flavor is more specifically the blend of taste, odor, and feeling sensations obtained from a substance in the mouth.

The subject of flavor is a complicated one since it depends on a number of factors, and since flavor itself has an elusive and highly individual nature. Ordinarily, we think of flavor as "taste," and it may come as a surprise that not only the sense of taste, but also the senses of smell and feeling are involved in determining a flavor. There have been many attempts at classifying the nature and work of the senses. But although much research has been done on hearing and vision, little has been done for tasting, feeling, and smelling, so that there are few basic definitions of the characteristics of these senses.

Speaking of taste, sweet, sour, salt, and bitter are the four usually accepted components which are detected by the taste buds in the mouth and pharynx. Taste is affected by temperature, by texture, and by a person's sensitiveness to its various components. For instance, when ice cream is melted to room temperature, it tastes much sweeter than when cold, and it is much more flavorful when eaten slowly in small spoonfuls, rather than quickly. To taste a food reliably for seasoning, it should be neither very hot nor very cold.

Smelling is also still a rather mysterious process and there is even disagreement as to where exactly it takes place in the back of the nose. Perceiving odors is a very personal business, so that there is no agreement as to how many basic odors there really are.

The sense of touch, of feeling, works in its own mysterious ways, too. Milk chocolate, for instance, doesn't taste right unless it is on the thick side, but the contrary applies to bittersweet chocolate.

The greatest age for the introduction of new flavors was the first part of the 17th century, when coffee, chocolate, tea, and a great number of exotic spices from such newly discovered areas as North America, Central and South America, and the Far East became widely known in Europe.

FLAVORING—A substance added to food to give it a particular flavor. Spices, condiments, grated fruit rinds, and liqueurs are considered flavorings, but more specifically, the word is used in reference to essences or extracts of spices, nuts, herbs, fruits, and some flowers in alcoholic solutions. Among the many available are: almond, anise, banana, brandy, celery, cherry, cinnamon, cloves, coconut, coffee, ginger, lemon, maple, mocha, orange, orange-flower, peach, peppermint, pineapple, pistachio, raspberry, rosewater, rum, sherry, spearmint, strawberry, vanilla, walnut, and wintergreen.

FLITCH—This is an English term for a whole side of salt pork or more specifically, a side of bacon.

FLOATING ISLAND—This poetically named dessert consists of a soft custard topped with puffs of meringue baked in the oven until slightly brown; or a soft custard topped with puffs of meringue which have been cooked until firm in scalding milk. Floating Island belongs to the group of creamy desserts that was so popular in Victorian and Edwardian days.

FLOATING ISLAND

    3 egg whites
       Salt
   10 tablespoons sugar
   1½ cups milk
    ½ cup light cream
    6 egg yolks
    1 teaspoon vanilla extract

Beat egg whites until foamy. Add ⅛ teaspoon salt, then 6 tablespoons sugar gradually, continuing to beat until stiff. Drop by heaping tablespoonfuls into ½ inch of boiling water in shallow baking pan. Bake in preheated slow oven (325°F.) for 10 minutes. Carefully remove meringues from water and let stand until cold. Meanwhile scald milk and cream in top part of double boiler over hot water or in a heavy saucepan. Beat egg yolks slightly, just enough to mix. Stir in ¼ teaspoon salt and remaining sugar, then slowly add the heated milk and cream. Return immediately to top part of double boiler over hot, not boiling, water and cook, stirring constantly, until thick enough to coat a metal spoon. Cool; add vanilla. Cover and chill. Serve topped with the meringue "islands." Makes 4 servings.

FLORENTINE—This is a cooking method which uses spinach as its base. Eggs, fish, or chicken are most often cooked à la Florentine. They are set on a bed of spinach, covered with a white or cheese sauce, sprinkled with cheese, and baked in the oven or cooked under the broiler.

CHICKEN FLORENTINE

    2 pounds fresh, or 2 boxes frozen
       chopped spinach
    ¼ cup butter
    1 garlic clove, mashed
       Dash each of ground marjoram and
       basil
    ¼ cup all-purpose flour
    ⅓ cup light cream
       Meat from one 5-pound chicken,
       poached
    ¾ cup light cream
    ¾ cup chicken stock
       Salt and pepper
    6 thin slices of Canadian bacon
    1 cup grated Parmesan cheese

Cook, drain and chop fresh spinach. Or, if frozen is used, cook as directed on the label and drain. Melt 1 tablespoon butter and in it cook the garlic, marjoram, and basil, stirring constantly, for 5 minutes. Add 1 tablespoon flour and mix well. Add ⅓ cup cream and the spinach and simmer for 5 minutes, stirring constantly. Put spinach into the bottom of a casserole. Cover with the chicken cut into slices. Melt remaining butter and blend in remaining flour smoothly. Add ¾ cup cream and the stock and stir until thickened. Season to taste with salt and pepper. Sauté the bacon in a lightly greased skillet and cut it into thin slivers. Add to sauce and pour over the chicken. Cover all with grated cheese and bake in preheated hot oven (400°F.) for 20 minutes, or until cheese is delicately brown. Makes 6 servings.

Note: Hot croissants are delicious with this dish. A salad of thinly sliced cucumbers, wilted in a good tart French dressing, is also an excellent addition.

FLOUNDER FLORENTINE

    2 cups water
       Salt
    1 pound flounder fillets
    1 pound fresh, or 1 box frozen
       chopped spinach
    3 tablespoons butter or margarine
    3 tablespoons flour
       Dash of cayenne
   1¼ cups milk
    ¼ cup heavy cream, whipped
    ¼ cup grated Parmesan cheese

Bring water to boil in skillet. Add 1 teaspoon salt. Simmer flounder in the water for 10 minutes, or until fish flakes easily with a fork. Remove from water. Cook, drain and chop fresh spinach. Or, if frozen is used, cook as directed on the label and drain. Put in shallow 1½-quart baking dish. Put fish on top. Melt butter, blend in flour, ½ teaspoon salt, and the cayenne. Gradually add milk and cook, stirring, until smooth and thickened. Fold in cream and pour over fish and spinach. Sprinkle with cheese. Put under broiler until delicately browned and heated. Makes 3 or 4 servings.

Note: Sole, cod, or other lean white fish can also be used.

EGGS FLORENTINE

    1 pound fresh, or 1 box frozen chopped
       spinach
    4 eggs, poached
   1½ cups medium white sauce
    ½ cup grated Parmesan cheese

Cook, drain and chop fresh spinach. Or, if frozen is used, cook as directed on the label and drain. Put in hot shallow broilerproof baking dish and make 4 depressions in it. Put 1 egg in each depression. Cover with white sauce and sprinkle with cheese. Put under broiler until delicately browned. Makes 4 servings.

FLOUNDER—The name is used for a large family of salt-water flatfish found in the coastal waters of the North and South Atlantic and in the southern part of the Pacfic Ocean. The flounder family includes gray sole, summer flounder (also called fluke), winter flounder, lemon sole, and dabs. The most common flounders are dark gray on top and white at the bottom. The eyes are on top.

Flounders are important food fish and in season all year. The flesh is lean and sweetly flavored. Their weight generally ranges from one-half to five pounds, although summer flounder may weigh as much as fifteen pounds.

Availability—Fresh flounder is available all year round, whole and in fillets. Frozen flounder is available in fillets, stuffed fillets, fillet dinners and may occasionally be available packaged whole.

Purchasing Guide—Whole fish should have bright, clear, bulging eyes, reddish gills, and tight shiny scales. Look for fillets that are firm fleshed and have a fresh odor. Avoid fish that is soft and flabby.

Storage—Fresh flounder is very perishable. Wrap fish in moisture-proof covering or place in a tightly covered container. Keep fish in the coldest part of the refrigerator. Frozen fish should be kept solidly frozen until ready to use. Once thawed, use it immediately.

☐ Fresh, refrigerator shelf: 1 to 2 days
☐ Fresh, refrigerator frozen-food compartment, prepared for freezing: 2 to 3 weeks
☐ Frozen, refrigerator frozen-food compartment: 2 months
☐ Fresh, prepared for freezing, or frozen, freezer: 1 year

Nutritive Food Values—Fish is a very good source of protein and contains iron, calcium and vitamins A and B.

☐ 3½ ounces, cooked = 202 calories

Basic Preparation—Wash fish quickly in cold, salted water. Do not allow fish to remain in water as it may lose flavor and nutrients. Frozen fish should be thawed in the refrigerator; allow about 8 hours for 1 pound of fish.

Flounder is a tender fish and may be cooked by either dry- or moist-heat methods. It may be broiled, baked, poached, fried, or steamed. See Cooking Methods, under Fish, page 683. Cook fish using low or moderately high heat until it flakes easily when tested with a fork. Avoid overcooking as it tends to make fish dry and tough. Use thawed frozen fish interchangeably with fresh fish in recipes. When cooking frozen fish without thawing, use a lower temperature and cook for a longer period of time.

To freeze, see Basic Preparation of Fish, page 683.

FLAKED FLOUNDER COCKTAIL
1½ cups flaked cooked flounder
½ cup chili sauce
1 tablespoon prepared white horseradish
1 tablespoon fresh lemon juice
½ teaspoon salt
⅛ teaspoon white pepper
4 lettuce leaves, shredded

Chill flounder for several hours. Combine remaining ingredients, except lettuce, to make sauce. Chill. Arrange fish on lettuce in chilled cocktail glasses. Top with sauce. Serve very cold. Makes 4 servings.

FLOUNDER MONTEREY
1½ pounds flounder fillets
Salt and pepper
⅓ cup dry white wine
Juice of 1 lemon
1 bay leaf, crushed
⅛ teaspoon ground ginger
¼ cup butter or margarine
1 tablespoon instant minced onion
2 parsley sprigs, chopped

Season fish with salt and pepper. Cut into serving pieces. Roll up and secure with toothpicks. Put remaining ingredients in skillet and bring to boil. Add fish and simmer, covered, for 10 minutes. Spoon some of sauce over fish once or twice. Makes 4 servings.

FLOUNDER AND SHRIMPS
2 cups water
Salt
1 pound flounder
3 tablespoons butter or margarine
2 tablespoons all-purpose flour
Juice of 1 lemon
1 egg yolk
½ cup heavy cream
1 cup cooked shrimps
Pepper
Chopped parsley

Bring water to boil in skillet. Add 1 teaspoon salt. Simmer fish in the water for 10 minutes, or until done. Remove fish to a hot platter; keep warm. Reserve 1¼ cups liquid. Melt butter. Stir in flour. Gradually stir in liquid. Cook over low heat, stirring constantly, until smooth and thick. Stir in lemon juice and egg yolk mixed with cream. Cook for 5 minutes longer. Add shrimps and season to taste. Heat and pour over fish. Sprinkle with parsley. Makes 4 servings.

FLOUNDER AND RICE CROQUETTES
2 cups flaked steamed fresh or frozen flounder fillets (about 1 pound raw)
1 small onion, minced
¼ cup margarine
⅓ cup all-purpose flour
1¼ teaspoons salt
⅛ teaspoon white pepper
1 cup tomato juice
1 teaspoon each of Worcestershire and prepared horseradish
1 cup cold cooked rice
¾ cup crushed cornflakes
1 egg
2 tablespoons cold water
Fat for deep frying

Mince fish fine. Cook onion in margarine until yellowed; blend in flour, salt, and pepper. Add tomato juice slowly and cook until thickened, stirring constantly. Add Worcestershire, horseradish, fish, and rice, and mix well. Chill for several hours. Shape into 8 croquettes. Roll in cereal and dip into beaten egg mixed with cold water. Roll in cereal again. Chill for 1 hour. Fry in hot deep fat (370° to 375° F. on a frying thermometer). Makes 4 servings.

FLOUNDER WITH TARTARE SAUCE
1½ pounds fresh or thawed frozen flounder fillets
¼ cup milk
⅓ cup fine dry bread crumbs
1 teaspoon salt
⅛ teaspoon white pepper
¼ cup melted butter or margarine
⅔ cup mayonnaise
½ teaspoon minced onion
1 teaspoon minced parsley
1 tablespoon each of chopped capers, pickle relish, and chopped stuffed olives
Dash of cayenne

Wipe fish with damp cloth or paper towel. Cut into serving pieces. Dip into milk; then roll in crumbs mixed with salt and pepper. Arrange on a greased cookie sheet. Pour butter over fish and bake in preheated slow oven (325°F.) for 25 to 30 minutes. Meanwhile, combine mayonnaise and remaining ingredients, chill, and serve cold on hot fish. Makes 4 servings.

FLOUR—Flour is finely ground meal made from grain. It is usually bolted (sifted) to obtain the very finest particles. When the term flour is used without any further description, it refers to white wheat flour. However, flours made from different grains are available. These include flours made from barley, buckwheat, corn, cottonseed, Lima beans, peanuts, potatoes, rye, rice, and soybeans.

Making flour is a process as old as civilization itself. As soon as man had begun to cultivate cereal grains for food instead of hunting and foraging for it, the milling of flour followed as a natural process. As we see in Egyptian wall paintings of 3,000 years ago, stone crushers were being used to grind grain into flour. The grain was placed in the hollow of a stone and pounded with another stone which, in time, was fashioned to fit the shape of the hand. This mortar and pestle method can still be seen in use in Mexico and wherever Indians grind their corn by hand.

In the course of time, this first primitive stone crusher developed into the saddle stone, a sloping stone placed on a pedestal slanting away from the grinder, so that as the flour was ground, it could be pushed into a receptacle below the stone. This was in use for thousands of years.

The Romans revolutionized flour-grinding with the invention of the quern, the forerunner of the millstone. The quern was round, with a grooved, flat or slightly convex surface and was stationary. On it, another grooved round stone was rotated, crushing the grain which was fed through a central hole. The stones were so arranged that the space at the rim was narrower than the space near the center. Thus the grain, fed in at the center, was first crushed, and as it traveled towards the rim, ground. In time, these grinding processes milled more flour through the use of larger stones. The people took their grain to state-owned mills to be ground, and this was the beginning of the professional millers and, later, bakers, who have played such a colorful and leading role in the history of the western world.

Millstones, specially hewn and dressed stones which had evolved from the quern, came into use about the 14th century and served until the 19th century. In 1870 the roller process, which is still in use, was introduced to the United States. In this process the grain is pulverized between corrugated and smooth steel rolls.

As for the power needed to grind grain into flour, for thousands of years it was supplied by man, or woman, and beast. The Greeks, around 100 B.C., invented the waterwheel, which substituted waterpower for man or animal power. It is not known who first thought of harnessing the wind for the job, but windmills were

known in Europe by the 12th century. Man, animals, water, and wind served until the invention of the steam engine. Steampower was first used in a flour mill about 1820.

The first mention of a wheat mill in the United States is in Governor Winthrop's *Journal* in 1632, which contains a notation that a windmill was moved from Newton (Cambridge) to Boston because it would not grind with a westerly wind. The first water mill of record was built at Dorchester in 1634; thereafter, wheat growing and milling expanded so rapidly that New England exported flour to other colonies as well as to the West Indies.

Today, flour milling is one of the major American industries, carried on in giant mills according to government specifications that include regulations as to the kinds of wheat or other grains used to produce certain flours and the way the flour is processed, enriched, and packaged.

Refining flour is the process of separating the endosperm from the bran and germ. The completeness of separation determines the resulting grade of flour. If the separation is so complete that only the heart of the endosperm is used, the resulting flour may be called a "fancy" or "short patent." Cake flour is fancy or short patent. Whole-wheat flour is unrefined because no separation of the three elements of the wheat kernel has occurred.

Flour, when it is first milled, has a slightly yellow color. In addition, freshly milled wheat flour does not bake as good a loaf of bread as a matured flour. Natural aging will bleach and mature the flour without the use of chemicals, but this requires several weeks for most flours. Chemicals are often used to bring about these changes quickly. An oxidizing agent —chlorine dioxide is a typical one—is used to increase the whiteness of the flour as well as to mature it. Chlorine-treated cake flours are said to make cakes that are less likely to fall and that will carry a higher percentage of shortening and sugar, thus producing sweeter and tenderer cakes. Bakers regard maturing of flour as more important than bleaching. Potassium bromate is a chemical which has no bleaching action but does have maturing action. Chemicals for bleaching or maturing are optional ingredients and flour in which they are used must be labeled "Bleached."

Availability and Purchasing Guide

Wheat Flour—This is available in the following forms:

Whole-Wheat, Graham, or Wheat Flour

—These terms are synonymous for flour made from any cleaned, unrefined, unbleached wheat other than durum or red durum wheat. The proportions of the natural constituents of the wheat (bran, endosperm, and germ) remain unaltered. *Gluten Flour* is a high-protein wholewheat flour from which the starch has been removed.

Flour, White, Plain, All-Purpose, or General-Purpose Flour—These terms are synonymous for refined wheat flour. It is available bleached and unbleached. It can be used in any recipe calling simply for "flour" with no other special qualification mentioned. Different blends of this flour are prepared to conform to the baking tastes of different areas. For example, a blend made from softer wheat is marketed in the South whereas a blend made from harder wheat is marketed in the North. *Bran Flour* is a flour into which bran is mixed. *Cracked-Wheat Flour* is a flour into which cracked wheat is mixed. *Wheat-Germ Flour* is a flour into which powdered wheat germ is mixed.

Cake Flour—This is a highly refined bleached flour so uniformly and finely ground that it feels soft and satiny. It is also the flour used, with other ingredients, in the many cake mixes available.

Self-Rising Flour—Refined bleached flour to which leavening ingredients and salt, in the proper proportion for home baking, have been added. It is available in all-purpose and cake flours.

Enriched Flour—This is refined bleached flour to which vitamins and minerals have been added. The amounts added per pound of flour are prescribed by Federal regulations. The standards used are set at a level to approximate whole-wheat flour, as follows:

	Minimum	Maximum
Iron	13.0 mg.	16.5 mg.
Niacin	16.0 mg.	20.0 mg.
Riboflavin	1.2 mg.	1.5 mg.
Thiamine	2.0 mg.	2.5 mg.

Enriched flour may also contain, per pound of flour:

	Minimum	Maximum
Calcium	500 mg.	625 mg.
Vitamin D	250 USP units	1,000 USP units

Instant-Type Flour—This flour represents the newest development in milling. Its granular structure makes it easier to pour and easier to measure without packing than other flours are. It does not need sifting and mixes into cold liquids without lumping. However, it is not as suitable for dredging as ordinary flour, and in baking, it is very important to use recipes specifically developed for it, since straight substitutions do not work in all recipes.

Other Flours—Flours made from other grains and seeds are available. Generally they are found in combination with wheat flour because, with the exception of rye, they lack the gluten-forming proteins necessary for baking. Many of them, however, are available pure (without the addition of wheat flour) in health-food stores.

Arrowroot Flour—Derived from the crushed root stocks of the maranta plant of tropical America. It is easily digested and is often used in commercially made cookies for children and invalids.

Barley Flour—Made by a process similar to that used for making flour. The flour lacks the acrid flavor of the whole kernel as this flavor is removed with the husk. Barley is lower than wheat in protein but is a nutritious grain and contains many minerals. It is more popular in Europe for making bread than in the United States. It lacks gliadin which makes it difficult to use in making yeast breads.

Buckwheat Flour—The finely ground product obtained by sifting buckwheat meal.

Carob Flour—The carob is a tree of the Mediterranean area, the long pods of which contain a sweetish pulp high in protein. The pulp is dried and the seeds removed in making the flour. The pods are also called "St. John's bread" or "locust pods."

Corn Flour—A by-product of the new-process method of making cornmeal. It may also be made by grinding and sifting white or yellow corn until the granules are as fine as those of wheat flour.

Cottonseed Flour—Made from the press cake left after the extraction of oil from specially treated cotton seeds.

Lima Bean Flour—Made from pulverized dried ripe Lima beans.

Oat Flour—Derived from oat kernels which are cleaned, kiln-dried, put through machines to remove the hulls, and then sterilized and ground. It lacks gliadin which makes it difficult to use pure in making yeast breads.

Peanut Flour—The product left after oil has been extracted from peanuts.

Potato Flour—Prepared from cooked potatoes that have been dried and ground.

Soy Flour—Full-fat soy flour is made by grinding treated soybeans that have only the hull removed. Low-fat soy flour is made from the press cake after all, or nearly all, of the oil is taken out of the treated soybeans.

Rice Flour—A white starchy flour milled from white rice.

Rye Flour—The finely ground product obtained by sifting rye meal.

Tapioca Flour—Made from the fleshy root stocks of the cassava or manioc plant which are heated to remove the moisture and then pulverized. It is high in nutritious starch.

Waxy Rice Flour—Milled from certain varieties of rice having waxen adhesive qualities. It is composed almost completely of amylopectin with little or no amylose. It acts as a stabilizer in sauces and gravies and is especially useful in preventing separation in these products when frozen.

Storage—Flour should be stored at room temperature in tight containers. In hot weather, only small amounts should be kept.

Nutritive Food Values—In white flour starch is present in greater proportion and is more digestible than it is in whole-wheat flour. Therefore, it is higher in caloric value. If enriched, white flour contains added thiamine, riboflavin, niacin, and iron. Calcium and vitamin D may also be added. Whole-wheat flour contains all the nutrients available in the whole grain.

The caloric values of 3½ ounces of the most commonly available wheat flours are:

- [ ] Whole-Wheat = 333 calories
- [ ] Flour, enriched or unenriched = 364 calories
- [ ] Cake = 364 calories
- [ ] Self-rising, enriched = 352 calories

The caloric values of 3½ ounces of the most commonly available flour made from other grains and beans are:

- [ ] Corn = 368 calories
- [ ] Rye, light = 357 calories
- [ ] Rye, medium = 350 calories
- [ ] Soy, full-fat = 421 calories
- [ ] Soy, low-fat = 356 calories

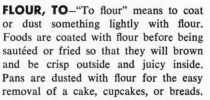

FLOUR, TO—"To flour" means to coat or dust something lightly with flour. Foods are coated with flour before being sautéed or fried so that they will brown and be crisp outside and juicy inside. Pans are dusted with flour for the easy removal of a cake, cupcakes, or breads.

Pastry cloths, boards, rolling pins, and hands are dusted with flour to keep the dough from sticking.

Dough is dusted with flour to prevent it from sticking when it is shaped.

FLUKE—A salt-water flatfish belonging to the flounder family. It is also known as the summer flounder. Fluke is a lean fish, with white meat, and it weighs between one and fifteen pounds. It lives in the North Atlantic between Maine and South Carolina, and it is a popular and spirited game fish.

Fluke is found in fish markets and food stores during the summer months only. It can be panfried, deep fried, steamed, and poached. If basted frequently, it can also be baked or broiled, and it can be used in any recipe calling for flounder.

FLUMMERY—An old New England dessert prepared by simmering berries in water and thickening with cornstarch. The dessert is sweetened and served cold with cream.

BLACKBERRY FLUMMERY

1 pint blackberries
Water
3½ tablespoons cornstarch
½ cup sugar
Cream

Simmer berries with 2 cups water for about 10 minutes. Blend cornstarch and ¼ cup water and stir carefully into berries. Simmer, stirring constantly, until smooth, thick, and clear. Add sugar, cool and chill. Serve with cream. Makes 4 servings.

Note: Other berries such as blueberries, strawberries or raspberries can be substituted for the blackberries in the recipe above.

FOIE GRAS—Literally translated, these two French words mean "fat liver." In culinary language, they are applied to the livers of geese which are bred to be used for *foie gras,* and are a specialty of Alsace and southwest France. Good *foie gras* also comes from Austria, Czechoslovakia, and Hungary. *Foie gras* is also made from duck livers. It is not as delicate, but it is less expensive. *Foie gras* is not made in the United States because the breeding procedure, which is cruel to the geese (they are fed to bursting and kept in tight coops to prevent them from exercising), is forbidden by law here.

Foie gras is one of the great luxury foods, and has been since Roman days. Gourmets swoon at the very thought of it, especially when the *foie gras* has been combined with truffles and cooked in brandy and Madeira.

There are a great many uses for *foie gras.* It is eaten as an appetizer spread, or as a main dish with a green salad; it is used in the making of aspics, and to stuff other meats; and it is cooked with meats and vegetables, usually with the addition of a fortified wine such as port or Madeira.

Pâté de foie gras is the most popular way of preparing the product. The goose livers are puréed, seasoned with wine, spirits, and herbs, and studded with truffles. Then the mixture is baked either in a pastry case for a *foie gras en croûte,* or in special casseroles called "terrines" which have been lined with pork fat. These dishes are baked and then served hot or cold. When served cold, *pâté* should be cut into ¼- to ½-inch slices and accompanied by buttered toast. A little chopped aspic sprinkled on the *pâté* or flanking it enhances the flavor and appearance of the dish.

Foie gras au naturel, plain cooked livers either whole or *puréed,* is available in cans. *Pâté de foie gras* is available in cans, jars, and crocks. These products can be found in specialty food departments or stores.

PÂTÉ DE FOIE GRAS
Stud goose livers with cut truffles and sprinkle with brandy. Season with salt and pepper. Let stand for 2 hours in refrigerator. Brown goose livers in very hot butter on all sides. Transfer to casserole. Moisten with a little brown gravy and Madeira combined. There should be about ⅓ inch of liquid in the casserole. Cover dish tightly so that no steam can escape. Simmer over lowest possible heat, or cook in preheated very slow oven (250°F.) for about 1 hour. Slice and serve hot or chilled.

PÂTÉ-AND-CUCUMBER SANDWICHES
Cut 24 thin slices peeled cucumber. Cut fresh white bread in rounds a little larger than cucumber slices. Spread bread with soft butter. Put cucumber slices on half of bread and top with a slice of *pâté de foie gras,* add a slice of cucumber and sprinkle with French dressing. Top with bread. Makes 12 small sandwiches.

HOT BISCUITS WITH FOIE GRAS
Make a rich biscuit dough and cut in tiny biscuits. Bake until brown and done. Split the biscuits and fill with *pâté de foie gras.* Serve warm as an hors-d'oeuvre.

ARTICHOKE HEARTS WITH FOIE GRAS
Heat drained canned artichoke hearts in about 1 inch of dry Madeira, basting them frequently. Have as many ¼-inch slices of *foie gras* or *pâté de foie gras* as there are artichoke hearts. Place hot artichoke hearts on heated platter and top each with slice of *foie gras.* Serve immediately with buttered toast fingers.

PÂTÉ DE FOIE GRAS IN ASPIC
    3 envelopes unflavored gelatin
    ½ cup cold water
    3 chicken bouillon cubes
    3½ cups boiling water
    3 hard-cooked eggs
    4 truffles
    1 jar (2½ ounces) pate de foie gras, mashed
      Lettuce
      French dressing

Soften gelatin in the cold water. Add bouillon cubes and boiling water. Stir until gelatin and cubes are dissolved. Pour enough of mixture into 1½-quart loaf pan or mold to make a layer ⅛ inch thick. Chill until almost firm. Arrange slices of 1 truffle and 1 egg in a pattern on the gelatin. Chill remaining gelatin mixture until thickened, but not firm. Dice remaining eggs and truffles and fold with *pâté* into second gelatin mixture. Pour into mold and chill until firm. Unmold and cut in slices. Serve on lettuce with French dressing. Makes 8 to 10 servings.

FOLD, TO—In culinary language the phrase "to fold" has several meanings. It can mean "to enclose," as when the dough is folded over the filling or over butter in puff pastry; "to mix," as when mushrooms are folded into a sauce; and, most often, "to incorporate," as when egg whites are folded into a soufflé or cake batter.

Folding in egg whites or whipped cream is a delicate process and should be performed with a light and quick hand. Spoon the egg white or cream over the mixture into which it is to be folded. Using a whisk, large spoon, spatula, or rubber scraper, cut down through the center of the mixture to the bottom of the bowl. Scrape along the bottom of the bowl towards the edge of the bowl and bring the utensil up the side of the bowl and over the top of the mixture back into the center again. Give the bowl a quarter turn and repeat the procedure until mixture is well blended. Work evenly and gently, taking care not to knock or mash the mixture so that the maximum amount of air will be incorporated.

FONDANT—A crystalline, soft, white candy made by cooking sugar, water, light corn syrup or cream of tartar to the "soft-ball" stage (234° to 240°F. on a candy thermometer). The mixture is then cooled to 110°F. and beaten and kneaded until it is perfectly white. It is used as a base for such candies as bonbons and chocolate creams. When softened by heat, it is used for icings. Many variations of fondant may be made by changing the flavor and adding color. There is also a variety of uncooked fondant, generally used in home candy-making.

Fondant flavors include orange, lemon, cherry, vanilla, chocolate, pistachio, cinnamon, peppermint, wintergreen, coffee, and maple. Fondant colors are usually yellow, orange, red, pink, and green. Fondant should be stored in a covered crock or glass jar and allowed to mellow for 2 to 3 days before using.

COOKED FONDANT
    3 cups sugar
    1⅓ cups water
    ¼ teaspoon salt
    ⅓ cup light corn syrup
    1 teaspoon vanilla extract

Mix first 4 ingredients in large saucepan. Bring to boil, stirring. Cover; boil for 3 minutes. Remove cover and cook until the mixture reaches 238°F. on a candy thermometer, or until a small amount forms a soft ball when dropped into cold water. During the cooking, wash down sides of pan several times with a pastry brush dipped into cold water, using up and down motion. Pour out onto an ungreased platter. Cool to lukewarm (110° F.). Add vanilla and beat until mixture turns cloudy. Gather into a ball and knead with lightly buttered hands until smooth and creamy. Put in bowl, cover with damp cloth, and store in cool place until needed. Makes about 2¼ pounds.

Fondant-Stuffed Dates
Color fondant, if desired. Shape into small rolls and use to fill pitted dates.

Fondant-Dipped Almonds
Tint fondant with pink and green food coloring. Flavor if desired. Melt each color in top part of double boiler over hot water. Dip rounded end of toasted almonds into fondant; put on wax paper and let stand until firm.

BONBONS
■ **To Make Center**—Flavor fondant, above, with rum, instant coffee powder, oil of peppermint or wintergreen, or other flavoring as desired. Shape in balls. If desired, pieces of nut meat or candied fruit can be pressed into the center of each ball. Leave on board, covered with wax paper until firm.

■ **To Dip**—Melt additional Fondant over hot water, flavor and tint with additional food coloring as desired. Do not allow Fondant to become hot. If too thick, add a few drops of cold water. Drop one center at a time into Fondant. Stir with a fork or candy dipper until center is entirely covered, lift up and put on wax paper. Make a swirl on the top of the bonbon with the fork or dipper. Stir the Fondant frequently.

CHOCOLATE CREAMS
Prepare Fondant centers as in Bonbons.

Melt squares of semisweet chocolate over hot, not boiling, water. Beat gently until chocolate feels a little cooler than the hand (80° to 85°F. on a candy thermometer). Working in a room with a temperature of about 65°F., dip centers one at a time, in chocolate. Stir with a fork or candy dipper until center is entirely covered, lift up and put on wax paper. Make a swirl on the top of the chocolate creams with the fork or dipper.

UNCOOKED FONDANT
⅓ cup soft butter or margarine
⅓ cup light corn syrup
½ teaspoon salt
 1 teaspoon vanilla extract
3½ cups (1 pound) sifted confectioners' sugar

Blend all ingredients except sugar; mix in sugar; knead until blended. Makes about 1⅓ pounds.

Almond Diamonds
Substitute almond extract for the vanilla in the Uncooked Fondant recipe. Add ½ cup chopped blanched and toasted almonds. Roll to ½-inch thickness. Cut into diamonds.

Toasted-Coconut Balls
Add ½ cup toasted flaked coconut to Uncooked Fondant recipe. Shape in ¾-inch balls.

Fig Logs
Add ½ cup finely chopped dried figs to Uncooked Fondant recipe. Shape in rolls 2 x ½ inches. Roll in chocolate shot.

Filbert Squares
Add ¾ cup chopped filberts to Uncooked Fondant recipe. Roll to about ½-inch thickness. Cut in squares.

FONDUE—The origin of this French word is *fondre,* that is, "to melt." In culinary language, it often means a hot dish made from melted cheese, into which pieces of bread are dipped. Fondue is the national dish of Switzerland.

FONDUE
and Other Swiss Dunking Dinners
by Jean Fogg

Who doesn't like to dunk? And how gay to have everyone sitting around the table and dunking their dinner together! And what fun to cook over a burner or open fire, each guest his own chef, cooking his dinner just to his own taste!

The Swiss, those happy folk blessed with one of the world's most beautiful countries, love a gathering full of *Gemütlichkeit* (a friendly congeniality) and are eager dunkers. They dunk their morning bread into chocolate or coffee with no compunctions about sticky fingers; they dunk sugar into their after-dinner coffee; and they have evolved a number of dishes and meals, just bubbling with *Gemütlichkeit* and conviviality, all of which call for the happy, hungry diners to gather around a fire and dunk their own.

All these dishes are as different and delectable as they are a snap for the hostess and a delight for the guests. Creamy, aromatic Cheese Fondue bubbling over the flame; Cheese *Raclette* turning to succulent softness before wood or charcoal fire; Fondue *Bourguignonne* with its tender beefsteak and spicy sauce assortment; or Potato Dabs for cool fall evenings: all of these can inspire mouth-watering talk, delicious eating, and a minimum of muss and fuss. They're perfect for teen-age parties where, table and ingredients ready, the young set can take over and cook its own, perfect for cookouts or backyard fireplaces.

The atmosphere created by a Fondue, *Raclette* or Dab is as bubbly and exciting as the savory mixture itself. Above all, a matter of fun and friendship, never to be served to cranks or bores or people who don't like something just a little different.

A Cheese Fondue in the center of the table is always surrounded by a ring of shining, expectant faces, young and old.

Fondue *Bourguignonne* captivates the men especially, because what man doesn't secretly think that he alone knows just how rare a rare steak should be, or get a secret joy if given a free hand with the sauce mixing.

Raclette belongs by an open fire, conjuring up visions of campfires, cookouts, and the heady smell of wood smoke. One of our Swiss friends declares that *raclette* is at its best if made outdoors while lots of pretty girls sit around on the grass. Another Swiss friend and *raclette*-lover makes it at his fireplace on festive party evenings and lets each guest hold the big half-moon of cheese in an American chef's mitt (potholder mitten) while making his own *raclette*.

The Potato Dab is given in just one of the many varieties of potato dunks which the Swiss like so much that they even manufacture special potato equipment: big, covered potato dishes with smaller matching dishes for the peels which are removed at the table, and special three-pronged potato spears for holding the hot things securely while peeling and eating. Country Swiss eat potatoes in their fingers at the table, dunking them into salt and pepper at each bite, or into sauces of whatever is handy; city cousins spear and peel, then put the potato on the dinner plate to be eaten with knife and fork.

CHEESE FONDUE

The true origin of Cheese Fondue is mysteriously hidden in legends. One story says that a war ended when fondue began: Army A had nothing left to eat but bread; Army B, nothing but milk. They patched up a temporary truce so they could dunk A's bread into B's milk, and found such mutual pleasure in dunking amicably together that they added a bit of cheese for flavor and presto, fondue had begun. However, the French-speaking part of the Swiss Alps is generally given credit for its discovery.

Fondue does not always mean a cheese fondue, since the French word *fondre* means "to melt." The recipes that follow take this into account, as well as the fact that some fondues contain white wine and kirsch and that others are non-alcoholic.

Fondue, Neuchâtel Style

FONDUE, NEUCHÂTEL STYLE

Neuchâtel Fondue takes its name from the dry white wine of Neuchâtel, which is the distinguishing ingredient. As for the cheese, don't worry about not being able to buy your cheese in Switzerland. Huge quantities of "Switzerland Swiss" cheese are exported to the States and are easily obtainable, or you may use domestic Swiss. Whatever the cheese, it should be fresh and also freshly grated. Prepared grated cheese should not be substituted; it is too finely grated. In the way of equipment, you'll need: Flameproof earthenware casserole and alcohol lamp or a chafing dish; long-handled fork for each guest; wooden fork or wire whisk for stirring.

    1   garlic clove
    ½   cup dry white wine per person
    1½ cups (5 to 6 ounces) grated Swiss
        cheese per person (if possible, half
        Emmentaler and half Gruyère)
    1   teaspoon all-purpose flour per person
    3   tablespoons kirsch per person
        Freshly ground pepper and/or
        nutmeg
        French bread or rolls

Rub the inside of the casserole or chafing dish with the cut garlic clove. Put in the wine and set over low heat. When the wine is warm enough to begin sending bubbles to the surface (but not hot), begin to add, a handful at a time, the cheese which has been dredged with the flour. Be sure to stir, without stopping, with either a wooden fork or a wire whisk. (Tradition says that one cannot stir around the pot but should use a back-and-forth or figure-eight motion. We discovered this only after having made several highly successful fondues by stirring round and round, so perhaps it is a questionable instruction.) When all of the cheese has been added and melted, and all is bubbling, slowly add the kirsch (if no kirsch is available, a very dry sherry can be used). If using a casserole, have someone light the alcohol lamp with a fairly high flame, and rush the bubbling pot to the table.

The fondue ritual begins with the addition, by the host, of freshly ground pepper and nutmeg (only a dash of the latter). Each diner helps himself to bread which has been cut into bite-size pieces, roughly 1½ inches square, preferably with a bit of crust on each piece. The method is to spear a piece of bread through the soft part and into the crust, dunk it into the fondue, turning it around to coat all sides, lift it out of the fondue, twirling the fork to keep it from dripping, convey carefully to a safe spot over your plate, and when cool enough to eat, take the whole piece at one delicious bite. As each guest dunks, he must stir the whole mixture a little with his fork to keep it from getting thick toward the bottom of the pan. Be careful not to lose the bread in the fondue; this calls for a forfeit. The Swiss make the careless one buy a bottle of wine for the table, but you can think up your own type of forfeit. Someone should keep an eye on the flame during the eating; the fondue should be kept bubbling and not allowed to cool off. If it cools, it will most probably separate into a rubbery-looking substance; warmed wine (but not cold) can be added a little at a time if this calamity should befall.

No other food is ever served with a fondue although one could, as a concession to American taste, serve not-too-hearty appetizers before. Cold drinks should be avoided with a fondue, but if chilled white wine is served, it should be sipped very slowly. The Swiss custom is to drink hot coffee or tea with it and to have small glasses of kirsch for everyone for the traditional glass halfway through, and another kirsch at the end.

FONDUE, GENEVA STYLE

This is a creamy, nonalcoholic variation of the standard recipe, excellent for young people or for those who don't like the taste of wine in their food. The same equipment used for the Neuchâtel Fondue is needed for this one.

8 egg yolks
2 cups (½ pound) grated Emmentaler or Gruyère cheese
10 tablespoons butter
½ cup light cream
Salt, pepper, grated nutmeg

In a flameproof casserole or chafing dish mix the egg yolks and cheese with a dash of salt and pepper and nutmeg to taste. Place over very low heat and, stirring constantly, add the butter bit by bit. When the mixture thickens, add the cream and stir until well blended. Then bring at once to the table to keep warm over a very low flame: do not allow to cook further. This can be eaten just as Neuchâtel Fondue with French bread to dunk, or pieces of fried toast can be dunked into the pot.

RACLETTE

Raclette, which means literally "a scraping" (although a *racleur* is not an eater of *raclette* but a "murderer of the violin") begins with a very large piece, preferably a half, of a whole cheese specially suitable for melting. In Switzerland, cheese from the Valais region is used: either a Gomser cheese or cheese from the Bagne valley.

To make this you'll need: Mitt; wide tongs for holding cheese; bricks or fireproof base for resting cheese; scraper or

handsome knife.

Large piece of cheese as described above
Freshly ground pepper or nutmeg
Boiled potatoes
Pearl onions
Sliced cucumbers

At the fireplace or outdoor fire, prop the cheese on bricks or stones, with cut side facing fire. When the surface begins to melt, each person in turn scrapes the melted part onto his plate, to be eaten with bites of boiled potato, onions, and cucumbers. Fresh pepper or nutmeg may be ground onto the *raclette.* Plates must be as warm as possible so the *raclette* won't harden.

Although this is not a dunking dish in the fondue sense of the word, the gathering-round spirit is the same as when a fondue is eaten, and each guest does dunk his knife into the creamy mass to scrape his own *raclette.* You can also make it at the table if you have a table-oven in front of which the cheese can be propped or held.

Chilled white wine usually is served with *raclette,* and the Swiss serve the potatoes piping hot in their jackets, to be peeled at the table. Since this dish is much more filling than it would seem, Swiss custom decrees that a prize is given to the one who makes the most *raclettes* (and eats them)!

FONDUE BOURGUIGNONNE

This is a cheeseless fondue that could rightfully be called "Fondue Feast" since it is another meal in itself complete with steak, individually cooked and flavored in the most festive and friendly setting imaginable, with everyone seated around the cooking pot, dunking his steak, and discussing the relative merits of rare or well-done meat, and preferences for sauces and condiments. With the flame of the burner for a focal point, the table is at its best with candles for light. Now is the time to bring out all the small extra dishes that are usually stacked at the back of the cupboard, and to exercise one's own imaginative taste in selecting the accompaniments for the meal. This could have a hearty onion-and-pickle flavor for that men's poker-night supper, or run to rare sauces and spices for an exotic offering to a special guest list.

If a multicourse meal is in order, a clear soup to start and a simple salad mixture with the steak is about all one needs. This is a most wonderfully easy meal to prepare in advance, then forget entirely until time to sit down at the table; fine for the hostess who likes to be with her guests.

You'll need: Chafing dish; long-handled forks or spears.

About ⅓ pound of the very best beefsteak per person
Peanut oil (Peanut oil is recommended, as olive oil has too penetrating a taste for the beef, and butter will burn)
Assortment of sauces and condiments (see suggestions below)

Guests, served with an empty plate and fork, help themselves to the raw steak which has previously been cut into bite-size chunks about 1 inch square and heaped on a platter or wooden board on the table. Condiments and sauces are passed and guests serve themselves to the ones of their choice. By this time the oil (about 1 inch deep in the chafing dish) is boiling gently and it is time to begin. Each guest spears one piece of steak and holds it in the boiling oil until done to his own particular preference. Since this dunking takes a minute or so, it is much cooler if the forks or spears have wooden handles; metal ones heat up very quickly. The steak morsel is then dunked into one or more of the sauces and popped whole into the mouth. Each bite is different! A mustard sauce bit followed by one dipped, for example, into a tart relish is a flavor contrast to make taste buds tingle.

The Restaurant Franziskaner in Zürich, which has long made a house specialty of this popular dish, serves the following "on the side":

Tartare sauce
Mustard mayonnaise
Béarnaise sauce
Paprika
Tiny pearl onions
Sour gherkins (Cornichons)
Preserved fruit in mustard sauce
A mixture of ground peanuts, grated coconut, and curry powder

We can think of some fine alternatives such as:

Minced Bermuda onions
Tomato relish
Pickled peaches
Dill pickles
Russian dressing
Sour-cream horseradish sauce
Prepared meat sauce
Chutney

A bottle of good red wine, the pot bubbling in the middle of the table, the sauces in colorful display in the candlelight, and a hungry group of steak lovers: the perfect recipe for a delectable and different dinner.

POTATOES AND DAB

The Swiss say, "potatoes in their bathrobes" instead of "in their jackets." Supper often consists of just potatoes with coffee or milk; sometimes the potatoes known as *Rösti,* made with boiled potatoes which have been peeled, put through the ricer, and finally fried like a pancake until golden brown and crusty; or plain

Fondue Bourguignonne

boiled potatoes to be speared whole, peeled at the table, and eaten in the fingers with butter and salt and one of several kinds of cheese.

The equipment needed: Small flameproof pan and alcohol lamp or candle heater or a chafing dish; long-handled spears or forks.

> Hot boiled potatoes (in their bathrobes)
> 3 tablespoons oil or melted butter
> 5 tablespoons vinegar
> 2 medium onions, minced fine
> Salt and pepper

One old German source we came across begins a description of this recipe with the colorful words: "Take a three-legged pot which will stand on the fire. . . ." The number of legs on the pot doesn't really seem to make a difference, nor do we feel it necessary to use an open fire. Any flameproof pan will do so long as it will stay hot on its own or can be placed over a heater. Pour oil or butter, vinegar, and onions into the pot, add salt and pepper to your taste, and heat all together until very hot. Bring to the table with a covered dish of hot boiled potatoes. Each person spears a potato, peels it at the table, then dips bite-size pieces into the pot for a "dab" in the sauce. This dish, in its very simplicity, can be delightfully varied with additions or changes in the "dab" according to personal taste. The substitution of chives or leeks for onions, the addition of an herb such as thyme or oregano, or a bit of minced bacon for example, are equally successful and may suggest other tasty variations. The lowly boiled potato can be glamorized!

COFFEE DUNK

And now, to top off your Swiss dunking dinner, or just for fun, how about a coffee dunk?

The Swiss love their kirsch, that distilled cherry spirit that goes into the fondue, and long ago invented this method of bringing together the friendly harmony of kirsch and coffee, just as we do with Cognac when making *Café Diable,* or other exotic coffee brews.

The dunking method could be applied to any favorite after-dinner liqueur or flavor. The kirsch is poured into any small dish and put into the center of the table. The *canardli* or "little duck" is the customary dish in Switzerland; these are usually made of glass or crystal; they sit on a tiny silver tray, and the kirsch is poured into the little hollow in the duck's back. With each *canardli* comes a miniature sugar tongs also of silver and about two inches long. The method is to take a lump of sugar in the tongs, dip it into the kirsch, pop it into the mouth, then

take a sip of black coffee. For this process very small lumps are best since repeated dunks are made. Without tiny tongs, this same system could easily be used with just a coffee spoon to hold the sugar lump, letting it down gently into the dish to soak up some of the liquid; if you're doing it this way, have a separate dish or wide-mouthed glass for each guest's dunking. We tried this once with coffee and Creme de Cacao—wonderful!

FOOD VALUE—This phrase is used to describe a nutrient, or element, of which food is composed. Protein, fat, carbohydrates, vitamins, and minerals are food values. Food values are needed for the growth, maintenance, and repair of the body tissues and for the production of energy. All the values that man requires are found in ordinary foods readily available in all parts of the country the year around.

A nutritionally adequate diet, one containing all the necessary food values, can be achieved without memorizing the nutrient content of foods. Simply choose foods from the four basic groups: milk, meat, vegetable-fruit, and bread and cereals.

The milk group is our richest source of calcium and a valuable source of protein and riboflavin. It also supplies vitamin D. Cheeses are included in this group.

The second group includes meat, fish, poultry, and eggs as well as such other protein foods as dried beans and peas and nuts. B vitamins, potassium, and iron are also supplied by this group.

The third group includes vegetables and fruits of all kinds and is a valuable source of vitamins A and C.

The last group includes all breads and cereals that are whole-grained, enriched, or restored. This group provides important food values such as thiamin, calcium, and potassium.

No single food will provide all the values needed. A varied diet is the best way to be sure of proper nutrition.

FOOL—This surprising word describes a very old but still popular English fruit dessert. It is based on a fruit purée (any soft fruit, especially berries, will do). The fruit is cooked with very little water, sweetened to taste, strained, and chilled. Just before serving, chilled whipped cream is added to the fruit purée, in the proportion of two parts whipped cream to one part fruit. The fool is served in sherbet glasses.

Fool is one of the most delicious of all summer desserts. Where the name comes from is obscure, but it may have been derived from the French *fol* or "mad," and perhaps refers to the fact that the fruit is all mixed up.

GOOSEBERRY FOOL

> 1 quart gooseberries
> 1 cup sugar
> 1 cup water
> Green food coloring (optional)
> 2 cups heavy cream, whipped

Remove stem and blossom end of berries. Wash them. Combine berries, sugar, and water. Cook over low heat until tender, stirring occasionally. Taste for sweetness; add more sugar if necessary. Strain berries through a fine sieve or a food mill. Stir in a few drops of green food coloring. Cool mixture. Fold whipped cream into gooseberry purée. Chill thoroughly. Makes 4 to 6 servings.

FORCEMEAT—Forcemeats, the French word *farce* is synonymous, are mixtures of finely chopped raw or cooked meats, raw or cooked poultry or game, fresh or canned fish, variety meats and game, all blended with herbs and spices into a thick, smooth paste. Forcemeats can also be made of potatoes, cornmeal, chestnuts, and even fruit. Fruit forcemeats are excellent for stuffing wild ducks or other poultry. Forcemeats are used to stuff other foods or as the basis of other dishes, and they can be as imaginative as the cook likes.

The main ingredient in a forcemeat must be ground several times to achieve as smooth a texture as possible. The remaining ingredients are then beaten in carefully to incorporate air and give the mixture lightness. The resulting mixture should be smooth and velvety with a delicate texture.

Forcemeats are used both cold and hot. When used cold, they are mixed with butter, cream, or gelatin to thicken the mixture, which is then poured into a decorative mold and chilled until firm. When used hot, either cooked or baked, they are mixed with bread, cream, or eggs for thickening. When baked, they form the basis of many pâtés, mousses, quenelles, terrines, and galantines, and are used for stuffings for boned poultry or other meats, whole fish, game, and some vegetables.

Forcemeats may be a blend of such meats as veal for lightness and pork for flavor. They may be layered with strips or cubes of meats of various colors, such as ham, and with thin slices of truffles. When these forcemeats are cut, a mosaic of pretty colors will result.

Many pâtés made with forcemeat are cooled after baking and then remolded with gelatin or aspic. If a forcemeat is baked in a pastry shell, that is *en croûte*, the meat will shrink during cooking within the pastry covering. After baking and cooling, the hollow within the pastry may be filled through a small hole in the top with appropriately flavored aspic.

CHICKEN FORCEMEAT

1 pound raw chicken meat, ground 3 times
1 cup fresh mushrooms
⅔ cup pistachio nuts
7 tablespoons dry sherry
1 tablespoon sliced truffles
3 eggs, beaten
7 tablespoons butter, softened
1½ teaspoons salt
Dash of white pepper
⅔ cup soft bread crumbs
½ cup milk
1 tablespoon brandy

Grind chicken with mushrooms and nuts. Add sherry, truffles, eggs, butter, salt, and pepper. Soak bread crumbs in milk and brandy. Add to chicken mixture. Beat well until very smooth. Makes enough stuffing for one 6-pound chicken.

FISH FORCEMEAT

1 pound raw halibut, cod, haddock, flounder, or shellfish
2 egg whites
1 teaspoon salt
¼ teaspoon white pepper
2 cups heavy cream

Remove any bones or shells from fish. Force through food chopper, using finest blade. Beat until smooth. Work in unbeaten egg whites. Add seasonings and beat until very smooth. Force through fine sieve. Gradually add cream, beating with electric mixer until cream is absorbed and mixture is very smooth. Use for Fish Pudding or Quenelles (see recipes in next column). Makes about 3 cups.

POTATO FORCEMEAT

2 cups hot mashed potato
1 teaspoon grated onion
¼ teaspoon paprika
¼ cup cream
1 tablespoon butter or margarine
½ teaspoon ground sage
2 egg yolks, beaten

Mix all ingredients thoroughly. Use as stuffing for a 4-pound roasting chicken. Makes about 2¼ cups.

FRUIT FORCEMEAT

2 apples, peeled and thinly sliced
¼ cup fine cracker crumbs
½ pound prunes, pitted
¼ cup seeded raisins
Boiling water
1 teaspoon sugar
1 egg, beaten
Salt to taste

Sprinkle apples with some of crumbs to keep from darkening. Cover prunes and raisins with boiling water and let stand for about 5 minutes; drain. Mix prunes and raisins with remaining crumbs. Add apples and remaining ingredients. Use as stuffing for wild duck or domestic duck or goose. Fill cavity only three-fourths full as mixture swells when cooked. Makes about 4½ cups.

FISH PUDDING

Prepare Fish Forcemeat (recipe at left). Pour into buttered 1½-quart casserole. Bake in preheated slow oven (325°F.) for 1 hour, or until firm. Makes 4 to 6 servings.

QUENELLES

Prepare 1 recipe of Fish Forcemeat (recipe at left). Drop from 2 tablespoons dipped in cold water into large skillet containing about 1 inch of lightly salted simmering water. Poach gently for 8 to 10 minutes, basting constantly with liquid in pan. Remove with a slotted spoon and put on paper towel to drain. Serve with Shrimp Sauce (page 695), Mornay Sauce or hollandaise. Makes 6 to 8 servings.

BAKED STUFFED PEPPERS

4 green peppers
Salt
1 recipe Potato Forcement (see recipe at left)
Fine dry bread crumbs
Butter or margarine

Cut peppers in half lengthwise and remove seeds and membrane. Simmer in boiling salted water for 5 minutes. Drain and put in shallow baking dish. Fill with Potato Forcemeat, sprinkle with crumbs and dot with butter. Bake in preheated hot oven (400°F.) for 20 minutes, or until tops are lightly browned. Makes 4 servings.

GALANTINE OF VEAL

1 boned breast of veal, about 3 pounds
Salt and pepper
1 tablespoon chopped mixed fresh thyme, marjoram, and rosemary
1 recipe Chicken Forcement (see recipe at left)
½ pound lean ham, cut in strips
2 hard-cooked eggs
Chicken stock
1 egg white
Water
1 egg shell, crushed
Parsley

Spread veal breast out flat and sprinkle with salt, pepper. and herbs. Spread with Chicken Forcemeat, leaving 1 inch around edge uncovered. Arrange ham strips down the length of the meat. Put eggs in center and roll meat tightly. Sew with thread. Wrap in cheesecloth and tie ends securely. Put in boiling chicken stock and simmer, covered, for 2 hours. Remove meat and unwrap. Add egg white beaten with 1 tablespoon water and crushed egg shell to stock. Boil for 2 minutes and strain. Pour into shallow pan and chill until firm. Wrap meat in dry cheesecloth, weight with a board and weight and chill overnight. Unwrap and remove thread. Chop firm stock and spread on a platter. Arrange meat on top and surround with parsley. Makes 12 servings.

TERRINE DE PORC, VEAU, ET JAMBON
(Pork and Veal Pate with Ham)

½ cup minced onion
2 tablespoons butter or margarine
½ cup brandy
¾ pound each of lean pork and lean veal, ground several times
½ pound fresh pork fat, ground several times
2 eggs, beaten
1½ teaspoons salt
⅛ teaspoon pepper
Dash of ground allspice
½ teaspoon crumbled dried thyme
1 garlic clove, mashed
½ pound lean veal, cut into ¼-inch strips
2 or 3 canned truffles, cut into ¼-inch cubes
3 tablespoons brandy
Salt and pepper
1 tablespoon minced green onion
½ pound fresh pork fat, ⅛ inch thick, or blanched salt pork or bacon
½ pound lean boiled ham, cut into ¼-inch strips
1 bay leaf

Sauté onions in butter until tender but not browned. Pour mixture into a mixing bowl. Add ½ cup brandy to skillet and boil until reduced to half. Pour this into mixing bowl. Add ground meat, ground pork fat, eggs, seasonings, and garlic. Beat mixture until well blended. Place veal strips in a bowl with truffles. Add 3 tablespoons brandy, salt and pepper to taste, and minced green onion. Marinate for 1 hour. Remove veal strips and truffles and beat marinade into pork and veal forcemeat. Use slices of pork fat, salt pork or bacon to line an 8-cup rectangular pan or oval terrine, reserving some slices to cover the top. (If using salt pork or bacon, cover with water and simmer for 10 minutes. Drain and pat dry (before lining pan.) Spoon one-third of the forcemeat into the mold. With wet fingers, flatten surface of the forcemeat. Cover with half the strips of veal and ham. Arrange cubes of truffles down the center. Top with a second layer of forcemeat and strips of meat. Top with a third layer of forcemeat. Place bay leaf on top. Cover with slices of pork fat. Cover tightly with aluminum foil. Place in a pan of hot water which should come halfway up the side of the mold. Bake in preheated moderate oven (350°F.) for 1½ hours, until pâté is shrunken from the sides of the mold and the fat and juices are clear yellow with no traces of pink. Remove foil and place a piece of wood or a pan into the mold on top of the pâté. Weight with cans or other weight and allow to cool at room temperature for several hours or overnight. Unmold on a platter and cut into serving slices. Makes 8 to 10 servings.

HAM MOUSSE
1 envelope unflavored gelatin
⅓ cup cold water
2 egg yolks
¾ teaspoon salt
Dash of cayenne
1 teaspoon powdered mustard
1 can (10½ ounces) condensed consommé
1 cup ground cooked ham
1 onion slice, minced
¼ cup mayonnaise
¼ cup heavy cream, whipped
Lettuce

Soften gelatin in cold water. Mix egg yolks, salt, cayenne, and mustard in top part of double boiler. Beat until thick and lemon-colored. Add consommé and cook, stirring, over boiling water until mixture thickens enough to coat a metal spoon. Add gelatin and stir until dissolved. Cool. Add ham, onion, mayonnaise, and cream. Pour mixture into a lightly oiled 1-quart mold. Chill until firm. Unmold on a bed of lettuce on serving plate. Makes 4 servings.

FORK—The fork is a table utensil consisting of a handle and two or more prongs, used for serving and eating food. Though ancient in origin, it did not make its appearance in the kitchen or on the dinner table for many centuries after its discovery. The first two-pronged forks were used to hold sacrificial meat.

Sophisticated Venetians became acquainted with the art of the fork from a Byzantine princess in the 11th century. Members of the aristocracy used the fork more as a lark than as a method of serious eating. Not until the 17th century did eating with forks catch on as the fashionable thing to do. Then people carried their precious forks in special cases with them when invited to dinner. The fork in many instances was as elaborate as a piece of jewelry. Wrought of silver, it still had two prongs. Later a third and then a fourth prong were introduced.

In 1608 an English traveler by the name of Thomas Coryate returned from a trip to Italy with samples of the fork. Governor John Winthrop of Massachusetts is credited with introducing the fork to the colonies. He arrived in 1630 bringing with him his personal knife and fork in a leather case.

FOWL—The term covers any large edible wild or domestic bird. Specifically, it is used to describe a mature female chicken, also called a hen or stewing chicken, more than ten months old and weighing three to six pounds. This bird is best cooked by moist heat.

CHICKEN SOUP
4 large onions, sliced
2 tablespoons butter or margarine
1 stewing chicken, about 4 pounds, cut up
2 quarts water
Salt and pepper to taste
2 cups sliced carrots
3 cups sliced potatoes
½ teaspoon monosodium glutamate

Cook 2 onions in the butter until golden. Add chicken and water. Bring to boil, cover and simmer for 3 hours, or until chicken is tender. Remove chicken. Add remaining onions, salt, pepper, carrots, and potatoes. Simmer until vegetables are tender. Remove skin and bones from chicken and cut meat in cubes. Add to soup with monosodium glutamate. Add more salt and pepper, if necessary. Makes 8 servings.

CHICKEN STEW WITH DUMPLINGS
1 stewing chicken (about 3 pounds), cut up
3 tablespoons butter or margarine
1 celery stalk, diced
1 medium onion, chopped
1 bay leaf
1 teaspoon seasoned salt
½ teaspoon pepper
4 cups water
3 tablespoons all-purpose flour
1 teaspoon monosodium glutamate
Dumpling batter

Wash chicken and dry on absorbent paper. Brown in butter. Add next 5 ingredients and water. Bring to boil and simmer, covered, for 3 hours, or until chicken is tender. Thicken stock with flour blended with a little cold water; add monosodium glutamate and more salt, if necessary. Drop Dumpling Batter by teaspoonfuls onto chicken pieces. Cover and steam for 10 minutes, or until dumplings are done when tested with a toothpick. Makes 4 servings.

Dumpling Batter
Combine 1 cup cake flour, 1 teaspoon baking powder, ½ teaspoon poultry seasoning, and ½ teaspoon salt. Cut in 1 tablespoon shortening and add 1 tablespoon minced parsley. With a fork beat in 1 egg and 3 tablespoons milk. Add to first mixture and stir until thoroughly blended.

CHICKEN FRICASSEE
1 stewing chicken (about 5 pounds), cut up
½ cup butter or margarine
Boiling water
1 small onion, quartered
Few celery tops
1 small carrot, sliced
1 bay leaf
4 peppercorns
Salt
¼ cup all-purpose flour
2 cups chicken broth, or broth and milk or cream
Pepper
Dash of Worcestershire

Brown chicken pieces on all sides in ¼ cup butter. Put in large kettle. Add boiling water to cover, onion, celery, carrot, bay leaf, and peppercorns. Bring to boil, cover and simmer for 1 hour. Add 2 teaspoons salt and simmer for 2 hours longer, or until chicken is tender. Remove from heat and let stand until fat rises to surface. Spoon off fat. Remove chicken and keep warm. Melt remaining butter and blend in flour. Gradually stir into broth and cook, stirring, until smooth and thickened. Season to taste with salt, pepper, and the Worcestershire. Pour some of sauce over chicken and pass remainder. Makes 6 servings.

FRANGIPANE—This is a name given to a mixture made with flour, egg yolks, butter, and milk. It is cooked like a cream-puff pastry and used for poultry and fish forcemeats.

A frangipane cream is a thick custard filling made with crushed macaroons or ground almonds and used for cakes, tarts, crêpes, and other desserts. The dessert filling is an old one and has been popular in France for centuries. These sweetened custards probably came from the Middle East where many creams and custards include ground almonds.

FRANGIPANE PIE
¾ cup sugar
½ cup all-purpose flour
¼ teaspoon salt
3 cups milk
3 egg yolks, slightly beaten
2 tablespoons butter or margarine
1 teaspoon vanilla extract
½ teaspoon lemon extract
⅓ cup fine dried almond-macaroon crumbs
9- inch baked pie shell
Whipped cream

Mix first 3 ingredients in top part of double boiler. Add 3 cups milk. Put over hot water, and cook, stirring constantly, until thickened, about 15 minutes. Add small amount of mixture to egg yolks. Stir mixture back into double boiler and cook for 3 minutes longer, stirring. Remove from heat and add remaining ingredients, except pie shell and cream. Cool and pour into shell. Chill and decorate with whipped cream.

**A collection of recipes featuring the versatile frankfurter
in appetizers, hearty soups and stews, casseroles,
kabobs, skillet main dishes, and salads**

FRANKFURTERS

FRANKFURTERS—Frankfurters (or weiners or hot hot dogs) are a type of sausage, made from beef, pork, and sometimes veal or combinations of these meats. The meats are combined with seasonings and curing nitrates and in some cases fillers; then stuffed into casings, smoked, cooked in steam, and quickly chilled. Although recipes vary, in general those labeled "all meat" are a combination of beef and pork but without fillers. Those ·labeled "all beef" contain only beef, are sometimes Kosher and frequently heavily seasoned with garlic. A large percentage of those sold in modern meat markets and food stores are called "skinless" as the cellulose casing is removed after they are fully processed, giving a more tender and more uniform product than those stuffed in animal casings. Sizes vary from the one-bite cocktail size to the "mile-long" twelve-inch frankfurter. The most common size is about six inches. Frankfurters are extremely versatile and easy to prepare. They may be barbecued, boiled, braised, broiled, fried, roasted, or steamed; used alone or with other foods, whole sliced or in chunks.

Availability and Purchasing Guide—Frankfurters are usually labeled "all meat" or "all beef." They are available in packages, in bulk by the pound, and in jars and cans. The best quality all-meat frankfurters are made of ground beef, veal, pork, and seasonings with no cereal filler added. Good quality all-beef frankfurters should be without cereal, too. Check ingredients listed on package, tag, or label.

Storage—Keep frankfurters in original package or wrap loosely in wax paper. Refrigerate. Do not freeze.
☐ Refrigerator shelf: 3 to 4 days
☐ In can or jar, kitchen shelf: 1 year

Nutritive Food Values—Good source of protein, some vitamins of B-group, thiamine, riboflavin, niacin. Fair source of calcium and iron.
☐ All meat, 3½ ounces = 296 calories

Basic Preparation
☐ **To Boil**—Place frankfurters in saucepan; cover with boiling water. Heat for 5 to 10 minutes, depending on type.
☐ **To Broil**—Slash each frankfurter diagonally in 4 to 6 places, about ¼ inch deep. Put on pan. Set 4 inches from source of heat. Turn once during broiling. Do not overcook.
☐ **To Panfry**—Add just enough shortening to skillet to grease bottom. Use frankfurters whole or slash them lengthwise but not all the way through. Fry slowly until slightly browned and thoroughly hot. Turn several times to brown evenly.

APPETIZERS

MARINATED APPETIZER FRANKFURTERS
½ cup soy sauce
1 tablespoon sugar
1 teaspoon instant minced onion
½ teaspoon ground ginger
¾ pound cocktail frankfurters

Combine all ingredients except frankfurters. Marinate frankfurters in mixture for 2 hours, turning and basting occasionally. Drain and reserve marinade. Place frankfurters in shallow baking dish. Pour marinade over them. Bake in preheated moderate oven (350°F.) for 15 to 20 minutes, or until thoroughly heated. Drain and serve on cocktail picks. Makes 8 to 10 servings.

FRANKFURTER-AVOCADO DIP
1 medium avocado
1 tablespoon fresh lemon juice
1 package (3 ounces) cream cheese
½ teaspoon instant minced onion
¼ teaspoon salt
⅛ teaspoon hot pepper sauce
3 skinless frankfurters, ground or very finely minced
¼ cup milk or dairy sour cream

Peel and mash avocado. Stir in lemon juice. Combine all other ingredients and blend thoroughly with avocado. Add more milk or sour cream if needed for proper dipping consistency. Makes about 2 cups.

APPETIZER KABOBS
¾ cup large pimiento-stuffed olives
½ pound cocktail frankfurters
2½ cups cooked or canned small white potatoes
⅓ cup French dressing

Thread olives, frankfurters, and potatoes on 6 skewers. Brush with French dressing. Broil 4 to 5 inches from source of heat, or cook on outdoor grill for 6 minutes. Turn once and baste or brush frequently with French dressing during cooking. Makes 6 servings.

FRANKFURTERS WITH CHEESE AND BACON
Cut frankfurters halfway through lengthwise. Spread with nippy cheese spread. Wrap a strip of bacon around each frankfurter and secure with toothpicks. Place in shallow baking pan and bake in preheated hot oven (425°F.) until bacon is crisp.

FRANKFURTER BITS
Cut pastry into strips (1 x 3 inches); roll around chunks of frankfurter. Sprinkle with chili powder. Bake in preheated hot oven (400°F.) for 15 minutes.

FRANKFURTER-EGG APPETIZERS
Partially split cooked frankfurter pieces. Fill with chopped hard-cooked eggs mixed with mayonnaise, and minced celery, olives, and onion.

FRANKFURTER STICKS
Cut frankfurters into quarters lengthwise and once crosswise. Brown in hot deep fat. Serve with dips such as mustard or chili sauce.

FRANK-ROLL SLICES
Cut ends off unsplit frankfurter rolls. Remove centers; spread inside with chive cream-cheese spread. Insert cooked frankfurter. Wrap in wax paper, chill, and slice crosswise.

SOUPS AND STEWS

FRANKFURTER AND CORN CHOWDER
(Shown on cover)
1 medium onion, chopped
1 cup chopped celery
¼ cup margarine
1 cup peeled and diced potatoes
2 cups water
1 teaspoon salt
1 pound frankfurters, sliced
½ bay leaf, crumbled
½ teaspoon dried thyme
3 cups cut fresh corn
3 tablespoons all-purpose flour
½ cup cold milk
1½ cups hot milk
½ cup cooked peas

Sauté onion and celery in margarine. Add potato, water, salt, frankfurters, bay leaf, and thyme. Cover and simmer until potatoes are almost tender. Add corn and simmer for 5 minutes longer. Blend flour and cold milk into a smooth paste. Add a little of the vegetable mixture to this and stir slowly into vegetable-frankfurter mixture. Simmer for 5 minutes. Add hot milk and blend. Garnish with peas. Makes 1½ quarts or 6 servings.

FRANKFURTER AND RICE SOUP
3 tablespoons butter or margarine
1 onion, chopped
¼ cup chopped green pepper
¼ cup diced celery
3 cups chicken bouillon
1 cup canned or stewed tomatoes
¼ cup uncooked rice
2 tablespoons chopped parsley
½ bay leaf
½ teaspoon salt
⅛ teaspoon pepper
½ pound frankfurters, sliced

Frankfurter with Macaroni and Cheese

Mexican Frankfurters and Eggs   **Frankfurter Succotash**

Melt butter and sauté onion, green pepper, and celery in it until soft. Add all other ingredients, bring to a boil, and reduce heat. Simmer, covered, stirring frequently, for 20 to 30 minutes. Makes about 1½ quarts.
Note: This is a satisfying one-dish meal.

FRANKFURTER AND PURÉED LENTIL SOUP
2 cups dried lentils
9 cups water
2 slices of bacon, diced, or 1 ham bone
1 medium onion, chopped
2 celery stalks, chopped
1 carrot, chopped
1 bay leaf, crumbled
1 teaspoon sugar
¼ teaspoon crumbled dried marjoram
2 tablespoons butter or margarine
2 tablespoons all-purpose flour
1 teaspoon salt, or more to taste
½ teaspoon pepper
1 pound cocktail frankfurters, halved, or large frankfurters, sliced
1 to 2 tablespoons white or cider vinegar
¼ cup chopped green onions

Soak lentils according to package directions; drain. Cook lentils with water and bacon in large kettle over low heat until tender, about 30 minutes; skim as needed. Add onion, celery, carrot, bay leaf, sugar, and marjoram to lentils. Cover and simmer for 30 minutes longer. Purée in electric blender or rub through sieve or food mill. Melt butter and stir in flour. Blend in a small amount of soup to make a smooth paste. Stir into soup. Season. Add frankfurters and cook over very low heat for 15 to 20 minutes, stirring frequently. Stir in vinegar, blending thoroughly. Serve sprinkled with green onions. Makes 3½ quarts.

QUICK SOUPS WITH FRANKFURTERS
When you need a hearty soup in a matter of minutes, try one of these. Any of them will make 4 servings as a soup course.
■ Make onion soup with 1 package of mix; add ½ pound frankfurters, peeled and diced, and sprinkle with grated cheese.
■ Make vegetable soup with 1 package of mix; add ½ pound frankfurters, cut into bite-size pieces, and simmer until frankfurters are warmed through, about 5 minutes.
■ Make tomato soup with one 10½-ounce can and equal amount of light cream or milk. Add 2 frankfurters, chopped, ½ teaspoon sugar, and pinch of ground rosemary.

FRANKFURTER STEW
6 onions, quartered
6 carrots, sliced
6 potatoes, peeled and cubed
2 pounds frankfurters
1 can (10½ ounces) tomato soup

Cook vegetables in small amount of boiling water until almost done; do not drain. Cut frankfurters into bite-size pieces. Combine all ingredients; simmer for 15 minutes, or until vegetables are tender. Makes 8 servings.

CASSEROLES

FRANKFURTERS WITH SHIRRED EGGS
6 to 8 cocktail frankfurters
2 teaspoons butter
1 cup tomato sauce or canned tomato soup
1 tablespoon chopped parsley
6 to 12 eggs
Salt and pepper

Cut frankfurters into ½-inch pieces and cook in hot butter for 5 minutes. Add tomato sauce and parsley. Pour into 6 shirred-egg or individual baking dishes. Break 1 or 2 eggs into each dish on top of sauce. Season eggs with salt and pepper. Bake in preheated moderate oven (350°F.) for 15 minutes, or until of desired doneness. Makes 6 servings.

FRANKFURTER AND CORN CASSEROLE
Butter or margarine
3 tablespoons all-purpose flour
1 teaspoon salt
¼ teaspoon white pepper
1½ cups hot milk
2¼ cups cooked fresh or canned whole-kernel corn, drained
3 eggs, beaten
¼ cup fine dry bread crumbs
¾ pound frankfurters
Chopped parsley

Heat 3 tablespoons butter and stir in flour. Blend thoroughly and add salt and pepper. Gradually stir in hot milk. Cook sauce until thick and smooth, stirring. Remove from heat and add corn. Slowly stir in beaten eggs. Pour mixture into 1½-quart casserole. Top with bread crumbs and dot with 2 tablespoons butter. Bake in preheated moderate oven (350°F.) for 45 minutes. About 15 minutes before dish is done, score frankfurters. Arrange on top. Finish baking. Sprinkle with parsley. Makes 6 servings.

FRANKFURTER EGGS FU YUNG
5 eggs
½ cup water

1 small onion, slivered
1 cup bean sprouts
2 cooked frankfurters, chopped
¼ cup sliced water chestnuts
Salt and pepper to taste
Soy sauce
Hot cooked rice

Beat eggs with water. Add all other ingredients except soy sauce and rice. Brown the omelet on both sides in well-buttered hot skillet. Serve with soy sauce and hot cooked rice. Makes 4 servings.

FRANKFURTER-MOZZARELLA SPAGHETTI
1 can (10½ ounces) meatless spaghetti sauce
¼ pound frankfurters, sliced
¼ cup chopped parsley
Salt and pepper
½ pound spaghetti, cooked
½ pound Mozzarella cheese, sliced

Combine spaghetti sauce, frankfurters, parsley, and salt and pepper. Turn spaghetti into 1½-quart casserole. Top with sauce and Mozzarella. Cover and bake in preheated moderate oven (350°F.) for 30 minutes, or until cheese is melted and dish heated through. Makes 4 servings.

FRANKFURTERS WITH MACARONI AND CHEESE
1½ cups scalded milk
1 cup soft bread crumbs
1½ cups grated Cheddar cheese
1 cup macaroni, cooked
3 eggs, separated
Salt
1 tablespoon grated onion
3 tablespoons melted butter or margarine
Paprika
4 frankfurters, halved and scored

Pour hot milk over the bread crumbs. Add cheese and cook over low heat until cheese is melted. Add macaroni and mix together. Add beaten egg yolks, salt, onion, and melted butter. Beat egg whites until stiff but not dry. Fold into mixture. Pour into buttered casserole. Sprinkle with paprika and top with frankfurters. Bake in preheated moderate oven (375°F.) for about 35 minutes. Makes 4 servings.
Note: If you need to double the recipe, bake in two casseroles.

FRANKFURTER-KRAUT CASSEROLE
1 pound frankfurters, cut into ½-inch pieces
2 cups, about (one 1-pound can) sauerkraut, undrained
1 package (10 ounces) frozen peas, thawed
1 can (10½ ounces) cream-of-mushroom soup

1 onion, minced
1 cup crushed potato chips

Combine all ingredients except potato chips and put in shallow 2-quart casserole. Top with crushed chips and bake in preheated moderate oven (350°F.) for about 30 minutes. Makes 6 servings.

FRANKFURTERS WITH SPANISH RICE
1 large onion, sliced
1 garlic clove, minced
¼ cup celery, chopped
¼ cup butter or margarine
3½ cups (one 1-pound, 13-ounce can) tomatoes
1 green pepper, minced
1½ teaspoons salt
½ teaspoon pepper
⅛ teaspoon ground thyme
1 bay leaf, crumbled
1 cup uncooked rice
1 pound frankfurters

Sauté onion, garlic, and celery in hot butter until soft. Add tomatoes, green pepper, and seasonings. Simmer, covered, for 10 minutes, stirring occasionally. Stir in rice. Simmer, covered, for 30 minutes longer, or until rice is tender. Stir occasionally; if mixture is dry, add a little hot water, 1 tablespoon at a time. Split frankfurters lengthwise or cut into 1-inch pieces. Arrange alternate layers of rice and frankfurters in 1½- to 2-quart casserole. Cover and bake in preheated moderate oven (350°F.) for about 25 minutes. If desired, sprinkle with grated cheese and put under broiler until cheese is bubbly. Makes 6 servings.

FRANKFURTER AND LIMA-BEAN CASSEROLE
1 pound dried Lima beans
1 garlic clove
4 onions, sliced
1 green pepper, diced
2 tablespoons fat
1 can (10½ ounces) condensed tomato soup
1 teaspoon salt
2 tablespoons brown sugar
¼ teaspoon hot pepper sauce
½ teaspoon powdered mustard
¼ teaspoon ground marjoram
1 tablespoon dried celery flakes
1 cup beef bouillon
1 pound frankfurters

Cook beans in usual manner with garlic clove until barely tender. Drain; remove garlic. Sauté onion and green pepper in hot fat until soft. Add beans and remaining ingredients except frankfurters. Mix thoroughly. Turn into shallow 1½-quart casserole. Bake in preheated moderate oven (350°F.) for 45 minutes. About 20 minutes before beans are done, arrange

frankfurters on top in spoke fashion. Finish baking. Makes 6 to 8 servings.

SCALLOPED TOMATOES AND FRANKFURTERS
Butter
2⅓ cups (1-pound, 3-ounce can) whole tomatoes, drained
4 frankfurters, cut into bite-size pieces
2 cups soft bread crumbs
Salt, pepper, and sugar to taste

In a well-buttered casserole combine tomatoes, frankfurters, and 1 cup of the bread crumbs. Add salt, pepper, and sugar. Butter remaining bread crumbs, and sprinkle on top. Bake in preheated hot oven (400°F.) for about 30 minutes, or until nicely browned on top. Makes 4 servings.

MAIN DISHES

FRANKFURTER, PRUNE, AND ONION KABOBS
String alternately on skewers diagonally cut pieces of frankfurters, plumped pitted prunes, green-pepper squares, and canned white onions. Brush with melted butter or margarine. Put in shallow baking pan and pour 1 tablespoon dark corn syrup or molasses over each skewer. Bake in preheated moderate oven (350°F.) for 20 minutes, or broil for about 7 minutes. Serve with yellow rice. Allow 2 skewers per person.
Note: To plump prunes, let stand in water to cover in refrigerator for 4 to 5 hours, or overnight.

BAKED FRANKFURTERS
1 pound frankfurters
⅓ cup chili sauce
1 tablespoon chopped parsley
1 tablespoon instant minced onion
¼ cup chopped celery
⅓ cup pickle liquid
¼ cup chopped pickles or pickle relish
Baked beans or home-fried potatoes

Prick frankfurters and arrange in shallow baking dish. Combine next six ingredients and pour over the frankfurters. Bake in preheated moderate oven (350°F.) for 20 to 30 minutes. Serve with baked beans. Makes 6 servings.

COUNTRY-STYLE FRANKFURTERS
4 cups sliced onions
1 garlic clove, minced
2 tablespoons fat
½ teaspoon salt
⅛ teaspoon pepper
2 tablespoons Worcestershire
1 tablespoon prepared mustard
1 pound frankfurters, split

Cook onions and garlic in fat until golden brown. Sprinkle with salt and pepper. Cover and simmer for 10 minutes, or until onion is tender. Add Worcestershire and mustard. Heat frankfurters in colander over boiling water, or brown lightly in small amount of fat. Put on hot platter and top with onion mixture. Makes 4 servings.

FRANKFURTERS WITH NEW POTATOES AND PEAS
2 pounds very small new potatoes
Boiling salted water
½ pound frankfurters, cut into 1-inch pieces
1 cup cooked green peas
½ teaspoon dried basil
⅛ teaspoon pepper
2 tablespoons butter or margarine
¼ cup light cream or undiluted evaporated milk
Pimiento strips for garnish (optional)

Scrape or peel potatoes. Cook, covered, in ½ inch of boiling salted water until half done, or about 15 minutes. Shake pan frequently. Add frankfurters and cook, covered, for 10 minutes. Shake pan frequently. If necessary, add a little more boiling water to prevent sticking. Add peas and heat through thoroughly. Add basil, pepper, butter, and cream and heat for 1 minute. Serve garnished with pimiento strips. Makes 4 to 6 servings.

FRANKFURTERS BUON GUSTO
2 slices of bacon, chopped
2 medium onions, minced
1 pound frankfurters, sliced
2 medium green peppers, cut into strips
12 stuffed olives, sliced
2 teaspoons capers
Salt and pepper
Pinch of oregano if desired
6 eggs
2 tablespoons milk

Cook bacon in heavy skillet until almost crisp. Add onions and cook for 3 minutes. Add frankfurters and peppers and cook for 5 minutes longer. Add olives, capers, and seasonings. Beat eggs with milk and pour over ingredients in skillet. Cook until eggs are set, stirring occasionally. Makes 6 servings.

FRANKFURTER AND SAUERKRAUT GOULASH
2 tablespoons margarine
1 pound frankfurters, sliced
¼ cup chopped onion
3½ cups (1 pound, 13-ounce can) sauerkraut
1 cup dairy sour cream
1 tablespoon caraway seeds or dillseeds
¼ teaspoon salt
1 teaspoon paprika, or more to taste

Heat margarine and cook frankfurters and onion in it for 5 minutes, stirring. Drain sauerkraut and rinse under running cold water. Drain again; add to frankfurters. Cook, covered, for 15 minutes. Add last 4 ingredients. Cook, uncovered, over low heat for 5 minutes longer. Makes 6 servings.

FRANKFURTERS WITH YELLOW PEAS, GERMAN STYLE

    4 cups (2 pounds) dried yellow split peas
    6 cups boiling water
    1 large onion, minced
    ⅓ cup bacon fat
    1½ teaspoons salt
    ½ teaspoon pepper
    ¼ teaspoon ground allspice
    12 ounces cocktail frankfurters

Cook peas in boiling water until almost soft, about 20 minutes. Cook onion in hot bacon fat until soft and barely golden. Add to peas. Add salt, pepper, and allspice. Simmer, covered, over low heat until peas are cooked, stirring frequently. Add more liquid if needed. When peas are cooked, add frankfurters and heat for 10 to 15 minutes. Makes 6 servings.

Note: This is a good cook-ahead dish for a picnic; reheat it on an open fire.

FRANKFURTERS BAVARIAN

    1½ pounds frankfurters
    2 tablespoons fat
    1 large onion, minced
    ¾ teaspoon salt
    3 tablespoons paprika
    ¼ teaspoon pepper
    2 cups dairy sour cream

Cut frankfurters diagonally into chunks. Brown in fat in chafing dish or large skillet. Add remaining ingredients except sour cream and cook slowly until onion is tender, stirring frequently. Add sour cream and heat, stirring constantly. Serve at once. Garnish with additional sour cream if desired. Makes 6 servings.

HAWAIIAN FRANKFURTERS

    ¼ cup butter or margarine
    1 large onion, chopped
    1 green pepper, slivered
    1 cup diced canned pineapple, drained
    2 small tomatoes, peeled and chopped
    2 tablespoons cornstarch
    ½ cup pineapple juice
    1 tablespoon white vinegar
    1 pound frankfurters, cut into 2-inch pieces
    Salt and pepper
    Hot cooked rice

Heat butter. Add onion, green pepper, pineapple, and tomatoes. Mix thoroughly. Cook over low heat for 7 minutes, or until heated. Blend cornstarch with pine-apple juice and vinegar. Stir into vegetable mixture. Add frankfurters and salt and pepper to taste. Simmer, covered, for about 10 minutes, stirring frequently. If necessary, add a little more pineapple juice or hot water, 1 tablespoon at a time. Serve with hot cooked rice. Makes 6 servings.

FRANKFURTERS IN PUNGENT SAUCE

    ¾ pound frankfurters, diced
    2 tablespoons cooking oil
    1½ tablespoons soy sauce
    2 carrots, diced
    2 green peppers, diced
    1 tablespoon brown sugar
    Cooked rice

Brown frankfurters quickly in hot oil. Sprinkle with soy sauce. Cook for 1 minute. Add carrots; cover and cook for 2 minutes. Add peppers. Cook, covered, for 3 to 4 minutes, stirring occasionally. Add brown sugar and mix well. Serve over rice. Makes 4 servings.

FRANKFURTER-STUFFED GREEN PEPPERS

    6 large green peppers
    ¼ cup butter or margarine
    1 onion, chopped
    ½ teaspoon instant minced garlic
    ¾ pound frankfurters, diced
    ½ cup grated Cheddar cheese
    2 cups cooked rice
    2 tablespoons chopped parsley
    ¼ teaspoon pepper
    Salt
    1 cup tomato juice

Cut stem ends off peppers and carefully remove the seeds and pith. Parboil for 5 minutes. Heat butter, and sauté onion and garlic in it until onion is soft. Add frankfurters and cook for 5 minutes, stirring. Add cheese, rice, and parsley. Blend thoroughly. Add pepper, and salt to taste. Cool mixture slightly and stuff peppers. Arrange peppers in greased baking dish and pour tomato juice around them. Bake in preheated moderate oven (350°F.) for 30 minutes, or until tender, basting occasionally. If peppers dry out, pour tomato juice around them as needed. Makes 6 servings.

HOT FRANKFURTER AND POTATO SALAD

    1 onion, chopped
    3 tablespoons bacon fat or butter
    1 tablespoon all-purpose flour
    1½ teaspoons salt
    1 tablespoon sugar
    ½ teaspoon powdered mustard
    3 tablespoons vinegar
    3 tablespoons water
    2 tablespoons sweet-pickle relish
    ⅓ cup diced celery
    2 tablespoons chopped green pepper
    4 cups diced cooked potatoes
    1 pound frankfurters, scored

Sauté onion in hot fat until soft. Combine flour, salt, sugar, and mustard, and stir into onions. Add vinegar and water and cook until thick, stirring. Combine remaining ingredients except frankfurters and blend with hot dressing. Turn into 1½-quart baking dish and top with frankfurters. Cover and bake in preheated moderate oven (350°F.) for 20 minutes. Makes 4 servings.

FRANKFURTER PILAF

    ¼ cup butter or margarine
    1 large onion, minced
    1 cup uncooked rice
    2½ cups hot chicken bouillon
    ½ pound frankfurters, sliced
    Salt and pepper to taste

Heat butter in heavy sauce pan that has a tight lid. Sauté onion in it until soft; add the rice and sauté until golden, stirring. Add hot bouillon and frankfurters. Cover tightly. Simmer over the lowest possible heat until rice is tender, 20 to 25 minutes. Season with salt and pepper. Makes 6 servings.

STUFFED BROILED FRANKFURTERS

    1 cup prepared bread crumbs
    3 tablespoons melted butter or margarine
    ¾ cup thick applesauce
    1 pound frankfurters
    Bacon slices

Combine bread crumbs, melted butter, and applesauce. Split frankfurters halfway through lengthwise. Fill with stuffing. Wrap a slice of bacon around each and fasten with toothpicks. Broil 3 to 4 inches from source of heat, or cook over outdoor grill for 7 minutes, turning to cook evenly. Makes 6 servings.

FRANKFURTERS WITH CABBAGE

    1 small head red or green cabbage, shredded
    2 unpeeled tart apples, cored and sliced
    2 tablespoons bacon fat
    1½ teaspoons salt
    ½ teaspoon pepper
    ½ pound frankfurters, halved or cut into 2-inch pieces
    Water
    3 tablespoons vinegar
    1 teaspoon sugar
    1 tablespoon all-purpose flour

Place cabbage in large skillet. Add apples, bacon fat, salt, pepper, frankfurters, and just enough water to cover. Bring to a boil. Reduce heat, cover and simmer, stirring frequently, until cabbage is tender but still crisp, about 15 minutes. Drain; reserve liquid. Combine vinegar, sugar,

Mustard Sauce

Frankfurter, Prune, and Onion Kabobs

Broiled Frankfurters

Frankfurter and Corn Casserole

Frankfurter and Corn Chowder

and flour and stir into cabbage liquid. Cook, stirring, until thick and smooth. Blend into cabbage mixture. Makes 4 to 6 servings.

FRANKFURTERS AND CREAMED ONIONS

- ¼ cup butter or margarine
- ¼ cup all-purpose flour
- ½ teaspoon salt
- ¼ teaspoon pepper
- 2 cups hot milk
- ¼ teaspoon ground marjoram
- 4 cups, about (two 1-pound cans) white onions, drained
- ¾ pound frankfurters, sliced
- 2 tablespoons sherry (optional)

Melt butter and stir in flour, salt, and pepper. Add milk slowly, stirring. Bring to a boil, stirring. Add marjoram, onions, and frankfurters. Simmer, covered, for about 10 minutes. Add sherry. Makes 6 servings.

FRANKFURTER TETRAZZINI

- 2 cans (4 ounces each) sliced mushrooms, drained
- 6 tablespoons butter or margarine
- 3 tablespoons all-purpose flour
- 2 chicken bouillon cubes
- 2 cups boiling water
- 1 cup undiluted evaporated milk
- 1 teaspoon steak sauce
- ¼ teaspoon pepper
  Salt to taste
- 1 pound frankfurters, cut into 1-inch pieces
- ½ pound (about 4 cups) uncooked noodles
- ½ cup grated Parmesan cheese
  Paprika

Brown mushrooms in 2 tablespoons butter in skillet. Remove mushrooms and add 4 tablespoons butter. Blend in flour. Dissolve bouillon cubes in boiling water and stir into flour mixture. Add milk; cook, stirring, until thickened and smooth. Add mushrooms, steak sauce, pepper, salt, and frankfurters. Simmer for 10 minutes. Cook noodles in boiling salted water. Drain. Turn noodles into shallow 2½-quart baking dish. Pour frankfurters and sauce on top. Sprinkle with cheese and paprika. Bake in preheated hot oven (425°F.) for 15 minutes, or until cheese is brown. Makes 6 servings.

FRANKFURTER AND TOMATO SCRAMBLED EGGS

- 1 frankfurter per person
  Butter
- 2 eggs per person
  Pepper
  Tomato juice

Peel and dice frankfurters and brown lightly in butter. Add eggs, beaten with freshly ground pepper and tomato juice.

Use as much liquid as you would use if scrambling eggs with milk. Cook slowly until eggs are of the consistency you like. There is no time limit. When they are the way you prefer, turn onto warm platter and serve.

FRANKFURTERS WITH FRUIT SAUCE

- ½ cup firmly packed brown sugar
- 1½ tablespoons all-purpose flour
- ½ teaspoon powdered mustard
- 1½ cups (one 12-ounce can) apricot nectar
- ¼ cup cider vinegar
- ½ cup raisins
- ¾ pound frankfurters, sliced

Combine all ingredients except frankfurters in saucepan and bring to a boil. Reduce heat; simmer, stirring, until thickened. Add frankfurters; cook for 5 minutes. Serve over noodles, if desired. Makes 4 servings.

SNACK AND LUNCHEON SPECIALS

CREAMED FRANKFURTERS AND CHICKEN

- 6 large hard rolls
- ¼ cup butter or margarine
- ½ cup diced celery
- ¼ cup all-purpose flour
- ½ teaspoon salt
- ⅛ teaspoon pepper
- 2½ cups milk
- 1 cup diced cooked chicken
- ½ pound diced cooked frankfurters
- 2 tablespoons chopped parsley

Scoop out hard rolls; reserve crumbs for other uses. Melt butter; sauté celery in it until tender. Stir in flour, salt, and pepper. Gradually add milk. Simmer until mixture thickens, stirring. Add chicken, frankfurters, and parsley; heat. Serve in hard-roll shells. Makes 4 to 6 servings.

FRANKFURTERS STUFFED WITH MASHED POTATOES, ONIONS, AND CHEESE

- 8 frankfurters
- 1½ cups mashed potatoes
- 1 tablespoon minced onion
  Salt and pepper to taste
  Butter
  Cheddar cheese, coarsely grated

Split frankfurters and stuff with mashed potatoes to which has been added onion, salt, pepper, and plenty of butter. Sprinkle with cheese. Broil until golden brown. Remove and serve immediately. Makes 8 servings.

SPLIT FRANKS COOKED WITH RELISH

Split frankfurters halfway through length-

wise. Spread slit with prepared mustard, fill with pickle relish, and broil to a sizzle.

CHEESE-TOPPED FRANKFURTERS

Spread prepared mustard between 6 split frankfurter rolls. Top each with split frankfurter and cheese mixture. (Cream ¼ cup margarine with 1 cup shredded sharp Cheddar. Fold in 2 stiffly beaten egg whites.) Bake in preheated hot oven (425°F.) For 15 minutes.

FRANKFURTER BOATS

Make 4 gashes in each frankfurter. Roll canned biscuits thin. Shape into boats around frankfurters; pinch ends. Bake in preheated hot oven (425°F.) for 10 minutes. Fill gashes with pickle relish.

MEXICAN FRANKFURTERS AND EGGS

For 4, cut up 1 green and 1 red pepper; cook in water until tender. Split ¾ pound frankfurters. Brown in butter. Scramble 8 eggs and top with peppers and frankfurters. Serve with cold tomato juice and toasted cornbread rounds.

FRANKFURTER-SQUASH LYONNAISE

For 4, split and steam 1 pound each zucchini and yellow squash in a little water. Brown 1 sliced onion in ¼ cup margarine. Add ¾ pound small frankfurters; brown. Add squash; heat.

CONEY ISLAND PICNIC FRANKFURTERS

- 8 frankfurters (about ¾ pound)
- ⅓ cup sweet pickle relish
- 2 tablespoons sweet pickle liquid
- 1 tablespoon melted margarine
- 1 teaspoon prepared mustard
- ⅛ teaspoon each of pepper, onion salt, and garlic salt
- 8 frankfurter rolls

Split frankfurters halfway through lengthwise. Fill with pickle relish and fasten with toothpicks. Combine all other ingredients except frankfurter rolls and mix well. Brush frankfurters with this mixture. Broil 3 to 4 inches from source of heat, or cook on outdoor grill for 5 to 7 minutes, brushing frequently with mixture. Serve in rolls. Makes 4 servings.

FRANKFURTERS AND CREAMED CORN

- 1 pound frankfurters
- 3 tablespoons butter or margarine
- 2 cups (one 1-pound, 1-ounce can) whole-kernel corn
- ½ can (10½-ounce can) cream-of-mushroom soup
- ¼ cup milk
  Pepper

Cut frankfurters into ½-inch slices. Melt butter; add franks and drained corn. Cover and cook for about 10 minutes. Stir this often. Add mushroom soup and milk and heat, stirring constantly, until the soup is thoroughly heated. Then add a bit of pepper. Makes 6 servings.

FRANKIE AND JOHNNY
- 1 cup coarsely ground white or yellow cornmeal
- 1 teaspoon salt
- Butter
- 1 cup boiling water
- ¼ cup milk
- 2 tablespoons fat
- 1 pound frankfurters

Mix cornmeal, salt, and 1 tablespoon butter in a bowl. Add actively boiling water and mix well. Stir in milk. Heat fat in baking pan (8 x 8 x 2 inches). Pour in batter and smooth to fill pan. Bake in preheated very hot oven (475°F.) for about 30 minutes. Cool in pan; cut into squares, split, and spread generously with softened butter. Brown under broiler. Slice frankfurters lengthwise and brown in butter. To serve, place frankfurters between squares of johnnycake, sandwich fashion. Makes 4 servings.

FRANKFURTERS IN THE ROUND
- Butter
- Hamburger buns
- Frankfurters (one to a bun)
- Cheddar cheese
- Relish

Butter the buns. Gash frankfurters and fasten ends together with toothpicks. Place frankfurters on bottom halves of buttered buns. Fill center of ring with cheese. Broil until frankfurter is done to your liking. Top with your favorite relish. Put on the top of the bun.

FRANKFURTER CHILI
Combine 1 pound sliced frankfurters with 2 cans chili with beans. Season with one teaspoon chili powder. Stir in ½ cup tomato juice, tomato sauce, or water. Simmer, covered, until frankfurters and chili are heated, about 15 minutes. Serve with plain cooked rice and a green salad. Makes 4 to 6 servings.

FRANKFURTER SUCCOTASH
Cook 2 packages (10 ounces each) frozen Fordhook Lima beans and 1 package (10 ounces) cut corn and stir together. Lightly brown ¾ pound small frankfurters in butter. Mix about half into succotash. Season. Top with remaining frankfurters. Serve with sliced tomatoes and watercress. Makes 6 servings.

FRANKFURTERS WITH CHEESE
Split frankfurters lengthwise and stuff with pimiento cheese spread. Broil until the cheese is oozy.

FRANKFURTERS IN SPAGHETTI SAUCE
Use a good canned spaghetti sauce. Add peeled diced frankfurters; heat. Serve on toast or spaghetti.

FRANKFURTERS IN OLIVE SAUCE
Add chopped olives to mayonnaise. Spread broiled split frankfurters with olive-mayonnaise mixture. Serve at once.

FRANKFURTER-CUSTARD TARTS
Line 6 tart pans with pastry; beat together 2 eggs, 1 cup dairy sour cream, ½ teaspoon salt, and dash of pepper; add ½ pound cubed frankfurters; fill pastry-lined tart pans. Bake in preheated hot oven (425°F.) for 20 minutes.

FRANKFURTERS IN A CRISPY CRUST
Split frankfurters and brush generously with mayonnaise; then roll in crushed potato chips. Use ½ cup mayonnaise and 5-ounce package potato chips to cover 6 to 8 frankfurters. Broil until golden brown.

FRANKFURTERS IN BLANKETS
Slit frankfurters and fill with pickle relish. Cut crusts from slices of fresh white bread. Roll a bread slice around each frankfurter; then roll a slice of bacon around each piece of bread. Bake in preheated hot oven (400°F.) for 15 minutes. Serve with onions, olives, and celery.

FRANKFURTER CORN STICKS
Make your favorite corn-stick batter; half fill hot greased corn-stick pans. Cut frankfurters into halves lengthwise. Top each batter layer with one piece; cover with more batter. Bake in preheated hot oven (400°F.) for 15 minutes.

SNAPPY FRANKFURTER-CHEESE ROLLS
Grind 1 pound frankfurters, ½ pound sharp cheese, 1 onion, 2 pimientos, ½ cup ripe olives. Add an 8-ounce can of tomato sauce and prepared mustard and Worcestershire to taste. Fill 12 split hard rolls with the mixture. Wrap rolls in foil and bake in slow oven (300°F.) for 25 minutes. Makes 6 servings.

FRANK-CHEESE BURGERS
Split hamburger rolls; toast. Put 2 slices of cheese on each bottom half. Cut frankfurters into fours and put 2 pieces on each roll. Bake in preheated hot oven (425°F.) for 8 minutes. Add tops.

FRANKFURTER RAREBIT
Arrange sliced peeled frankfurters on well-buttered toast in individual ramekins. Top with Cheese Sauce (below) and a good dash of Worcestershire. Slip under broiler until bubbly and nicely browned.

FRANKFURTERS WITH BRUSSELS SPROUTS
Allow 2 frankfurters for 4 servings of Brussels sprouts. Add sliced frankfurters to sprouts about 5 minutes before sprouts are cooked.

SAUCES AND RELISHES TO SERVE WITH FRANKFURTERS

CHILI BARBECUE SAUCE
- 2 medium onions, chopped
- 2 green peppers, chopped
- ⅔ cup sweet pickle relish
- ½ cup cider vinegar
- 2 cups chili sauce
- ¼ cup firmly packed brown sugar
- 1 tablespoon prepared mustard
- ¼ teaspoon hot pepper sauce

Combine all ingredients. Simmer, covered, for about 10 minutes, stirring frequently. Makes about 3 cups sauce, enough to serve with 3 pounds grilled or boiled frankfurters.

CHEESE SAUCE
In greased skillet combine ¼ pound sliced process American cheese, ½ cup milk, and dash each of garlic salt and cayenne. Cover and heat for 5 minutes. Remove cover and stir vigorously until blended. Makes about 2 cups.

CURRY-ONION SAUCE
Cook 1 minced small onion in 1 tablespoon butter or margarine until lightly browned. Add 1 tablespoon curry powder, ¼ cup each of ketchup, milk, and water, and ¼ teaspoon salt. Cook for 5 minutes, stirring frequently. Remove from heat and add 1 tablespoon each of fresh lemon juice and heavy cream. Makes ¾ cup.

ENGLISH MUSTARD
Mix equal parts powdered mustard and water, stirring to break up all lumps. Let stand for 10 minutes to develop pungent

flavor. Add dash each of salt and sugar.

HORSERADISH SAUCE

Mix well 1 cup mayonnaise, 3 table-spoons prepared horseradish and ½ tea-spoon prepared mustard. If you like a stronger horseradish flavor, add more.

MUSTARD SAUCE

In saucepan combine ¾ cup undiluted evaporated milk, ¼ cup prepared mus-tard, 1 grated onion, 2 teaspoons sugar, and ¾ teaspoon salt. Heat. Makes 1 cup.

PIQUANT BARBECUE SAUCE

In saucepan combine ½ cup butter or margarine, 1 teaspoon each of salt and sugar, 2 tablespoons vinegar, 1 table-spoon Worcestershire, 1 teaspoon onion salt, ¼ teaspoon pepper, and ½ cup water. Heat until butter is melted. Makes about 1 cup.

WINE BARBECUE SAUCE

In saucepan combine 1 minced garlic clove, 1 minced onion, 1 beef-bouillon cube, dash of cayenne, 1 teaspoon chili powder, 1 cup each of dry white wine and water, and 1 can (15½ ounces) meatless spaghetti sauce. Bring to boil and simmer, uncovered, for 30 minutes, stirring constantly. Makes 2 cups.

CABBAGE-BEET RELISH

Mix 2 cups chopped pickled beets, 3 cups chopped green cabbage, 1 chopped onion, 2 teaspoons salt, and 1 tablespoon celery seeds. Store, covered, in refrigerator for several days before serving. Makes 5 cups.

CURRIED TOMATO RELISH

Peel 3 medium tomatoes, cut into small pieces, and simmer for 10 minutes. Add 1 teaspoon sugar, ¼ teaspoon garlic salt, 2 teaspoons each of curry powder and vinegar, and ½ teaspoon salt. Cook for 5 minutes; cool. Makes about 1 cup.

HODGEPODGE RELISH

Add ¼ cup hot vinegar to ⅔ cup diced cucumber, 1 cup diced tomato, ½ cup chopped onion, and ¼ cup chopped cel-ery. Add ½ teaspoon each of celery and mustard seeds. Makes about 2 cups.

MARINATED ONION RINGS

Peel and slice very thin 6 to 8 small white onions. Separate into rings. Heat ½ cup well-seasoned French dressing and pour over onions. Cool. Makes about 1½ cups.

FRAPPÉ—Literally translated, this French word means "beaten." In culinary lan-guage, it refers to a drink or a dessert, partially frozen and stirred. Frappés are served in glasses and are very pleasant hot weather fare. At the end of a meal, a frappé can double as a drink and a des-sert.

Liqueurs, poured over a glass of shaved or cracked ice, are also called *frappé*.

GRAPE-LIME FRAPPÉ

2 cups water
1 cup sugar
1 cup grape juice
Juice of 2 small limes

Set refrigerator control for fast freezing. Boil water and sugar for 5 minutes; cool. Add fruit juices. Pour into refrigerator tray and partially freeze. Remove from tray to chilled bowl. Beat until fluffy and light in color. Makes about 4 servings.

TANGERINE FRAPPÉ

1½ cups (two 6-ounce cans) frozen tangerine juice, undiluted
1 envelope unflavored gelatin
½ cup sugar

Set refrigerator control for fast freezing. Blend tangerine juice with 3 juice cans water. Sprinkle gelatin on ½ cup juice and let stand for 5 minutes. Put over low heat and stir until dissolved. Add gelatin and sugar to remaining juice. Pour into refrigerator trays and freeze until mushy, stirring occasionally. Remove to cold bowl and beat with rotary beater until fluffy. Makes 4 servings.

DEEP SOUTH CAFÉ FRAPPÉ

1 cup sugar
4 cups strong hot coffee
1 cup heavy cream
Whipped cream

Set refrigerator control for fast freezing. Add sugar to coffee while hot. Stir until completely dissolved. Cool. Add cream. Pour into refrigerator trays. Freeze until mushy; beat until fluffy. Serve as a des-sert-drink in tall glasses decorated with whipped cream. Makes 4 servings.

FREEZE, TO and FROZEN FOODS—

The freezing of food is the process of chilling a liquid, or a solid which con-tains varying amounts of liquid, until it is hardened. The lower the freezing tem-perature, the faster the freezing, the smaller the ice crystals formed in the food, the less breakdown of cellular structure of foods, and so the greater re-tention of flavor and firm texture in the final product.

Although water freezes at 32°F. at sea level, and a refrigerator frozen-food stor-age compartment which maintains tem-peratures of 20°F. to 32°F. is adequate for storing already frozen foods, 0°F. or less is much better for the storing and the freezing of meats, fruits, vegetables, and other foods in the home for more than a few days. Food freezers and true freezers in the combination freezer-re-frigerators are designed to freeze and store frozen foods properly. Commercial freezing is done at even lower tempera-tures and commercially frozen foods are either ready for cooking or already cooked, needing only reheating. In some cases, defrosting is all that is needed. There are hundreds of frozen foods and food combinations available, from sim-ple vegetables and fruits to elaborate gourmet dishes. Most of them are excel-lent in quality and add quick and wel-come changes to the daily diet. It is ad-visable to read the package instructions for their most satisfactory use. As for storing, they are to be treated like home-frozen foods. Thawing times vary; a rule of thumb is to allow approximately four to six hours in the refrigerator, or over-night, two to three hours at room tem-perature, and twenty to thirty minutes under running water.

Home freezing is very easy and satis-factory, and there is no one set of direc-tions that covers how much or what to freeze or how large or small the freezing device should be. Each family must de-cide for itself which system will result in the greatest time, labor, and cost sav-ings. There is a wide choice of equip-ment available: chest-type freezers, a combination refrigerator-freezer, locker space away from home, or a small freezer at home, are among them.

BASIC RULES FOR SUCCESSFUL HOME FREEZING

■ **Be Selective**—Don't waste time freez-ing fresh foods which are not of high quality and at the peak of perfection, or which your family doesn't favor.

■ **Freeze Foods Quickly**—Plan to freeze in quantities that can be handled in a short time. The secret of success with fresh foods is to freeze them as quickly as possible. With few exceptions fresh foods will not improve, in fact they deteriorate, on standing. Check procedures, equipment, your own time schedule and plan work so quick handling is possible. (You can't have 12 quarts of strawberries picked or purchased and ready to freeze, then go off for an afternoon of shopping.)

See that quantities to be frozen are never greater than the size of the fast-freeze plate or the shelves for freezing them. When food freezes too slowly, loss in quality, even spoilage, may take place. Put in no more food than will freeze in 24 hours, preferably in even less time. Follow freezer manufacturer's directions about quantity and placement of foods. Be sure packages make contact with freezer plate or shelves and are spaced out. Limiting the amount frozen at any given time will also prevent temperature increases in the rest of the freezer.

■ **Choose Suitable Packaging Materials and Pack According to Directions**—All items in freezer must be kept airtight. Drying out will affect all foods; "freezer burn," dried-out white spots, will affect meat; air holes in fruit and vegetable packages may cause collapsing, flavor and color changes, and loss of nutrients. Even bread dries out and stales quickly after defrosting if not properly wrapped. Improperly wrapped foods may also absorb foreign odors and flavors. All this can be avoided with present-day freezing materials. They must be moisture- and vapor-proof or resistant. They are made of aluminum foil, laminates, or polyethylene films. The laminates are polyethylene, cellophane, pliofilm or glassine laminated to kraft paper or aluminum foil laminated to a paper base. When using these, allow enough extra paper for generous folding at the joining and seal with freezer tape. The clear films cling so that it's easy to exclude air, but for long storage, overwrap and seal with freezer tape.

Drugstore Wrap, Single—Place meat, poultry, or other solid food in the center of a suitable freezer wrapping, enough to make a three-fold seal when wrapping. Place a double thickness of moisture-proof dividers between steaks, chops, and cut-up foods when two or more pieces are put into the same package. This makes it possible for pieces to be taken apart readily without complete thawing. Bring the two edges of the wrapping material together above the food. Fold down in about 1-inch folds until the wrapping is snug against the food. Wrap tightly. Mold wrap firmly against the food and smooth out to remove all air. Fold ends in the same way and pull under the package. Fasten securely. Tie with twine, or tape with odorless freezer tape. Aluminum foil, if tightly folded, needs no tape or twine. Label package and freeze quickly.

Butcher Wrap, Double—This wrap requires about 20 per cent more material than the drugstore wrap. Place food on the paper so there is enough paper at each corner of the food to equal or be greater than its thickness. Turn the food completely over twice, pulling the paper tight as you turn. Be sure all surfaces are covered by two or more thicknesses of paper. Fold in sides and ends to exclude air. Pull paper tightly and tie or tape. Label and freeze.

Bags—They are transparent, pliable at low temperatures and come in various sizes to meet many requirements. Bags are polyethylene plastic, easy to expel air from (press food in bag lightly) and easy to seal. Give top a quick twist, fold it over, and secure with rubber band or string. Watch for punctures. To reuse, sterilize by soaking for 10 to 15 minutes in 1 teaspoon chlorine solution in 1 quart water. For cellophane bags, heat-seal or seal with freezer tape. Watch out for sharp-edged foods and for splitting or tearing.

Containers—Most of these are reusable. The polyethylene and plastic types should be sterilized as noted above. Glass and metal containers should be sterilized in boiling water. Containers commonly available are polyethylene boxes, polyethylene bags in boxes, glass freezer jars, plastic boxes, aluminum-foil containers, and waxed and treated paper containers.

Pack or wrap as directed for each type of food, adjusting sizes of packages according to your family needs. Most foods frozen in airtight containers will need ½ inch or more of headspace unless otherwise directed, because foods expand during freezing.

■ **Keep Food to Be Frozen Cool**—If the food has been heated or cooked, chill it quickly. See directions for each type of food. In general, when cooling scalded fresh foods, chilling water should be very cold and plentiful. Use ice in the water if necessary. Frequent water changes may be required. Cooked food can be set in pans in cooling water.

■ **Label and Date All Foods**—It is helpful to many women to keep a checklist of the foods placed in freezer and the dates they were placed there. There is a storage timetable for all frozen foods varying from 1 week to 1 year (see page 728). Be familiar with these times and use foods when at their peak. When large quantities of foods are stored at home, or in lockers away from home, the running inventory may be helpful. Checklist forms are available for those who wish to keep an inventory. Be sure to use up foods as you go along. If you have no inventory, rotate them in the freezer so that you will use first the ones stored longest.

■ **Store at 0°F. or Lower**—This is the temperature agreed upon by all authorities to maintain quality in frozen foods. Temperature variations may occur in freezers according to the location of foods and the way they are used. It is a good practice to keep a thermometer in the spot known to be the warmest for checking. Some freezers are equipped with controls which can be turned to coldest position before a load is frozen and kept there during freezing period. A well-packed full freezer will maintain uniformly low temperature better than a half-filled one.

Commercially frozen foods are handled in the freezer during their storage in the same way as home-frozen foods. See that they are frozen solid when purchased, and keep the time from store to home freezer at a minimum.

■ **Defrost and Clean Freezer as Directed**—Some freezers are self-defrosting and need only occasional cleaning. Others should be defrosted and cleaned thoroughly once a year, or twice, if humidity causes a large build-up. A build-up of frost may not affect operating efficiency, but it will cut down on space in freezer and is inconvenient.

■ **Take Special Care During Power Interruptions**—If power goes off or freezer fails, food in a loaded freezer cabinet ordinarily will remain frozen for 2 days providing door is kept closed. In cabinets with less than a half-load, food may not stay frozen even for 1 day. Dry ice, used properly, may help if power is off for 2 or 3 days. But better still, if a long interruption is anticipated, try to find other available freezer space or put foods in a locker plant; do this before foods begin to thaw.

■ **Do Not Refreeze Foods**—Refreezing of any food is not advisable. However, food may be refrozen if food is still partially frozen, or if its temperature has not gone above 40°F. (thawed, but still feels

MAXIMUM STORAGE TIMES FOR FROZEN FOODS AT 0°F.

PRODUCT	MONTHS
Meat, Fresh	
Beef, steaks or roasts	9 to 12
Beef, ground	4 to 6
Beef or lamb liver	3 to 4
Heart, all varieties	3 to 4
Kidney, all varieties	3 to 4
Lamb	9 to 12
Lamb, ground	4 to 6
Pork	4 to 6
Pork, ground	1 to 3
Pork liver	1 to 2
Pork, sausage	1 to 3
Tongue	3 to 4
Veal	9 to 12
Veal, ground	4 to 6
Meat, Smoked	
Bacon, slab	1 to 3
(Do not freeze sliced bacon)	
Frankfurters	1 to 3
Ham, whole	1 to 3
Sausage	1 to 2
Poultry, Fresh	
Chicken, ready-to-cook	12
Ducks, geese, ready-to-cook	6
Giblets	2 to 3
Turkey, ready-to-cook	6
Fish and Shellfish	
Lean fish	4 to 6
Fatty fish, clams, oysters, scallops, raw shrimps	3 to 4
Cooked crabmeat and lobster meat	2 to 3
Cooked shrimps	1 to 2
Other Foods	
Butter and cheese, except cottage cheese	6 to 8
(Do not freeze cream cheese.)	
Eggs, yolks and whites separated	12
Fruits and vegetables	10 to 12
Fruit juices	up to 16
Heavy cream, cottage cheese	3 to 4
Ice cream	1 to 2
Margarine	12
Cooked or Prepared Foods	
Baked pies, biscuits, muffins, waffles, cream puffs, spongecake	2
Baked quick breads (muffins, etc.)	2
Baked yeast bread and rolls	6 to 8
Cakes (frosted) loaves, doughnuts, pie and cookie dough, unbaked pies	4 to 6
Cakes (unfrosted) fruit cakes, unbaked fruit pies	6 to 8
Leftovers, fried foods, newburgs, thermidors, pasta dishes	1
Roast beef, lamb, veal, and chicken, beans	4 to 6
Roast pork and turkey, stews, cooked vegetables, foods in sauces and gravy, chow mein, meat pies, meatballs and loaves, hash, gravies	2 to 4
Sandwiches	1 to 4 weeks
Soups	6
Turkey pies, stuffing, chili con carne	1 to 2
Unbaked biscuits, muffins	2 weeks
Unbaked yeast dough	2 weeks

very cold). Above this temperature, food should not be refrozen: vegetables will spoil rapidly, fruits begin to ferment, meat and fish may spoil.

Fruits, fish, precooked dishes, and vegetables can be cooked from the frozen state. Soups, stews, chowders, and creamed dishes can be reheated slowly in covered pot or skillet, in a double boiler, or in a covered dish in the oven. Heavy foil can be used as a cover. The makers of some glass baking ware guarantee it can be put in the oven direct from freezer.

Meats, poultry, or other bulky frozen foods should be thawed or partially thawed to cook properly. If possible, remove foods from freezer several hours ahead of reheating and let them warm up to room temperature, or leave for a longer period in the refrigerator. Many dishes can be heated from the unthawed state.

TO FREEZE FRUITS

Almost all fruits can be frozen satisfactorily, although quality will vary somewhat with the kind of fruit. But most of the quality of frozen fruits is within the control of the person doing the freezing. For fruit especially, freezing quickly at the time when the fruit is best for eating, when it is uniformly ripe and free from signs of spoilage, is the best safeguard.

Bananas should be mixed into a creamy mixture such as ice cream. Avocados must be frozen mashed only, and pears and grapes should not be frozen alone but only in combination with other fruits.

■ Wash fruits in cold water. For delicate ones such as berries, handle only a small quantity at a time and as little as possible. A wire basket is helpful here. Always keep fruit cool. Lift all fruit out of the water and drain thoroughly. Never let fruit stand in water.

■ Preparation of fruit for freezing is about the same as for serving: peel, pit, slice, etc. However, it may be frozen in more than one form as chart beginning on page 730 indicates; the choice is yours. Soft fruit may be crushed with a wire potato masher, a pastry fork, or even a slotted spoon. Some very firm fruits may be put through a chopper. A colander, food press, or strainer is useful in making purées. If fruit must be put in large containers or heated during the process, aluminum, earthenware, enamelware, glass, nickel, stainless steel, or good-quality tinware will be a good choice. Watch out for galvanized ware for, in direct contact with fruit or juices, the acid may dissolve the zinc, which is poisonous. Metallic off-

flavors may come from iron utensils, chipped enamel, or old tinware.

■ Fruit may be frozen in dry sugar or sugar syrup, or it may be packed without sweetening. The freezing chart following lists all three. Choice will depend on individual preferences or needs. Unsweetened packs of some fruits, although they usually result in lower quality, may be necessary for special diets. Among the fruits which will have as good quality with or without sugar are gooseberries, currants, cranberries, rhubarb, and figs.

Syrup packs are most often used for firm fruits such as apricots, cherries, peaches, and plums. A 40 per cent sugar syrup is most commonly used; however a lighter syrup may be desirable for mild-flavored fruits, a heavy syrup for the very sour ones. This becomes a matter of individual taste.

To make syrup packs, dissolve sugar in either cold or hot water and then cool. In either case, syrup should be made up ahead of time and chilled in refrigerator. It will take ½ to ⅔ cup of syrup for each pint of packed fruit.

Type Syrup	Cups of Sugar*	Cups of Water	Yield In Cups
30% syrup	2	4**	5
35% syrup	2½	4	5⅓
40% syrup	3	4	5½
50% syrup	4¾	4	6½
60% syrup	7	4	7¾
65% syrup	8¾	4	8⅔
70% syrup	11	4	9⅓

* To make a syrup of sugar and corn syrup combined, replace ¼ of the sugar with light corn syrup.
** 4 cups = 1 quart.

To make sugar packs for the softer, juicier fruits: Cut measured or weighed amounts of fruit into a bowl, or spread out in a shallow pan. Sprinkle the quantity of sugar given in chart over fruit and mix gently with a large spoon or pancake turner until juice flows and sugar is dissolved. When packing sugared fruits in containers, cover top of fruit with a piece of crumpled parchment or freezer wrapping material to hold fruit under juice. Put cover in place and seal.

There are three ways to pack fruit without sugar or syrup: 1) Pack prepared fruit into containers and seal; 2) Pack fruit and cover with water containing ascorbic acid; 3) Crush or slice fruit and pack in its own juice. Again, cover top with paper, close, and seal.

To make a loose pack, freeze fruits spread out singly on a tray. Pour frozen fruits into a container and seal. Good for small families who only wish to use half of a package at one time. To prevent darkening of fruit, use ascorbic acid or the ascorbic-acid mixtures. This provides vitamin C and preserves flavor and nutritive value as well as color. It is tasteless. Ascorbic acid is used at two points during freezing: When fruit is being prepared, slices may be put into water containing ascorbic acid or into vinegar or citric-acid solution (see Apples on Chart for Freezing Fruit) which is poured off and thrown away. Or the ascorbic acid is mixed directly with sugar or put into syrup for the frozen product.

Ascorbic acid is available in drug stores in crystalline, powdered, or tablet form. Ascorbic-acid mixtures are readily available in food stores. There are two types: mixed with sugar, or mixed with sugar and citric acid. *Follow directions given on the label when using these.* To use, sprinkle any one over fruit before adding sugar; or stir it into chilled syrup shortly before using; or stir directly into fruit juices or purées. In unsweetened packs, it may be sprinkled directly over fruit, or added to water if this is used. Also, to prevent darkening, lemon and other citrus juices can be used, but these must not be used in such quantities that they can be tasted. For some fruits, such as apples, steaming or treatment with sodium sulfite or sodium bisulfite may help prevent darkening.

● ● ● ● ●

·· Chart for Freezing Fruit ··

FRUIT	PREPARATION	PACKING Dry Sugar Pack	PACKING Syrup Pack	Unsweetened
APPLES 1 bushel (48 lbs.)=32 to 40 pints. 1¼ to 1½ pounds=1 pint	Full-flavored firm and crisp, not meaty, apples are best for freezing. Wash, remove bruises and decayed spots, peel, quarter and core. Cut each quarter into 3 slices. To prevent discoloration during preparation, slice apples into a solution of ½ cup salt to 1 gallon of water. After 15 to 20 apples have been sliced, remove them from the brine, rinse in cold water, drain and rinse again. Pack with sugar or forty percent sugar syrup. (Sugar pack or unsweetened is best for pies. Syrup pack is preferable for fruit cup or uncooked dessert). To prevent darkening during freezing when packed in sugar, submerge apples for not more than 5 minutes in a solution made by dissolving 1 teaspoon sodium bisulfite (USP grade) in 1 gallon of water at 60° to 70°F. (Buy sodium bisulfite in the drug store.) This amount of solution is enough for one half bushel of apples. Drain apples and mix with sugar. Let stand a few minutes until sugar dissolves. Stir carefully to coat apples with sugar solution. Pack.	½ cup sugar per quart of apples	Omit sulfite bath. Mix apples with a 40% sugar syrup, adding ½ teaspoon ascorbic acid per quart of syrup.	Freeze apples after treating with sulfite solution. Freeze as for Dry Sugar Pack, omitting sugar.
APPLESAUCE	Make as preferred; add sugar to taste. Pack leaving ¾- to 1-inch headspace.	½ cup sugar per quart fruit. To prevent darkening, add 1½ teaspoons ascorbic acid for each cup of sugar.	Use 40% syrup.	Freeze as for Dry Sugar Pack, omitting sugar.
APRICOTS 1 bushel (48 lbs.)=60 to 72 pints. ⅔ to 4/5 pound=1 pint.	Select firm ripe uniformly yellow fruit. Sort, wash, halve, pit. Peel and slice if preferred. (If unpeeled, heat in boiling water for ½ minute, then cool.) Puréed: Peel, pit, and quarter. Press through sieve or heat to boiling point in just enough water to prevent scorching, then purée.	Add ½ cup sugar to each quart whole fruit; 1 cup per quart puréed fruit	Use 40% syrup; add ¾ teaspoon ascorbic acid to each quart syrup.	Add ¼ teaspoon ascorbic acid to each quart fruit.
AVOCADOS	Select soft ripe, but not mushy, fruit with unblemished rinds. Peel, cut into halves, remove pit, mash pulp. (Does not freeze satisfactorily whole or sliced.) Unsweetened for salads, sandwiches. Sweetened for ice cream or milk shakes.	Add 1 cup sugar to each quart purée	No syrup pack.	Add ¼ teaspoon ascorbic acid to each quart purée.
BERRIES, SOFT (Blackberries, Boysenberries, Dewberries, Loganberries, Youngberries) 1 crate (24 qts.)=32 to 36 pints. 1⅓ to 1½ pints fresh=1 pint frozen.	Select fully ripe but firm plump berries with glossy skins. (Green berries may cause off-flavor.) Sort; remove any leaves or stems. Wash in cold water; drain by lifting from water.	Add ¾ cup to each quart whole berries; 1 cup sugar per quart purée	Use 40% to 50% syrup that must cover berries.	Dry-loose pack: Spread berries in a single layer on a tray, freeze firm, and then pour into freezer container.
BERRIES, FIRM (Blueberries, Elderberries, Huckleberries)	Select firm fully ripe berries of uniform size with tender skins. Sort, wash, drain. (May be steamed for 1 minute, then chilled. This softens skins.)	½ cup sugar per quart whole berries; 1 cup per quart purée	Use 40% syrup.	Dry-loose pack: see above.
CHERRIES Sour 1 bushel (56 lbs.)=36 to 44 pints. 1¼ to 1½ pounds=1 pint.	Select bright red tree-ripened fruit. Stem, sort, and wash. Drain and pit. Crushed. Purée, juice.	For pies and cooking ¾ cup per quart whole fruit; 1 to 1½ cups per quart crushed. Add 1 teaspoon ascorbic acid to each cup of sugar.	To serve uncooked use 50% to 70% sugar syrup.	No unsweetened pack.
Sweet (For quantity see above.)	Red varieties best for freezing. Well-colored tree-ripened fruit best for freezing. Sort, stem, wash, and drain. May pit or not, as preferred. Note: All cherries should be handled quickly to prevent browning around pit cavity.	No sugar pack.	Use 40% to 50% syrup; add ½ teaspoon ascorbic acid per quart syrup.	No unsweetened pack.

FRUIT	PREPARATION	PACKING Dry Sugar Pack	Syrup Pack	Unsweetened
CRANBERRIES ½ pound=1 pint.	Choose firm deep-red berries with glossy skins. Wash, drain, dry. Will freeze well without sugar or syrup. Pack into containers leaving ¾- to 1-inch headspace. A syrup pack may be used.	No sugar pack.	Use 50% syrup.	Dry-loose pack best method of freezing cranberries.
CURRANTS 2 quarts (3 lbs.)=4 pints. ¾ pound=1 pint.	Pick plump, fully ripe, bright-red currants. Wash, remove stems, dry. Whole Will freeze well without sugar or syrup. Pack into containers, leaving ¾- to 1-inch headspace. They may be used in recipes like fresh. Or pack in sugar or syrup. Crushed Crush after draining and stemming. Juice For beverage select ripe fruit; for jelly mix in some underripe. Wash, stem, and drain. Crush, then warm to 165°F. over low heat to start flow of juice. Do not boil. Press hot fruit in jelly bag to extract juice. Cool.	¾ cup sugar per quart whole fruit 1⅛ cups per quart crushed; ¾ to 1 cup per quart juice	Use 50% syrup. No syrup pack.	Dry-loose pack. No unsweetened pack.
GOOSEBERRIES	Choose fully ripe gooseberries for pie, a little underripe for jelly or jam. Sort; remove stems and blossom ends. Wash.	⅔ cup sugar per quart	Use 50% syrup.	Dry-loose pack.
GRAPEFRUIT, ORANGES	Select firm tree-ripened fruit, heavy for its size and free from soft spots. Wash, then peel. Section, removing membrane and seeds. Slice oranges if desired. Juice Squeeze juice from fruit using squeezer that does not press oil from rind. To prevent off flavors, freeze in glass or citrus-enamel tin cans.	No sugar pack. 2 tablespoons sugar per quart juice plus ¼ teaspoon ascorbic acid	Use 40% to 70% syrup. Add ½ teaspoon ascorbic acid to each quart syrup. No syrup pack.	No loose pack. No unsweetened pack.
GRAPES	Select firm grapes. Wash and stem. Whole or halves Leave seedless grapes whole; cut table grapes with seeds into halves and remove seeds. Purée Prepare as above, then crush. Heat to boiling. Drain off free juice and freeze or can separately. Cool pulp and press through a sieve. (If tartrate crystals form in freezer, they will disappear when purée is heated.) Juice For beverages, select as above. For jelly, select as recommended in jelly recipe. Prepare as above. Crush and strain through jelly bag. Let stand overnight in refrigerator while sediment sinks to bottom. Pour off clear juice for freezing. If tartrate crystals form in frozen juice, thaw, then strain before using.	No sugar pack. ½ cup sugar per quart purée ½ cup to 1 cup sugar per gallon of juice	Use 40% syrup. No syrup pack. No syrup pack.	Dry-loose pack. No unsweetened pack. No unsweetened pack.
MELONS (Cantaloupe, Crenshaw, Honeydew, Persian, Watermelon) 1¼ pounds=1 pint.	Select firm-fleshed good-colored ripe melons for freezing. Cut into halves, remove seeds, and peel. Slices, cubes, or balls Cut pulp as preferred. Crushed. Cut up pulp and crush or put through coarse blade of food chopper.	2 cups sugar over 3 quarts melon, 1 tablespoon ascorbic acid per quart	Use 40% syrup.	No unsweetened pack.
NECTARINES	See apricots, halves and slices.			
PEACHES 1 bushel (48 lbs.)=32 to 48 pints. 1 to 1½ pounds=1 pint.	Select firm ripe fruit with no green color in the skins. Sort, wash, peel, and pit. (A better frozen product will result if peaches can be peeled without a boiling-water dip.) Place ½ cup syrup into container or sugar into bowl. Slice peaches into sugar or syrup to prevent darkening. Halves or slices As preferred. Crushed or purée Peaches may be dipped into boiling water for ½ to 1 minute to loosen skins. The riper the fruit, the less scalding needed. Cool quickly in cold water, remove skins, and pit. Crush peaches coarsely, or press through sieve. Or heat pulp for 4 minutes with just enough water to prevent scorching. Then press through sieve.	For halves or slices: ⅔ cup sugar per quart For crushed or purée: 1 cup per quart, ¼ teaspoon ascorbic acid per quart, plus 1 package dry powdered pectin	Use 40% syrup. Add ½ teaspoon ascorbic acid to each quart syrup plus ½ bottle liquid pectin or 1 package powdered pectin No syrup pack.	Substitute water for syrup. Add 1 teaspoon ascorbic acid to each quart water. No unsweetened pack.

FRUIT	PREPARATION	PACKING Dry Sugar Pack	Syrup Pack	Unsweetened
PINEAPPLE 5 pounds=4 pints.	Select firm ripe fresh pineapple with full flavor and aroma. Pare; remove core and eyes. Cut into any desired size or shape, or crushed. Do not store for a long time as it has a tendency to develop an off-flavor.	No sugar pack.	(Pack tightly) in 40% to 70% syrup.	Dry pack or substitute water for syrup.
PLUMS, FRESH PRUNES 1 bushel (56 lbs.)=38 to 56 pints. 1 to 1½ pounds=1 pint.	Excellent for pie, jam, salad, or as a dessert fruit. Select tree-ripened fruit with deep color. Sort and wash. Cut into halves or quarters, or leave whole. Whole or Pieces Pack into containers. To serve, dip frozen fruit into cold water for 5 to 10 seconds, peel, cover with 40% syrup. Let thaw. Purée Use fully ripe fruit. Wash, cut into halves; pit. Press unheated through sieve if soft, or add 1 cup water for each 4 quarts plum halves. Bring to a boil, cook, press through sieve. Juice For beverages, select ripe fruit. For jelly making, select as recommended in jelly recipe. Wash and simmer in water barely to cover until soft. Strain through jelly bag. Cool.	Whole or Pieces: No sugar pack. Purée: Use 1 cup sugar to each quart Juice: 1 to 2 cups per quart juice, if desired	Use 40% to 70% syrup. Add ½ teaspoon ascorbic acid to each quart syrup. No syrup pack. No syrup pack.	Dry pack. No unsweetened pack. No unsweetened pack.
RASPBERRIES 1 crate=24 pints. 1 pint fresh=1 pint frozen.	Freeze fully ripe juicy berries. Seedy berries may be used for purée. Sort, wash carefully, and drain by lifting from water. Crushed or purée Prepare as above; crush or press through sieve. Juice For beverages use ripe berries; for jelly select as directed in recipe. Crush berries and heat slightly to start flow of juice. Strain through jelly bag.	No sugar pack. Use ¾ cup sugar per quart Use ¾ to 1 cup sugar per quart, ½ to 1 cup per quart juice.	Use 40% to 65% syrup. No syrup pack. No syrup pack.	Dry pack when berries are to be used for jam. No unsweetened pack. No unsweetened pack.
RHUBARB 15 pounds=15 to 22 pints. ⅔ to 1 pound=1 pint.	Choose well-colored firm tender stalks with few fibers. Wash, trim, cut into ½- to 1-inch pieces, or into lengths to fit package. May be frozen plain. Or heat for 1 minute in boiling water; cool immediately in cold water to help to retain color and flavor. Purée Add 1 cup water per 1½ quarts rhubarb. Boil 2 minutes. Cool; press through sieve. Juice Use for beverage or jelly. Cut into pieces. Add 1 quart water for each 4 quarts (5 pounds) rhubarb. Bring just to boiling. Press through jelly bag. Cool.	Use 1 cup sugar to each quart ⅔ cup sugar per quart purée ½ cup per quart juice, if desired	Use 40% to 60% syrup (raw or preheated). No syrup pack. No syrup pack.	Dry pack, raw or preheated. No unsweetened pack. No unsweetened pack.
STRAWBERRIES 1 crate (24 qts.)=38 pints. ⅔ quart=1 pint.	Choose firm ripe red berries. Sort, wash, drain, and remove hulls. Halve or quarter large berries. Sliced or crushed. Prepare berries as above. Slice or partially crush. Purée Prepare as above. Put through sieve. Juice Use fully ripe berries. Prepare as above. Crush, then strain through jelly bag.	¾ cup per quart ⅔ cup per quart ⅔ to 1 cup per quart	Use 40% to 50% syrup. No syrup pack. No syrup pack.	Loose pack. With strawberry juice or water, add 1 teaspoon ascorbic acid to each quart water or juice. No unsweetened pack. No unsweetened pack.

TO FREEZE VEGETABLES

Just as for fruits, the quality story for vegetables is the fresher the vegetable the more satisfactory the frozen product.

■ Washing is the first important step. Wash vegetables in cold water and lift them from the water so grit will settle to the bottom of sink or pan. It is usually easier to wash peas, Lima beans, and similar vegetables in the pod, then shell. They will not need further washing if they are kept clean.

■ Sort or arrange vegetables according to size and pare, trim, or cut up as directed or desired.

■ Preheating is required for almost all vegetables. This is called "blanching," "scalding" or merely "cooking in boiling water or steam." The purpose of this is to stop all enzyme action. The enzymes which helped the vegetables grow and mature in the garden, if allowed to continue their action now, will cause loss of flavor and color. While vegetables must be heated enough to stop this, they must not be overcooked as this also results in

colorless and flavorless products. The Chart for Freezing Vegetables on page 734 gives the timing information; this varies with the vegetables and the size of the pieces.

To scald or cook in boiling water you will need a large kettle with a cover, fitted with a fine-mesh wire basket. This is known as a blancher. Allow 1 gallon of boiling water for each pound of prepared vegetables. Scald only about this amount of food at one time; too large quantities will cool down cooking water.

Have water rapidly boiling. Put the vegetables in the basket and lower into the boiling water. Put the lid on the kettle and start counting the time immediately. If vegetables are of the type that will float, a fine-mesh wire rack will hold them down, or the blanching basket may be agitated once or twice during boiling time. Keep heat high so the water is boiling actively. (If you live at altitudes of 5,000 feet or more, add 1 minute to the heating times specified in chart.)

Heating in steam is recommended for a few vegetables (see chart). Use a regular large steamer or a kettle with a tight lid and a rack that will hold a steaming basket at least 3 inches above the bottom of the kettle. Put an inch or two of water in the kettle and bring to rapid boil. Put vegetables in the basket, a single layer only so steam will reach all parts quickly. Cover kettle, keep heat high, and start counting steaming time as soon as the lid is on. (At altitudes of 5,000 feet or higher, steam for 1 minute longer than the time specified.)

Often it is convenient first to bake pumpkin, sweet potatoes, or winter squash, especially if freezing in large quantities. It prevents these vegetables from becoming watery. Mushrooms may be heated in fat in a skillet, and prepared summer squash may be skillet-fried or oven-baked.

■ Prompt cooling is imperative. As soon as time is up, vegetables should be plunged into cold running water at 60° F. or below. It may be necessary to add ice to bring the water down to this temperature. It is advisable to have auxiliary baskets in the cold water so heated vegetables from blanching basket can be poured into them. Then the next load can be heated while the previous load is cooling. Also the blanching basket does not cool down. It will take at least as long to cool the vegetable as it did to heat it. But do not let the vegetables soak. As soon as they feel cold to the fingers, lift them out and drain thoroughly. If vegetables were cooked in a skillet or in the oven, transfer the food to another pan or dish set in the cold water. The food will cool more quickly, and there is no point in wasting cold water on the hot pans.

■ Pack and freeze speedily. Since most vegetables are packed in rigid containers with covers, leaving headspace is important. About ½ inch is the usual allowance. Stalk vegetables such as asparagus or broccoli may be packed in bags with or without protective carton; other vegetables such as corn or peas may also be packed in bags in family-meal portions.

Many of the small vegetables such as kernel corn or peas may be spread out on trays and frozen quickly, then placed in bags. All packages must be completely sealed.

TO FREEZE MEAT

The amounts of meat to be frozen will depend on the number in the family and on family preferences; on the availability of meat for freezing; and on the size of the freezer. There are periods of special buys in meats which will encourage stock-piling. The convenience of having meat handy in the freezer is another consideration.

■ Home-produced meats require special handling, and directions should be acquired from the United States Department of Agriculture or from the local state extension departments. Many householders who routinely freeze their own meat take advantage of local locker plants where meat can be processed, cut, wrapped, and even prefrozen if that is desired. Some keep meat there, taking into the home freezer only a few weeks' supply at a time.

■ Purchased meats usually come by the cut and all that is required at home is to wrap them properly (food stores seldom sell meat wrapped for freezing) and freeze as soon as possible. In general, few rules are needed outside of proper packing, but there are some suggestions that are helpful.
1. Meat should be ready to cook, that is, cut into sizes ready for oven or pan.
2. Roasting-size pieces of meat or large pot roasts should have exposed bones well padded with freezer or wax paper so they will not pierce wrapping. They can then be wrapped with any of the freezer sheet material or slipped into a large polyethylene bag. All air should be removed and the bag should be securely tied. Thawing is usually recommended before cooking large cuts and this is done before unwrapping, preferably in the refrigerator. Roasts may be cooked in the frozen or half-frozen state, providing roasting time is lengthened accordingly. The exception is pork which, most authorities say, should always be completely thawed before cooking.
3. Steak- and chop-size pieces may be wrapped and frozen individually, or grouped in meal quantities and packaged. It is more convenient to put double pieces of freezer paper between each piece of meat, for then one or more can be removed at will.
4. Ground meat may be molded into sizes and shapes for final cooking, meat, loaf, for instance, or individual patties.

It is best to have these pan-ready, and to season when cooking. Stewing meat or other small pieces may be put in bags in meal-size portions.
5. The rib ends of standing rib roasts can be collected and frozen until there is enough for a meal of short ribs.
6. The excess fat from beef roasts can be trimmed, packed and frozen separately to use with other beef cuts which may not have enough fat.

■ Large game is frozen as is any other meat, after proper preliminary treatment.

■ Sausage meats, bologna, bacon, ham, and frankfurters (any cured meats) should not be frozen for any length of time as the salt in these meats causes development of rancidity.

■ Variety meats can be frozen if the suggestions below are followed.
1. Brains may be frozen cooked or uncooked. Do not use those with any blood clots. Since most recipes call for precooked brains, it may be more convenient to freeze them cooked. Wash brains and simmer in water to cover with 1 tablespoon vinegar and 1 teaspoon salt to each quart of water. Drain, cool, and divide in meal-size portions.
2. Freeze hearts uncooked. Remove large arteries and trim off any hard parts, then wash thoroughly. Leave whole or cut into pieces according to use planned.
3. Freeze kidneys uncooked. Remove all fat and tubes; wash and split through the center. Wrap whole kidney individually, or cut in pieces as desired.
4. Freeze livers uncooked. Wipe with a damp cloth. Slice beef and veal livers about ½ inch thick and put sheets between slices before packaging. Pork and lamb livers may be sliced or cut into pieces, depending on use planned.
5. To freeze sweetbreads follow directions for preparing brains. If any membranes are present, remove them after the sweetbreads have been cooked. Drain, cool, and divide in meal-size portions.
6. Beef and veal tongues may be frozen fresh although the preferred method is to have them corned or smoked in advance. Freeze them whole, including the roots. Pork and lamb tongues may be pickled in brine and frozen.
7. Tripe should be cooked before freezing. Cover with water and simmer for about 2 hours. Drain and chill. Cut in bite-size pieces.
8. Freeze oxtails uncooked. Select those with a generous covering of white fat around the jointed bones. Cut apart at the joints.

·· Chart for Freezing Vegetables ··

VEGETABLE AND APPROXIMATE YIELD	SELECTION AND PREPARATION	HEATING METHOD, TIME AND PACKING	
ASPARAGUS 1 crate (ten 2½-lb. bunches)=15 to 22 pints. 1 to 1½ pounds=1 pint.	Tips should be tender, stems snap easily. Freeze within 2 to 3 hours of cutting. Wash thoroughly in cold water. Cut or snap off woody parts of stalks. Remove large scales if desired; wash again. Sort spears according to thickness. Freeze whole, or cut into 2-inch lengths. For flat packs of spears, alternate ends and tips.	<u>Boiling Water</u> Small: 2 minutes Medium: 3 minutes Large: 4 minutes (Time by thickness of spears)	Chill in cold water for 3 to 5 minutes. Drain. Pack alternating tips and stem ends. Headspace, ½ inch.
BEANS, Lima 1 bushel (32 lbs.)=12 to 16 pints. 2 to 2½ pounds=1 pint.	Beans should still be green, not white or starchy. Wash pods in cold water. Shell and sort according to size. If hard to shell, shears may be used to cut off tough pod edges. Remove any white overmature beans; these may be frozen separately or cooked immediately. If a large quantity is being handled, keep shelled beans in refrigerator until scalded.	<u>Boiling Water</u> Small: 2 minutes Medium: 3 minutes Large: 4 minutes	Chill in cold water for 5 minutes. Drain. Headspace, ½ inch. Can use loose pack.
BEANS, Shelled Green	Select pods while they are still plump, not dry or wrinkled. Shell and wash.	<u>Boiling Water</u> 1 minute	Chill in cold water for 3 minutes. Drain. Headspace, ½ inch.

BEANS, Snap Green or Wax
1 bushel (30 lbs.)=30 to 45 pints.
⅔ to 1 pound=1 pint.
	Use tender young beans that will snap when broken.
	Wash thoroughly; snap off or cut off ends.
	   Cut into 1- or 2-inch pieces.
	   Cut lengthwise for "French" style.
	   Whole, use only young immature beans.
		<u>Boiling Water</u>
		
		3 minutes
		3 minutes
		3 minutes
			Chill in cold water for 3 to 5 minutes. Drain. Headspace, ½ inch. Can use loose pack.

BEETS 1 bushel (52 lbs.)=35 to 42 pints. 1¼ to 1½ pounds=1 pint.	Choose only young small beets, not more than 3 inches in diameter. Wash, trim tops to 1 inch, and sort according to size. After cooking, cool quickly in cold water; peel, and cut into slices or cubes.	<u>Boiling Water</u> Small: 25 to 30 minutes Medium: 45 to 50 minutes	Chill until cool to center. Drain and prepare. Headspace, ½ inch.
BROCCOLI 1 crate (25 lbs.)=24 pints. 1 pound=1 pint.	Select uniformly compact dark green heads. Cut off large leaves and tough stalks; separate into uniform pieces not more than 1½ inches across. Wash thoroughly. Examine for insects and, if necessary, soak, head down, in salted water (1 tablespoon salt to 2 quarts water) for 30 minutes.	<u>Steam</u> (preferred) 5 minutes <u>Boiling Water</u> 3 minutes	Chill in cold water for 4 to 5 minutes. Drain. Headspace, none.
BRUSSELS SPROUTS 4 quart boxes=6 pints. 1 pound=1 pint.	Heads should be green, firm, and compact. Examine for insects and, if necessary, soak in salt water (see Broccoli). Trim, remove coarse outer leaves, and wash thoroughly.	<u>Boiling Water</u> Small: 3 minutes Medium: 4 minutes Large: 5 minutes	Chill in cold water for 6 to 8 minutes. Drain. Headspace, none.
CAULIFLOWER 2 medium heads=3 pints. 1⅓ pounds=1 pint.	Select snow-white firm tender heads. Break or cut apart into pieces about 1 inch across. Wash, check for insects and, if necessary, soak in salt water (see Broccoli). Note: If purple cauliflower is used, it will turn a pale green during boiling.	<u>Boiling Water</u> 3 minutes (Add 4 teaspoons salt per gallon water.)	Chill in cold water for 4 to 5 minutes. Drain. Headspace, none.
CORN (In Husks) 1 bushel (35 lbs.)=14 to 17 pints. 2 to 2½ pounds=1 pint.	Freeze when kernels are plump and tender and milk is sweet and thin. If milk is thick, corn is better frozen as cream-style. Freeze corn as soon as picked. Husk, remove silk, wash ears. <u>Corn-on-Cob</u> Cook in boiling water. For kernels cut from ear, heat ears in boiling water for 4 minutes and proceed as below: <u>Whole kernels</u> Cut kernels from cob at ⅔ depth of kernel. <u>Cream-style</u> Cut corn at about the center of kernels, then scrape cobs with the back of a knife to remove milk and heart of kernels.	<u>Boiling Water</u> Small ears: 7 minutes Medium ears: 9 minutes Large ears: 11 minutes	Chill in cold water for 10 to 12 minutes. Drain. Whole ears wrapped separately. Cut or cream-style corn, headspace, ½ inch. Kernel corn can be frozen loose pack.

VEGETABLE AND APPROXIMATE YIELD	SELECTION AND PREPARATION	HEATING METHOD, TIME AND PACKING	
GREENS (Beet, Chard, Collards, Kale, Mustard, Spinach, Turnip) Average: 1 to 1½ pounds=1 pint.	For freezing, pick only young tender leaves. Wash well, lifting leaves from washing water. Take out any tough stems and imperfect leaves. Cut any large leaves into pieces of desired size. Scald beet greens, kale, chard, mustard, and turnip greens. Scald collards. Scald spinach. Scald all very tender leaves.	<u>Boiling Water</u> 2 minutes 3 minutes 2 minutes 1½ minutes	Chill in cold water for 5 minutes. Drain. Headspace, ½ inch.
OKRA	Select very young and tender green pods. Wash well. Cut off stems, taking care not to cut open seed cells. Pods may be left whole for freezing or sliced crosswise.	<u>Boiling Water</u> Small: 3 minutes Large: 4 minutes	Chill in cold water for 3 to 5 minutes. Drain. Headspace, ½ inch.
PEAS 1 bushel (30 lbs.)=12 to 15 pints. 2 to 2½ pounds=1 pint.	Watch peas for maturity; do not use immature or tough starchy ones. Pick bright-green plump pods with sweet tender peas.	<u>Boiling Water</u> 1½ minutes	Chill in cold water for 3 minutes. Drain. Headspace, ½ inch. Can use loose pack.
PEPPERS, Green ⅔ pound (3 peppers)=1 pint.	Select firm crisp thick-walled peppers. Wash, cut out stems, cut into halves, and remove seeds. Cut into rings if desired. For use in uncooked foods, MAY BE FROZEN WITHOUT HEATING. Or, if preferred for cooking, heat.	<u>Boiling Water</u> Halves: 3 minutes Slices: 2 minutes	Chill in cold water for 3 to 4 minutes. Drain. Headspace, ½ inch.
PEPPERS, Hot	Wash, stem, and pack into small containers. MAY BE FROZEN WITHOUT HEATING.	No heating necessary	Headspace, ½ inch.
PUMPKIN 3 pounds=1 pint.	Select full-colored mature pumpkin with fine rather than coarse or stringy texture. Wash outside, cut into pieces, and remove seeds. Cook until soft in boiling water, in steam, or in a pressure cooker, or bake in covered pan in oven. Remove pulp from rind; mash or press through a sieve. Cool in a pan set in cold water; stir occasionally.	No additional heating necessary	Cool thoroughly. Headspace, ½ inch.
RUTABAGAS AND TURNIPS	Select small to medium-size, firm yet tender, mild-flavored vegetables. Cut off tops, wash, peel, then cut into ½-inch cubes. Or, cook cubes in small amount of boiling water, drain, and mash.	<u>Boiling Water</u> 2 minutes	Chill in cold water for 3 to 4 minutes. Drain. Headspace, ½ inch.
SQUASH Summer: 1 to 1¼ pounds=1 pint. Winter: 3 pounds=2 pints.	1. <u>Winter</u> See Pumpkin. 2. <u>Summer</u> Pick out young tender squash with small seeds. Wash. Cut into ½-inch slices with some sliced onion if desired, or fry slices in oil or cooking fat in skillet on top of stove, or bake in a shallow baking pan in oven until almost tender. Set pan in cold water to cool.	<u>Boiling Water</u> 3 minutes	Chill in cold water for 5 minutes. Drain. Headspace, ½ inch.
SWEET POTATOES ⅔ pound=1 pint.	Choose medium- to large-size potatoes that have been cured. Sort according to size and wash. Cook until almost tender in boiling water, in steam, in a pressure cooker, or in the oven. Cool. Peel, cut into halves, and slice or mash. A little orange or lemon juice will keep them from darkening, or use ½ teaspoon ascorbic acid to 2½ pints water; or roll cooked potatoes in sugar, then pack; or pack whole or sliced in freezing containers and cover with a cold syrup (equal parts sugar and water).	No additional heating necessary	Cool thoroughly. Prepare. Headspace, ½ inch.

TO FREEZE POULTRY

All poultry may be frozen at any state of maturity, whole, in halves or pieces, as you prefer. Special methods of preparation are necessary for home-produced poultry.

■ All poultry purchased for freezing should be unwrapped, examined for feathers and hairs, and checked internally for excess fat or forgotten bits of lungs. After these are removed, the birds are washed quickly and dried; they can then be left whole or cut up in any way desired. Finally they are wrapped or put into bags and sealed for freezing.

■ Giblets are washed well, examined, and rewrapped separately. They may be placed alongside the roaster in its package, or put into bags and frozen separately if you prefer to cook them at another time.

■ If they have not been so prepared at the food store, young birds may be split down the center of the back and along the keel or breastbone, ready for broiling. Put two pieces of freezer wrapping material between the halves before packaging them for freezing, for then they can be separated while still frozen.

Cut-up poultry for frying is more convenient if each piece is wrapped separately before packaging. Then as many pieces as you wish may be selected for cooking. Older chicken pieces for stewing need not be wrapped individually.

Again, if more than one bird is being frozen, legs and thighs, the white meat pieces, and the bony pieces may be packaged and frozen separately. If freezer space is valuable, bony pieces may be cooked, the meat taken from the bones, meat and broth cooled, put into containers, and frozen. The meat not only takes less freezer space, but it is ready to heat and use without further preparation.

■ Duck, turkey, chicken, and game birds, providing they are ready to cook, are all frozen in the same way. Even the small game such as rabbit or squirrel, after they are properly cleaned and prepared, are frozen exactly as is poultry.

Truss bird to make it compact. Do not stuff, as stuffing encourages growth of bacteria. Seal, excluding air, and close with tape.

TO FREEZE SEAFOOD

Most fresh fish is prepared for freezing exactly as it is for cooking. Most purchased fish will be ready except for washing and drying. Game fish will have to be scaled, eviscerated, head and fins removed, then washed thoroughly and drained. Small fish may be frozen whole, and a couple of sheets of freezer wrap may be inserted in the body to keep sides from freezing together. Large fish may be cut into chunks, steaks, or fillets.

Again, put two sheets of freezer wrapping material between the pieces so they can be separated easily before cooking.

Fish may be wrapped and sealed, or put into bags or containers for freezing.

■ Oysters and clams in or out of shell and scallops may be frozen in cartons after cleaning. Pack, then cover with own liquid or with a brine (1 tablespoon salt to 1 cup cold water).

■ Lobster and crab should be steamed or boiled for 15 to 20 minutes, the meat removed, cooled, and packed in airtight freezer cartons.

■ Shrimps are more tender if frozen uncooked. Remove heads and tails and package. If cooking is preferable, cook in boiling salted water for 2 to 5 minutes in a covered saucepan; cool, shell, and package.

■ Lean cut-up fish should be immersed for 20 to 30 seconds in a salt solution (¼ cup salt to 1 quart water).

■ Fatty cut-up fish should be dipped into an ascorbic-acid solution (1½ teaspoons ascorbic acid to 1 quart water).

■ Cleaned whole fish may be ice-glazed. Freeze fish until hard. Dip fish into near-freezing water. Refreeze. Repeat 3 to 4 times to form a coating of ice ⅛ inch thick.

TO FREEZE DAIRY PRODUCTS

■ Butter or lard packages may be slipped into freezer bags, sealed, and frozen.

■ Heavy cream, 40 per cent or more of butterfat, may be frozen safely if it is sure to be used within a few months. However, it will need homogenizing before using. Whipped cream, if handled in a special way, is easily frozen and is handy. Whip cream as usual; sweeten or not as you prefer; drop in small mounds from a teaspoon or tablespoon onto a cookie sheet or other large pan and freeze quickly. As soon as frozen, put mounds in freezer bags or cartons. As you wish to use them, take a few, drop on the top of a dessert like warm apple cobbler, and serve immediately.

■ Cheese is apt to lose flavor with freezing, and the Cheddars become crumbly. It is safe to freeze, however, and it may be used in sandwiches. Do not freeze cream cheese.

■ Ice cream should be packed in moisture-proof containers (commercial ice cream should be rewrapped) with headspace of 1 inch.

■ Eggs—do not freeze hard-cooked eggs.

To package raw eggs, shell and pack into containers that hold as much as is needed at one time. Shell whole eggs, and beat slightly. For use in sweet cooking add 1 tablespoon corn syrup to each cup. For nonsweet use add 1 teaspoon salt to each cup. Beat egg slightly to combine well but do not incorporate air.

Egg whites—Package egg whites as is, in small amounts.

To package egg yolks—Add 1 tablespoon corn syrup or 1 teaspoon salt to each cup of yolks. Beat egg yolks slightly to blend well but do not incorporate air.

1 tablespoon egg yolk = 1 egg yolk
1½ tablespoons egg white = 1 egg white
2½ tablespoons whole egg = 1 whole egg

TO FREEZE COOKED FOODS

There are many dishes which can be partially or fully prepared, cooked, and frozen for future use. Often it is no trouble to double or triple a recipe, eat some, and freeze the rest. Or if the family is very small, perhaps the average-size recipe will make enough for two meals. Leftovers need not be a problem if frozen until there is a special use for them.

■ Almost anything can be frozen. It's easier to list the exceptions.

Salads—Do not freeze salads which contain greens and other raw vegetables, mayonnaise, cream cheese, or hard-cooked egg whites.

Sandwiches—Avoid those with the "don't freeze" ingredients listed for salads.

Main Dishes—Skip those made with sauerkraut or hard-cooked egg whites. If space is limited, freeze only the long cooking part of mixtures and add the bulky quick-cooking macaroni, potatoes, or rice at reheating time. Whole cooked potatoes do not freeze well, anyway. Store smoked meats or a mixture containing them for a few weeks only. Flavor deteriorates quickly in these salty and spiced meats if they are frozen.

■ Do not slice meats before packaging. If sliced, cover with gravy or sauce before packaging.

■ Beat gravies and sauces well before freezing to prevent curdling during thawing.

■ Freeze meat, fish, or poultry loaves or pies before baking. Freezing after baking offers no time advantage.

■ Fried foods must be thoroughly cooled

before freezing.

■ Black pepper, cloves, onion, and garlic become stronger when frozen. Add monosodium glutamate to preserve flavor, ¼ teaspoon to every portion.

■ Use only converted rice for freezing.

■ Cook pasta for freezing only until it reaches firm stage as it softens during freezing.

■ Add whole potatoes after reheating since they do not freeze well.

■ Concentrate soups before freezing to reduce volume.

■ In packaging cooked foods for freezing you can use pliofilm and polyethylene wrappings or bags, freezer-weight aluminum foil and plastic wrap, moisture-proof cellophane, freezer paper, plastic containers, glass freezer jars, paper freezer containers, coffee cans, milk cartons (if they can be tightly taped or sealed).

If storing in baking ware, be sure to wrap or seal with freezer tape, or wrap container completely. In order not to tie up all of your loaf pans or casseroles, line them with foil before filling. Freeze, then turn contents out, wrap or slide into pliofilm bags, and store in freezer. To reheat or cook, unwrap contents of bag and return it to the container it fits. There are heavy foil pie plates, baking dishes, and casseroles, too, which are inexpensive; some are reusable. Paper pie plates for freezer are usually good for one usage. Broth, vegetable cooking water, gravy, soups, stews, sauces, and creamed dishes can be frozen in loaf pans or ice-cube trays, the contents then removed and wrapped or put in bags. Leave ice-tray divider in while freezing liquids without solids, and store cubes in bags. Storage in cube form reduces thawing time and then, too, it's easy to use just as much at a time as desired.

TO FREEZE SANDWICHES AND CANAPÉS

■ Wrap sandwiches as directed for all frozen foods but do not freeze near walls or bottom of freezer or in direct contact with shelves as this will make the sandwich soggy because of formation of ice crystals on bread.

■ Use day-old bread.

■ Spread both slices of bread with butter to prevent sogginess.

■ Do not freeze sandwiches containing salad dressing, hard-cooked eggs, crisp salad greens, jellies, or jams.

■ Thaw sandwiches wrapped.

■ Prepare party sandwiches or canapés on a platter with dips and sauces, or prepare sandwich loaf and frost before serving. Wrap and freeze until the party. Add

crisp vegetable garnishes such as parsley, radishes, watercress, or cucumbers just before serving.

TO FREEZE DESSERTS AND BAKED PRODUCTS

■ Frozen desserts may include cooked fruits, dessert sauces, puddings, ice cream, sherbets, and fruit salads.

■ Almost any kind of already-baked product can be frozen. The exceptions are popovers and custard pies.

■ Certain ingredients should be used in the preparation if you are planning to freeze the product:

1. Use pure vanilla extract as the synthetic acquires a bitter flavor with freezing.

2. Frosted cakes—Use only confectioners'-sugar frosting made with plenty of shortening. Use fillings other than cream fillings.

■ Fill cream puffs or éclairs with cream filling after defrosting before serving, or fill with ice cream and freeze.

■ Rolls may be frozen partially baked. To do so bake in very slow oven (275° F.) for 20 to 30 minutes. Cool thoroughly and package. Thaw for 15 minutes in wrapper. Unwrap and bake in preheated hot oven (400°F.) for 5 to 10 minutes.

■ Pies can be cut into serving pieces and wrapped and frozen.

■ Cool thoroughly before freezing.

■ Large firm items should be wrapped in moisture- vapor-proof material.

■ Frosted cakes, meringue-topped pies, and other sticky foods should be frozen first, then wrapped, as should small or soft items. Some cakes, pies, cookies, and other small baked items are still squashable when frozen. Store in a protected spot. Allow them to thaw wrapped to prevent sogginess.

■ The procedure for thawing varies depending on the product:

Thaw yeast products wrapped for 15 to 30 minutes. Heat unwrapped in a preheated slow oven (300°F.) for 10 to 15 minutes.

Thaw unfrosted cakes and cupcakes unwrapped; use as soon as possible, as thawed cakes dry out more rapidly.

With frosted cakes, loosen the wrapping, but do not uncover while thawing. Thaw in refrigerator to prevent a grainy frosting.

Angel food and spongecake cannot be frozen unbaked, but other products may be. To do so there are some special rules to follow:

■ Certain ingredients should be used in

the preparation if you are planning to freeze before baking:

1. Use double-acting baking powder.

2. Freeze only rich yeast doughs.

3. Extra thickening is needed in fruit pies to be frozen; add 1 tablespoon flour or ½ tablespoon cornstarch more.

4. Add ¼ teaspoon ascorbic acid to each pie containing fruits that darken.

■ Freeze muffin batter in paper cups. Thaw for 1 hour before baking as usual.

■ Biscuits and cookies should be shaped before freezing except in the case of refrigerator-type cookies which are shaped into rolls.

■ Piecrusts and pies can be frozen unbaked, but two-crust pies may have a soggy crust after freezing and custard pies should not be frozen.

■ Meringues should be put on pies before serving.

■ Cake batters must be thawed before baking.

FREEZE-DRY—This is a newly developed process for food preservation. Water is removed from cooked or uncooked frozen foods by a procedure called sublimation. The food is placed in a vacuum chamber and the ice in the frozen food is changed from a solid to vapor leaving the solid with its flavor and color. To serve such foods, water or other liquid, hot or cold, is added, and the product is allowed to stand for about thirty minutes. It is then ready to eat or to cook.

In flavor, these foods have been found to be superior to the ones preserved by other drying methods, and the nutritional value is similar to the original. They are light in weight and small in volume, thus cutting distribution problems. One pound of beefsteak will weigh only four ounces, two pounds of chicken stew just six and a half ounces. When properly packaged, they can be stored at room temperature in any climate for as long as two years. Among the freeze-dry products first on the consumer market were some of the dried soup mixes containing meat, poultry, onion, and mushrooms which were dried by this process. Since the lightweight food is especially attractive to campers, hunters, hikers, and other sportsmen, they were sold first in sporting goods stores. The armed forces are using them. Other foods now available are meat and fish—beef cubes to pork chops, crabmeat and shrimps, chicken—and vegetables such as asparagus, green beans and peas, and mushrooms.

French cuisine
reflects that country's
long and great
tradition of treating
cookery as a fine art

FRENCH COOKERY By James A.
Beard—Many people think of French cooking as being "fancy" and unusually rich. Actually French cuisine has great variety, probably more than any other cuisine in the world. It includes elegant dishes, it is true, but the average French family, particularly in the countryside, eats homely peasant-style dishes, flavorful and satisfying. Some of these recipes are purely regional, others are known throughout France, but each area has its own version.

I find this hearty peasant cuisine very popular, and a number of small French restaurants in the United States make a specialty of it. They are crowded with appreciative patrons. Several of the most successful hostesses I know do not hesitate to offer a simple *Pot-au-Feu* for a company dinner.

The French cook manipulates seasonings and flavorings in much the same way that the conductor controls a symphony orchestra. He may prepare a *daube,* using garlic, wine, several herbs and vegetables, all blended together to give a subtle, rich taste. Or he may emphasize one particular herb in a dish such as *Poulet à l'Estragon* (chicken tarragon), or a particular flavor, such as garlic in *Sauce Aïoli.*

You may be startled to find that many of the meat recipes from France call for very long cooking. French meat is not so tender as ours, not so well marbled with fat. You can usually cut the cooking time by one third or even one half.

Here is a collection of these popular regional recipes from France.

SOUPS

SOUPE À L'OIGNON AU GRATIN
(Onion Soup with Cheese)

Extremely good onion soup comes in cans or packages. But if you like to make your own soup, here is one of many versions. I find it simple and tasty.

- 6 medium onions, rather thinly sliced
- 6 tablespoons butter or half butter and half cooking oil
- 1 teaspoon sugar
- 1 teaspoon salt
  Dash of ground nutmeg
- 7 cups strong beef bouillon
- ¼ cup sherry or port
- 6 thick pieces of French bread, dried out in the oven
  Grated Switzerland Swiss cheese
  Grated Parmesan cheese

Sauté onion in butter until soft. Add sugar, salt, and nutmeg and toss well. Cook down slightly but do not let the onions get too dark. They should be a golden brown. Add hot bouillon and

bring to boil. Reduce heat and simmer for 10 minutes. Add wine and adjust seasoning. Ladle the soup into 6 ovenproof casseroles or pots, and top each with a piece of French bread. Spoon about 2 tablespoons grated Swiss cheese on top of each. Cook in preheated slow oven (300° F.) for 10 minutes, or until cheese is melted and bubbly. Serve with additional Swiss cheese, Parmesan cheese, and toast. Makes 6 servings.

GARBURE BASQUE
(Ham and Bean Soup with Vegetables)

Each Basque housewife has her own recipe for this dish. Here is a flavorful version, ideal for winter meals.

- 1 pound dried navy or pea beans, washed and drained
- 6 cups water
- 1 ham butt, 3 to 4 pounds, or a smoked tenderloin
- 6 onions, sliced
- 8 garlic cloves, chopped
- 1 green pepper, cut into strips
- 1 hot pepper
- 1 pound fava beans or Lima beans, or 1 package (10 ounces) frozen Lima beans
- 4 carrots, sliced
- 6 turnips, sliced
- 1 cabbage, shredded
- 1 pound peas or 1 package (10 ounces) frozen peas
  Salt and pepper
- 12 to 16 pork sausages

Cover dried beans with water, bring to boil, and boil for 2 minutes. Cover and let stand for 1 hour. Then cook until just tender. Add ham, onions, garlic, green pepper, hot pepper, beans, carrots, turnips, and more water if necessary. Cover kettle and simmer gently for 3 to 4 hours. Add cabbage, peas, and any other vegetable you may have. Cook until vegetable mixture is a thick purée. Season to taste. Remove ham from soup when tender; cut into slices and keep warm. Grill the sausages. Serve big bowls of this thick soup with slices of ham, sausages, and plenty of crusty bread. This is a good rib-sticking winter dish. Makes about 4 quarts or 8 servings.

POTAGE PARMENTIER
(Potato Soup)

Parmentier was the French agriculturalist who made the potato popular in his country and many potato dishes are named for him. This soup, a genuine masterpiece, is one of them; perfect for lunch or supper.

- 1 pound potatoes, peeled and cut up
- 2 leeks, washed thoroughly and cut into sections
- 2 onions, peeled and sliced
- 1 carrot, peeled and sliced
- 1 celery stalk, cut into pieces
- 1 parsley sprig
- 2½ quarts water
- 1 tablespoon salt
  Pepper
- ¼ cup butter
- ½ cup heavy cream
  Chopped chives

Combine all the vegetables and put in kettle with water. Cover and cook over low heat for about 2 hours. Season with salt and pepper to taste. Drain vegetables, reserving liquid. Put vegetables through food mill or coarse sieve, or whirl in blender. Return mixture to the liquid and add butter and cream. Reheat and add more seasoning if necessary. Serve topped with chives. Makes 2 quarts or 6 servings.

Potage Au Cresson
(Watercress Soup)

Prepare Potage Parmentier; just before serving, add a bunch of watercress, finely chopped. Heat for 3 to 4 minutes and serve topped with additional chopped watercress.

SEAFOOD

COQUILLES ST. JACQUES

- 1½ pounds sea scallops
  Butter or margarine
- 6 shallots or green onions, chopped
  Bouquet garni (parsley, celery, thyme, bay leaf)
- 1½ cups dry white wine
  Salt
- 12 mushrooms, chopped fine
- ⅓ cup water
  Juice of 1 lemon
  Pepper
- 3 tablespoons all-purpose flour
- 4 egg yolks
- 1 cup heavy cream
  Grated Parmesan cheese
  Fine, dry bread crumbs

Wash scallops well and dry on paper towels. Place in saucepan with 2 tablespoons butter and shallots. Add *bouquet garni* and barely cover with white wine. Season with a little salt. Bring to boil and simmer for 4 or 5 minutes, or until scallops are just tender. Drain and save broth for the sauce. When scallops are cool enough to handle, cut in small pieces or slices. Sauté mushrooms in 2 tablespoons butter for 2 or 3 minutes. Add water, lemon juice, ½ teaspoon salt, and ¼ teaspoon pepper, and simmer gently for a few minutes, or until mushrooms are tender. Drain and reserve liquid. Blend 3 tablespoons butter and 3 tablespoons flour. Knead in small balls about the size of peas. Combine liquids from scallops and mushrooms and heat. Stir in butter-flour mixture and cook and stir until sauce is thickened and smooth. Cook for 2 or 3 minutes and add scallops. Heat through. Beat egg yolks and mix with cream. Add this to sauce and cook gently, stirring, until smooth and thick. Do not let sauce boil. Add mushrooms and season to taste. Spoon into individual ramekins or shells, sprinkle with Parmesan and crumbs and glaze under broiler. Makes 6 servings.

QUICHE DE LANGOUSTE
(Lobster Pie)

2 lobsters (1½ pounds each) cooked, or 3 or 4 lobster tails, cooked, or 1 can (12 ounces) frozen lobster meat, thawed
Pastry for 1-crust 9-inch pie, unbaked
2 tablespoons chopped onion
¼ cup butter
¼ cup brandy or whisky
Salt and pepper
Lobster coral and tomalley, if you use whole lobster
1 to 1¼ cups heavy cream
4 eggs
Dash of ground nutmeg

Remove lobster meat from shells and cut into convenient pieces. If you are using whole lobsters, remove coral and tomalley and reserve. Roll out pastry and use it to line a 9-inch pie pan. Chill. Place a piece of foil over pastry in pan and fill with dry beans to weight down pastry. Bake in preheated hot oven (425°F.) for 10 minutes. Take out foil and beans. Sauté onion in butter until tender. Add lobster and heat through. Add brandy and season to taste with salt and pepper. Arrange lobster and onion in pastry-lined pie pan. Put coral and tomalley, if any, in pan in which you heated lobster; add 1 tablespoon cream. Cook for 1 or 2 seconds and pour over the lobster. Beat eggs and remaining cream together and season with salt. Pour over lobster; dust top with a little nutmeg. Bake in preheated moderate oven (375°F.) for 35 minutes, or until firm. Serve at once. This will serve 6 for a first course or 4 for a luncheon main course.

BOURRIDE
(Fish Stew)

This is a Mediterranean specialty, a fish stew thickened with Sauce Aïoli.

4 cups water plus a little white wine
Dash of vinegar
1 onion
1 parsley sprig
1 bay leaf
1 carrot
Few fennel or dill leaves
Salt and pepper to taste
3 pounds white fish (2 or 3 kinds: bass, sole, or whitefish) filleted or cut into thick slices
3 egg yolks
2 cups Sauce Aioli
6 to 8 thick slices of French bread, toasted

Put liquids and seasonings in kettle and bring to boil. Cook for 10 minutes. Add fish to boiling broth and poach for 5 to 10 minutes, or until fish flakes easily. Do not overcook. Remove fish to a hot platter and strain broth. Cook down to 1½ cups. Beat egg yolks in top part of double boiler. Gradually add hot broth, then set pan over hot, not boiling, water. Cook and stir until thickened. Gradually and carefully stir in about 1 cup *Sauce Aïoli* and blend until mixture is creamy and heated through. Warm 6 soup plates and

place a piece of toast in each. Top with cooked fish and pour some of the sauce over all. Pass the rest of the *Sauce Aïoli*. This dish is eaten with a spoon and a fork. Makes 6 servings.

Sauce Aioli
(Garlic Mayonnaise)

Formerly this sauce was made in a marble mortar. The garlic was pounded with a pestle, the egg yolks were added, and then the oil, and the mixture was beaten until it resembled mayonnaise. It's far simpler if you make it in an electric blender. Prepare a good olive-oil mayonnaise, substituting fresh lemon juice for the vinegar. Omit sugar. Add 2 to 6 garlic cloves or more, even to 12 (according to taste), crushed, for each pint of sauce. Or, put 2 to 6 garlic cloves in blender, add ¼ cup commercial mayonnaise, and 1 tablespoon fresh lemon juice. Blend well. Add 1¾ cups mayonnaise.

MEAT AND POULTRY

POT-AU-FEU
(Boiled Beef with Vegetables)

5 pounds cross rib, short rib, or brisket of beef
1½ pounds salt pork
1 marrow bone
10 medium onions, peeled
4 whole cloves
9 leeks, well washed
10 carrots, peeled and sliced
1 bay leaf
1 teaspoon dried thyme
2 or 3 parsley sprigs
1 teaspoon salt
¼ teaspoon pepper
8 small turnips, peeled
1 medium cabbage, cut into quarters or sixths

Put meat, salt pork, marrow bone, 2 onions stuck with cloves, 3 leeks, 2 carrots, and the herbs in heavy kettle. Add enough water to come 1½ inches above meat. Bring to boil and boil rapidly for 5 minutes. Skim off any scum that forms on top, add salt and pepper, and cover kettle. Lower heat and simmer for 2 to 2½ hours, or until meat is tender. Remove meat and keep warm. Add remaining vegetables except cabbage to the broth and cook until done. Add cabbage for the last 12 minutes. Cut salt pork and beef into slices and arrange on a hot platter. Surround meat with vegetables and garnish with marrow from marrow bone. Coarse salt, mustard, and horseradish are traditional with this dish. Potatoes cooked in jackets and good pickles are also a nice addition. Adjust seasoning of the broth. Pour broth into bowls and serve separately. Makes 8 servings.

FILET DE BOEUF BOUQUETIÈRE
(Beef Fillet with a Bouquet of Vegetables)

This is a simple dish to prepare, yet it

makes a spectacular main course for company dinners.

1 fillet of beef (5 to 6 pounds)
Butter
Salt and pepper
Crumbled dried thyme or rosemary
5 or 6 strips of mild bacon or salt pork
Vegetables in season
Sauce Madère

Ask butcher to trim all fat and tissue from the fillet. Rub well with melted butter, salt, pepper, and a little thyme, and top with strips of bacon. Roast in preheated very hot oven (450°F.). After 20 minutes, remove salt pork or bacon and brush fillet with more melted butter. Fillet should be done in 30 to 40 minutes, or when it reaches an internal temperature of 125°F. This is rare beef, and fillet should be rare to be at its best. Remove fillet to a hot platter and surround with a bouquet of vegetables. The elegance of this dish depends on the array of vegetables. They should be tiny and perfect: tiny new potatoes or potato balls sautéed in butter; tiny peas; cauliflowerets cooked until just done but still crisp and white; tiny green beans; cherry tomatoes heated in the top part of a double boiler with butter and basil; sautéed mushroom caps; tiny slices of zucchini sautéed in butter seasoned with garlic. These are suggestions. You can have as varied a list as you like. Be sure vegetables are ready just as meat is done and make the arrangement as eye-appealing as possible. Brush fillet with melted butter before bringing it to the table. Serve with *Sauce Madère*. Makes 8 servings.

Note: To complete this dinner, serve a simple soup for the first course, and finish with cheese and fresh fruit. A bottle of good red wine is a nice complement.

Sauce Madère
(Madeira Sauce)

Skim excess fat from pan juices and combine with 1¼ cups brown sauce (1 can beef gravy can be used). Add ¼ cup Madeira and simmer for 2 or 3 minutes. Adjust seasoning and add a dash of fresh lemon juice.

STEAK AU POIVRE
(Pepper Steak)

Buy 4 small minute steaks or 1 large steak to serve 4 persons. Crack 2 or 3 tablespoons peppercorns. You can roll them with a rolling pin or pound them in a mortar; or buy cracked peppercorns in jars. Press pepper into both sides of steak with heel of your hand. Then let steaks stand for 10 minutes. Heat a heavy skillet, a big black iron one is best, and rub with a little beef fat until the surface is just barely greased. Sear steaks quickly on both sides and then finish cooking, turning often until done to your taste. Season with salt as they cook. Remove steaks to a hot platter and top each with a piece of softened butter. Rinse pan with a little red wine or brandy and pour over the steaks. Serve at once with *Pommes Frites*, page 744.

STEAK AU POIVRE FLAMBÉ À LA CRÈME
(Flamed Pepper Steak with Cream)

Follow the *Steak au Poivre* recipe. When the steaks are just done, pour ⅓ cup brandy into pan and ignite. Remove meat to a hot platter and add 2 tablespoons beef bouillon or red wine to skillet. Cook it for 1 minute. Remove pan from heat and add 1 tablespoon butter. When melted, stir in ⅔ cup dairy sour cream. Heat but do not boil. Pour over steaks. Makes 4 to 6 servings.

STEAK BORDELAISE

Prepare steak by your favorite method. Remove it to a hot platter and top with a good dab of butter and slices of *Moelle Pochée*. Serve with *Sauce Bordelaise*.

MOELLE POCHÉE
(Poached Marrow)

Ask butcher for marrow bones cut into small sections so that you can scoop out the marrow. Or ask him to extract it for you. Cut marrow in slices about ¼ inch thick and poach in boiling salted water for about 2 minutes. Remove and place on the *Steak Bordelaise*.

Sauce Bordelaise

Cook 1 cup dry red wine, 1 finely chopped green onion or shallot, and 1 parsley sprig together. Boil to reduce the liquid to ⅓ cup. Stir in 1¼ cups brown sauce (canned gravy can be used) and bring to boil again. Let the sauce bubble for about 4 minutes. Add freshly ground black pepper and a little chopped parsley. Pour over the steaks.

CHATEAUBRIAND, SAUCE BÉARNAISE

A Chateaubriand is a thick section cut on the diagonal from the thickest part of the tenderloin or filet of beef. It should weigh 1 to 1¼ pounds and makes 2 servings. Rub it well with salt, pepper, and softened butter. Broil, turning often to brown on all sides. It will take 10 to 12 minutes for rare filet. Cut into thin slices and serve with Sauce Béarnaise.

Sauce Béarnaise

- 2 shallots or 3 small green onions, chopped
- ½ cup wine vinegar
- 1 teaspoon dried or 1 tablespoon chopped fresh tarragon
- 3 egg yolks
- 1 tablespoon warm water
- ½ cup butter, softened but not melted
  Salt

Put shallots, vinegar, and tarragon in a pan and bring to boil. Cook down until it is merely a glaze. Put egg yolks and warm water in a bowl over hot, not boiling, water. Water beneath bowl must be just below the boil and kept at that point over low heat. Whisk egg yolks and then slowly add soft butter, 1 tablespoon at a time. Keep whisking as you add butter. When sauce thickens, add glaze and salt to taste. If sauce is too thick, thin with a little heavy cream. Taste for seasoning and if it needs more zest, add a little fresh lemon juice and a dash of hot pepper sauce.

Note: You can make sauce in an electric blender. Put egg yolks, glaze, and a little salt in blender and flick it on and off quickly. Melt butter and heat until bubbly but not boiling. Turn blender on at high speed and dribble hot butter into beaten egg yolks until sauce thickens. Makes about ½ cup.

DAUBE D'AGNEAU
(Lamb Daube)

- 1 cup dry red wine
- ⅔ cup olive oil
- 1 tablespoon salt
- 1 teaspoon pepper
- 1 teaspoon each of dried oregano and rosemary
- 1 bay leaf
- 2 cloves
- 1 carrot, cut up
- 4 garlic cloves
- 1 shoulder of lamb (4 to 5 pounds), boned and rolled
- 2 onions, stuck with 2 cloves
- 1 teaspoon dried tarragon
- 1 green pepper, finely sliced
- 3 tablespoons tomato paste
- 24 black olives, pitted

Place first 9 ingredients for marinade in a pot and bring to boil. Lower heat and simmer for 5 minutes. Remove from heat and cool.

Cut garlic into slivers. Make tiny slits in the flesh of the meat and insert garlic slivers. Soak lamb in marinade for 12 to 24 hours. When ready to cook, put meat in braising pan or heavy Dutch oven and add onions, tarragon, and green pepper. Strain marinade and pour over the meat. Cover pot and cook in preheated moderate oven (350°F.) for 1 hour. Reduce heat to slow (300°F.), add tomato paste and olives, and adjust seasoning. Cook for 45 to 60 minutes, or until lamb is tender. Remove meat. Strain sauce, chill, and skim off fat. Reheat lamb, covered, in sauce. Slice meat; serve sauce separately. Makes 8 servings.

LE GIGOT QUI PLEURE
(Weeping Leg of Lamb)

- 1 leg of lamb (6 to 7 pounds)
- 3 garlic cloves, slivered
  Salt and pepper
  Crumbled dried rosemary
  Butter (about ¼ cup)
- 3 to 3½ pounds potatoes, peeled
- 3 garlic cloves, minced
- ½ teaspoon dried thyme
- 3 tablespoons chopped parsley

Put lamb on rack in shallow roasting pan. Stud meat with slivers of garlic (see *Daube d'Agneau*, above) and rub with salt, pepper, and rosemary. Butter meat well. Insert a meat thermometer through fat side into center of lamb. Roast in preheated slow oven (325°F.) for 1 hour. Cut potatoes into thin even slices. Butter a large shallow baking dish and put a layer of potatoes in the bottom. Dot with butter and sprinkle with a little garlic, salt, pepper, rosemary, and thyme. Repeat until all potatoes are used. With baster remove some of the fat from the pan in which the lamb is roasting and sprinkle on potato. Put potatoes in oven with lamb and bake for 1½ to 1¾ hours, or until potatoes are done and meat thermometer registers 175°F. (medium). Slice lamb and arrange slices on top of potato. Pour juices from slicing over the dish. Serve with *Céleris Braisés*, page 745. Makes 6 to 8 servings.

1. Coquilles St. Jacques—2. Sauce Madère
3. Pot-au-Feu—4. Oignons à la Monégasque
5. Salade de Tomates—6. Céleris Braisés
7. Filet de Boeuf Bouquetière
8. Coq au Riesling
9. Soupe à l'Oignon au Gratin

JAMBON PERSILLÉS
(Parsleyed Ham)

    3 cups beef or chicken bouillon
1½ tablespoons unflavored gelatin
    3 cups diced cooked ham (½-inch
      cubes)
      About 1 cup chopped parsley
      Sauce Moutarde

If you do not have bouillon or clear stock, dissolve 3 bouillon cubes in 3 cups boiling water. Dissolve gelatin in hot bouillon and mix well. Cool slightly. Mix diced ham with parsley and press firmly into a mold or bowl. Pour the cooled gelatin mixture over ham until it just reaches top. Cover with a plate and top with a weight. Chill thoroughly. Unmold on platter and slice. Serve with *Sauce Moutarde*. Makes 6 servings.

Note: This dish from Burgundy is delicious in summer. It's perfect for a picnic.

Sauce Moutarde (Mustard Sauce)

Combine ½ cup Dijon mustard with ½ cup chopped gherkins, sweet and sour mixed. Chop the pickles very fine. This sauce is delicious with many cold meats.

PIEDS DE PORC ST. MENEHOULD
(Grilled Pig's Feet)

    6 pig's feet (long ones with knuckles, if
      available)
    2 garlic cloves
    1 onion, stuck with 2 cloves
    1 teaspoon thyme
  ¼ cup vinegar
      Salt and pepper
      Butter
      Bread crumbs
      Sauce Diable

Wrap each pig's foot in cheesecloth and tie securely. Put the garlic, onion, thyme and vinegar in a large kettle and add enough water to cover the pigs' feet. Bring to boil and boil for 20 minutes. Season to taste with salt and pepper and place the pigs' feet carefully in the broth. Cover and simmer for 3 to 3½ hours. Remove the feet and cool slightly. When cool enough to handle, unwrap and put in deep dish. Pour some of the broth over pigs' feet and chill for several hours. When ready to use, remove the feet from the jelly and brush with melted butter. Then roll in crumbs until they are well coated. Put on a rack in broiling pan and roast in preheated hot oven (400°F.) for 25 minutes, turning carefully once during the roasting. If not browned, run under the broiler for a few minutes. Baste once with melted butter during the broiling. Serve with Sauce Diable. Makes 6 servings.

Sauce Diable

1¼ cups brown sauce (canned gravy
      can be used)
    1 tablespoon wine vinegar
1½ teaspoons powdered mustard
      Dash of Worcestershire
    1 teaspoon freshly ground pepper

Combine all ingredients, bring to boil and simmer for 4 or 5 minutes, stirring occasionally. Makes 1¼ cups.

POULET À LA CRÈME
(Chicken with Cream)

- 2 roasting chickens, about 4 pounds each
- 1 pound of gizzards, or 2 to 3 pounds of necks and backs
- 1 carrot
- 1 onion, stuck with 2 cloves
  Sprig of parsley
- 2 garlic cloves
  Salt and pepper
  Butter or margarine
  Tarragon or rosemary
  Ginger
- 3 tablespoons all-purpose flour
  Nutmeg
- ¼ cup brandy (optional)
- 3 egg yolks
- ½ cup heavy cream

Put the chicken giblets and the extra gizzards in a pot and cover with water. Add the carrot, onion, parsley, and garlic, and season to taste with salt and a little pepper. Simmer for 2 hours. Strain the broth, chill and skim off the fat. (Do this a day ahead, if possible.) Put a good lump of butter and some tarragon inside each chicken. Rub well with salt and a little ginger. Poach gently in the hot broth until just tender. Remove to a hot platter and pour a little melted butter over each one. Reduce 2 cups broth to about 1½ cups. Melt 3 tablespoons butter and blend in the flour. Slowly add the hot broth, stirring constantly. Cook and stir until smooth and thickened. Simmer for 5 minutes. Taste for seasoning and add a touch of nutmeg. Stir in a little brandy, if desired. Beat the egg yolks with the cream and blend with a little sauce. Stir into the sauce slowly, over very low heat. Do not boil. Stir until well blended, heated, and slightly thickened. Makes 8 servings.
Note: Good accompaniments for this dish are well-buttered noodles or rice.

COQ AU RIESLING
(Chicken with Riesling)

Everywhere one goes, one finds the red-wine version of this dish, the *coq au vin*. This chicken in wine comes from Alsace and calls for the delicious white wine of that region; California Riesling can be used.

- 2 roasting chickens (3 to 4 pounds each), cut into quarters, or 6 chicken breasts
  All-purpose flour
  Salt and pepper to taste
  Butter (about ⅔ cup)
- 2 tablespoons cooking oil
  Dash of ground nutmeg
- 1 teaspoon dried thyme
- 1 leek, well washed
- 1 parsley sprig
- 1 onion, stuck with 2 cloves
- ⅓ cup brandy, slightly heated
- 1½ cups Riesling or other dry white wine
- 2 slices of salt pork
- 12 mushroom caps
- 18 small white onions, peeled
- 2 teaspoons sugar (about)
- 3 egg yolks
- ¾ cup heavy cream
  Chopped parsley

Dredge the chicken pieces with flour seasoned with salt and pepper. Heat ¼ cup butter and the oil in a heavy skillet and place the chicken in the hot fat, skin side down. Put in dark meat first, for these pieces take a little longer to cook. Brown the chicken well and turn to brown the other sides. When chicken is well browned, add nutmeg, thyme, leek, parsley, and onion. Pour brandy over all and ignite. When flame dies down, add wine and bring to boil. Reduce heat to simmer, cover, and cook gently for 20 to 25 minutes, or until chicken is tender. While chicken is cooking, cut the salt pork into small pieces and sauté in a little butter. When just golden, add to pan with chicken. Sauté the mushroom caps in pan in which salt pork was cooked. Sauté onions in ¼ cup butter. Sprinkle with a little sugar to glaze and season with salt. Cover the pan and steam gently until tender. Keep warm. When chicken is done, remove to a hot platter and garnish with the onions and mushrooms. Reduce the sauce to 1½ cups. If you like a creamy sauce, beat egg yolks with cream and beat in a little sauce. Add mixture to the sauce slowly, cooking over very low heat. Cook and stir until smooth and creamy. Do not boil. Serve sauce separately, garnished with chopped parsley. Makes 6 servings.
Note: With this chicken dish, serve buttered noodles and chilled Riesling.

POULET À L'ESTRAGON
(Roast Chicken with Tarragon)

This is a classic dish. In northern France, where tarragon is a garden herb, it is often the choice for Sunday dinner. Choose a fine plump roasting chicken or capon weighing 5 to 6 pounds. Rub inside and out with a cut lemon and salt. Put 5 to 6 tablespoons butter and a large sprig or two of fresh tarragon into the cavity. Or rub a little dried tarragon in your hand and add it to the butter, mixing together before putting them in the cavity. Rub skin of bird with butter and a little tarragon. Put chicken on its side on rack in roasting pan and roast in preheated moderate oven (375°F.) for 20 minutes. Remove and turn to the other side. Baste with drippings and a little additional melted butter. Roast again for 20 minutes. Remove chicken and turn on its back. Baste again and roast for 20 minutes. Chicken should be done. Test to see if legs move easily at the thigh joint. Serve with the pan juices and *Pommes de Terre Sautées* (at right). Makes 4 servings.

CANARDS AUX NAVETS
(Ducklings with Turnips)

- 2 ducklings, about 4 pounds each
  Salt and pepper
- 2 small onions
- 2 parsley sprigs
- ¼ pound mushrooms, sliced
  Butter or margarine
- 1 cup small green olives
- 12 to 14 young turnips, peeled
- 1¼ cups brown sauce (canned gravy can be used)
- ⅓ cup sherry or Madeira

Rub ducklings with salt and pepper and place an onion and a sprig of parsley in each. (Save the duck livers to use in an omlet the next day. They are delicious.) Put the ducklings on a rack in a shallow roasting pan and roast in preheated slow oven (325°F.) for 1½ hours, basting from time to time. After 1 hour, puncture the skin of the breasts with a fork. During the last 15 minutes, increase the heat to between 450°F. and 475°F. and puncture the breast skin again. This will make the ducklings crisp. While the ducklings are cooking, sauté mushrooms in ¼ cup butter. Season to taste and add the olives. Cook for 3 or 4 minutes. Cook turnips in boiling salted water until just tender. Season to taste and add 3 to 4 tablespoons butter. Remove the ducklings to a hot platter and keep warm. Skim the fat from the juices, blend in the brown sauce and bring just to a boil. Add the mushrooms, olives, and sherry. Lower the heat and simmer for 2 or 3 minutes. Serve ducklings on a platter and surround them with the turnips. Serve the sauce separately. Good accompaniments are rice and a very crisp salad or watercress. Makes 4 generous servings.

VEGETABLES

POMMES FRITES
(Fried Potatoes)

For frying, the French use waxy potatoes about the size of our new potatoes. Use these for best results. Peel and cut into quarters. Drop into hot deep fat (365°F. on a frying thermometer) and cook just until they start to turn color. Remove and drain on absorbent paper. Heat fat to 370°F. and cook potatoes a second time until they are crisp on the outside and smooth and creamy on the inside. Drain on absorbent paper and keep hot. Season with salt.

POMMES DE TERRE SAUTÉES
(Sautéed Potatoes)

For each person, peel 1 large potato and slice. Wash potato slices and dry on absorbent paper. Melt 6 tablespoons butter in heavy skillet and arrange potato slices, overlapping each other a little, in a spiral pattern. Cook over medium heat for 15 minutes, or until potatoes are brown and crusty on the bottom. Turn and brown on the other side, adding more butter if necessary. Shake pan from time to time to keep potatoes from sticking. Season with salt and pepper to taste as they cook. Turn out on hot plate and serve.

POMMES DE TERRE EN SALADE
(Hot Potato Salad)
2 pounds small new potatoes, washed and scraped
Salt
⅓ cup salad oil
2 tablespoons vinegar, or to taste
Pepper
½ cup finely chopped onion
¼ cup chopped parsley

Cook potatoes in boiling salted water until just tender. Drain and cut into halves or quarters. Heat oil and vinegar with salt and pepper to taste and when hot add onion and parsley. Pour over hot potatoes and toss well. Serve at once. Makes 6 servings.

CÉLERIS BRAISÉS
(Braised Celery)
3 small bunches of celery
1¼ cups chicken bouillon (canned or made with bouillon cubes)
⅓ cup butter
Salt and pepper

Cut base from celery bunches and separate into stalks. Cut each stalk into halves. Poach celery gently in bouillon until just tender. Remove from heat, pour off liquid, and reserve. Add butter to pan with celery and melt it. Cook for a few minutes, browning celery in the butter. Season to taste. Add a little of the reserved liquid and cook down quickly. Makes 6 to 8 servings.

OIGNONS À LA MONÉGASQUE
(Onions, Monaco Style)
3 to 4 dozen tiny white onions, peeled
1½ cups dry white wine
1 tablespoon vinegar
1 teaspoon salt
Pepper to taste
3 lemon slices
2 tablespoons tomato paste
½ cup sultana raisins
¼ cup white raisins

Put onions in skillet with wine, vinegar, salt, pepper, and lemon slices. Simmer until onions are just tender but still crisp in the center. Stir in tomato paste and raisins and cook for several minutes. Remove the onions to a dish. Let the juices cook down with the raisins until the liquid is almost a glaze. Pour over the onions and chill. Serve as an hors-d'oeuvre or with cold meat. Makes 8 to 12 servings.

SALADE DE TOMATES
(Tomato Salad)
4 to 6 very ripe tomatoes
2 heads endive
1 tablespoon each of chopped parsley, chives, and fresh basil
3 tablespoons olive oil
1 tablespoon wine vinegar
Salt and pepper

Plunge tomatoes into boiling water for a second and then let them cool. Peel and cut into very thin slices. Arrange leaves of endive around edge of serving dish; add tomatoes and sprinkle with chopped herbs. Top with the oil and vinegar and add salt and freshly ground black pepper to taste. Makes 6 servings.

PISSALADIÈRE
This is the French pizza. It is lighter and more digestible than the Italian.
1 recipe Brioche Dough
½ cup olive oil (it must be olive oil)
8 medium onions, coarsely sliced
Anchovy fillets
Soft black Mediterranean olives

Heat olive oil and add onions. Cook gently for 4 minutes, or until onions melt down and become very soft. Do not let them fry. Spread two 12-inch pizza pans with Brioche Dough and spoon onion mixture on top. Make a lattice pattern of anchovy fillets and put an olive in the center of each square. Bake in preheated hot oven (400°F.) for 15 to 20 minutes, or until crisp and brown.

■ **Variation**—Spread dough with tomato paste and sprinkle with a little fresh basil, if available. Then add the onions, anchovies, and olives.

Brioche Dough
1 package active dry yeast
½ cup warm water
4 cups sifted all-purpose flour
1½ teaspoons salt
2 tablespoons sugar
6 eggs
1 cup melted butter or margarine

Dissolve yeast in water and mix with 1 cup flour. This makes a spongy mixture. Cover with a towel and set aside in warm spot to rise until doubled in bulk. Meanwhile, blend rest of flour, salt, and sugar and mix in 3 unbeaten eggs. Gradually add melted butter and keep stirring until smooth. Add the other 3 eggs, one at a time, beating well after each addition. When yeast sponge has doubled, add to dough and blend thoroughly. Cover and place in warm spot to rise until doubled in bulk. Punch dough two or three times to deflate, and chill until ready to use. Can be kept for several days.

SAUCE

SAUCE VINAIGRETTE
This is what we call "French dressing." A true sauce vinaigrette is nothing more than 3 or 4 parts olive oil, 1 part wine vinegar, and salt and pepper to taste. There are numerous variations. Most of them consist of adding special seasonings. For example, French Dijon mustard to taste; chopped herbs: basil for tomatoes, tarragon for greens, chervil for potato salad, dill for cucumbers, a blend of herbs for mixed salads. For boiled meats, a combination of herbs, a good amount of chopped parsley, chopped hard-cooked egg, chopped garlic and capers can be added to vinaigrette sauce. This makes a rather thick dressing that goes well with boiled beef, calf's head, etc.

DESSERTS

TARTES AUX FRUITS
(Fruit Tarts)

French fruit tarts are made in two ways. Pastry is baked in flan rings and then filled with pastry cream, topped with fresh fruit, and glazed; or, if the fruit is especially delicious, it can be put into the tart shell without the pastry cream and glazed. Here are examples of each type; both are equally delicious.

TARTES AUX FRUITS AVEC CRÈME PÂTISSIÈRE
(Fruit Tarts with Pastry Cream)

Rich Pastry Dough:

2 cups all-purpose flour
3 tablespoons sugar
1 teaspoon grated lemon rind
3 hard-cooked egg yolks, mashed
½ cup butter at room temperature
¼ cup shortening
2 raw egg yolks
¼ teaspoon salt

Heap flour in bowl or on work surface. Make a well in center and place all other ingredients in well. Using finger tips and working quickly, mix them in with the flour to make a firm ball of paste. Roll pastry between sheets of wax paper, turning frequently to shape it, and loosening top sheet of paper each time you turn. Fit into two 9-inch pie pans or tart pans. Fit it well around the edges. This is very rich dough and may break a bit here and there. Don't worry. Simply patch with your finger tips. Chill pastry. Line with foil and fill with dry beans or rice. Bake in preheated very hot oven (450°F.) for 10 minutes. Reduce heat to 400°F. and bake until pastry is done. This will take 5 to 8 minutes. Remove foil and beans. Makes two 9-inch pastry shells.

Pastry Cream:

5 egg yolks
⅔ cup sugar
⅓ cup all-purpose flour
2 cups hot milk
1 teaspoon vanilla extract
Strawberries, or blueberries, or other seasonal fruit

Beat yolks until thick and gradually beat in sugar. Continue beating until mixture forms a ribbon when you lift the beater. This can be done with an electric mixer. Beat in flour. When well blended, add hot milk in a thin stream, beating constantly. Put mixture in top part of double boiler over simmering water. Stir with a wire whisk until mixture is smooth and flour is cooked. Remove from heat and beat in vanilla, or any other flavoring you choose. Cool cream slightly.

Spoon a layer into bottom of tart shells. Any leftover cream can be stored in refrigerator and used for other tarts or cakes. Top cream with ripe strawberries, blueberries, or other seasonal fruit. Glaze with Apricot Glaze (see *Poires Glacées,* below).

FRUIT TARTS, SECOND METHOD

Prepare tart shells as above. Sprinkle cooked shells with ground almonds and fill with sweetened ripe fruit. You can use strawberries, raspberries, sliced or halved peaches, pitted cherries, grapes, etc. Brush with Apricot Glaze or Currant Glaze, below, and top with sweetened whipped cream, if you like.

Currant Glaze

Melt a 10-ounce jar of currant jelly and, when it boils, add a few tablespoons brandy or kirsch. Cook for 2 minutes. Cool slightly and brush on top of the fruit in the tart shells.

POIRES GLACÉES
(Stuffed Pears with Apricot Glaze)

12 ripe pears
   Simple sugar syrup: 1 cup sugar, 2 cups water, 1 teaspoon vanilla extract
1 can or jar (10½ ounces) whole chestnuts in syrup
   Apricot Glaze
   Candied violets
   Pistachio nuts, chopped

Peel pears and remove core from bottom of each pear, leaving a cavity at base. Prepare a simple syrup with sugar, water, and vanilla, and cook together for 5 minutes. Add pears and cook until just tender, spooning syrup over them as they cook. You can poach pears in two or more batches using the same syrup over again. Drain pears and cool. Break up chestnuts and when pears are cool, stuff cavities with broken chestnut meats. Arrange on serving dish. Spoon or brush Apricot Glaze over surface of pears. Chill thoroughly and decorate with candied violets and chopped pistachio nuts. Makes 12 servings.

Apricot Glaze

Put 2 cups (1 pound) apricot preserves in small saucepan and bring to boil over medium heat. Add 2 tablespoons brandy and cook for 3 minutes, stirring. Put preserves through sieve and cool slightly. Makes 2 cups.

POMMES BONNE FEMME
(Apples Baked on Toast Rounds)

6 large cooking apples
½ to ¾ cup sugar
6 rounds of buttered toast
   Vanilla extract
   Melted butter

Core apples and peel ¼ of the way down from the stem end. Rub with some of the sugar. Arrange the toast rounds in a baking pan and top each with an apple.

Into each apple spoon enough sugar to come to the top of the cavity. Add a few drops of vanilla and 1 to 2 tablespoons melted butter to each. Bake in preheated moderate oven (350°F.) until apples are tender, basting from time to time with more melted butter. Bake for 30 to 45 minutes, depending on size and type of apple used. Serve with heavy cream. Makes 6 servings.

SOUFFLÉ MOKA
(Mocha Soufflé)

   Butter (about ¼ cup)
   Sugar (about ⅔ cup)
3 tablespoons all-purpose flour
¾ cup milk
6 egg yolks, slightly beaten
3 teaspoons instant coffee powder
¼ cup crème de cacao
8 egg whites
½ cup heavy cream, whipped
1 tablespoon brandy

Butter a 2-quart soufflé dish or straight-sided baking dish and sprinkle with sugar. Melt 3 tablespoons butter over low heat and blend in flour to make a *roux*. Slowly add milk and cook, stirring, until smooth and thick. Simmer for 3 minutes. Cool slightly; add egg yolks, ¼ cup sugar, and the coffee. Return to heat and cook gently, stirring, until mixture is well blended. Do not boil. Cool again and add *crème de cacao*. Beat egg whites until almost stiff. Gradually beat in ¼ cup sugar. Gently fold into mocha mixture. Pour into buttered and sugared soufflé dish and bake in preheated hot oven (400°F.) for 25 minutes, or until puffy and brown on the outside and still slightly runny in the center. Serve with sweetened whipped cream flavored with brandy. Makes 6 servings.

MOUSSE AU CHOCOLAT
(Chocolate Mousse)

6 ounces (1 small package) semisweet chocolate pieces
6 egg yolks
   Grated rind of 1 orange
⅓ cup sugar
6 egg whites
   Whipped cream

Melt chocolate in top part of double boiler over hot water. Beat egg yolks lightly and stir into chocolate. Heat for several minutes, but do not let water in double boiler come to a boil. Add orange rind and sugar and cool slightly. Beat egg whites until stiff and fold into the chocolate mixture thoroughly. Pour into individual serving dishes and chill for several hours. Serve with sweetened whipped cream. Makes 6 servings.

GÂTEAU DE MARRONS AU CHOCOLAT
(Chestnut Chocolate Cake)

The French call this a cake but actually it's a molded dessert. It's so rich that small servings suffice.

1. Baba au Rhum
2. Gâteau de Marrons au Chocolat
3. Mousse au Chocolat
4. Poires Glacées
5. Tartes aux Fruits

1 can (1-pound, 5 ounces) unsweetened
    whole chestnuts, drained
¾ cup sugar
½ cup sweet butter, melted
8 ounces (two 4-ounce bars) sweet
    cooking chocolate, melted and cooled
    Whipped cream

Force chestnuts through food chopper, using fine blade. Stir in sugar and butter. Add chocolate and mix well. Pour into 1-quart mold and chill for several hours, or until firm. Turn upside down on serving plate and cover mold with a cloth wrung out of hot water. Shake mold with plate slightly, if necessary to loosen. Decorate with whipped cream. Makes 10 to 12 servings.

Note: Chestnuts can be bought in specialty food stores or food sections of large department stores.

BABA AU RHUM
(Rum Cake)

There are many versions of this typically French dessert. Some contain currants, raisins, or candied fruits, others are glazed after the rum syrup is poured over them. Here is a simple but delicious recipe.

1 package active dry yeast
½ cup warm water
2 cups unsifted all-purpose flour
4 eggs
¼ cup sugar
1 teaspoon grated lemon rind
½ teaspoon salt
½ cup soft butter
    Rum Syrup
    Whipped cream

Soften yeast in the warm water. Add ½ cup flour and beat until smooth with a rotary or electric beater. Add eggs, one at a time, beating very thoroughly after each addition. Then beat in remaining flour, sugar, lemon rind, and salt. Cover and let rise in warm place for 45 minutes. Add butter, a small amount at a time, beating after each addition until thoroughly blended. Pour into a well-buttered 5-cup fluted mold with a tube and let stand for 10 minutes. Bake in preheated moderate oven (375°F.) for 35 to 40 minutes. Let stand for 5 minutes, then turn out on serving plate. Prick with fork and spoon *Sirop de Rhum* over Baba, making sure all surfaces are covered. Let stand until syrup is absorbed. Fill center with whipped cream. Makes 6 to 8 servings.

Sirop de Rhum
(Rum Syrup)

Put 1 cup sugar and ½ cup water in saucepan. Bring to boil and cook, stirring, until sugar is dissolved. Cool; stir in ⅓ cup rum.

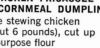

FRICASSEE—This is the French word for hash. In culinary language, a fricassee,

though not a hash in the American sense, is an extremely thrifty dish of fowl, veal, and other meats, which generally utilizes the less-tender cuts. These are first cooked in fat until a pale gold; then a liquid, such as bouillon, water, milk, or wine, is added to the dish, along with vegetables and seasonings.

CHICKEN FRICASSEE WITH
CORNMEAL DUMPLINGS

1 large stewing chicken
    (about 6 pounds), cut up
    All-purpose flour
    Salt and pepper
¼ cup fat
    Celery tops
1 onion, peeled
1 bay leaf
4½ cups water
2 chicken bouillon cubes
    Cornmeal Dumpling Batter

Wash chicken pieces. Drain and pat dry. Dredge pieces with flour mixed with salt and pepper. Brown chicken on all sides in hot fat. Add celery tops, onion, bay leaf, 4 cups water, and bouillon cubes. Bring to a boil, lower heat, cover, and simmer for 1½ hours, or until chicken is tender. Blend 6 tablespoons flour with remaining water. Stir mixture gradually into hot liquid. Cook until thickened, stirring constantly. Season to taste with salt and pepper. Make Cornmeal Dumpling Batter and drop by teaspoonfuls into gently boiling fricassee. Cover and simmer for 12 minutes, or until dumplings are done when tested wtih a toothpick. Makes 4 servings.

Cornmeal Dumpling Batter

1 egg, beaten
¼ cup milk
1 tablespoon cooking oil
½ cup yellow cornmeal
¼ teaspoon poultry seasoning
½ cup all-purpose flour
1 teaspoon baking powder
½ teaspoon salt

Mix egg with milk, oil, cornmeal, and poultry seasoning. Sift in remaining ingredients. Blend well. Makes 12 to 16 small dumplings.

VEAL BREAST FRICASSEE

2 pounds veal breast
¼ cup soy sauce
1 tablespoon vinegar
½ teaspoon salt
½ teaspoon pepper
¾ teaspoon ground ginger
¼ cup all-purpose flour
3 tablespoons fat
¾ cup boiling water
1 cup small white onions, peeled

Cut veal into 8 pieces. Place in bowl. Combine soy sauce, vinegar, and seasonings. Pour over veal and let stand for at least 30 minutes. Lift veal from sauce. Roll in flour and brown in hot fat. Add soy sauce mixture and water. Cover and simmer over low heat for about 2 hours, or until veal is tender. Add onions dur-

ing last 30 minutes of cooking. Makes 4 servings.

FRITTER—This is a small amount of batter which may be mixed with chopped cooked fish, meat, vegetables, or fruits, or used to coat these foods. Whichever method is used, fritters are always fried in deep fat or sautéed. They are an excellent way of utilizing leftovers.

The trick of making successful fritters lies in having the food dry and, if it is to be coated with the batter, making sure that it is very completely coated so that the food can't ooze out during frying. The fat must also be of a temperature to insure crispness without and juiciness within.

Dessert fritters are highly regarded in English, French, and Italian cooking. Fruit fritters are an example. They are served very well drained, very hot, and sprinkled with powdered sugar.

BASIC FRITTER BATTER

1 cup all-purpose flour
1½ teaspoons baking powder
½ teaspoon salt
2 eggs, well beaten
⅓ cup milk

Sift flour with baking powder and salt. Beat egg with milk. Stir flour into egg mixture. Beat until smooth and well blended. Makes about 1 cup batter.

Note: This batter can be used with pieces of cooked vegetables, chopped meat, chicken, fish, and fruits.

OCEAN-PERCH FRITTERS

2 cups (about 1 pound raw) flaked
    cooked fresh or frozen ocean-perch
    fillets
1 cup all-purpose flour
1 teaspoon salt
⅛ teaspoon white pepper
    Dash of paprika
1 teaspoon baking powder
1 egg, separated
⅔ cup milk
1 tablespoon melted margarine
    Fat for deep frying

Sift together flour, salt, pepper, paprika, and baking powder. Mix egg yolk with milk and add to dry ingredients; beat well. Add margarine. Fold in stiffly beaten egg white and fish flakes. Drop by tablespoonfuls into hot deep fat (370° to 375°F. on a frying thermometer) and fry until golden brown on both sides. Drain on absorbent paper. Serve at once with horseradish and ketchup or chili sauce. Makes 4 servings.

Note: These fritters can also be made with mullet, pike, fluke, halibut, salmon, or flounder.

MEAT FRITTERS

1 cup unsifted all-purpose flour
1½ teaspoons baking powder
½ teaspoon salt
　Dash of pepper
1 egg, well beaten
½ cup milk
¾ cup finely diced cooked meat
　(chicken, beef, or lamb)
1 teaspoon minced onion (optional)
　Gravy

Mix dry ingredients. Add egg to milk and add to first mixture, beating until smooth. Fold in meat, and onion, if desired. Drop by tablespoonfuls into hot deep fat (375° F. on a frying thermometer) and fry until golden brown on both sides and done. Drain on absorbent paper. Serve with heated gravy. Makes about 12 fritters, or 4 servings.

PARSLEYED CORN FRITTERS

2 eggs, beaten
¾ cup milk
1 teaspoon grated onion
1 tablespoon chopped parsley
2½ cups sifted all-purpose flour
2 teaspoons baking powder
1 teaspoon salt
2 tablespoons melted margarine
2 cups (one 1-pound can) cream-style
　corn
　Fat for deep frying

Combine eggs, milk, onion, and parsley. Add sifted dry ingredients, margarine, and corn; mix well. Drop batter by tablespoonfuls into hot deep fat (375°F. on frying thermometer). Fry until golden brown. Drain on absorbent paper. Serve hot, with butter and syrup if desired. Makes 2 dozen fritters.

Note: Fritter batter may be dropped by tablespoonfuls onto hot greased griddle. Brown both sides.

THIN FRITTER BATTER FOR FRUITS

1 cup all-purpose flour
1 teaspoon salt
¼ teaspoon ground nutmeg
2 eggs, separated
2 tablespoons fresh lemon juice
　Grated rind of 1 lemon
1 tablespoon melted butter or
　margarine
¾ cup water

Sift flour with salt and nutmeg. Combine egg yolks with lemon juice, lemon rind, and melted butter. Add water. Blend well. Stir in flour mixture and beat until smooth. When ready to use, fold in egg whites beaten stiff but not dry. Makes about 1½ cups batter.

Plum Fritters

Use pitted fresh or well-drained canned plums. Sprinkle with sugar and a dash of ground cloves or nutmeg. Cover and let stand for 30 minutes. Drain well and dry on paper towel. Dip fruit into Thin Fritter Batter. Deep fry in fat heated to 375°F. on a frying thermometer for 2 to 3 minutes. Drain on absorbent paper.

Sprinkle with confectioners' sugar.

Orange Fritters

Peel oranges. Remove white skin. Cut oranges into ¾-inch slices. Carefully remove seeds. Sprinkle with sugar. Drain slices and dry on paper towel. Dip into Thin Fritter Batter. Fry in deep fat or oil (375°F. on a frying thermometer) for 2 to 3 minutes. Drain on absorbent paper. Sprinkle with confectioners' sugar.

APPLE FRITTERS REGINA

3 large apples
½ cup granulated sugar
2 tablespoons brandy
1 teaspoon each of grated lemon and
　orange rind
1½ cups sifted all-purpose flour
¼ teaspoon salt
2 eggs, well beaten
1 teaspoon olive oil
⅓ cup beer
　Fat for deep frying
　Confectioners' sugar

Core and peel apples; cut into ½-inch rings. Reserve ends for use in salad. Mix ¼ cup granulated sugar, the brandy, and grated rinds. Pour over apples and let stand for 2 hours. Mix remaining granulated sugar and other ingredients except last 2. Let stand for 1 hour. Dip apples, 1 ring at a time, into the batter mixture. Fry in hot deep fat (375°F. on a frying thermometer) until golden brown. Drain on absorbent paper and sprinkle with confectioners' sugar. Serve warm. Makes 1 dozen.

VIENNESE JAM FRITTERS

4 cups unsifted all-purpose flour
4 teaspoons baking powder
1 teaspoon salt
2 eggs, separated
1 cup sugar
1 cup milk
½ cup melted butter or margarine
　Strawberry, apricot, peach, or
　other jam

Sift flour with baking powder and salt. Beat egg yolks until thick and lemon-colored and stir in sugar. Add flour and milk alternately, mixing well after each addition. Mix in melted butter. Fold in egg whites beaten until stiff but not dry. Shape dough into a ball in mixing bowl. Wrap in wax paper and chill for 2 hours. Roll out dough on a lightly floured board to ¼-inch thickness. Cut with 2-inch cookie cutter or doughnut cutter. Place a small spoon of jam on half of the rounds. Moisten edges of dough with water and top with remaining rounds of dough. Press edges to seal. Fry in hot deep fat or oil (375°F. on a frying thermometer) for 2 minutes, or until browned on both sides. Drain on absorbent paper. Serve sprinkled with confectioners' sugar. Makes about 18 fritters.

FROG'S LEGS—The hind legs of the frog are eaten as a delicacy in Europe and in the United States. Their taste resembles chicken in texture and flavor but is more delicate.

Fresh frogs' legs are available year round at fish stores. They are usually sold skinned and ready to cook. They are also available frozen. If it is necessary to dress them, cut off the hind legs close to the body and wash them well in cold water. Remove feet. Chill before skinning. Beginning at the top, strip off the skin as you would a glove. Soak again for one to two hours in cold water or in milk. Drain and dry before cooking.

Frogs' legs can be broiled, sautéed, cooked with a sauce, or deep fried; since they are small, they take only a short time to cook. Allow two large or six to eight small frogs' legs for each serving.

Nutritive Food Values—Frogs' legs contain substantial amounts of riboflavin and thiamin.

3½ ounces, raw = 73 calories

FROGS' LEGS POULETTE

12 pairs frogs' legs
2 tablespoons butter
2 tablespoons all-purpose flour
½ cup dry white wine
　Salt and pepper
1 tablespoon chopped parsley
1 tablespoon minced onion
1 egg yolk
1 tablespoon water

Soak frogs' legs in cold water for 2 hours. Drain and dry thoroughly. Sauté frogs' legs in hot butter for 2 minutes on each side. Sprinkle with flour. Stir to blend flour with pan juices. Add wine, salt and pepper to taste, parsley, and onion. Simmer, covered, over moderate heat for 10 to 15 minutes, or until tender. Remove to hot serving dish and keep hot. Beat egg and water. Remove sauce from heat. Add a little of the hot pan liquid to egg and blend thoroughly. Pour egg mixture into remaining sauce and stir over lowest possible heat or in top part of double boiler over hot water until thickened. Do not boil again. Pour sauce over frogs' legs and serve immediately. Makes 4 to 6 servings.

FROST, TO and FROSTING

FROST, TO and FROSTING—In culinary language "to frost" means to coat a cake, cookie, or pastry with a frosting. Frostings are made of sugar combined with water, milk, or egg whites, flavorings, and often coloring. They can be uncooked or cooked and should be soft enough to spread easily but firm enough to keep from running off. They should also remain soft and creamy. Another word much used for frosting is icing.

For many people, and not only children, the frosting is what makes a cake worthwhile; to them the cake is only the vehicle for the frosting. Making good frostings is an art that will bring countless large bouquets to a cook.

The thick, fluffy frostings so beloved by Americans are a typically American food. Europeans do not make them nor do they make the high fluffy cakes which are so often the base for our luscious frostings. This is entirely their loss, for a tall, noble, light-as-a-feather cake decorated with lavish swirls of creamy frosting is a true culinary treat.

Frostings should be applied when the cake is fresh. In order to keep crumbs from mixing with the frosting, the cake should be crumbed or be spread over with a thin layer of frosting which is allowed to dry before the remainder is put on. If the frosting is thick, it can be spread evenly by dipping the spatula used for applying it into hot water. To apply finished layer of frosting, frost sides first and then frost top. Apply frosting in rough strokes, or shape swirls and peaks on top.

Frostings generally fall into one of these four categories:

■ **Cooked Fluffy Frostings**—Seven Minute and Sea Foam Frostings are examples of this type. Sugar, egg whites, and water are beaten over boiling water until the mixture stands in stiff peaks. A similar frosting, called Boiled Frosting, is made by cooking a sugar-water syrup to a given temperature, then beating it slowly into whipped egg whites.

■ **Buttercream Frostings**—For these frostings a syrup is made from sugar, cream of tartar, salt, and water. The syrup is poured over egg whites. Soft butter and flavoring are added. These frostings spread like cream and have enough body to be piped in swirls and rosettes with a cake decorator. They are ideal for all special-occasion cakes.

■ **Cooked Fudge Frostings**—These are actually soft fudges spread on cakes. A sugar mixture is cooked to a certain temperature, usually soft-ball stage, cooled and beaten until creamy.

■ **Uncooked Frostings**—These frostings use confectioners' sugar. The finer the sugar, the moister the frosting will be and stay. The sugar is added in small amounts to a creamed butter or butter mixture, then beaten to a good spreading consistency. Frequently whole eggs, egg whites or yolks are added as part of the liquid for a creamier consistency.

COOKED FLUFFY FROSTINGS

SEVEN-MINUTE FROSTING

1½ cups sugar
⅓ cup water
¼ teaspoon salt
2 egg whites
1½ teaspoons light corn syrup
1 teaspoon vanilla extract

Combine all ingredients, except vanilla, in top part of double boiler. Beat about 1 minute to mix thoroughly. Then put over boiling water and beat constantly with rotary beater or electric mixer for 7 minutes, or until frosting will stand in stiff peaks. (Stir frosting up from bottom of pan occasionally.) Remove from over boiling water and add vanilla. Beat until of proper spreading consistency. Makes 5⅓ cups.

Cherry Frosting

Use recipe for Seven-Minute Frosting, adding 3 tablespoons maraschino cherry juice with the egg white. Substitute 1 teaspoon grated lemon rind for the vanilla.

Coffee Frosting

Use recipe for Seven-Minute Frosting, adding 2 to 3 teaspoons instant coffee powder to mixture before beating.

Marshmallow Frosting

Use recipe for Seven-Minute Frosting. Remove frosting from over hot water and stir in 1 cup miniature marshmallows or 16 large marshmallows, cut up.

Coconut-Marshmallow Frosting

Use recipe for Marshmallow Frosting. Stir ½ cup flaked or toasted coconut into Frosting before spreading on cake. Additional coconut can be sprinkled on top of frosted cake, if desired.

Peppermint Frosting

Use recipe for Seven-Minute Frosting, substituting ¼ teaspoon peppermint extract for the vanilla. Tint Frosting pale pink with red food coloring. Sprinkle frosted cake with crushed peppermint candy.

Sea Foam Frosting

Use recipe for Seven-Minute Frosting, substituting 1½ cups firmly packed brown sugar for the granulated sugar. Omit corn syrup.

Maple Sea Foam Frosting

Use recipe for Sea Foam Frosting. Substitute ½ to ¾ teaspoon maple flavoring for the vanilla.

Praline Frosting

Use recipe for Sea Foam Frosting. Just before spreading, fold in ¾ cup chopped pecans.

BOILED FROSTING

2 cups sugar
¾ cup water
¼ teaspoon salt
¼ teaspoon cream of tartar
2 egg whites
½ teaspoon vanilla extract

Combine sugar, water, salt and cream of tartar in saucepan. Cook and stir over medium heat just until clear. Then cook without stirring until a little of the syrup forms a soft ball when dropped in very cold water (240°F. on a candy thermometer). Beat egg whites until soft peaks form. Add syrup in a very thin stream, beating constantly. Then beat until frosting stands in stiff peaks. Add vanilla. Makes 2¾ cups.

Lime or Lemon Boiled Frosting

Use recipe for Boiled Frosting, omitting cream of tartar and vanilla and substituting ¼ cup fresh lime or lemon juice

FROSTING AMOUNTS NEEDED FOR BUTTERCREAM UNCOOKED, AND FUDGE-TYPE FROSTINGS*

	Between layers	Sides	Top	Total
8-inch 2-layer cake	½ cup	1 cup	¾ cup	2¼ cups
9-inch 2-layer cake	⅔ cup	1¼ cups	¾ cup	2⅔ cups
8-inch square	———	⅔ cup	⅔ cup	1⅓ cups
9-inch square	———	1 cup	1 cup	2 cups
13 x 9-inch cake	———	1 cup	1⅓ cups	2⅓ cups
24 cupcakes	———	———	2¼ cups	2¼ cups
10-inch tube cake	———	1½ cups	¾ cup	2¼ cups

For Cooked Fluffy Frostings about twice the amounts shown above are needed

for ¼ cup of the water. Add ½ teaspoon grated lime or lemon rind and, with food coloring, tint frosting pale green or yellow.

BUTTERCREAM FROSTINGS

BASIC BUTTERCREAM FROSTING
1 cup sugar
⅛ teaspoon cream of tartar
Dash of salt
¼ cup water
2 egg whites
1 teaspoon vanilla extract
⅔ cup butter

Combine sugar, cream of tartar, salt, and water in saucepan. Bring to boil and cook until a little of the syrup forms a soft ball when dropped in very cold water (240°F. on a candy thermometer).

Beat egg whites with rotary beater or electric mixer at high speed until stiff but not dry. Add syrup very slowly to egg whites, beating constantly. Add vanilla. Cool thoroughly.

Cream butter well. Add egg-white mixture to butter, 2 or 3 tablespoons at a time, beating well after each addition. If desired, sprinkle with chopped nuts, shredded coconut, crushed peanut brittle, or crushed peppermint candy. Or decorate frosting with shaved chocolate or candied cherries. Makes about 2 cups.

Butterscotch Buttercream Frosting
To Buttercream Frosting add ½ cup thick butterscotch sauce. Beat until well blended.

Cherry Buttercream Frosting
To Buttercream Frosting add ¼ cup cut maraschino cherries and 2 teaspoons cherry juice. Beat until well blended.

Chocolate Buttercream Frosting
To Buttercream Frosting add 3 ounces (3 squares) unsweetened chocolate, melted and cooled. Beat until well blended. Or add ½ cup very thick chocolate sauce or bought chocolate syrup. Beat until well blended.

Coffee Buttercream Frosting
To Buttercream Frosting add 1 tablespoon instant coffee powder. Beat until well blended.

Mocha Buttercream Frosting
To Buttercream Frosting add 2 ounces (2 squares) unsweetened chocolate, melted and cooled, and 2 teaspoons instant coffee powder. Beat until well blended.

Cooked Orange Buttercream Frosting
Use Buttercream Frosting recipe, but omit vanilla and add 1 teaspoon grated orange rind and ¼ cup fresh orange juice. Beat until well blended.

Pineapple Buttercream Frosting
To Buttercream Frosting add ½ cup pineapple jam. Beat until well blended.

Strawberry Buttercream Frosting
To Buttercream Frosting add ½ cup strawberry preserves. Beat until well blended.

COOKED FUDGE FROSTINGS

CHOCOLATE FUDGE FROSTING
3 cups sugar
3 tablespoons light corn syrup
1 cup milk
4 squares unsweetened chocolate
⅓ cup butter or margarine
1 teaspoon vanilla extract

Put the sugar, corn syrup, milk and chocolate in large saucepan. Cook over medium heat, stirring until sugar is dissolved. Cook until a small amount of mixture forms a very soft ball in very cold water (232°F. on a candy thermometer), stirring occasionally to prevent scorching. Remove from heat, add butter without stirring and cool until lukewarm, about 1 hour. Add vanilla and beat until frosting is creamy. Spread quickly on cake. Makes about 3 cups.
Note: If frosting stiffens before spreading is completed, add ½ to 1 teaspoon water and beat until smooth.

CARAMEL FUDGE FROSTING
⅔ cup butter or margarine
1 cup firmly packed brown sugar
⅓ cup milk
3 cups sifted confectioners' sugar (about)

Melt butter in saucepan. Add brown sugar and cook over low heat for 2 minutes, stirring constantly. Add milk and cook, stirring, until mixture boils. Remove from heat and cool for 10 minutes. Gradually add confectioners' sugar, beating until frosting is of good spreading consistency. Makes 2 cups.

White Fudge Frosting
Use recipe for Caramel Fudge Frosting, substituting granulated sugar for the brown sugar. Stir in 1 teaspoon vanilla before spreading.

Raisin Fudge Frosting
Use recipe for White Fudge Frosting, adding ½ cup chopped raisins just before spreading.

SEMISWEET FUDGE FROSTING
¼ cup butter or margarine
⅓ cup milk
1 package (6 ounces) semisweet chocolate pieces
1 teaspoon vanilla extract
2¼ cups sifted confectioners' sugar

Combine butter and milk in saucepan and bring just to a boil. Add chocolate and vanilla and stir until smooth. Gradu-

ally add sugar, beating until of good spreading consistency. Makes 1½ cups.

MAPLE-NUT FUDGE FROSTING
1½ cups maple sugar, crumbled
1 cup dairy sour cream
1 cup chopped nuts

Combine maple sugar and sour cream. Cook, stirring constantly, until a small amount of mixture forms a soft ball when dropped in very cold water (234° F. on a candy thermometer). Remove from heat and beat in nuts. Makes 2 cups.

UNCOOKED FROSTINGS

FLUFFY BUTTER FROSTING
⅓ cup soft butter or margarine
¼ teaspoon salt
1 teaspoon vanilla extract or other flavoring
1 pound (about 3½ cups) sifted confectioners' sugar
2 egg whites, unbeaten
1 tablespoon milk (about)

Cream butter, salt, and vanilla until light and fluffy. Add sugar alternately with egg whites, beating well after each addition. Add milk and beat until smooth and of spreading consistency. Makes 2¼ cups.

Fluffy Chocolate Butter Frosting
Use recipe for Fluffy Butter Frosting, adding 3 squares unsweetened chocolate, melted, to the sugar-egg white mixture. Beat well. Increase milk to 2 to 3 tablespoons, add to chocolate mixture and beat until of spreading consistency. Makes about 2½ cups.

Plain Confectioners'-Sugar Frosting
Use recipe for Fluffy Butter Frosting, omitting egg whites. Increase milk to ¼ cup, or enough to make frosting of good spreading consistency. Makes 1½ cups.

Mocha Butter Frosting
Use recipe for Plain Confectioners'-Sugar Frosting, substituting strong coffee for the milk, and adding 2 tablespoons cocoa.

UNCOOKED ORANGE BUTTERCREAM FROSTING
Grated rind of 1 orange
Grated rind of 1 lemon
¼ cup fresh orange juice
¼ cup butter or margarine, softened
1 egg yolk
⅛ teaspoon salt
2 teaspoons fresh lemon juice
3½ cups (1 pound) sifted confectioners' sugar

Combine orange rind, lemon rind, and orange juice. Let stand for 10 minutes; strain, if desired. Cream butter until light. Add egg yolk, salt, and lemon juice. Gradually beat in confectioners' sugar. Makes 2½ cups.

CREAM CHEESE FROSTING

1 package (3 ounces) cream cheese
1 tablespoon warm water
1 teaspoon vanilla extract
3 cups sifted confectioners' sugar

Mash cream cheese until softened. Add water and vanilla. Gradually add sugar, beating until smooth and of good spreading consistency. Makes 1½ cups.

Orange Cream Cheese Frosting

Use recipe for Cream Cheese Frosting, substituting fresh orange juice for the water and 1 teaspoon grated orange rind for the vanilla.

CHOCOLATE CREAM CHEESE FROSTING

2 packages (4 ounces each) sweet cooking chocolate
2 packages (3 ounces each) cream cheese
2 tablespoons light cream
2 cups sifted confectioners' sugar
¼ teaspoon salt
1 teaspoon vanilla extract

Put chocolate in small bowl and set over hot water until melted. Cool slightly. Add cream cheese and cream; blend. Gradually add sugar, beating well. Then add salt and vanilla. Makes 2 cups.

HUNGARIAN CHOCOLATE FROSTING

4 or 5 squares unsweetened chocolate
2¼ cups sifted confectioners' sugar
¼ cup hot water
2 egg yolks or 1 whole egg, unbeaten
6 tablespoons soft butter or margarine

Melt chocolate, remove from heat and put in bowl. Add sugar and water at same time and blend. Add egg yolks and beat well. Add butter, 1 tablespoon at a time, beating thoroughly after each addition. Makes 2 cups.

WEDDING OR ANNIVERSARY CAKE FROSTING

1 cup butter or margarine (as pale as possible)
8 cups sifted confectioners' sugar
¾ cup milk (about)
4 teaspoons vanilla extract
½ teaspoon salt

Cream butter until fluffy. Gradually add half of sugar, beating after each addition until smooth. Add remaining sugar alternately with milk, beating until of good consistency to spread. Add vanilla and salt. (While frosting cake, cover bowl of frosting with a damp cloth to keep frosting moist.) Makes about 5 cups.

■ **To Decorate**—Mix ¼ recipe of Wedding Cake Frosting, using only 1½ tablespoons milk. Use in cake decorator.
Note: Frostings can be tinted with food coloring, if desired.

CHOCO-SOUR-CREAM FROSTING

12 ounces (1 large package) semisweet chocolate pieces
1 cup dairy sour cream
⅛ teaspoon salt

Melt chocolate over hot water. Beat in sour cream and salt. Makes 2 cups.

FROSTED—In culinary language, the word has several meanings. It is used to describe foods whose taste or appearance reminds one of frost. Frosted fruit is one of the best-known frosted foods.

The word is also used to describe a cold thick drink made from syrup, a little milk, and plenty of ice cream, whirled in a blender until smooth. It may refer to an accumulation of frost as on mint-julep tumblers, or to the rims of glasses coated with a thin layer of crystalline sugar. Finally, it may refer to any coating over a food such as a frosting on a cake or a mashed-potato frosting on a meat loaf.

FROSTED FRUIT FOR DECORATIONS

Beat egg whites until frothy. Dip washed and dried fruit into the egg whites. Coat all surfaces. Roll fruit in granulated sugar. Place on a rack to dry. Small bunches of grapes, small clusters of currants, and fresh cranberries can be frosted in this way.

FROSTED CHOCOLATE

Beat ½ cup milk with 2 tablespoons chocolate syrup. Beat in 2 small scoops of vanilla or any other desired ice cream. Beat until smooth. Makes 1 serving.

FROSTED GLASSES

Dip rim of glass about ¾ inch deep into water or lemon juice. Drain slightly and dip into granulated or confectioners' sugar. Place glasses in freezer or refrigerator frozen-food compartment for a few minutes to harden sugar and to frost glasses. Fill glasses carefully to avoid wetting the frosted rim.

FRUIT—This is the reproductive body of a seed plant. Although, strictly speaking, acorns, beans, peas, chestnuts, and tomatoes are all fruits, when we think and speak colloquially of fruits, we mean the more or less sweet-pulped products of vines, shrubs, or trees, ranging from apples to tangerines.

Fruit has always sustained and delighted mankind, whether he found it wild, or grew it scientifically. Aside from its health-giving properties and its culinary versatility, it is the most ravishing of the products of nature, appealing to the eye as much as to the senses of smell and taste. Fruit has been an inspiration to painters and poets alike; it needs a poet's words to do justice to the glories of this food:

What wondrous life is this I lead!
Ripe apples drop about my head;
The luscious clusters of the vine
Upon my mouth do crush their wine;

The nectarine and curious peach
Into my hands themselves do reach;
Stumbling on melons, as I pass,
Ensnared with flowers, I fall on grass.
Meanwhile the mind, from pleasure less,
Withdraws into its happiness;
The mind, that ocean, where each kind
Does straight its own resemblance find;
Yet it creates, transcending these,
Far other worlds, and other seas;
Annihilating all that's made
To a green thought in a green shade.
Here at the fountain's sliding foot,
Or at some fruit-tree's mossy root,
Casting the body's vest aside,
My soul into the boughs does glide;
There, like a bird, it sits and sings,
Then whets and combs its silver wings,
And, till prepared for longer flight,
Waves in its plumes the various light.
Andrew Marvell (1621-1678)

Availability—Available all year round, although some fruits are seasonal, such as berries and melons. Some fruits can be grown in any section of the country, but in recent years they have been localized to take advantage of the proper soil and climatic conditions. Fruits which require a tropical climate such as bananas are imported.

Fruits can be bought fresh, frozen, canned, or dried, or in the form of fruit butters or juices. Some fruits are sold minted, pickled, spiced, brandied, or mixed as in fruit cocktail or salad.

Purchasing Guide—Fresh fruits are sold by weight or by the piece. Frozen or canned fruits are packed whole, halved, sliced, and diced, packed in syrup or in water.

When buying fresh fruits, select firm, bright-colored fruits with a fresh unwrinkled appearance. Citrus fruit should feel heavy with good-textured skins. The color and degree of maturity desirable depends on the type of fruit.

Buy fruits that are in season in nearby areas or in surplus. Buy fruits which suit the purpose for which they are to be used. Large perfect fruits may not be the best buy if small fruits with blemishes that do not affect quality or flavor can be used. In dishes where fruits are peeled and cut up, a small size that is not perfect may be the better bargain.

Examine prepackaged fruits to make sure that the quality is uniform and the package holds the full amount of fruit. Handle fruits carefully since bruised fruits spoil easily.

Storage—Fresh fruits should be stored in a cool dry place or in the refrigerator. Bruised or spoiled fruit should be discarded. Do not wash before storing since

this increases the chance of spoilage. Unripe fruits should be allowed to ripen at room temperature. For storage times, see chart.

Nutritive Food Values—Fruits add important vitamins, minerals, and bulk to the diet. They are rich in sugar to provide energy.

Vitamins supplied are ascorbic acid, some vitamins B, A, and G.

Minerals supplied are calcium, phosphorus, manganese, copper, and iron.

Fresh raw fruits are higher in vitamins and minerals than the frozen or canned versions. The dried fruits, which are concentrated, are higher in calories, minerals, and vitamins than fresh fruits, and canned and frozen fruits in sugar packs are higher in calories than fresh fruits. However, all processed fruits, whether canned, frozen, or dried, are a great deal lower than fresh fruits in ascorbic acid.

Basic Preparation—Wash fresh fruit thoroughly to remove chemical sprays and dust.

☐ **To Serve Raw**—Peel or cut fruit into desired shape and size or leave whole. Some fresh fruits darken on standing unless sprinkled with citrus fruit juice. Chill and serve.

☐ **To Cook**—Fruit may be cooked in syrup, stewed, or made into sauces. To retain the full nutritive value, cook, covered, in a small amount of water as quickly as possible. Sugar should be added to the fruit during cooking if the shape of the fruit is to be retained. But if you want the fruit to be soft throughout, add the sugar after cooking since the inclusion of sugar retards the cooking of the fruit.

Fruit can be baked, browned under the broiler, fried, and deep fried; it can be mixed, cooked or raw, into baked products and endless other dishes.

☐ **To Serve Frozen Fruits**—If they are to be served without any further preparation, they taste better when still slightly frozen.

☐ **To Freeze**—See Chart for Freezing Fruit, beginning on page 730.

FRUIT COCKTAILS

■ **Fresh Fruit Wedges with Orange Juice**—Place wedges of fresh pineapple, pears, apples, peaches, or green seedless grapes in fruit-juice glasses. Fill with fresh orange juice. Spear fresh fruit pieces with toothpicks.

■ **Fruit Sherbet with Fruit Juice**—Place a small scoop of fresh-fruit sherbet in fruit-juice glasses. Fill with fresh orange or grapefruit juice.

■ **Melon Balls with Citrus Fruit Juice**—Place fresh cantaloupe or honeydew balls in fruit-juice glasses. Fill with equal parts of fresh orange and grapefruit juice. Spear melon balls with toothpicks.

■ **Fresh Orange Sections with Watermelon Juice**—Put watermelon through a sieve. Add fresh lemon juice and sugar to taste. Chill. Place chilled fresh orange sections in fruit-juice glasses. Fill with watermelon juice.

■ **Fresh Fruit Medley**—Combine orange and grapefruit segments, pineapple sticks, unpeeled pear slices, halved strawberries, banana chunks, pitted grapes, and mint sprigs. Dip bananas and pear slices into lime juice to prevent darkening.

■ **Frozen Fruit Cup**—Combine packages of mixed fruit, melon balls, peaches, pineapple, raspberries. Flavor with grenadine, Cointreau, or cranberry juice.

■ **Fresh Fruit Dinner Cup**—Arrange fresh pineapple wedges, sliced fresh strawberries, and fresh orange sections in layers in sherbet glasses, using 1 cup of each fruit. Combine ½ cup fresh orange juice, ¼ cup fresh strawberry purée, 2 tablespoons fresh lemon juice, and ¼ cup sugar. Mix well. Pour over the fruit. Chill. Spoon into sherbet glasses and garnish each with a whole uncapped fresh strawberry. Makes 6 servings.

■ **Summer Fresh Fruit Cup**—Combine 2 cups chilled cantaloupe balls, 1 cup watermelon balls, 1 cup diced fresh peaches, ½ cup fresh blueberries, 3 tablespoons sugar, and 3 tablespoons fresh lime juice. Pile lightly into sherbet glasses or cantaloupe shells. Garnish with fresh mint. Makes 6 servings.

■ **Minted Fruit Cup**—Prepare any combination of sliced or diced fruit. Add chopped fresh mint, Cointreau, and confectioners' sugar to taste. Use a cantaloupe or honeydew melon as a fruit "bowl." Cut slice from top, remove seeds, fill with fruit, chill.

■ **Fruit Sherbet Cup**—Top fresh fruit with a small scoop of lemon, lime, pineapple, or orange sherbet. Or serve the sherbet in hollowed-out lemon or orange shells with a fresh fruit plate.

■ **Double Fruit Cup**—Pour cranberry, orange, grapefruit, pineapple, or other fruit juice or nectar over fruit cup. Or top each serving with 1 tablespoon frozen juice concentrate; orange juice concentrate in the hollow of a cored pear half, for instance.

■ **Fruit Spikes**—Put a melon ball, 1 chunk of frozen pineapple and 1 strawberry on a long wooden pick. To serve, stick picks into a bowl of crushed ice. Allow 1 pick for each serving.

FRUIT SALADS

FIVE-FRUIT SALAD PLATE

For each serving arrange on plate sliced unpeeled apple, quartered banana, slices of pear, a peach half, and a spoonful of cottage cheese topped with chopped nuts. Garnish with raspberries and watercress. Serve with a honey-lime dressing made by mixing equal parts of fresh lime juice and honey. Add a little salt.

CHEESE-STUFFED APPLE SALAD
3 ounces cream cheese
¼ cup crumbled Roquefort or
    blue cheese
4 ripe apples, unpeeled
1 tablespoon fresh lemon juice
    Lettuce leaves
    Green seedless grapes for garnish
    Fresh Orange French Dressing

Mix cream cheese with Roquefort. Wash and core apples. Brush insides with fresh lemon juice to prevent discoloration. Stuff cavities with cheese mixture. Wrap in foil and chill for several hours or overnight. To serve, cut into quarters and arrange on lettuce. Garnish with grapes. Serve with Fresh Orange French Dressing. Makes 4 servings.

Fresh Orange French Dressing
Mix ¼ cup salad oil, ⅓ cup fresh orange juice, and 1 tablespoon fresh lemon juice. Add salt and pepper to taste. Makes about ¾ cup.

STORAGE TIMES FOR FRESH FRUIT				
TYPE OF FRUIT	AT ROOM TEMPERATURE	ON REFRIGERATOR SHELF	IN REFRIGERATOR FROZEN-FOOD COMPARTMENT	IN FREEZER
Fresh:				
Soft	1 to 4 days	3 to 14 days	2 to 3 months	1 year
Hard	1 to 4 weeks	1 to 4 months	2 to 3 months	1 year
Cooked	1 to 2 days	4 to 5 days	2 to 3 months	1 year
Canned:				
Unopened	1 year	—	—	—
Opened	—	4 to 5 days	2 to 3 months	1 year
Frozen	—	1 week	3 months	1 year
Dried	6 to 8 months			

1 banana
½ teaspoon fresh lemon juice
Lettuce
¼ cup fresh grapefruit sections
¼ cup seeded grape halves
4 fresh orange sections
Whipped cream or mayonnaise

Peel banana and halve lengthwise. Sprinkle with lemon juice. Place on a bed of lettuce. Combine grapefruit and grapes and spoon over top of split banana. Garnish with fresh orange sections. Serve with whipped cream or mayonnaise. Makes 1 serving.

Note: Any fresh fruit in season may be substituted for grapefruit and grapes.

MOLDED WINTER FRUIT SALAD

3 envelopes unflavored gelatin
¾ cup cold water
1½ cups boiling water
¾ cup sugar
¼ teaspoon salt
¾ cup fresh lemon juice
1 cup fresh grape juice
2 fresh tangerines
6 fresh unpeeled apple slices
1 cup dairy sour cream
5 cups mixed diced fresh fruits such as apples, pears, oranges, grapes, bananas
Salad greens
Mayonnaise

Soften gelatin in cold water. Add boiling water. Stir until dissolved. Add sugar, salt, fresh lemon juice, and grape juice. Rinse a 6½-cup ring mold in cold water and pour ½ cup of the mixture into the mold. Chill until firm. Peel and section tangerines and arrange over chilled gelatin around the mold. Place an unpeeled apple slice, cut to fit width of mold, between tangerine sections. Pour in an additional ½ cup clear gelatin mixture. Chill until firm. In the meantime, chill remaining gelatin until slightly thick. Beat in sour cream. Chill until the mixture begins to thicken. Stir in 2 cups of the mixed diced fruits. Pour into the mold. Chill until firm and ready to serve. Unmold onto a serving plate. Fill center with the remaining diced fruit. Garnish with salad greens as desired. Serve with mayonnaise. Makes 12 servings.

FRUIT PLATE WITH PISTACHIO CHEESE

Blend 8 ounces softened cream cheese, ¼ cup crumbled blue cheese, 1 tablespoon fresh lemon juice, and ½ teaspoon salt. Tint pale green with food coloring. Add ½ cup skinned shelled pistachio nuts. Fold in ¼ cup heavy cream, whipped. Put in refrigerator tray, smoothing top. Turn refrigerator control to coldest setting and freeze until firm. Cut into squares and arrange in center of large plate. Around edge put orange slices, frozen peach slices, frozen melon balls, and/or other fruit. Makes 6 servings.

WATERMELON COOLER—Pour watermelon juice over fresh orange segments.

FRUIT CUP—Combine sliced peaches, watermelon and cantaloupe balls, grapes, and blueberries, and garnish with mint.

Fresh fruit,
sunny-ripe and cool to the tongue,
each one an individual
taste treat

Nectarines, Grapes, Bananas, Sour Cherries,
Blueberries, Gooseberries, Apples, Oranges, Currants,
Plums, Pineapple, Peaches, Mangoes,
Apricots, Pears, and Strawberries

PINEAPPLE-STRAWBERRY SALAD
4 large slices of pineapple
 Watercress
1 pint strawberries
2 tablespoons fresh lime juice
1 tablespoon honey
2 tablespoons salad oil

Arrange pineapple and watercress on 4 individual salad plates. Wash and decap all but 4 berries. Cut decapped berries into lengthwise slices; arrange petal fashion on pineapple; top each salad with a whole berry. Mix last 3 ingredients for a dressing. Makes 4 servings.

FRUIT DESSERTS

SUMMER-FRUIT COMPOTE
1½ cups sugar
½ lemon, sliced
4 pears
8 plums
4 peaches
4 apricots
1 cup blueberries

To sugar and lemon add ¾ cup water; bring to boil. Add pears, peeled, halved, and cored; plums, cut into sections through to pit, pulp left attached to pits; peaches, peeled, halved, and pitted; and apricots, halved and pitted. Cover and cook very slowly until tender. Remove fruit as it becomes tender and put in serving dish. Add blueberries and simmer for 1 minute. Pour into serving dish; cool. Compote will keep for several days in refrigerator. Makes 8 servings.

FRUITS ROUGES
1½ quarts large ripe strawberries
2 packages (10 ounces each) frozen raspberries, partially thawed
1 cup heavy cream
 Powdered sugar

Clean strawberries and arrange in pyramid in serving dish. Sprinkle lightly with sugar. Drain raspberries and whirl in blender long enough to make a thick purée. Strain and spoon over the strawberries. Serve with sweetened whipped cream, flavored with liqueur if desired. Makes 6 servings.

CANNED FRUIT COMPOTE
Use figs, pear and peach halves, whole apricots, dark sweet cherries, and greengage plums. Drain fruits and cook syrups with grated orange rind and a cinnamon stick for 10 minutes. Remove cinnamon and pour syrup over fruits.

BANANAS IN CREAM
2 large bananas, sliced (1¾ cups)
⅓ cup green seedless grapes
¼ cup diced peeled fresh oranges
1 cup dairy sour cream
2½ tablespoons sugar
 Grated orange rind

Place all ingredients except orange rind in a mixing bowl. Toss lightly. Serve in sherbet glasses garnished with grated orange rind. Makes 4 servings.

PEARS IN ORANGE SAUCE
Core 4 fresh pears and peel one third of the way down from the top. Put in 2-quart casserole. Mix ¾ cup sugar, 1 cup water, ½ cup fresh orange juice, 2 teaspoons grated orange rind, juice of ½ lemon, and dash of salt in saucepan. Boil for 5 minutes. Pour over pears. Cover; bake in preheated hot oven (400°F.) for about 30 minutes. Remove pears; pour syrup into saucepan and boil for 10 minutes. Pour over pears. Chill; serve plain or with sour cream. Makes 4 servings.

PEACH, PLUM, AND APRICOT MEDLEY
 Juice of 1 lime
½ cup honey
3 medium peaches, peeled and sliced
3 large apricots, peeled and sliced
2 plums, sliced
 Mint sprigs

Mix lime juice and honey. Pour over peaches and apricots. Put in serving dishes. Arrange a few plum slices on each serving. Garnish with mint. Makes 4 servings.

BERRY CHARLOTTE
1 envelope unflavored gelatin
¼ cup cold water
½ cup boiling water
1 cup crushed fresh blueberries, strawberries, raspberries, or other soft berries
1 tablespoon fresh lemon juice
½ cup sugar
½ cup heavy cream, whipped
¼ teaspoon salt
2 egg whites
1 dozen ladyfingers or one 8-inch spongecake layer, cut into strips

Sprinkle gelatin on cold water to soften. Dissolve in boiling water. Add berries, lemon juice, and sugar; stir until sugar is dissolved. Chill until partially set. Fold in cream and stiffly beaten salted egg whites. Turn into mold or dessert dishes lined with ladyfingers. Chill until set. Makes 4 to 6 servings.

SCANDINAVIAN FRUIT PUDDING
½ cup pitted dried prunes
½ cup seedless raisins
½ cup dried apricots
3½ cups water
1 cinnamon stick
2 tart apples, peeled and sliced
2 fresh pears, peeled and sliced
2 cups (one 1-pound can) pitted red sour cherries
1 box (3 ounces) cherry-flavored gelatin
 Whipped cream

Put first 7 ingredients in saucepan and bring to boil. Cover and simmer for 15 minutes, or until fruit is tender. Add undrained cherries and bring to boil. Add gelatin and stir gently until dissolved. Cool; then chill. Pudding will be soft. Serve with whipped cream. Makes 6 to 8 servings.

FRUITED RICE PUDDING
3 cups cooked rice
¾ cup milk
½ cup juice drained from fruit cocktail
2 eggs, well beaten
½ cup sugar
½ teaspoon grated lemon rind
2 cups drained fruit cocktail
⅓ cup firmly packed dark brown sugar
⅓ cup finely chopped nuts
2 tablespoons all-purpose flour
3 tablespoons butter or margarine

Mix rice with milk, juice drained from fruit cocktail, eggs, sugar, and lemon rind. Spoon mixture into well-greased 1½-quart casserole. Top with fruit cocktail. Mix brown sugar with nuts and flour and cut in butter until mixture is crumbly. Sprinkle crumbs over the fruit. Makes 6 servings.

CALIFORNIA FRUIT ROLL
Select a mixture of uncooked dried fruits such as raisins, figs, apricots, pears, peaches, pitted prunes, and dates. Sprinkle with a little fresh lemon juice and force fruits through food chopper, using fine blade. Add a little more juice if needed to handle easily. Shape into rolls 2 inches thick and coat with finely chopped nuts. Wrap in wax paper; refrigerate.

FRUITCAKE—The term is applied to a cake which is composed mainly of fruits and nuts, held together with a rich batter. In some cakes there is just enough batter to hold the fruit and nuts together, in others, considerably more. The fruits used are dried, candied, or crystallized.

Fruitcakes range from the very dark ones containing molasses or brown sugar and a large varied amount of spices to those called golden or light, in which a lighter-colored batter, generally made with granulated sugar, lighter-colored fruits, and no spices, is used.

Fruitcakes are traditional Thanksgiving and Christmas cakes. The dark rich cakes that spell "fruitcake" to so many of us are typical of England, from where they emigrated to America. Cakes rich in fruit were baked for Christmas not only in England but in all of Europe. The custom goes back to the days when a cake, and one rich in precious fruit, was indeed a delicacy and very often one that could not be afforded at other times of the year. Currants, raisins, dates, candied peels, and spices are not luxury items to us, but to our ancestors, whose children prized a single orange as a Christmas gift beyond compare, they stood as a symbol of the wonderful riches of distant lands, where these fruits grew in the warm golden sun.

Our colonial ancestors, especially those of the southern states, served their holiday fruitcakes with pride and spoke of them as the finest fare their homes could offer. They competed in blending fruits and spices in new and delicious ways, and to this day, the great fruitcakes of our South are among the finest ever made.

Fruitcakes are baked at very low temperatures for a long period of time to allow heat to penetrate the heavy mixture. Some fruitcakes are covered with foil during baking and uncovered for the last hour of baking to brown. A pan of warm water should be placed in the oven to keep cakes moist. Because of their excellent keeping quality, these cakes are often made weeks ahead of the time they will be eaten; storage improves their flavor.

Fruitcakes are popular Christmas gifts. They may be baked in small baking pans or small glass casseroles, greased and lined with brown paper, and greased again. The brown paper keeps the outer crust of the cake from getting too brown.

In the preparation of a fruitcake, citron, orange, and lemon peel are usually finely sliced and cut up. Other candied fruits are cut larger. Currants and seedless raisins are left whole. Nuts should be coarsely cut. When measuring the raisins and fruits, remember that a half pound equals one and a half cups. Candied fruits and peels are available already cut up in cans, packages, or glass jars. If using scissors for cutting fruit, dip scissors into water for greater ease. Mix dried fruits such as figs, prunes, raisins, dates, apricots, and nuts with a little of the flour in the recipe to keep fruits and nuts from sinking in the cake.

To store a fruitcake, allow it to cool, then wrap it in wax paper or plastic wrap, and store it in an airtight container in a cool place. For added flavor and to insure its moist quality, brush it from time to time with sherry, brandy, fruit juice, or cider. Another popular method of adding flavor is to saturate a piece of cheesecloth with sherry or brandy and wrap it around the cake before wrapping it in paper. Thus stored, a fruitcake will keep for many months and be improved by this ripening.

DARK FRUITCAKE

    1 box (15 ounces) seedless raisins
    1 box (11 ounces) golden raisins
    ¾ pound citron
    ½ pound each candied cherries, lemon, and orange rind
    ¼ pound candied pineapple
    2 cups coarsely chopped walnuts or pecans
 2¼ cups sifted all-purpose flour
    1 cup shortening
    1 cup sugar
    ½ cup molasses
    5 eggs, slightly beaten
    ¾ teaspoon salt
    ½ teaspoon soda
 1½ teaspoons cinnamon

    ½ teaspoon each cloves and mace
    ½ cup fruit juice
    1 cup jam or preserves
      Glaze
      Candied pineapple, cherries, and angelica or citron for decorating

Force fruits through coarse blade of food chopper. Add nuts, and mix in 1½ cups flour. Cream shortening until fluffy. Gradually add sugar and molasses. Beat in eggs; add remaining flour, sifted with salt, soda, and spices; mix well. Stir in fruit and nuts, fruit juice, and jam. Turn into 2 deep 9-inch tube pans, greased and waxed-paper-lined. Bake in preheated slow oven (275°F.) for about 3½ hours. Cool slightly; remove from pan, and peel off paper. Cool. Spread Glaze over cake, and decorate with candied pineapple, cherries, and angelica.

Glaze

Bring to boil ½ cup light corn syrup and ¼ cup water. Cool. Makes ⅔ cup.

OLD ALABAMA FRUITCAKE

    2 cups (1 pound) butter
    2 cups (1 pound) sugar
   12 eggs
    1 cup molasses
    1 cup brandy, rum, or bourbon
    1 cup rosewater
    4 cups (1 pound) sifted all-purpose flour
    ¼ pound candied orange peel, chopped
    2 pounds currants
    2 pounds raisins
    2 pounds candied citron, chopped
    1 pound shelled almonds, blanched and cut into small pieces
    1 tablespoon ground nutmeg

Cream butter until light. Gradually beat in sugar, a little at a time. Add eggs, one by one, beating well after each addition. Stir in molasses, brandy, and rosewater. Sprinkle flour over fruits and nuts and add nutmeg. With hands mix fruits and flour so that fruits are well coated with flour. Add floured fruits to batter and mix thoroughly. Grease two 10-inch angel-food-cake pans or four loaf pans (9 x 5 x 3 inches). Line pans with heavy unglazed brown paper and grease paper. Spread batter into pans. Bake in preheated very slow oven (250°F.) for about 3 hours, or steam first for 1 hour and bake for remaining time. Cake will be crumbly. Cool cake in pans overnight to set. Let cake get very cold. If at all possible, ripen from 1 week to 3 months before using. Makes about 12 pounds rich dark fruitcake.

Note: The flavor will vary depending on whether you use brandy, rum, or bourbon. You can buy the rosewater in a gourmet food store. It should not be omitted since it adds a subtle taste to the cake.

GOLDEN FRUITCAKE

    ½ cup butter or margarine
    1 cup sugar
    ½ teaspoon grated lemon rind

 1¼ cups sifted all-purpose flour
    1 teaspoon baking powder
    ¼ teaspoon salt
    ½ cup milk
    1 cup each golden raisins and chopped dates
    ¼ cup chopped citron
    ¾ cup candied cherries and pineapple
    ¾ cup chopped blanched almonds
    ½ cup shredded coconut
    3 egg whites, stiffly beaten
      Glaze
      Split blanched almonds, candied cherries and citron for decorating

Cream butter and sugar until light and fluffy. Add lemon rind. Sift dry ingredients, and add alternately with milk to creamed mixture. Add fruits and nuts; mix well. Fold in egg whites. Pour into greased and waxed-paper-lined 9 x 5 x 3-inch loaf pan. Bake in preheated slow oven (275°F.) for 2½ hours, or until done. Cool slightly, remove from pan, and peel off paper. Just before serving, spread Glaze over top of cake; arrange split almonds, cherries, and citron in flower design.

Glaze

Combine 1 jar strained apricot-and-apple baby food with ¼ cup sugar. Cook, stirring until mixture thickens. Makes about ½ cup.

CANDIED LIGHT FRUITCAKE

    2 cups sifted all-purpose flour
    2 teaspoons baking powder
    ½ teaspoon salt
 2½ cups (1 pound) coarsely chopped candied pineapple
    2 cups (1 pound) whole candied cherries
 3½ cups (1¼ pounds) pitted dates, cut coarsely
    4 eggs
    1 cup sugar
    8 cups (2 pounds) pecan halves

Sift flour with baking powder and salt. Add fruits and mix well with the hands to coat thoroughly each piece of fruit. Beat eggs until frothy. Gradually beat in sugar. With hands mix in nuts. Grease two 9-inch springform pans. Line with unglazed brown paper and grease again. Divide dough between pans and press mixture down firmly with the fingers. Bake in preheated slow oven (275°F.) for about 1¼ hours. Let cake stand in pans for about 5 minutes. Turn out on racks and pull off brown paper. Cool cake before slicing. Makes about 6 pounds of fruitcake.

Fruit-filled French pastry, not only good to eat,
but a treat for the eye as well. The rectangular tart is cherry,
the round one apple. The tartlets are filled with luscious strawberries
brushed with jelly glaze and peaches topped with shredded coconut.

How to Cook Superbly:
Fruit Tarts and Tartlets
by Helen Evans Brown

Have you ever admired the beautiful fruit tarts on a restaurant's dessert wagon or in the window of a French *pâtisserie,* and wondered how those upright pastry sides and lovely amber or ruby glazes were achieved? It's easy when you know how, and you will if you follow these directions. Soon you will be turning out spectacular desserts almost as easily as you used to whip up a cake with a packaged mix. There are, of course, several different kinds of pastry: regular piecrust for American two- or one-crust pies, puff paste *(pâte feuilletée)* from which Napoleons, *vol-au-vents,* and other high-rising pastries are made, and *pâte brisée* or *pâte à flan,* which is used for the open-faced straight-sided quiches and flans so popular in Europe. The one we are going to concentrate on is a sweet pastry called *pâte brisée sucrée* or *pâte sucrée,* meaning "sweet pastry," and that's what we will call it here. It is tender, yet not as fragile as some pastries because it must be firm enough to support the filling. This, as well as the careful arrangement and glazing of the fruit, is what gives them their splendor. The glaze itself, though it does so much for the tart, is actually simple to make.

EQUIPMENT

For the pastry you will need a worktable with a hardwood or marble top, or a large pastry board, the usual mixing bowls, measuring cups and spoons, a rolling pin, a strainer, and either an 8-, 9-, or 10-inch flan ring. A flan ring, which sometimes isn't a "ring" at all, but a rectangle or square, is a metal hoop or frame, with perpendicular sides from ¾ inch to 1¼ inches high. It has no bottom, so a cookie sheet is used under it when baking. A flan ring or rectangle can be improvised by folding several layers of heavy aluminum foil into the desired shape and height, or straight-sided cake pans can be used. If you are making tartlets, you will also need tart pans, either plain or fancy ones. For the fillings the only thing you'll need in addition to everyday kitchen equipment is a whip for making *crème pâtissière* and a pastry brush for glazing the fruits or gilding pastry strips. A pastry wheel, or jagger, to cut strips for latticed tarts is handy but not essential. A good idea for novices is to make a gauge for measuring the thickness of the pastry when rolling it. This is simple: cut off the pointed end of a toothpick, making it square. Then using a very sharp pencil, mark it off in fractions of an inch: 1/16, 1/8, 3/16, and 1/4. It's easy to stick this into the rolled pastry at several spots to measure the thickness and evenness.

PÂTE SUCRÉE
(Sweet Tart Pastry)

Note: The larger amount of butter naturally produces a richer crust, but it is also slightly more fragile. If you're not used to handling pastry, perhaps you'd better use the lesser amount given here as an alternative first time you try.

    2 eggs
    2 cups unsifted all-purpose flour
    ½ teaspoon salt
    2 tablespoons sugar
    ⅔ cup butter or ¾ cup butter (see Note above)

This is enough for two 8- or 9-inch flan rings, or one 10-inch, plus lattice tops on 2 to 3 dozen tartlets.

Hard-cook 1 egg yolk. To do this bring a small panful of water to a boil; turn down to simmer. Carefully break and separate eggs. Put one unbroken yolk in the water and cook for 10 minutes. Force through a strainer. Have butter firm but not hard, and cut it into pieces. Combine all ingredients, including the 2 unbeaten raw egg whites and both the raw and cooked yolks. Using your finger tips, mix quickly until thoroughly blended, with an even texture and color. Overmixing will toughen the pastry. Form into a ball, flatten slightly to hasten chilling, wrap in wax paper, foil, or plastic, and chill for several hours in the refrigerator, or for at least 1 hour in the freezer.

☐ **To Roll Dough**—Have flan ring or tart shells arranged on cookie sheet. Lightly flour table or board and do the same with the rolling pin (or use wax paper; see below). Put chilled dough on the board and roll it away from you, pressing it evenly and lifting the pin as you get to the edge of the pastry. Give dough a quarter turn several times during the rolling: this keeps the dough from sticking; sprinkle a tiny bit more flour under

the dough and on the pin if it starts to stick, spreading it evenly. Try to roll the dough into the shape desired and to get the thickness as uniform as possible. If you have to patch, moisten the edge of the extra dough lightly before rolling together. It should be rolled from 1/8 to 3/16 inch thick for tarts (flans), 1/8 inch thick for tartlets.

Note: If you prefer, try rolling between sheets of wax paper, lifting paper occasionally while rolling to eliminate wrinkles. You need no flour for this method, but it is a little harder to get uniform thickness. When the pastry is of the desired thickness, roll it up on the pin, then lift to the edge of the flan ring, and unroll so that the pastry lies over the top of the flan ring. Lift the edges, allowing it to settle to the cookie sheet below. Press the bottom firmly onto the sheet, and work the sides down, molding the pastry so that it is slightly thicker at the sides than on the bottom. This is easier than it sounds as the pastry is plastic and easy to handle. Now press thickened sides against the inside of the ring and gently pass the rolling pin over the top. This cuts off surplus overhanging pastry. If you are using a foil ring or a cake pan, cut surplus pastry off with scissors. Decorate edges of pastry by pressing with the back of a knife, the prongs of a fork, or by pinching little scallops into it with your fingers. Using the forefinger of the left hand, push a little of the pastry toward the outside of the ring and pinch this together with thumb and forefinger of the right hand—if you're right-handed, that is. When making tartlets, do one shell at a time, cutting a piece of pastry not only large enough to fit the bottom and sides of the pan but also large enough to give a little surplus. Proceed as for the flan. If you work slowly, it's better to keep the pastry in the refrigerator, removing enough for 2 or 3 tartlets at a time. When finished, chill for at least 3 hours in the refrigerator or for 1 hour in the freezer.

☐ **To Bake**—Prick bottoms of tarts thoroughly with a fork. To keep sides from collapsing during the baking, fold a strip of foil an inch longer than the circumference of the flan ring into a 2-inch wide strip and fold over edge of the pastry, having it come to the bottom on the inside with at least 1/4 inch folded down over the top. Chill again briefly, then put in preheated moderate oven (375°F.). Look at it after 3 or 4 minutes, and if the bottom has puffed up, prick it so that it collapses, repeating once or twice for the first 10 minutes. When the pastry has set, in about 10 or 12 minutes, carefully remove foil and continue baking until nicely browned, about 10 or 12 minutes

longer. Bake tartlet shells in exactly the same way but without the foil collar. If, after 5 minutes, the pastry has slipped down, press it back into place with a fork or butter spreader. Bake tartlets in preheated moderate oven (375°F.) for 15 to 18 minutes, or until lightly browned. Cool slightly before removing flan ring or turning out from tartlet pans. If a cake pan has been used, it can easily be turned out when cool.

☐ **To Bake Partially**—Sometimes the tart crust is partially baked, then filled and the baking finished. In this case make exactly as above, but do not return to oven after the foil collar has been removed; it will be sufficiently baked by that time.

☐ **To Fill Baked Tart Shells**—There are several different ways to do this. The simplest is to half fill the baked shell with cut-up sugared fruits or berries, then arrange whole berries or halved sliced fruit on top in a symmetrical pattern. Brush light-colored fruits such as apples, peaches, pears, or pineapple with apricot glaze, and strawberries or other red fruits with currant or other red-jelly glaze. Another way is to put a layer of soft custard (*Crème Pâtissière,* see below) or sweetened whipped cream at the bottom of the baked shell and arrange and glaze the fruit as above.

☐ **To Fill Partially Baked Tart Shells**—Sometimes a half-baked shell is used with partially cooked or canned fruits, or even with raw fruits, then baked further and glazed as above. The Apple Tart, below, is made this way.

☐ **To Fill Unbaked Shells**—When a latticed crust is desired, an unbaked shell is filled with desired fruit, either raw, cooked, or canned; the lattice, made with strips of egg-washed pastry, is put over the filling, then the tart is baked. If desired, a glaze may be brushed on the top between the pastry strips, but this is not necessary. See Cherry Tart, page 763.

CRÈME PÂTISSIÈRE

In heavy saucepan combine 2 tablespoons all-purpose flour, ½ cup sugar, and pinch of salt. Stir in 1 cup milk until smooth. Cook over medium heat, stirring, until mixture is thick. Simmer for 5 minutes. Stir a little of hot sauce into 3 egg yolks. Then return to saucepan, stirring. Return to low heat, add 1 tablespoon butter, and heat until thickened. Do not boil. Add 1 teaspoon vanilla extract, or flavor with 1 teaspoon brandy, rum, kirsch, or Cointreau. Cover until cool.

APRICOT OR RED-JELLY GLAZE

Melt ½ cup (for an 8-inch tart) or ¾ cup (for a 10-inch tart) of strained apricot jam or red jelly (currant, strawberry, or raspberry). Cook, stirring, for 2 or 3 minutes, or until bubbly, and paint, while hot, over the top of fruit tarts or tartlets. A tablespoon of rum or brandy may be added before cooking.

STRAWBERRY TART
Bake an 8-inch shell and paint with slightly beaten egg; allow to dry. Then spread bottom with 1 recipe of *Crème Pâtissière* (page 762). Arrange on the top, stem side down, 1 pint of perfect whole strawberries, which have been washed, hulled, and allowed to dry. Put the largest berries in the center and arrange the remaining ones in circles around them, having the smallest at the outer edge. Paint with hot red-jelly glaze and serve within an hour or two. You can substitute sliced sugared berries, flavored with a liqueur such as Cointreau, if you wish. You can also use whipped cream instead of the custard. For a 10-inch tart, double the amounts of filling and make the larger amount of glaze.

APPLE TART
Partially bake a 10-inch tart shell. Cool and brush with apricot glaze or slightly beaten egg, leaving the paste in the metal ring and on a cookie sheet. (Note: If you have baked your shell in a cake pan, it will have to be removed from the pan before filling. Make sure it has set and cooled before removing it from the pan. Place it on a cookie sheet and fasten a double strip of foil around the outside before filling and finishing the baking.) Peel and core 4 pounds cooking apples. Slice 2 large ones (or 3 smaller ones) into ⅛-inch slices, sprinkle with lemon juice, cover with plastic wrap to keep from discoloring, and set aside. Cut the remaining apples into pieces, put in a heavy saucepan with 3 tablespoons of water, cover, and bring to a boil. Turn heat low and simmer for 20 minutes, or until the apples are tender and the water has evaporated. Stir in ¼ cup butter, ¾ cup sugar, and 2 tablespoons Jamaica rum or brandy, or 2 tablespoons vanilla extract, and cook slowly until thick, stirring constantly. Cool and pour into shell. Arrange reserved apple slices in overlapping spiral or concentric circles and brush with melted butter. Cut a circle of aluminum foil to fit over the sliced apples. Put on the upper shelf of preheated moderate oven (375°F.) and bake for 20 minutes. Remove foil and continue baking until the apples are tender and slightly gilded, 10 to 15 minutes longer. Slide tart, ring and all, onto a serving plate, and paint with hot apricot glaze. Remove ring and serve warm or cool, but not chilled. Whipped cream or

heavy cream may be served.

CHERRY TART
Line a 9-inch flan ring with pastry and chill. Pit a quart of sweet cherries, sprinkle with ½ cup sugar (double amount if cherries are tart), and mix lightly. Paint bottom of chilled pastry shell with red fruit glaze or slightly beaten egg. Roll surplus pastry ¼ inch thick and brush with egg glaze (1 egg beaten slightly with 1 tablespoon water or milk). Cut into strips 3/16 to ¼ inch wide. Fill shell with sugared cherries, then moisten edge of pastry with water and make lattice on top with the pastry strips, pressing them down firmly at the edge and trimming evenly. Put on bottom shelf of preheated moderate oven (375°F.) and bake for 1 hour, or until the cherries bubble slightly and the top is brown. If desired, brush cherries with red-jelly glaze, taking care not to paint the latticed crust. This same recipe may be used for fresh sliced peaches or apricots.

FRESH PEACH TART
Partially bake a 9-inch shell and brush the bottom with 2 tablespoons Apricot Glaze, then sprinkle with 2 tablespoons chopped blanched almonds. Blanch 4 or 5 ripe peaches (depending on their size) by dipping them into boiling water for 20 seconds. Cut into halves, remove pits, and place, round side up, on the tart shell, arranging attractively. Sprinkle with ¾ cup sugar and brush with 3 tablespoons melted butter. Bake in preheated moderate oven (375°F.) for 30 minutes, or until the peaches are tinged with amber. Put half a blanched almond on each peach half and brush with remaining apricot glaze.

FRUIT TARTLETS
These are most satisfactory if the shells are prebaked. They may be filled with sliced and sugared fresh fruit, or with canned or stewed fruit. The fruits, as in the larger tarts, may be arranged symmetrically and glazed; they can be topped with whipped cream; or *Crème Pâtissière* may be put in the bottom of the shells, the fruits on top. And if you want some extra special goodies to serve at a tea party, make tiny tart shells and in each one put a huge whole ripe strawberry. Paint with red-jelly glaze that has been flavored with brandy. Sublime!

Notes on Measurements and Servings
The pastry recipe given here makes about 18 ounces of pastry. A 10-inch tart shell takes about 12 ounces of pastry; a 9-inch one 7 to 8 ounces; and an 8-inch one about 6 ounces. A 3-inch tart shell takes about ¾ ounce of pastry, and a 4-inch

one about 1½ ounces. As for filling, a 10-inch tart shell takes 5 to 6 cups filling, a 9-inch one 4 to 5 cups, and an 8-inch one 3 to 4 cups. Small tart shells take 3 tablespoons to ¼ cup filling, and larger tart shells up to ½ cup.

An 8-inch tart will make 6 servings, a 9-inch tart, 6 to 8 servings, and a 10-inch tart, 8 servings.

FRY—As a noun, the word "fry" is used to describe the young of fishes and also an internal part or organ of an animal usually eaten fried, for example, pig's liver. As a verb, "to fry" means to cook food, in pieces or serving-size units, in fat or oil. When only a small amount of fat is used, the process is called "panfrying" or "sautéing." Sometimes the fat is supplied by the food itself, as is the case with bacon or salt pork. When larger amounts of fat are used, enough to cover the food, the process is called "deep frying" or "deep-fat frying."

Frying is one of the oldest and most economical of cooking processes. For one thing, it needs simple equipment and it can be done quickly under the most primitive circumstances. Even more importantly, frying requires comparatively little fuel since the food is cooked in small pieces in a short time. When fuel is scarce and expensive, as it still is in the many parts of the world with little gas and electricity and with limited supplies of such natural fuels as wood or coal, frying is the prevalent way of cooking. This is so in parts of southern Italy, France, and Spain and especially in China and Japan, fuel-short countries.

Properly prepared fried foods are delicious, for frying, by adding a crisp outer crust to juicy foods, makes for a most pleasant flavor and texture contrast.

Panfrying or sautéing is done in a skillet or frying pan and involves a relatively short cooking period. The skillet may or may not be covered during the cooking. Foods are cooked in this way when browning or a crisp crust are desired. Examples of foods cooked in this manner are hamburgers, steaks, ham, bacon, sausage, liver, fish, chicken, potatoes and other vegetables.

Deep frying is done in a kettle, deep heavy saucepan or electric deep-fat fryer filled about three-quarters full with fat. Foods are cooked by this method include doughnuts, fritters, croquettes, vegetables such as French-fried potatoes, chicken, and fish. Foods prepared in this way are crisp outside, moist inside. To prevent large fat absorption, the foods should cook quickly or be precooked.

FUDGE—This creamy smooth confection is one of the basic candies; it is also one of the best-loved ones, and one that is frequently made at home, to the joy of all concerned.

Fudge is made from sugar, water, corn syrup (or some other acid) to which butter, chocolate, coffee, cocoa, coconut, brown sugar, etc., are added. (Corn syrup, honey, or cream of tartar is needed to keep mixture creamy.) The ingredients are cooked to the "soft-ball" stage (234°F. to 240°F. on a candy thermometer, or until a small amount of syrup, dropped into very cold water, forms a soft ball which can be shaped with the fingers). The mixture is then cooled to lukewarm (110°F.). When lukewarm, flavorings and nuts or raisins are added and the fudge is beaten until creamy and thick. Then the mixture is poured into a buttered pan, cooled or chilled until firm, and cut into squares.

Fudge comes in a variety of flavors and nuts, raisins, candied fruits, peanut butter, crushed mints, gumdrops, or coconut may be beaten into fudge before pouring mixture into the buttered pan.

Caloric Values

☐ 3½ ounces, vanilla = 398 calories
☐ 3½ ounces, vanilla with nuts = 424 calories
☐ 3½ ounces, chocolate = 400 calories
☐ 3½ ounces, chocolate with nuts = 426 calories

OLD-FASHIONED CHOCOLATE FUDGE
2½ ounces (2½ squares) unsweetened chocolate
2½ cups sugar
¼ teaspoon salt
1 cup undiluted evaporated milk
6 tablespoons butter or margarine
1 tablespoon vanilla extract

Melt chocolate in saucepan. Add sugar, salt, and milk. Cook, stirring, until sugar is dissolved. Continue cooking without stirring until a small amount of mixture forms a soft ball when dropped into very cold water (234°F. on a candy thermometer). Remove from heat and let stand until lukewarm (110°F.). Add 2 tablespoons butter and the vanilla. Beat until mixture is thick and loses its gloss. Turn out on wax paper and let stand until cool enough to handle. Knead in 4 tablespoons butter. Press into buttered pan (8 x 8 x 2 inches), and let stand until firm. Cut into squares. Makes about 1¾ pounds.

BURNT-SUGAR FUDGE
3½ cups sugar
½ cup hot water
2 cups light cream
2 tablespoons corn syrup (light or dark)
¼ teaspoon salt
2 tablespoons butter or margarine

1 teaspoon vanilla extract
1 cup chopped nuts

In heavy saucepan, melt and burn ½ cup sugar until it forms a dark golden syrup. Remove from heat and let cool a few minutes. Add hot water very gradually. Stir in remaining sugar, cream, corn syrup, and salt. Cook without stirring until a small amount of mixture forms a soft ball when dropped in very cold water (238°F. on a candy thermometer). Remove from heat and add butter, vanilla, and nuts. Cool slightly, then beat until mixture thickens and begins to lose its gloss. Pour into buttered pan (8 x 8 x 2 inches), and let stand until firm. Cut into squares. Makes about 2¼ pounds.

LAYERED FUDGE
1½ cups undiluted evaporated milk
2 cups sugar
½ teaspoon salt
1 package (6 ounces) butterscotch pieces
1 package (6 ounces) semisweet chocolate pieces
Walnut halves

In saucepan, mix ¾ cup of the milk, 1 cup sugar, and ¼ teaspoon salt. Bring to full rolling boil, stirring. Boil for 5 minutes, stirring. Remove from heat and stir in butterscotch pieces. Turn into pan (8 x 8 x 2 inches) lined with 2 strips of foil with 2-inch overhang on each side. Repeat cooking process with remaining ingredients, cooking mixture for only 4 minutes. Stir in chocolate pieces and pour over first mixture. Chill. Lift from pan with strips of foil. Cut into squares and press a nut half on each chocolate square. Makes about 2 pounds.

KNEADED CHOCOLATE FUDGE
2 tablespoons butter
2 ounces (2 squares) unsweetened chocolate
1 cup milk
3 cups sugar
¼ cup honey
⅛ teaspoon salt
1 teaspoon vinegar
1 teaspoon vanilla extract
½ cup chopped nuts

Melt butter and chocolate in milk in saucepan. Beat to blend. Add sugar, honey, and salt. Bring to boil; cover and boil for 2 minutes. Uncover and cook, without stirring, until a small amount of the mixture forms a soft ball when dropped in very cold water (238°F. on a candy thermometer). Remove from heat and add vinegar. Let stand until lukewarm. Then add vanilla and beat until mixture is thick and loses its gloss. Add nuts; turn out on buttered plate. Let stand until lukewarm. Knead for 4 to 5 minutes. Shape into 2 rolls about 2 inches in diameter. Wrap in wax paper and store in cool place until ready to serve. Cut into slices. Makes 1½ pounds.

COCOA FUDGE
4 cups sugar
⅔ cup cocoa
1½ cups milk
2 teaspoons light corn syrup
¼ teaspoon salt
6 tablespoons butter
2 teaspoons vanilla extract

Measure sugar, cocoa, milk, corn syrup, and salt into a 3-quart saucepan. Mix well. Place over medium heat and stir until sugar is melted and mixture is thoroughly blended. Bring to a boil and cook until a small amount of mixture forms a soft ball when dropped in very cold water (234°F. on a candy thermometer). Stir occasionally to prevent sticking. Remove from heat; add butter and vanilla. Let cool, without stirring, until lukewarm (110°F.). Beat mixture until it becomes very thick and loses its gloss. Quickly pour into a buttered 8-inch square pan. When firm, cut into squares. Makes about 4½ dozen pieces.
■ **Variations**—Add 1½ cups broken nuts to fudge while still in beating stage, before it loses its gloss.

Or sprinkle ½ cup chopped nuts over top after fudge is in pan. Press nuts lightly into surface of fudge. Or try toasting the nuts first.

Or make small balls of fudge by rolling in palms of hands. Then roll in chopped nuts or flaked or grated coconut.

QUICK FUDGE
1 can (6 ounces) evaporated milk, undiluted
1¾ cups sugar
½ teaspoon salt
⅔ cup chopped walnuts
1½ cups miniature marshmallows
1½ cups semisweet chocolate pieces
1 teaspoon vanilla extract

Combine evaporated milk with sugar and salt. Bring to a boil, and simmer for 5 minutes. Remove from heat, and add remaining ingredients. Stir until marshmallows melt. Pour mixture into buttered square pan (9 inches). Cool. Makes about 2 pounds.

VANILLA FUDGE
3 cups sugar
3 tablespoons light corn syrup
1½ cups light cream
¼ teaspoon salt
1½ teaspoons vanilla extract

Mix all ingredients, except last 2, in saucepan. Bring to boil and cook without stirring until a small amount of mixture forms a soft ball when dropped in very cold water (236°F. on a candy thermometer). Remove from heat and let stand until lukewarm (110°F.). Add salt and vanilla, and beat until mixture thickens and loses its gloss. Pour into buttered pan (8 x 8 x 2 inches), and let stand until firm. Cut in squares. Makes about 1½ pounds.

GALANTINE—A galantine is a French dish made from boned poultry, meat, or fish which has been stuffed, pressed into a symmetrical form, cooked in a broth, and covered with aspic. Galantines are served cold and in slices. The dish is a decorative one, trimmed with truffles, pistachio nuts, vegetable cutouts, olives, etc., which show up prettily on both the whole dish and in the cut slices.

Galantines take time and some skill to make. The results are worth it.

HOW TO BONE AND PREPARE A CHICKEN, DUCK, OR TURKEY FOR A GALANTINE

The first step in preparing fowl for a galantine is to remove all the bones, leaving the skin in one piece with flesh attached. Next the meat is removed from the skin and put aside to be used in making the stuffing. The skin is then placed on a flat surface and spread with a stuffing. The skin is rolled around the stuffing and sewed into place. The galantine is then cooked, sewed side down, glazed with aspic, and served cut in thin slices.

To bone poultry use a small, sharp, thin knife. Start by cutting a slit down the back of the carcass from the neck to the tail. With your knife, scrape and cut away the skin and flesh from one side of the carcass, working with small slashes. Always turn the sharp side of the knife toward bone, rather than toward flesh and skin, so that the skin is not accidentally pierced. When the wing and leg ball joints are reached, cut through them leaving the leg and wing attached to the skin. Continue cutting until the breastbone is reached. Cut very carefully here, as the skin is very thin and is easily pierced. Repeat on the other side of the carcass. When this is completed, the skin will be in one piece with the wings and legs attached, and the skin still attached to the ridge of breastbone. Cut very carefully along the ridge of the breastbone to remove the skin in one piece. Remove the wing tips. Then cut the meat from the leg and wing bones, discarding the bones. There will be no more bones. The skin will be flat, like an open book, with the meat attached to the top of it. With a sharp knife, and pulling with your fingers, remove all the meat from the skin, leaving the skin in one piece, ready to be filled.

GALANTINE OF CHICKEN

2 chickens (about 5 pounds each)
1 pound lean veal, ground
1 pound lean pork, ground
1 pound salt pork, cubed
¼ cup brandy
1 cup heavy cream
3 tablespoons salt
    Pepper to taste
1 teaspoon crumbled tarragon leaves
1 teaspoon ground nutmeg
½ pound unsalted fatback, cut into strips
½ pound cooked tongue, cut into strips
1 cup shelled pistachio nuts
2 carrots, 2 celery stalks, and 2 sprigs parsley
    Chicken broth made from bones removed from chicken

Bone chickens or have them boned by the butcher. With a sharp knife remove all the meat, leaving the skins in one piece. Grind chicken with veal and pork several times until mixture is very fine. Combine meat with salt pork, brandy, cream, and seasonings. Lay the chicken skins, outside down, on a board. Spread half of the mixture on each skin. Top with alternate rows of fatback strips and tongue strips. Sprinkle top with pistachios. Shape the skins into a sausagelike roll and sew edges of skin together. Heavily butter 2 pieces of linen or cheesecloth and place a galantine on each cloth. Roll cloth tightly and tie at the ends and in the middle. Make sure the rolls are smooth and even. Place rolls in a large kettle and add carrots, celery, parsley, and enough chicken broth to cover. Cover, bring to a boil, and simmer for 1½ to 2 hours. Cool galantines in the liquid. Remove from broth. Remove galantines from cloth and wrap in another cloth. Weight with a heavy plate for 2 hours. Remove threads and glaze galantines with an aspic made from the stock in which the galantines were cooked. Chill and then cut into thin slices.

■ **To Prepare Aspic**—Strain hot broth. Use 3 cups hot broth to 1 envelope unflavored gelatin. This amount will make enough to cover as necessary. Soak gelatin in cold water for 5 minutes and then dissolve in hot broth. Chill the broth until syrupy and chill the galantines. Place the galantines on a wire rack and cover with a thin coat of gelatin. Cover the top of each roll with cutouts of truffles, slices of stuffed olives, and other thinly sliced garnishes for decoration. Cover with a second coating of gelatin and chill until firm. Makes 10 to 12 servings.

GALANTINE OF VEAL

1 breast of veal or boned shoulder of veal with a pocket
1 pound ground veal
1 pound ground lean pork
½ pound calves' liver, ground
1 onion, grated
2 small garlic cloves, minced
1½ teaspoons dried basil
½ cup chopped parsley
1 cup fine dry bread crumbs
1 teaspoon salt
1 teaspoon pepper
3 eggs
    Brandy
4 thick slices cooked smoked tongue, cut in finger shapes
6 ripe olives, diced
1 bay leaf
½ teaspoon dried thyme
1 parsley sprig
2 cups dry white wine
1 cup water
4 envelopes unflavored gelatin
2 egg shells

If using veal breast, ask the butcher to remove the flat bones. Trim the edges. Mix next 11 ingredients and ¼ cup brandy. Arrange half the mixture in pocket of meat, patting very flat. Arrange the tongue and olives in a pattern on the stuffing. Cover with remaining stuffing and sew edges of veal firmly together. Brown lightly in preheated very hot oven (450°F.) for about 15 minutes. Add remaining ingredients, except last 2. Cover and roast in preheated very slow oven (325°F.) for 1½ to 2 hours, or until tender. Remove meat and flame with ⅓ cup brandy. Add the liquid from the flaming to the pan liquid. Cool juices and skim off excess fat. Cool roast thoroughly, then chill. Measure 4 cups liquid into saucepan. (If necessary, add enough stock or water to make 4 cups.) Sprinkle with gelatin and let stand for 5 minutes. Add egg shells and heat, stirring until gelatin is dissolved. Strain through cheesecloth. Chill until the consistency of raw egg white. Brush on meat, chill and brush again. Chill until firm. Cut in thin slices. Makes 10 to 12 servings.

GALANTINE OF EEL

1 large eel
3 cups soft stale-bread crumbs
    Milk
¼ pound flounder, whiting, or other white-meated fish, chopped fine
3 tablespoons butter or margarine, melted
1 tablespoon each chopped chives, chervil, and parsley
2 eggs
    Salt, pepper, and nutmeg to taste
    Water
1 quart dry white wine
1 teaspoon dried thyme
2 onions, stuck with cloves
2 carrots, diced
2 garlic cloves
1 bay leaf
3 envelopes unflavored gelatin
2 egg shells
    Parsley sprigs

Cut head and tail from eel. Clean eel, and remove skin and bones. Soften bread crumbs in a little milk and squeeze dry. Add fish, butter, chopped herbs, eggs, salt, pepper, and nutmeg. Stuff eel with the mixture, distributing the stuffing evenly. Reshape eel to original appearance. Cook eel head and bones in 4½ cups water for 30 minutes. Strain and season with salt and pepper. There should be about 4 cups. Add wine, thyme, onions, carrots, garlic, and bay leaf. Bring to boil and simmer for 20 minutes. Wrap eel in cheesecloth, cutting fish in several pieces if necessary. Tie ends of cloth and add eel to hot mixture. Poach for 10 minutes, or until done. Remove, unwrap, and put eel under a weight in the refrigerator until thoroughly chilled. Strain liquid and, by boiling, reduce to 4 cups. Cool ½ cup of the liquid and sprinkle with the gelatin. Add to remaining liquid with egg shells and heat, stirring, until gelatin is dissolved. Strain through cheesecloth. Chill until the consistency of raw egg white. Put eel on serving platter and brush with mixture. Chill, then brush again. Chill until firm. Garnish with parsley sprigs. Makes 6 servings.

GALANTINE OF PORK

1 pork shoulder with knuckle and foot (about 5 pounds)
1 cup white wine
2 medium onions, sliced
4 carrots, diced
1 garlic clove, minced
1 tomato (or 1 cup canned)
1 celery stalk
1 leek
2 bay leaves
¼ cup chopped parsley
¼ teaspoon lemon rind
1½ teaspoons salt
6 peppercorns
4 juniper berries, crushed
2 egg whites

Ask the grocer to bone the shoulder, remove rind, tie the meat, and split the knuckle and foot. In kettle combine meat, rind, knuckle, foot and bones, wine, vegetables, and seasonings. Add almost enough water to cover, bring to boil and simmer, covered, for 2 to 2½ hours, or until meat is tender. Remove meat and cool. Continue cooking the remaining ingredients for 1 more hour; strain. Cut meat in bite-size pieces and cut half of rind a little smaller. (Reserve remaining rind for later use.) Pack into 2-quart bowl. The bowl should be three-fourths full. Add about 1 cup stock while meat and stock are still warm. Cover with plate and weight down; chill. Meanwhile, chill remaining stock until fat is solid. Remove fat. Beat 2 egg whites and combine in saucepan with stock. Heat just to boiling and simmer for 5 to 10 minutes. Strain through cheesecloth into bowl or refrigerator dish. Chill until firm. To serve, slice galantine in thin slices. Cube gelatin from remaining stock and serve with the meat. Makes 12 servings.

GAME *by James A. Beard*—Game literally means any wild bird or quadruped judged to be suitable for table use. It should also encompass many of the game birds which have been domesticated for the market. Such birds include quail, pheasant, turkey, partridge, and pigeons, to name only a few.

Because of strict game laws in the United States, there is little real game for sale in retail food stores. It is available only by hunting or through the kindness of the hunter. The deep freeze has been one of the greatest blessings to the game lover for it enables him to have his game and keep it, too.

Formerly, once it was bagged and killed, one had to "hang the game" sometimes to a state of putrefaction or else give a large part of it to friends. With freezing, it may be plucked, and made oven-ready, and packed for future use in quantity.

We in America are quite realistic about game and prepare it in great varieties of ways. Many of the recipes date back to pioneer times when game was a most important part of the diet. In England, it is prepared with little imagination but with great reverence. One always finds birds roasted and served with bread sauce and currant jelly; all furred game is usually braised and served with currant jelly and a brown sauce. The French, on the other hand, use all sorts of imagination when preparing and serving game in a fashion that is very different from we Americans.

Game holds many delights for the good eater. It also provides a magnificent opportunity to match good food and good wine, for the two are one of the happiest of gastronomic marriages.

Caloric Values—All caloric figures are based on 3½ ounces, edible portions.

☐ Beaver, roasted = 248 calories
☐ Duck, raw, flesh only = 138 calories
☐ Muskrat, roasted = 153 calories
☐ Opossum, roasted = 221 calories
☐ Pheasant, raw = 162 calories
☐ Quail, raw = 168 calories
☐ Rabbit, raw = 135 calories
☐ Raccoon (coon), roasted = 255 calories
☐ Turkey, roasted = 190 calories
☐ Venison, raw, lean meat = 126 calories

PREPARING GAME

The flavor of game and game birds depends on the age of the animal and the type of diet it lived on. The more tender cuts come from the back, behind the shoulder. Leg muscles and shoulders are less tender. When preparing game the carcass must be bled, cooled, and dressed as quickly as possible; then properly wrapped and prepared for easy transport home.

■ **To Dress**—Hang the carcass head down. Cut the jugular vein and allow the blood to drain. After the blood is drained, hang carcass head up. Slit the belly and remove the internal organs. Cut around the anus and tie to prevent contents of the intestines from spilling over the meat. Use a sharp thin knife and make clean, straight, firm cuts. Examine the internal organs to make sure the animal is healthy.

Open the carcass so that air will circulate inside and outside of it. Wipe carcass with a clean dry cloth or with dry grass. Do not use water to wash the carcass as this starts bacterial action which causes spoilage. Hang carcass and cover with cloth or canvas to keep off insects, and allow to dry and hang until completely cooled. Skin meat. Meat should hang for 12 to 14 days at just above freezing temperature. Then the meat can be cut, wrapped, and frozen for later use. Aging of meat makes it tender. Storage in freezer is from 6 months to 1 year, depending on the type of game. Young game is usually roasted, broiled, panbroiled, or fried. Rib and loin sections can generally be cooked by the same dry-heat methods. All fat from all game should be trimmed off before cooking.

■ **Older Game**—This is usually drier and tougher and must be larded or barded before cooking. Moist-heat methods of cooking are generally used. To remove gamy taste, meat should be soaked in salt, vinegar, and water for several hours or overnight. To remove the fishy taste found in waterfowl which feed on fish, such as wild goose, soak in milk. Drain and then marinate for several hours or even days, using herbs, spices, juniper berries, etc. Salt is added to game before cooking, and some of the meat may be pounded for extra tenderness. Use 1 teaspoon salt and 1 tablespoon vinegar to every quart of water when soaking meat. When marinating or soaking meat with acids of any kind, use only enamelware or stoneware pots or pans.

■ **Small Game**—This should be bled and eviscerated immediately. Wear rubber gloves when handling rabbits to avoid tularemia. Skin animals after evisceration. Remove all excess fat. Remove musk glands carefully to avoid spillage. These are present in beaver, opossum, raccoon, squirrel, woodchuck, skunk, rabbit, hare, and muskrat. Game should be soaked as for large game and cooked in the same way.

■ **Birds**—If to be used at once, birds should be bled and eviscerated as soon as possible. Remove crop. Rub dry inside and out with a clean dry cloth or dry grass. When removing entrails handle gall bladder carefully to avoid breakage. Pluck feathers and singe pin feathers. Plucking can be done best dry, by pulling out feathers, starting at the base of the neck, and singeing them down with a small flame; or else birds can be plucked by dipping into water heated to 165° to 175°F. until feathers loosen. However, of all methods used, dry plucking is far superior and results in a bird of excellent eating quality. After plucking, remove head and feet. Hang carcasses singly and protect against dirt and insects until cool. Hang for 4 to 8 days. Birds should be soaked and marinated as for game, using the same methods of cooking. Young birds spoil more easily. Undrawn birds keep longer. This must be considered when refrigeration is not available.

■ **To Prepare for Cooking**—Game is apt to be lean, with a tendency to dry out during cooking. It is often advisable to lard large and small game, that is, insert strips of bacon or salt pork with a larding needle (obtainable at fine housewares stores) or by pushing it through with a knitting needle.

Game birds, especially the bigger ones, should be trussed before cooking, like any chicken or turkey. Some game birds, such as pheasant, quail, and grouse should be barded. That is, a thin sheet

or slices of blanched salt pork or bacon should be laid over the bird's breast, and tied to it, or held close by the fowl's trussing. The fat should be removed when the bird, depending on size, is half or three quarters cooked, so that it may be delicately browned.

■ **Cooking Time**—The cooking time of all game animals depends on the size of the animal, its age, and the diet it fed on. In many cases, the only accurate gauge is to test the game for tenderness. Wild duck should be cooked to be on the underdone side; some people like it almost raw at the bone.

■ **Number of Servings**—Game birds come in a variety of sizes. Some are tiny, such as woodcock and snipe; others, such as pheasant and wild turkey, are bigger. Their weights also vary, so that it is impossible to say for certain how many servings your bag will make. This also depends on your appetite and the kind of meal at which these birds are served. Roughly speaking, allow 1 pound game bird for each serving.

For other game, allow ⅓ to ½ pound *boneless* meat, and *at least* ½ pound of meat with some bone in it for each serving.

There is a similarity in cooking methods for all game cookery. A small amount of practice will help to determine the accurate amount of stuffing, sauce, or other ingredients needed for each bird or quantity of meat in a recipe.

The following recipes are from *The Wild Game Wild Fowl Cook Book* by Martin Rywell, Pioneer Press, Harriman, Tennessee. They have not been tested by the *Woman's Day Kitchen,* and are based upon the personal collection of the author, which accounts for the individual way in which they are presented.

BREADED BEAR CHOPS

4 bear chops cut from loin
2 tablespoons melted butter
1 teaspoon onion juice
1 tablespoon fresh lemon juice
1 hard-cooked egg yolk, riced
2 tablespoons chopped parsley
2 tablespoons bread crumbs
  Salt and pepper to taste
2 tablespoons sherry

Marinate chops for 24 hours. Remove. Wipe dry. Mix melted butter, onion juice, and lemon juice. Combine egg yolk, parsley, bread crumbs. Dip chops in butter mixture, then in crumb mixture. Dust each chop with salt and pepper. Cut 4 squares of parchment paper, brush paper with sherry, and wrap each chop in wet paper. Tie with string. Place in baking dish in preheated moderate oven (375° F.) for 50 minutes.

ROAST HAUNCH OF BEAVER, HOTEL LEXINGTON

Haunch of young beaver
¼ cup vinegar
⅛ cup brown sugar
1 teaspoon salt
2 tablespoons all-purpose flour
½ cup melted butter
½ cup tomato ketchup
2 tablespoons Worcestershire
1 garlic clove, mashed
1 onion, chopped fine
1 cup water

Rub haunch with vinegar and brown sugar. Then rub haunch with salt. Dredge with flour. Place on roasting pan rack and brown. Mix melted butter, ketchup, Worcestershire, garlic, onion and 1 cup water. Pour this mixture over meat. Baste frequently. Cook until tender. Allow 35 minutes per pound.

ROAST COON

Clean, draw, and age by keeping in refrigerator for 2 to 3 days. Parboil. Prepare the following stuffing:

3 large sweet potatoes boiled, skinned, and mashed
2 cups day-old bread, crumbled into pieces
1 cup peeled, cored, diced apples
¼ cup sorghum
½ cup seedless raisins
Bunch celery leaves
2 tablespoons pecans, crushed
¼ cup melted margarine
½ teaspoon paprika
1 teaspoon salt

Blend and mix thoroughly all ingredients except last 2. Stuff cavity. Skewer. Sprinkle with paprika, and dust with salt. Place on greased rack. Roast in preheated moderate oven (350°F.) for 40 minutes per pound.

ROAST COOT

Draw. Keep only the liver. Chop off head, legs, tail, pinion. Do not pick feathers since it is too much of a job. Instead, remove the skin. Cut a slit and pull skin off. Wash with cold water. Dust with pepper. Palce in refrigerator overnight. Remove. Wipe off pepper. Parboil for 10 minutes in water to which add ½ teaspoon baking soda. Stuff with slices of peeled and cored raw tart apple. Place in roaster. Add 2 tablespoons butter and ½ onion, minced. Bake in preheated very hot oven (450°F.) until tender. Baste often with butter.

WESTERN DEER STEW

2 pounds deer meat, cut into cubes
1 cup grape juice
1 bay leaf
1 garlic clove, minced
1 teaspoon salt
½ teaspoon pepper
2 tablespoons bacon drippings
1½ cups bouillon
1 celery stalk, diced
8 whole cloves
1 tablespoon parsley
½ teaspoon crumbled dried thyme
Cornstarch

Place meat in deep bowl. Add grape juice, bay leaf, garlic, salt and pepper. Place in refrigerator for several hours. Turn frequently. Drain the meat. Keep the grape juice mixture. Brown the meat thoroughly in bacon drippings. Simmer together for 10 minutes the grape juice mixture, the bouillon and a cheesecloth bag tied in which you place celery, cloves, parsley and thyme. Add meat, cover, and simmer till tender or about 3 hours. Add boiling water if necessary. If desired add vegetables and cook until they are tender. Discard cheesecloth herb bag. Remove meat. Thicken gravy with cornstarch. Use ½ tablespoon cornstarch for each cup of broth. Add a little cold water to cornstarch and make into a smooth paste. Boil up broth and stir cornstarch mixture into broth. Cook, stirring for 2 minutes. Serve with meat.

BRAISED WILD GOOSE

Wild goose
1 apple
Dash of nutmeg
Salt and pepper
Bouquet Sauce

Clean. Singe. In the cavity place apple, peeled, cored and sliced, dash of nutmeg, salt, pepper. Place in covered earthenware pot. Cover tightly. Bake in preheated very hot oven (450°F.) for 25 minutes. Reduce heat to moderate 350°F. Add Bouquet Sauce. Heat for 30 minutes. Cook until tender.

Bouquet Sauce

2 tablespoons butter
1 carrot, cubed
1 onion, minced
¼ cup lean pork, finely diced
1 teaspoon chopped parsley
1 bay leaf
⅛ teaspoon ground thyme
1 whole clove
1 garlic clove, mashed
⅛ teaspoon salt
⅛ teaspoon pepper
½ cup veal stock
1 teaspoon paprika

Sauté in butter for 10 minutes cubed carrot, minced onion, diced pork, parsley, bay leaf, thyme, clove, garlic, salt, pepper. Stir frequently. Pour over this veal stock, paprika. Simmer 10 additional minutes.

MARYLAND MUSKRAT

Muskrat
Boiling salted water
1 slice onion
1 bay leaf
3 cloves
½ teaspoon thyme
3 slices bacon
1 cup boiling water

Skin, draw, and clean carefully. Remove without breaking musk sac and kernels in small of back. Hang in air for several days. Parboil for 2 hours in kettle of boiling salted water to cover to which add onion, bay leaf, cloves, thyme. Remove and drain. Place in Dutch oven. Cover with bacon, add 1 cup boiling water. Cover tightly. Cook slowly.

ROAST OPOSSUM

Skin. Draw. Remove head and tail. Reserve liver. Chop liver finely and set aside. Parboil meat in salted water and change water several times. Rinse well in clear boiling water. Stuff with following mixture:

½ pound chestnuts, roasted and peeled
¼ cup fine bread crumbs
½ cup apple sauce
⅛ teaspoon ground mace
¼ teaspoon cayenne

Fasten with skewers. Place in roaster. Add 1 can (10½ ounces) consommé and finely chopped opossum liver. Roast in preheated moderate oven (350°F.) for 2 hours. Baste frequently. Skim fat from gravy.

RABBIT, GERMAN STYLE

1 young rabbit
3 smoked pork sausages
½ cup claret
½ cup beer
¼ cup cider vinegar
1 cup consommé
1 cup browned bread crumbs
1 teaspoon caraway seeds
½ lemon peel, grated
1 teaspoon brown sugar
Salt and pepper

Cut rabbit into small serving pieces. Clean, rub with damp cloth. Parboil. Drain. Place pork sausages in large skillet. Cover with claret and beer. Simmer for 30 minutes. Remove sausages. Skim off fat. Add rabbit pieces to skillet. Add cider vinegar, consommé, browned bread crumbs, caraway seeds, lemon peel, brown sugar, salt and pepper to taste. Stir. Cover. Simmer gently for 2 hours. Just before it is done return sausages to reheat. Serve.

CANADIAN SNIPE

Snipe
Oil Marinade
All-purpose flour
Salt
Pepper
Bacon drippings
Onion, slices
Mushrooms

Soak snipe in marinade for 2 to 4 hours. Remove from marinade; dry. Roll in flour. Season, salt and pepper to taste. Place in frying pan with bacon drippings. Brown. Reduce heat. Add onion slices and mushrooms. Cook for about 5 minutes. Cover with Oil Marinade. Tightly cover frying pan. Slowly simmer for two hours.

Oil Marinade

1 cup salad oil
½ cup fresh lemon juice
1 tablespoon Worcestershire
½ teaspoon garlic salt
½ teaspoon fresh ground pepper

GAME

BRUNSWICK STEW

3 squirrels
1½ gallons boiling salted water
½ pound bacon, chopped
1 cup green Lima beans
1 cup chopped tomatoes
  Salt, pepper
1½ cups corn, fresh cut with milk
  scrapings
1 tablespoon butter
1 cup diced boiled potatoes
½ cup diced carrots
½ cup diced celery
½ cup grated cabbage

Clean squirrels, draw, soak in cold salted water for 3 hours. Parboil in salted water and then place in boiling water in iron kettle with bacon. Cook until meat loosens from bones. Take out squirrels. Remove bones and return meat to kettle. Add Lima beans and tomatoes. Season. Cook until beans are done. Add corn, butter, potatoes, carrots, celery, cabbage. Stir and cook until ingredients appear as one. Serve hot.

WILD TURKEY IN MOLE SAUCE

1 wild turkey
1 teaspoon lemon juice
1 teaspoon onion juice
  Salt and pepper
  Water
  Mole Sauce

Clean turkey, disjoint, freeze for 48 hours. Rub inside and outside with lemon juice. Dust with salt and pepper. Cover with water, add onion juice, salt and pepper, and simmer, covered for 2 hours, or until tender. Drain turkey and reserve 2 quarts of turkey broth for sauce. Cut turkey into serving pieces and add to Mole Sauce. Simmer until very thick and then serve.

Mole Sauce

5 chiles anchos
2 chiles pasilla
4 chiles mulatos
⅔ cup lard
2 tortillas, shredded
2 raw red tomatoes
2 raw green tomatoes
1 tablespoon pumpkin seeds
1 tablespoon roasted almonds, crushed
1 tablespoon roasted peanuts, crushed
1 tablespoon sesame seeds
1 tablespoon chile seeds
2 cloves
1 teaspoon cinnamon
1 teaspoon pepper
2 garlic cloves, mashed
2 ounces (2 squares) unsweetened
  chocolate
2 quarts turkey broth
1 tablespoon brown sugar

Remove veins from chiles. Fry lightly in ⅓ cup lard. In remaining lard fry the tortillas, red tomatoes, green tomatoes, pumpkin seeds, almonds, peanuts, sesame, chile seeds. Mix and grind all these ingredients together with fried chiles. Add cloves, cinnamon, pepper, garlic and again grind together. Now fry mixture in

Western Deer Stew

Rabbit, German Style

Braised Wild Goose

lard and stir. When it begins to boil, add chocolate, 1 quart of turkey broth and 1 tablespoon brown sugar. Reduce heat and simmer until dry. Add another quart of turkey broth.

WOODCHUCK IN CREAM

Parboil meat until it slips from bones. Remove it and cut into small pieces.

- 2 hard-cooked eggs
- 2 tablespoons butter
- 1 teaspoon prepared mustard
- 1 teaspoon all-purpose flour
- ½ cup heavy cream
- ⅛ teaspoon ground nutmeg

Mash egg yolks and mix with butter, mustard, flour, cream. Add egg whites, coarsely cut. Season with nutmeg. Boil for a minute, stirring constantly. Add meat. Mix well. Simmer for 20 minutes. Serve.

■ Baked, Gypsy Style—Drawn, rolled in clay, baked in ashes.
■ Broiled, Gypsy Style—Split open, skewered back, and broiled.

GAME CAN BE FINE FOOD

by Harry Botsford

Game is probably the most expensive meat that comes into the kitchen of the average home, considering all the incidental costs attached to bagging it. The meat can be the finest that ever graced a table, but much depends on how it is cooked and served. When this is properly and competently done, the result is something you really can cheer about.

Most people, however, don't know how. They figure if they know how to cook chicken, the same recipe is adequate for grouse, pheasant, or quail. If beefsteak is cooked in a certain manner, why isn't that a perfectly good way to prepare venison steak?

My answer would be to take such a person into a certain New York restaurant. If I am permitted to order, there

will presently be placed before us a glorious steak in a seductive sauce. The steak will be meltingly tender, and it will taste divine. Yet it is simply venison steak—a dish you could serve in your home.

Rabbit is high on the casualty list of all game killed. A resident of every state, rabbit is one of the finest game animals that can appear on the family table, as I discovered when I first met *Hasenpfeffer* in the bright and cheerful kitchen of a farmhouse near Bird in Hand, Pennsylvania. My hostess used a formula that is almost ageless, a method that was in vogue when William Penn ruled the territory. The rabbits were cleaned, washed, and all shot was removed; then they were cut into serving pieces. The pieces went into a crock and were covered with equal parts of vinegar and water, to which were added sliced onions, cloves, bay leaves, basil, salt, and pepper. After 2 days in the marinade, the rabbit pieces were removed, drained, and fried crisply in butter until brown, with frequent turnings to get them an even color. About 1 cup of the marinade in which the meat was pickled was gradually added and the meat simmered on the back of the stove until tender—usually about 30 minutes. Just before serving, 1 cup of thick dairy sour cream was stirred into the sauce. The result was *Hasen-pfeffer*, a joy and a treat to eat, especially when served with mashed potatoes, coleslaw, and a plate of biscuits, hot and fresh from the oven.

The French know how to do nice things to game, too, such as *lapin sauté à l'estragon*—and don't let the name throw you. It simply means rabbit sautéed with tarragon. To make this delectable dish, cut the rabbit into serving pieces and dust them very lightly with flour and salt. Melt ½ cup butter in a frying pan; add the rabbit and let it brown quickly. Reduce heat; cover with dry white wine and simmer for about 45 minutes, or until the meat is tender. Add 2½ tablespoons fresh tarragon leaves (or 1 teaspoon dried tarragon that has been moistened in white wine for a few minutes); turn the meat so it will absorb the tarragon flavor—about 5 minutes over low heat. Now remove the meat to a hot platter; add ½ tablespoon meat glaze or beef extract to the frying pan; stir, and add 2 tablespoons dairy sour cream. When the mixture bubbles, pour it over the rabbit, and serve. Teamed with tender young peas, a garden salad with Roquefort-cheese dressing, and toasted English muffins, this is a combination hard to beat.

Rabbit stew is a very pleasant dish to

find on the dinner table of a cold night. Marinate the cut-up rabbit as you would for *Hasenpfeffer*. Then slice 6 small onions; fry in butter with 1 tablespoon all-purpose flour. When they are brown, add the rabbit and cook until the meat is brown. Add several carrots, scraped, washed, and cut into small pieces, a bay leaf, a tiny pinch of curry powder, and one of ground sage; mix and cover with dry red wine. Clamp the lid on the pot; place it over very low heat and cook for about 30 minutes, or until the meat is tender. Remove meat; thicken gravy with a little flour; spice it with some beef-steak sauce and lemon juice; correct the seasoning if necessary. Cover the meat with gravy, and serve.

So scorn not the rabbit. It can be fried, roasted, stewed, or broiled—and if the job is done with a reasonable amount of culinary skill, you will have fine tender, appetizing meat.

Venison figures prominently in any consideration of game, big and small, as each year's deer kill represents tons of prime meat. Much of it spoils; a lot of it is improperly cooked. All of which is a burning shame, for venison can be a most delicious meat. Basically —and this any experienced hunter knows —the deer should be cleaned and hung immediately after the kill. After that, it should be skinned, and the surface of the meat wiped to remove all hairs and every vestige of blood. For tender meat, the deer should be hung in a cool place for a minimum of 2 weeks, then cut into cooking pieces and refrigerated.

In preparing venison, remember to remove all fat, as venison fat is far from palatable. Removal of the fat means that it must be replaced in cooking by larding or by adding butter.

A roast saddle or a haunch of venison can become banquet fare, the saddle being the better of the two. Place the saddle in a big crock and cover with a marinade of ⅔ cheap red cooking wine and ⅓ water; add mustard seeds, bay leaves, a pinch of ground thyme, peppercorns, a crushed garlic clove, and salt. Let the saddle repose in this light pickle for 24 to 30 hours, and turn the meat from time to time. Remove; lard generously with salt pork. Sear in preheated very hot oven (450°F. to 500°F.) for about 15 minutes; then reduce heat to slow (325° F.). Baste frequently. As a rule, 25 minutes per pound is sufficient time in the oven, but more time may be needed if the animal was elderly. When the meat is tender, remove to a hot platter. Add a small glass of red wine to the pan essence and boil until it is reduced about one third. Now add a glass of currant jelly; when it has melted and blended, stir in about 1 cup dairy sour cream to give the gravy a creamy color. Strain the gravy and serve separately. Garnish the venison platter with slices of orange and currant jelly.

With my venison, I serve traditional dishes—baked Hubbard squash, mashed and heavily buttered, served in the shell; small potatoes, dressed in cream; boiled whole beets, lightly glazed; watercress salad in French dressing. Hot biscuits are almost a necessity, and a bottle of good Burgundy helps to give the meal a special festive touch.

Venison steaks or cutlets can be wonderful. They must not be overcooked, however, I brush the steaks, a little less than 1 inch thick, with olive oil and season them with salt and pepper. Then I put them in a very hot broiler, close to the source of heat, to sear on each side; then I brush them again with olive oil and broil them for precisely 2 minutes on each side. I place the meat ceremoniously on a hot platter and spread it with a mixture of butter, chopped parsley, salt, pepper, and fresh lemon juice. Meltingly tender, these steaks can actually be cut with a fork. They make a very nice breakfast item, with hot muffins and plenty of marmalade, or with pancakes.

A camp cook I once knew did a neat trick with venison steaks that I find works equally well in a New York apartment. He rubbed each steak with a crushed garlic clove and seasoned it with salt and pepper. The steaks were basted with melted butter, broiled for about 5 minutes on each side, and the juice was salvaged in the broiler pan. When the steaks were nearly done (he liked them 2 inches thick), the juice was poured into a frying pan, heated, and thickened with a little flour and hot water. In another pan, fresh mushrooms were cooked for a few minutes in butter, then plopped into the bubbling gravy. The seasoning was corrected, and the gravy was poured over the waiting steaks.

Cuts of venison not readily adapted for cookery are a challenge to the person who abhors waste. A friend grinds these pieces with smoked sausage, forms the meat into small, hamburger-size cakes, wraps each in wax paper, and puts them in the freezer. When they emerge, they are thawed, quickly fried or broiled, placed between slices of buttered bread, and spread with mustard or relish. Here is a sandwich filling that has some real substance and a thoroughly good taste— much better than hamburger.

Pheasant is a real problem to the cook, for if it is cooked in the same way as chicken, the meat will be dry and tasteless. Cooked with a little culinary wisdom, however, roast pheasant can be gloriously tender and juicy, and the meat will have a delicate flavor.

First off, the birds should be hung in a cool place for several days after they have been killed and cleaned. A few sturdy gourmets have distinct ideas as to the length of time a bird should be hung. I do not subscribe to some of their theories, since I dislike the cherished high taste of overhung game, as do most Americans, I believe.

The trick of cooking a pheasant or grouse so it comes out tender lies in the dressing. It must be properly compounded. I slice and dice equal portions of onion and crisp cabbage and season them with salt and pepper. Then, using a wooden spoon, I beat and mix them in a wooden salad bowl until each ingredient takes on some of the characteristics of the other. I now blend in 3 lightly beaten eggs and enough evaporated milk to make a very wet, almost liquid dressing. The body cavity of pheasant or grouse is fairly small, and you may end up with too much dressing; but don't let this worry you. Stuff the bird rather compactly and sew up. Rub the outside with flour and butter; place strips of fat bacon on the breast and roast in a covered baking dish in preheated slow oven (325° F.) for 45 minutes to 1 hour. When the bird is nearly done, place the balance of the dressing in the baking dish alongside the bird; baste frequently with the essence. Remove the cover and the bacon strips for the final 15 minutes of cooking.

The wet dressing does the trick; when it becomes hot, the steam it generates permeates the flesh of the bird, tenderizing it and giving it essential moisture. The bird should arrive at the table with a crisp, crackly exterior and interior tender as a dream. Serve a generous dollop of dressing with each portion. With roast pheasant or grouse, I serve small baked yams, split open, buttered lavishly, with a freckle of paprika for color; green beans in a thin mustard sauce; plenty of authentic chutney; hot corn muffins; and a green salad.

Pheasant cooked in a heavy casserole becomes a superlative dish. To make it, use properly hung birds, cleaned and cut into serving portions. Coat the pieces with all-purpose flour, ground sage, salt, pepper, and a pinch of curry powder. Brown in bacon fat and butter; quickly transfer to a hot casserole, and top with links of smoked sausage. Melt ½ cup butter in a separate pan; thicken with 6 tablespoons all-purpose flour and 4 cups milk; bring to a slow boil, stirring vigorously. Pour over the pheasant and sausage, and then bake in preheated very slow oven (225°F. to 275°F.) for 2 hours. The result is rich, tender, and tasty. With this dish I serve glazed carrots; a salad of sliced cucumbers, radishes, and onion rings in sour-cream dressing; and toasted English muffins. Scads of strong coffee, or if it's a company meal bottles of ale or beer, are perfect companions.

Duck—Many hunters want their ducks roasted briefly, and with this I disagree. I like my ducks cooked, and I suspect you also like them that way.

If it's mallard, pluck and clean the bird; stuff with a sliced onion and a quartered lemon. Refrigerate overnight; then remove and discard the stuffing; it has fulfilled its purpose—to absorb any fishy flavor that may have been in the bird. Wipe interior with a clean cloth dipped into vinegar. Stuff with sauerkraut that has been marinated in red wine. Sew up the bird; chop off wing tips; truss; place on a trivet in an uncovered baking pan in preheated slow oven (325°F.). Since your mallard may be old, roast until tender is the best rule—but do not overcook. Serve with a tart jelly, a salad of grapefruit and oranges in French dressing, a green vegetable, wild rice cooked in consommé and lightly seasoned.

Roast duck with beans is a dish fit for a king. Cut the duck into serving por-

tions; rub lightly with seasoned olive oil, and broil under high heat for 15 minutes. The beans are pea beans; they must be soaked overnight in cold water, then cooked in slightly salted water with a bouquet of parsley, thyme, and a bay leaf, tied together. When the beans are almost soft, drain, and discard the bouquet. Rub the inside of a deep casserole with a garlic clove; line the bottom with strips of fat bacon. Now come a thick layer of beans, then the pieces of duck, and a final layer of beans. Moisten with a cup of stock or water; clamp the lid on the casserole and bake for 1 to 1½ hours, depending on the age of the duck, in preheated slow oven (about 300°F.). Lift the lid only when the casserole reaches the table; a small cloud of appetizing steam will arise. Serve generously with spicy coleslaw, toasted chunks of French bread, and bottles of cold beer or ale. This is a sturdy, masculine dish, but I have yet to see a frail woman falter when she asked for a second helping. An ideal meal to serve at an informal gathering or outdoors, close to the barbecue grill.

Quail and woodcock are small, but their flesh has long been a favorite of gourmets the world over. Woodcock meat is wholly dark, but in both birds the breasts represent about 90 per cent of the meat.

These birds are at their best when broiled and there isn't much of a trick to it. Rub the birds with lightly seasoned olive or salad oil; broil quickly—about 8 minutes—basting with the oil. Serve 1 bird to a person. Place the bird on a slice of buttered toast; garnish with a parsley sprig and a modest slice of lemon—that's all. These are exquisite trifles, endowed with a taste that is delicate and memorably good. With these serve a green vegetable, a small baked potato or small boiled potatoes in parsley butter, a green salad with Roquefort-cheese dressing, and fruit for dessert.

Quail and woodcock when steamed are also an epicure's dish. Always have them perfectly cleaned. For 4 birds, rub lightly with salt and place in a Dutch oven. Pour over them 1 cup of equal parts boiling water and butter; let them steam for 30 minutes. Add 2 tablespoons meat sauce, 1 cup chopped fresh mushrooms, and ½ cup sherry; dust lightly with flour and steam until tender. Sprinkle lightly with paprika, and serve. With these I am partial to a plate of crusty scones, fresh from the oven, and beet salad in sour cream, with a sprinkle of chopped chives.

Leftovers have attained new significance in cookery these days. The trick is to

prepare them in such a way that they won't taste like leftovers. This wild-fowl salad is one solution. In it you can use cold grouse, pheasant, quail, duck, or woodcock. Cut the meat into pieces about the size of the end of your finger; stop at 2 cups. Add ½ cup chopped roasted walnut meats; ½ cup finely diced celery; ¼ onion, minced; a pinch of ground oregano; and a modest dusting of ground nutmeg. Toss lightly in a tart boiled dressing. Serve at once on a platter of crisp lettuce leaves; sprinkle with paprika; garnish with slices of hard-cooked eggs. Do not refrigerate. An ideal luncheon dish, this salad is perfect with steamed brown bread. Much superior, too, to the conventional chicken salad.

Soup—Game shines in soups, gives a delicate, entrancing flavor. Squirrel soup, for example. Clean 4 squirrels; place them in a gallon of water with 1 tablespoon salt, a pinch each of dried thyme and oregano, and 1 bay leaf. Cover the pot, and simmer until the meat falls from the bones. Remove all bones; add 3 potatoes, finely diced; 3 carrots, diced; 2 onions, sliced; 1 small turnip. Cook until vegetables are tender. Thicken soup with butter and flour mixed to a paste. Correct seasoning by adding a few drops of hot pepper sauce, and salt and pepper to taste. Bring to a sharp boil, and serve instantly with croutons.

GARLIC (Allium sativum)—The garlic, a hardy bulbous plant, is a member of the lily family, which also includes leeks, chives, onions, and shallots. Like the onion, the edible bulb of the plant grows beneath the ground. This compound bulb is made up of small sections or bulblets called "cloves" which are encased in thin papery envelopes. The flat grayish-green tapered leaves reach a height of one foot, and the scape, a leafless flowering stem that rises from the ground, can be as tall as three feet. Garlic flowers

are a tiny mass of white blooms.

Garlic is widely cultivated in both temperate and hot climates. The bulbs are harvested when their tops are beginning to dry out. The bulbs are dried for a short time and stored in a cool, well-ventilated place. Sometimes the bulbs are plaited by the tops into garlands, or tied in bunches.

Garlic has been cultivated for thousands of years. A king of ancient Babylon grew it in his garden as early as 721 B.C. and the Egyptian slaves who built the Great Pyramid in the 5th century B.C. lived on garlic and onions. Virgil, the Latin poet, recommended that reapers eat garlic to help them stand up under their strenuous work in the sun.

From the days of antiquity, garlic has been used for medicinal purposes. As a cure for toothache, a tiny piece of it was placed in the cavity. It was also believed that garlic would cure consumption, "shrew-mouse" bites, and poisoned-arrow wounds. There is a collection of 15th-century prescriptions by medieval pharmacists which advocate garlic as a cure for dog bites and the stings of venomous worms. And a late 18th-century French writer, Bernardin de Saint Pierre, said: "Garlic, the smell of which is so dreaded by our little mistresses, is perhaps the most powerful remedy in existence against the vapours and nervous maladies to which they are subject."

Garlic has also proved useful in repelling evil. Demons, witches, and especially vampires are said to vanish at garlic seeds on their fields to protect their young plants. Birds would eat the garlic seeds and fall asleep. They could then be trapped easily by the farmer.

Garlic has often been considered a love potion; one of the characters in Boccaccio's *Decameron* sent his lady love garlic from his own garden to win her favors—which he did.

Garlic has also proved useful in repelling evil. Demons, witches, and especially vampires are said to vanish at the sight of it. The belief in this is so strong that to this day, in many parts of the world including the United States, people wear garlic around their necks or keep it in their houses to ward off the evil eye and other spells.

Nowadays garlic is one of the most important seasonings, and can be used in practically all nonsweet dishes according to taste. It has a powerful flavor and odor. These tend to diminsh in cooking; a little garlic, crushed into salads, has a more intense smell and taste than considerably more garlic, cooked.

To use garlic break off a clove from the bulb and remove the outer skin. Chop or mince the clove or put through a garlic press before adding to food. Use to flavor stews, pot and cream cheese, omelettes, pickles, sauces, dressings, vinegars, sausages. Put slivers of garlic in roast beef, lamb, or pork before cooking. Halve a clove to rub inside a salad bowl or on bread. Use it, sparingly, as a seasoning and in marinating mixtures.

Availability—Sold loose, in strings, or packaged in pairs in cellophane boxes. Also available in some food stores in small cellophane bags containing a few cloves.

Garlic is also available in dried powdered form and in flakes. It is often called instant garlic. Since this kind of garlic is dehydrated, it needs moisture to restore its full flavor. When used for sauces, stews, or other dishes cooked with a liquid, this liquid will be sufficient to reconstitute the garlic. When used in salads, or in dishes that are dry, soak the dehydrated garlic in a little water before using.

Garlic salt is a mixture of garlic powder and table salt with an anticaking agent added. The color is white and the flavor mildly salty and garlicky.

Purchasing Guide—Look for firm, plump bulbs with clean, dry, unbroken skins. A broken skin or softness may be caused by sprouting. A dirty bulb may conceal defects; a shriveled bulb, the presence of dry rot. Purchase in small amounts.

Storage—Keep away from other foods because of its strong odor. Put in a cool, dry place in a small wire or plastic open basket. Do not refrigerate.

Caloric Value

□ 1 garlic bulb = 1 calorie

GARLIC SEASONING
Mix 2 garlic cloves, peeled and pressed, ½ cup salt, 1½ teaspoons each of black pepper and ground ginger. Let stand for several days in covered jar before using on meats or vegetables.

GARLIC BUTTER
Cream ½ cup butter. Crush 1 or more garlic cloves (to taste), and blend into butter. Spread on crusty Italian bread or use on snails, boiled fish, or vegetables. Makes ½ cup.

PESTO ALLA GENOVESE
(Genoese Garlic Sauce)
- 4 to 6 garlic cloves, minced
- ⅓ cup fresh basil leaves, tightly packed
- ¼ cup chopped fresh parsley
- ¾ cup grated Parmesan cheese
- 1 tablespoon butter, melted
- ½ cup olive oil
- ¼ cup boiling water

Combine all ingredients in a bowl. Crush

and blend with wooden spoon until the consistency of thin paste. Or place in mortar and crush with pestle. Use for pasta, boiled fish, meats, and vegetables. Makes about 1 cup sauce or enough for 4 servings of pasta.

Note: The basil must be fresh or the sauce won't taste right. The sauce may be stored in a covered jar in the refrigerator for 10 days. Blend before using.

ITALIAN GARLIC SOUP
- 5 garlic cloves, peeled and pressed
- 1 tablespoon olive oil
- 2 quarts rich chicken bouillon
  Salt and pepper
  Pinch each of ground thyme and rosemary
- ½ cup light cream
- 3 egg yolks, beaten
  Toast
- ¼ cup grated Parmesan cheese

Sauté garlic in oil until light brown. Heat the bouillon and add the garlic and seasonings to it. Simmer for 1 hour; strain and return to heat. Add cream to egg yolks, then add a little of the hot liquid; then add eggs to soup. Remove soup from heat after 5 minutes, and pour over toast in tureen. Sprinkle with grated cheese. Makes about 2 quarts.

GARLIC-GINGER SHRIMPS
Split and clean jumbo shrimps. Marinate for 3 to 4 hours, turning occasionally, in equal parts of sherry or sake, soy sauce, and peanut or sesame oil, to which 1 pressed garlic clove and 1 tablespoon grated fresh or crystallized gingerroot have been added. Broil in range or over charcoal for 4 minutes on each side.

SHRIMP SAUTÉ
Shell and devein desired number of shrimps. For each pound, melt ½ cup butter or margarine; add 1 crushed garlic clove and shrimps. Cook quickly until pink; add ¼ cup brandy, flame, season, and serve at once on toast. Add ½ cup heavy cream if you wish more sauce. Prepare 1 pound shrimps for 4 servings.

BEEF ALLA ITALIANA
- 1 garlic clove, minced
- 2 tablespoons olive oil
  About 2 cups (one 1-pound can) tomatoes
- 1 can (8 ounces) tomato sauce
- ¼ teaspoon pepper
- ¾ teaspoon salt
- ½ teaspoon dried oregano
- 2 cups diced cooked beef
  Chopped parsley
  Hot cooked spaghetti or noodles

Cook garlic in oil until lightly browned. Add tomatoes, tomato sauce, pepper, salt, and oregano. Cook for 25 minutes. Add beef. Cook over low heat for about 15 minutes. Sprinkle with chopped parsley. Serve with spaghetti. Makes 4 servings.

CHICKEN WITH OLIVE AND CAPER SAUCE
- 1 frying chicken (about 2½ pounds), cut up
- ¼ cup all-purpose flour
- 1 teaspoon salt
- ¼ teaspoon pepper
- 3 tablespoons butter or margarine
- 2 garlic cloves, minced
- ½ cup sliced stuffed green olives
- 2 tablespoons capers
- 1 tablespoon caper liquid
- 2 tablespoons water
- ¼ cup chopped parsley

Roll chicken in flour seasoned with salt and pepper. Brown in butter. Cover and cook slowly for 40 minutes. Add remaining ingredients; heat. Makes 4 servings.

ALGERIAN-STYLE EGGS
- 1½ cups drained canned tomatoes
- 2 garlic cloves, crushed
- 1 green pepper, sliced
- 2 tablespoons butter
- 6 eggs
- 1 teaspoon salt
  Dash of pepper

Heat tomatoes with garlic. Put in buttered 8-inch pie pan. Cook green pepper in butter until tender. Put on top of tomatoes. Beat eggs with salt and pepper until well mixed. Pour over tomatoes. Bake in preheated moderate oven (350° F.) for 25 minutes, or until set. Makes 4 servings.

BROCCOLI, ITALIAN STYLE
- 2 tablespoons cooking oil
- 1 garlic clove, halved
  Dash of cayenne
- 1 bunch of broccoli, cooked

Heat oil, garlic, and cayenne for 5 minutes; remove garlic, and pour oil over hot broccoli. Makes 3 or 4 servings.

SUPPER SALAD
- ½ pound chicken livers, diced
- 2 tablespoons butter
  Salt
- 1 garlic clove
- 4 cups broken salad greens
- 1 red onion, thinly sliced
- 3 hard-cooked eggs, cubed
- ½ cup crumbled blue cheese
- ½ cup French dressing

Cook chicken livers in the butter until lightly browned. Sprinkle lightly with salt; cool. Rub salad bowl with cut garlic clove. Mix all ingredients except garlic; toss. Makes 4 to 6 servings.

ITALIAN GARLIC BREAD
Cut a loaf of Italian or French bread into thin, diagonal slices, *almost* through to bottom crust, but so that loaf still holds together. Spread cut surfaces with Garlic Butter (recipe at left). Wrap in aluminum foil, leaving foil open partially at one end. Bake in preheated moderate oven (375°F.) for 15 to 20 minutes. Serve hot.

GARNISH

GARNISH—The word is used to describe an ornament, which should be edible, added to a finished dish for the purpose of enhancing its appearance and appeal. Garnishing is an art practiced all over the world, for the appeal of food depends, to a great extent, upon its presentation. For this reason, the finest chefs must be masters in the skills of garnishing. The homemaker and hostess, too, should stress the appearance of the dishes she serves to her family and guests.

GENERAL RULES

■ Don't overlook the beauty of the food itself. When carefully selected and well prepared, food is attractive by virtue of its natural goodness and freshness and its verying textures, colors, and aromas. Just a row of thinly cut, beautifully roasted meat slices, delicately crusted, covered with a silky shimmer of sauce, and garnished with mushroom slices and fresh perky bunches of watercress, is beautiful to look at. Good food, good design involving color, form, and pleasing combinations all add up to successful garnishing.

■ Be sure the garnishes are in keeping with the food itself, and that the food is arranged on platters or in dishes suitable to it.

■ Arrange the food attractively. making sure the color and texture combinations are pleasing to the eye and the palate. Neat geometric arrangements, as well as casual tumbled arrangements, are all delightful if the combinations are fresh, bright, and appetizing.

NONSWEET GARNISHES

■ **Raw Garnishes**—These include the vegetable garnishes: carrot curls, slices, shreds and sticks and whole baby carrots; celery curls and sticks; chopped chives; cucumber slices, strips, and twists; dill sprigs; green pepper dices and rings; crisp greens; mint sprigs and chopped mint; mushrooms, whole and quartered, crowns and slices; onion rings; parsley sprigs and chopped parsley; radish curls, roses, and slices; scallions; tomato roses, slices, and wedges; watercress sprigs.

Other garnishes include thin slices of cheese and cottage cheese balls.

■ **Cooked Garnishes**—These include as-

paragus tips; gelatin aspics; crisp bacon, crumbled or in strips; pickled beets; whole baby carrots; croutons; dumplings; hard-cooked eggs, sieved, sliced, and whole; frankfurter slices; liver balls; meatballs; mushrooms; noodles and small pasta; mashed potatoes; molded rice; sauces and dressings such as tartare, hollandaise, and mayonnaise; toast points; broiled tomatoes.

■ **Prepared Garnishes**—Some of these you can make yourself, others are available in jars and cans. They include: almonds slivered and toasted; anchovies; artichoke bottoms and pickled artichoke hearts; butter balls and curls and such butters as anchovy or nut butter; capers; caviar; chutney; coleslaw; horseradish;

green, black, and pimiento-stuffed olives, sliced and whole; paprika; pickled mushrooms; pickled onions; pickles and relishes; pimiento slices and strips; potato chips; truffles.

FRESH FRUIT GARNISHES

Among the fruit garnishes are: apple cups, slices, and wedges; avocado slices; banana slices; cherry clusters; grape clusters; grapefruit halves and sections; lemon, lime, and orange baskets, sections, slices, twists, and wedges, and curled peel; melon balls, halves, and slices; nuts; pineapple cups and slices; raspberries; strawberries.

SWEET GARNISHES

These include angelica; sautéed bananas; candies, marshmallows, and mints; can-

died and preserved fruits and nuts; black, sour, and maraschino cherries; chocolate, chopped and shaved or cut into curls; cranberry sauce; dates; crushed and frozen fruits and spiced fruits such as apples, peaches, and pears; chopped crystallized gingerroot; scoops of ice cream and sherbet; jams and jellies, kumquats; prunes, raisins; sundae syrups; whipped cream.

DECORATIVE VEGETABLE GARNISHES
Beets and Turnips

■ **Cups**—Cook medium-size beets or turnips and peel. With a sharp knife trim out the center of the beet leaving a ½-inch shell. Fill as desired.

■ **Roses**—For beets: Parboil large beets for 10 minutes, or until skins slip off.

Cool. With sharp knife cut petal-shape scallops around lower end of beet; turn point of knife down and in. Cut around beet, removing ¼ inch from sides above petals. Start from a point ¼ inch above and midway between 2 petals of first row, cut down and in until knife touches tops of first row of petals. Continue around to form second row of petals. Cut around beet, removing ¼ inch from sides above second row of petals, as in first row of petals. Continue making rows of petals until rose is complete, making 4 or 5 rows of petals depending on size of beet.

For turnips: Pour boiling water over white turnips and let stand for 5 minutes. Peel and follow procedure for beets. To color roses, dip cut turnips into beet liquid or food coloring. Wrap roses and refrigerate until serving time.

Carrots

■ **Balls**—Cut small balls of cooked carrot with a melon baller. Use remainder of carrot for mashing.

■ **Cups**—Cut large carrots into 1½-inch pieces. Cook until tender, and carefully scoop out pulp and fill with sauce or vegetables.

■ **Curls**—Use large fat carrots to make these. They should be fresh and at room temperature. Peel carrot; then cut off a lengthwise slice that is ¼ to ½ inch thick at the top. This gives a broad flat surface with a generous showing of lighter-colored core. Using a vegetable peeler, cut thin strips from the flat surface, starting at the tip end. Strips sometimes curl themselves; if not, curl around finger and fasten with a toothpick. Drop into cold water and refrigerate for several hours, or put in bowl of ice water for 1 hour before serving.

■ **Flowers**—Cut scraped raw carrots into thin crosswise slices. Cut V-shape notches into the edge of the slice. Crisp in ice water.

■ **Lattice**—Cut lattice slices of raw carrot with a fluting knife. Cut the carrot and then turn it halfway round and make a second cut. Cut thinly to achieve an open lattice. Simmer gently and handle carefully. Can be used raw as well.

Celery

■ **Curls**—Cut celery into ½-inch lengths. With a sharp knife cut one end of the piece of celery into thin slices. Place in ice water to crisp and curl. Scallions may be cut in the same way.

■ **Roses**—Break celery stalks apart; wash and trim leaves. Fill celery stalks with softened cream cheese or an herb blend of cheeses. Put filled celery stalks back together. Tie with string and chill. Cut celery crosswise into ½-inch slices and serve.

Cucumbers

■ **Boats**—Cut a peeled or unpeeled cucumber into halves length wise. Scoop out pulp leaving a ½-inch thick shell to be filled with any mixture desired.

■ **Chains**—Cut thin slices of unpeeled cucumber. Cut a small round out of the center to form a ring. Cut each ring from one outside edge to the center and link cucumber slices together to form a chain.

■ **Flowers**—Cut off ends of an unpeeled cucumber. Cut cucumber into 2-inch pieces. On each piece scoop out pulp, then cut peel partially to form 5 petals. Place in ice water to curl peel into petals. Fill center with a carrot slice or shredded carrots.

■ **Fluted Slices**—Run the tines of a fork down the length of the cucumber so that the entire surface is scored. Cut into thin slices and crisp in ice water. This can be done with peeled and unpeeled cucumbers.

■ **Twists**—Cut thin slices of unpeeled cucumber. Cut each slice from one outside edge to the center. Pull the cut pieces in opposite directions to form an S-shape twist. Hold in place with a toothpick and chill in ice water.

Onions

■ **Chrysanthemums**—Use a medium-size red onion; peel and cut onion into thin slivers from the pointed end down, leaving the bottom attached. Place in ice water to crisp and flare the petals.

■ **Cups**—Cook whole large peeled onions until tender but still firm. Scoop out center pulp leaving a ½-inch shell. Fill as desired.

■ **Rings**—Peel onion and cut into thin slices. Separate into rings and use raw or dip into batter and deep fry.

Potatoes

■ **Balls**—Cut balls of raw peeled potato and simmer carefully in salted water until tender.

■ **Baskets**—Baskets can vary in size from very small to large. Shred raw potatoes and wash well in cold water. Place shreds in a layer in a sieve. Press another sieve into the first sieve. Lower into deep fat or oil and fry until crisp. Remove from oil and carefully pull out basket. Drain on absorbent paper. Fill as desired.

■ **Lattice**—See Carrot Lattice; potatoes are usually deep fried.

■ **Mashed**—Use a large star-tipped pastry bag filled with sweet or white potatoes to decorate planked dishes, to shape Duchess potatoes, and to fill orange cups. Potatoes can be scooped out of their shells after baking, mixed with seasonings, and restuffed.

■ **Sticks**—Cut peeled potatoes into long thin matchstick pieces and deep fry until brown and crisp.

Radishes

■ **Crisscross**—Make parallel cuts from tip to stem of fat squat radish. Give radish a quarter turn, make second set of cuts. Put in bowl of ice and water.

■ **Doublecut**—Cut circles from tip and 4 sides of radish. Make parallel cuts on sides to form 4 petals. Put in a bowl of ice water.

■ **Fan**—Make thin parallel cuts, not quite to stem end, on long oval radish. Let stand for about 30 minutes at room temperature. Spread fanlike. Crisp in ice water before serving.

■ **Rose**—Use firm, oval-shape radishes of a good size. Using a sharp knife with a thin point, thinly slice the outer red skin into petals. Place in ice water and the petals will fan out during chilling. The white inside part of the radish may be cut flat and a coil of pimiento strips used for the inside of the rose.

■ **Tulip**—Make cuts through peel only from tip to stem around radish. Cut peeling back to make petals. Put in bowl of ice and water.

Tomatoes

■ **Cups**—Make zigzag diagonal ½-inch cuts into the side of the tomato all the way around the center of the tomato. Pull apart. May be used as is or scooped out and filled. Cut off a thin slice from top and scoop out pulp for a larger and deeper tomato cup. It may be necessary to remove a thin slice from the bottom to keep tomato steady on the plate, or cut tomato, peeled or unpeeled, into wedges, leaving them jointed at the bottom. Spread open and fill as desired.

■ **Rose**—Cut the peel from a large tomato in one long strip, having the strip about 1-inch wide. Coil the strip into a tight roll, keeping the bottom part a little tighter than the top part. Use parsley sprigs or other green leaves to decorate rose.

To make a Tomato Cheese Rose, whip cream cheese. Wash and dry small tomatoes. Fill a teaspoon with the cream cheese and level it off with a knife. To form cheese petals, hold the filled teaspoon against the side of the tomato. Press the cheese onto the tomato with a downward stroke of the spoon. Place sieved egg yolk in the center of the flower. Chill before serving. Petals can be shaped around the tomato, repeating the process for a second and third tier of petals.

Other Vegetable Garnishes

■ **Bouquet**—Cut off one third of a grapefruit. From remaining piece scoop out about half of center. Tie parsley together to make a tight bouquet to fit into grapefruit. Stick strong toothpicks into bottoms of beet and turnip roses and radish flowers and arrange on parsley. Add other garnishes.

■ **Daisies**—With sharp knife tip, cut out v-shape sections from edge of a slice of carrot, white turnip, or cucumber. Put a small round of contrasting color in center; use carrot on white, ripe olive or black grape on color.

■ **Pickle Fans**—Thinly slice medium-size sweet pickle lengthwise to within ¾ inch of end. Spread to form fan.

■ **Sliced Vegetables**—Thinly slice 1-inch pieces of carrot, cucumber, or whole radishes to within ⅛ inch of opposite

side. Put in ice water for several hours to open.

DECORATIVE FRUIT GARNISHES
Lemons and Limes

Note: In addition to garnishes listed below, any orange garnish can be used for lemons and limes.

■ **Baskets**—Slice off top of fruit. Place tip of knife almost in center of cut section of fruit. Slice all the way around, gradually thickening slice to ¼ inch and continue halfway around again, gradually thinning slice. Lift the 2 cut edges to rest against each other. Garnish with mint.

■ **Cross**—Remove 4 vertical wedges from a whole fruit. Then cut fruit into thick

slices; garnish with capers.

■ **Curls**—Cut fruit into thin slices. Remove pulp from half of each slice, then curl the free strip of rind.

■ **Scallops**—Cut fruit into halves crosswise. Scallop edges with a sharp paring knife and garnish with capers.

■ **Twists**—Use a thick slice of fruit. Cut once from outer edge to center; twist cut edges.

■ **Twists of Peel**—Cut a long slice of peel by paring around fruit. Twist gently so as not to break peel.

■ **Wedges**—Cut fruit into lengthwise wedges. Sprinkle the sides of the wedges with chopped parsley.

Carrot Curls   **Turnip Roses**   **Doublecut, Fan, and Rose Radishes**

Fruit and vegetable garnishes: simply sliced or cunningly shaped

Melons

■ **Balls**—Cut peeled melon into balls with a melon-ball cutter.

■ **Halves, Scalloped**—Prepare as you prepare scalloped tomato halves.

■ **Slices**—Cut melon into 1-inch thick slices crosswise. Remove seeds and slice peel from melon. Fill center with sherbet or berries.

Oranges

Note: Use seedless oranges when making orange garnishes.

■ **Baskets**—Mark the outline of the basket on the orange peel, making a handle about ⅓ inch thick. Cut away the two upper sections forming the handle and the bottom of the basket, taking care not to cut through the handle. The edge of the basket may be left plain or scalloped. Grapefruit can be prepared in the same way.

■ **Cups**—See Tomato Cups. Grapefruit can be prepared in the same way.

■ **Daisies**—Cut thin slices of unpeeled orange. With a sharp knife cut v-shape sections from the orange rind, notching the skin all the way around the slice.

■ **Flowers**—Cut thin slices of unpeeled orange. With a sharp knife cut into the slice cutting out v-shape sections of peel and fruit; repeat around slice, forming longer petals than when making daisies.

■ **Roses**—See Tomato Roses; cut peel of orange in one strip and shape it into a rose. Grapefruit can be prepared in the same way.

■ **Twists**—Cut ¼-inch slices of orange with the peel; see Cucumber Twists.

Pineapple

■ **Halves**—Cut pineapple into halves lengthwise, including the leafy top. With a sharp knife cut out pulp, leaving a shell ½ inch thick. Cube pulp and and fill shell with pulp and other fruits, as desired.

■ **Wedges**—Cut pineapple into 8 to 10 wedges lengthwise including the leafy top. With a sharp knife cut fruit away from outer skin, leaving the fruit within the skin. Cut fruit into ½-inch slices crosswise for easier eating.

Other Fruit Garnishes

■ **Apple Cups**—Cut off top quarter of unpeeled apple. Carefully, with a sharp knife, scoop out pulp and core, leaving a shell about ½-inch thick. Brush inside of apple with lemon juice to prevent darkening.

■ **Grapes, Frosted**—Cut grapes into tiny bunches. Wash and dry well. Beat egg whites until slightly foamy. Brush grapes lightly with egg whites, making sure all grapes are well coated. Roll grapes in granulated sugar. Let dry in a cool dry place. Do not store in the refrigerator.

OTHER DECORATIVE GARNISHES

■ **Almonds, Blanched**—Poor boiling water over nuts and let stand for a few minutes. Rub skins off the nuts. Dry well. May be toasted or used plain. Almonds may be halved.

■ **Almond Slivers**—After blanching almonds, and while they are still moist, cut them with a sharp knife into thin lengthwise slivers.

■ **Butter Curls**—Have sticks of butter or margarine as cold as possible. Use a chilled butter curler. Run butter curler down the length of a stick of butter, cutting a thin slice which will curl as it is cut. Drop into ice water or place on top of crushed ice.

■ **Butter, Pressed**—Use a chilled wooden butter mold which has been dipped into ice water. Knead butter under ice water or running cold water until it is waxy. Press small amounts firmly into wet wooden mold. Push butter out with the plunger. Drop molds into ice water until ready to serve.

■ **Truffles**—Drain; cut into thin slices. Use very tiny cutters to cut desired designs. Place cutouts on food in arrangements as desired.

GARNISHING ASPICS

Make Aspic for Garnishing (recipe at right) and use the cooled mixture to glaze and coat a chilled dry food. Chill until firm. It may be necessary to coat food 3 to 4 times to give a thick enough coating. Before coating the food for the last time, the vegetable garnishes, cut as thinly as possible, should be placed on the food. Give the food a final coating and chill until firm.

STABILIZED MAYONNAISE

2 teaspoons unflavored gelatin
2 tablespoons water
1 cup mayonnaise

Add gelatin to water and let soak for 5 minutes. Place gelatin over low heat and stir until dissolved. Add dissolved gelatin to mayonnaise. Spoon mixture over foods to coat. It may be necessary to give foods 2 to 3 coatings. Mixture may be pressed through a pastry bag. Chill after decorating.

Note: May be used for coating chilled completely dry foods and may be piped through a pastry tube for garnishes. Work quickly since this type of mayonnaise will set at room temperature.

STABILIZED WHIPPED CREAM

1 teaspoon unflavored gelatin
2 tablespoons water
2 cups heavy cream

Soften gelatin in the water. Dissolve over hot water or very low heat. Whip cream until it just begins to thicken. Beat in gelatin and whip until cream is stiff. Fill pastry bag and garnish as desired. Chill after garnishing.

ASPIC FOR GARNISHING

2 cans condensed consommé
2 tablespoons sherry or Madeira
1 envelope unflavored gelatin
¼ cup cold water

Combine consommé and wine and boil for 5 minutes. Soften gelatin in the cold water and stir into consommé mixture. Cool; then chill until consistency of raw egg white. Use for brushing on foods. Or chill until firm in a shallow dish. Cut aspic in shapes, chop or rice. Makes about 2½ cups.

GASTRONOME, GASTRONOMY—

These culinary terms derive from the Greek words *gaster* and *nomos*, "belly" and "law." Gastronomy means the art of good food and a gastronome is a person who recognizes good food and takes great pleasure in it.

GÂTEAU—

The literal translation of this French word is "cake," and the French use it as casually as we use the word cake, there being *grands gâteaux* and *petits gâteaux,* that is, big and little cakes, which can be as plain or as fancy as desired.

In American culinary language, a *gâteau* is a splendid creation destined to add glamour to a party; in no way does it resemble a casual, family-type cake. A *gâteau* can be served as a dinner party dessert, or at tea parties, coffee parties, receptions; whenever the occasion demands a beautiful, elegant cake.

Heirloom Gâteaux
•••
by Paula Peck

As little as fifty years ago, many kitchen appliances which we take for granted today were unheard of. Life proceeded at a far easier pace than it does now, and even without mixers, blenders, toasters, and vacuum cleaners, women had time to cook and bake for their families. In most homes in France, Switzerland, Austria, and other countries renowned for their culinary arts, the lady of the house had at least one recipe for an extra-rich, delicate *gâteau* which was truly her *spécialité*. These confections were reserved for occasions: birthdays and anniversaries. Even fifty years ago they would have been too expensive and time-consuming to make for everyday use.

Not only were electric appliances unknown; many ingredients which today are packaged and sold in food stores had to be prepared in the kitchen. Nuts were always shelled and ground or sliced at home; preserves had to be made; cake flour had to be blended. Baking powder was an almost unheard-of ingredient. Cakes were leavened with the air beaten into them or, on occasion, with yeast.

With the passage of time, many special-occasion recipes have been lost. The few that are still known by some women are considered to be heirlooms.

Today, many European confections can be made without the enormous expenditure of time formerly necessary. Many of us own electric mixers. For these cakes, a mixer is a necessity unless you want to beat by hand for forty to sixty minutes.

In learning to make air-raised butter cakes, perhaps the best one to begin with is a *Gâteau Praliné,* which uses as its base the *génoise*. This classic cake, originally from Italy, was quickly adopted by France. When you have mastered the technique for putting it together, you will have acquired a whole repertoire of elegant desserts. In fine French bakeries the *génoise* is used to make *petits fours*. Change the flavors of your buttercreams, change the color of your decorations, add a liqueur, and you will have a completely new cake. Omit ½ cup flour and

add, instead, ½ cup dark, unsweetened cocoa, and you will have a feathey chocolate butter sponge.

GÂTEAU PRALINÉ
Génoise

6 large eggs
1 cup sugar
1 cup sifted all-purpose flour
½ cup sweet butter, melted and clarified (see below)
1 teaspoon vanilla extract

Grease and lightly flour two 9-inch layer-cake pans. In a large bowl combine eggs and sugar. Stir for a minute, or until they are just combined. Set bowl over a saucepan containing 1 or 2 inches of hot water. Water in pan should not touch bowl; nor should it ever be allowed to boil. Place saucepan containing bowl over low heat for 5 to 10 minutes, or until eggs are lukewarm. Heating eggs helps them whip to greater volume. They should, however, be lightly stirred three or four times to prevent them from cooking at bottom of bowl.

When eggs feel lukewarm to your finger and look like a bright yellow syrup, remove bowl from heat and begin to beat, preferably with an electric mixer. Beat at high speed for 10 to 15 minutes, scraping sides of bowl with a rubber spatula when necessary, until syrup becomes light, fluffy, and cool. It will almost triple in bulk and resemble whipped cream. It is the air in the eggs that gives *génoise* its lightness.

Sprinkle flour, a little at a time, on top of the whipped eggs. Fold in the flour gently, adding slightly cooled clarified butter and vanilla. Folding can be done with electric mixer turned to lowest speed, or by hand (see Note below). Don't overmix.

Pour batter into prepared pans. Bake in preheated moderate oven (350°F.) for 25 to 30 minutes, or until cakes pull away from sides of pans and are golden brown and springy when touched lightly on top. Remove from pans at once and cool.

Note: Folding by hand is especially effective because you can get the actual feel of the mixture with which you are working. When hands are used for folding, it is often possible to combine ingredients which would ordinarily become almost flat if a spatula were used. If ingredients are both liquids, pour the least fluffy one on top of the other. If dry ingredients are to be folded in, sprinkle them on top of the fluffy mixture.

To fold, keep the fingers of the right hand spread slightly apart. Cut down through batter gently, going to the bottom of the bowl. Twist your hand slightly, scrape it across the bottom of

the bowl, scraping the bottom and the sides. Bring up your hand, turning over some of the batter you've picked up at the bottom. Cut down through batter again in a different place. Repeat the entire process, folding the batter over and over with the hand until the ingredients are combined but still light.

■ **To Clarify Butter**—Melt ½ cup sweet butter over low heat. Allow the butter to cook very slowly for about 10 minutes, or until the remaining foam on top begins to look slightly tan around the edges. Skim off foam. Pour off fat to use in cake; leave sediment in pan.

When a large amount of butter is being clarified, it is a good idea to strain it through cheesecloth. Naturally, a large amount of clarified butter will take longer.

Clarified butter can be kept in the refrigerator for many months. It is excellent for greasing pans and for sautéing, as well as in many delicate cakes. It does not burn as readily as whole butter.

Nougat Buttercream

1 cup sugar
¾ cup coarsely chopped blanched almonds or filberts
1 tablespoon fresh lemon juice
1¼ cups butter
2 egg yolks
1 teaspoon vanilla extract

Combine sugar, nuts, and lemon juice in a heavy skillet. Cook over low heat, stirring constantly with a wooden spoon. When mixture is a deep golden color and sugar is completely dissolved, pour out on a *very well-oiled* pan. After nougat has cooled and hardened, grate fine with a nut grater, or pulverize in blender.

Cream butter until it is soft and fluffy. Beat in egg yolks and vanilla. Then, beat in about ½ cup nougat powder, or as much as the cream will take while still remaining a fluffy cream. Be sure to reserve some nougat powder for decorating sides of the *gâteau*.

Note: The nougat powder used in this recipe can be prepared days, or even weeks, ahead of time and kept in a covered jar.

How to Assemble Gâteau Praliné

First, prepare the top layer so that it has time to cool before you set it in place. Place a layer of *génoise* on a piece of well-greased wax paper (this will make the clean-up job easier). In a heavy skillet, over low heat, combine ¾ cup sugar with 2 teaspoons fresh lemon juice. Stir constantly until sugar has melted and is a golden-brown liquid. Pour at once over cake layer, spreading with a greased spatula. Work fast, as this melted sugar

Swiss Classic

hardens rapidly. Before it has hardened, cut through the glaze, using a well-oiled knife, to make 12 serving-size wedges. This will help later when the *gâteau* is served. (If you cannot work as quickly as required, spread the sugar glaze on a greased piece of wax paper 9 inches in diameter. Using a well-oiled knife cut into wedges, while still warm. Let dry thoroughly. Remove wedges and place on cake.)

Spread the remaining layer of *génoise* with half the buttercream. Place glazed layer on top. Spread sides with remaining buttercream. Using your hand, coat sides with the extra nougat powder. Makes 12 servings.

SWISS CLASSIC
Swiss Broyage

3 egg whites
⅛ teaspoon cream of tartar
Pinch of salt
1 teaspoon vanilla extract
¾ cup sugar
¼ cup blanched almonds, finely grated
⅓ cup sifted cornstarch

Grease and flour a large cookie sheet. Press the rim of a 9-inch layer-cake pan lightly into the flour on sheet twice to mark 2 circles as guides for shaping *broyage*.

Combine egg whites, cream of tartar, salt, and vanilla in a large bowl. Beat until egg whites hold soft peaks. Add ½ cup sugar, 1 tablespoon at a time, beating constantly. Continue beating until meringue is very stiff and dull.

Combine grated almonds, cornstarch, and remaining sugar. Fold into meringue. Divide mixture between floured guides on baking sheet. Spread evenly within circles. Or fill a pastry bag, fitted with a No. 3 or 5 round tube, with *broyage*. Starting in center of each circle, press out batter in a long continuous pencil-thick strip, curling it round and round until circle is completely filled in. Press out batter slowly, holding bag at least 1 inch away from sheet.

Bake in preheated slow oven (325° F.) for 35 to 40 minutes, or until layers are sand-colored and crisp. Remove from baking sheet and cool on a rack.

Almond Butter Cake

3 eggs
2 egg yolks
½ teaspoon vanilla extract
½ cup sugar
1 teaspoon grated lemon rind
¼ cup almond paste
¾ cup sifted all-purpose flour
¼ cup butter, melted and clarified
   (to clarify butter, see page 781)

Set oven at moderate (350°F.). Grease and flour one 9-inch layer-cake pan. In a bowl combine whole eggs, 1 egg yolk, vanilla, sugar, and grated lemon rind. Follow directions in *Génoise* recipe, page

781, for heating eggs and sugar over hot water. While eggs are warming, cream almond paste with remaining egg yolk until it is soft, smooth, and fluffy. When eggs feel warm and look like a bright yellow syrup, beat them well. Beat as for *Génoise*, until eggs are almost tripled in bulk and resemble whipped cream.

Pour softened almond paste over egg mixture. Sprinkle flour on top. Fold all gently together, adding slightly cooled clarified butter. Be careful not to overmix.

Pour batter into prepared pan. Spread it evenly. Bake for 15 to 20 minutes, or until cake is golden brown and springy to the touch. Remove from pan and cool on rack.

Speedy Chocolate Buttercream

½ cup soft butter
6 ounces semisweet chocolate, melted and cooled
1 egg yolk
½ teaspoon vanilla extract
2 teaspoons brandy

Cream butter briefly until it is soft and fluffy. Beat in cooled melted chocolate, egg yolk, vanilla, and brandy.

How to Assemble Swiss Classic

Using fingers or spoon, sprinkle Almond Butter Cake with ¼ cup brandy.

Place a layer of Swiss Broyage on a plate. Spread it with ½ cup raspberry jam. Set Almond Butter Cake on top. Spread cake with ½ cup jam. Place second layer of Swiss Broyage on top.

Spread sides of cake with Chocolate Buttercream, reserving enough to make a rosette border around top of cake. Press 1½ cups coarsely chopped or sliced nuts (walnuts, almonds, pecans, filberts) into buttercream sides. (Nuts have a better flavor if they have been lightly toasted in the oven for 10 to 15 minutes before using.)

Decorate top of cake with a border of tiny buttercream rosettes, if desired. Dust with confectioners' sugar. Makes 12 servings.

CHOCOLATE CHESTNUT SLICES
Basic Sponge Sheet

4 eggs
Pinch of salt
¼ cup sugar
½ teaspoon vanilla extract
¼ cup sifted cornstarch
¼ cup sifted all-purpose flour

Grease a jelly-roll pan (1 x 10 x 15 inches) and line with wax paper. Grease and flour paper.

Separate eggs. Beat egg whites with salt until they hold soft peaks. Gradually beat in sugar, sprinkling it in 1 tablespoon at a time. Continue beating until whites are very firm, about 5 minutes in all.

Stir yolks with a fork to break them up. Add vanilla. Fold one quarter of the stiffly beaten egg whites thoroughly into egg yolks. Pour yolk mixture on top of remaining stiffly beaten whites. Sprinkle cornstarch and flour on top. Fold all very gently together until no pieces of egg white show. Be careful not to overmix.

Pour into prepared pan. Spread batter evenly. Bake in preheated hot oven (400° F.) for 10 to 12 minutes, or until cake is very lightly browned. Be careful not to overbake. Loosen sides and remove cake from pan at once. Cool on a rack before peeling off paper. Cake should be flexible from end to end.

Chestnut Cream

1 can (2 pounds) whole chestnuts
½ cup soft butter
¾ cup sifted confectioners' sugar
1 ounce (1 square) unsweetened chocolate, melted
¼ cup brandy

Heat chestnuts in their liquid. Drain well. Mash to a fine purée. Cool. Cream chestnut purée with butter. Add confectioners' sugar, melted chocolate, and brandy. Chill until firm enough to mold.

Shape chestnut cream into 2 rolls, each 15 inches long and not more than 1 inch in diameter. If cream is very soft, wax paper helps mold it. Chill rolls until needed or, if desired, they can be frozen.

Apricot Glaze

1 cup sieved apricot jam
2 to 4 tablespoons brandy

Heat apricot jam in saucepan until it is boiling. Stir in brandy. Use while hot.

Bitter Chocolate Glaze

1 cup dark unsweetened cocoa, sifted
Pinch of salt
⅔ cup heavy cream
⅓ cup sweet butter
1⅓ cups sugar
1 teaspoon vanilla extract

Combine all ingredients except vanilla in a heavy saucepan. Cook over low heat, stirring constantly, until smooth and thick, about 5 minutes. When mixture has stopped bubbling, stir in vanilla. Use glaze while still hot. Be sure any cake containing a buttercream filling has been well chilled, or even frozen for an hour or two, before the hot glaze is poured over it.

How to Assemble
Chocolate Chestnut Slices

Cut Basic Sponge Sheet into halves lengthwise, making 2 rectangles 15 inches long. Sprinkle each piece with a little brandy. Spread with Speedy Chocolate Buttercream (recipe at left), dividing it evenly between the two rectangles.

Place roll of Chestnut Cream in center of each cake. Roll cakes lengthwise around chestnut centers, turning seams to the bottom. Brush with Apricot Glaze; chill.

When well chilled, place rolls on cake rack. Pour Bitter Chocolate Glaze over top and sides of each roll. Use a spatula, if necessary, to avoid bare spots.

Chill rolls. Cut in ¾-inch slices, wiping knife after cutting each slice. Decorate each slice with a bit of crystallized violet. Makes about 32 servings.

Note: This cake, except for glazes, can be assembled and frozen for up to 3 months. Neither the Apricot nor Chocolate Glaze can be frozen; they must be prepared and used promptly after cakes have been taken from freezer.

MELTING TEA CAKE

½ cup whole blanched almonds
1 teaspoon vanilla extract
1 teaspoon grated lemon rind
1 cup butter, melted
4 whole eggs
4 egg yolks
1 cup sugar
1½ cups sifted all-purpose flour
2 tablespoons cornstarch
⅛ teaspoon ground mace

Grease and dust lightly with flour a 9-inch kugelhopf pan or a deep 9-inch tube pan. Arrange blanched almonds around bottom of pan.

Add vanilla and grated lemon rind to butter melted over low heat and cooled to lukewarm, but not clarified.

In a large bowl combine eggs, egg yolks, and sugar. Beat for 1 minute. Set bowl over a saucepan of hot water and place saucepan over low heat for 10 minutes, or until eggs are slightly warmer than lukewarm. Do not let water boil. Stir eggs occasionally while they are being heated to prevent them from cooking on bottom of bowl. When eggs are warm, beat until they are cool, thick, and tripled in bulk. (See *Génoise,* page 781.) Sprinkle flour, cornstarch, and mace on top. Fold in gently, adding butter at the same time. Continue to fold until there is no trace of butter. Be careful not to overmix.

Pour batter into prepared pan. Bake in preheated moderate oven (350°F.) for 45 minutes, or until cake is golden brown and comes away from sides of pan. Cool on a rack. Makes 12 servings.

GÂTEAU MANON
Savarin Dough

1 package active dry yeast
¼ cup warm water
¼ cup lukewarm milk
2 tablespoons sugar
4 eggs, slightly beaten
½ teaspoon salt
2 cups sifted all-purpose flour (about)
⅔ cup soft sweet butter

Dissolve yeast in water according to directions on package. Add milk, sugar, eggs, salt, and then enough flour to make

a soft thick batter. Beat vigorously for 8 minutes with a wooden spoon. Cover bowl. Let batter rise for about 40 minutes, or until it has doubled in bulk. Stir it down. Beat in softened butter.

Grease a 1-quart mold. A round charlotte mold or deep metal bowl works fine.

Pour batter into prepared mold. Let rise until it has doubled in bulk. Bake in preheated hot oven (400°F.) for 10 minutes. Reduce heat to moderate (350° F.) and bake for 25 to 30 minutes longer, or until cake is golden brown. Cool on a rack.

Pastry Cream

2 tablespoons all-purpose flour
1 cup light cream or milk
⅛ teaspoon salt
6 tablespoons sugar
4 egg yolks
1 teaspoon vanilla extract

Combine flour with ¼ cup of the cream. Stir until smooth. Gradually add remaining cream. Place in a heavy saucepan. Stir in salt and sugar. Cook over medium heat, stirring, until mixture becomes as thick as a medium white sauce. Stir a little of the hot sauce into egg yolks. Then pour egg yolks into saucepan, stirring briskly. Return pan to low heat for a few minutes to thicken the sauce a little more, continuing to stir. Be careful not to let the sauce boil after the yolks have been added. Remove from heat. Add vanilla. Cool as quickly as possible.

In order to prevent a skin from forming on top of the pastry cream while it is cooling, melted butter can be brushed over it. Stir pastry cream before using.

Divide pastry cream into halves. To one half add 1 ounce (1 square) unsweetened chocolate, melted. Leave the remaining pastry cream as it is.

How to Assemble Gâteau Manon

When baked Savarin Dough has cooled, cut it into 5 thin layers. Brush both sides of each layer with kirsch. About ⅔ cup kirsch will be needed. It can be diluted slightly with water, if desired.

Sandwich cake together, using alternating layers of vanilla Pastry Cream and chocolate Pastry Cream. Leave the top plain.

Brush cake all over with hot Apricot Glaze (page 783). Cover glaze with 2 cups sliced almonds or filberts. (Sliced nuts will taste better if they have been lightly toasted in a moderate oven, 350° F., for about 15 minutes before using.) Before serving, dust cake with confectioners' sugar. Makes 8 to 10 servings.

GELATIN, GELATINE—A protein substance which swells on contact with a liquid, dissolves in hot water, and forms a jelly when it cools. The words gelatin and jelly both come from the Latin *gelatus,* meaning "frozen." In cookery gelatin is used as a thickening agent.

Edible gelatin is made, by a scientific process, from animal tissues, chiefly from veal and beef. Good gelatin is odorless and tasteless; when dissolved, it should make a clear solution.

For the wide variety of gelatin dishes made by modern homemakers attractive large molds are available in many shapes and sizes. There are shells, pineapples, fish, and many other shapes. However, square cake pans, loaf pans, or mixing bowls can also be used. Mixtures can be unmolded and cut into squares or slices, or scooped out with an ice-cream scoop.

A variety of scalloped, fluted, and other shapes is available in molds for individual servings. Mixtures can also be molded in custard cups, coffee cups, or even paper cups. Some mixtures need not be molded but can be spooned directly into sherbet or parfait glasses before chilling.

There are two main types of gelatin. The alkaline type is found in unflavored gelatin and the acid type is used in the flavored gelatin.

UNFLAVORED GELATIN

Unflavored gelatin is used as a jelly base for soups, salads, aspics, and desserts; as an emulsifying agent in the making of such candies as Turkish paste; in frozen desserts to prevent the formation of large ice crystals so that a smoother texture will be obtained.

Purchasing Guide — Unflavored gelatin comes in granular form for household use. It is packaged in sealed envelopes.

Each envelope contains ¼ ounce or about 1 tablespoon, the amount of gelatin needed to gel 2 cups of liquid.

Unflavored gelatin is sometimes sold in sheets. Six medium sheets, each measuring 4½ by 6 inches, correspond to 1 ounce of gelatin, enough to gel 2 quarts of liquid.

Storage—Packaged gelatin keeps indefinitely in a cool dry place.

Dishes prepared with gelatin should be refrigerated.

Nutritive Food Values—Gelatin is pure protein, easily digested. It contains seven essential amino acids. However, it is not a complete protein as are meats, egg, cheese, and milk proteins, It is useful as a protein supplement.

☐ 1 envelope = 28 calories

Basic Preparation

☐ **To Dissolve**—Sprinkle gelatin on cold

Vegetable Salad

liquid to soften (¼ cup liquid to 1 envelope gelatin). Let stand for 2 or 3 minutes. (a) Add the hot liquid and stir until dissolved, *or* (b) place over low heat, stirring constantly, until dissolved, *or* (c) place over boiling water, stirring occasionally, until dissolved. If more than 1 tablespoon sugar is mixed with the gelatin, hot liquid may be added directly, stirring until the gelatin dissolves. Or, the gelatin-sugar mixture may be combined with other ingredients and heated until dissolved, as in a chiffon or Bavarian, etc.

□ **To Fold in Solids, or To Whip**—Stirring occasionally, chill a gelatin mixture until it is the consistency of unbeaten egg white, or until it is slightly thickened. Then fold in the solids or fold the gelatin mixture into whipped cream and/or beaten egg whites. If it is to be used in making a whip or snow, however, the gelatin mixture should be chilled until it is *slightly thicker* than unbeaten egg white before it is beaten.

□ **To Gel Pineapple**—A protein-digesting enzyme in raw pineapple prevents gelation. Pineapple must be boiled for 2 minutes to destroy this enzyme before using in a gelatin mixture.

□ **To Layer Gelatin Dishes**—Chill each layer until set but not quite firm before adding next layer which should be cold so it won't soften the set layer. Build up to 3 layers; chill until firm.

□ **To Layer Fruit Molds**—Some fruits sink and some float in gelatin mixtures. Pour liquid gelatin into a mold and add a fruit that will sink. Then add a floating fruit. Stir fruit in gently to distribute evenly and chill until firm. Fruits that sink: those canned in heavy syrup, fresh grapes, plums, oranges, and cooked prunes. Fruits that float: apple cubes, banana slices, grapefruit, peach and pear slices, strawberries, melon balls, blueberries, mandarin oranges.

□ **To Make Designs in Molds**—Spoon or pour a thin layer into bottom of mold. Chill until slightly thickened. Arrange design with fruit. Chill until set, but not firm, to hold fruit in place. Cover with remaining gelatin and chill until firm.

□ **To Chill Partially and Quickly**—Place bowl of gelatin mixture in container of ice cubes and water; stir frequently until of desired consistency. Or place in freezer, stirring occasionally until of desired consistency, about 10 minutes.

□ **To Unmold**—Loosen edges of gelatin with tip of pointed knife. Dip mold briefly into lukewarm, not hot, water; remove and shake gently. Moisten a plate with cold water. This will make it easier to center the mold by sliding it into position. Or place a doily over mold. Place plate on top of mold with or without

doily. Hold firmly together and turn over. Shake gently and lift off mold. Center gelatin.

FLAVORED GELATIN

Flavored gelatin is a commercial mixture of unflavored gelatin, sugar, salt, acids, natural and artificial flavorings, and U. S. certified coloring.

Purchasing Guide—Flavored gelatins are available in 3-ounce or 6-ounce packages in many flavors. A 3-ounce package gels 2 cups liquid; a 6-ounce package gels 4 cups liquid.

Storage—Packaged flavored gelatin keeps for at least a year in a cool dry place.

Prepared dishes should be refrigerated and used as the foods contained therein indicate. Do not freeze prepared gelatin unless recipe specifies doing so.

Nutritive Food Values—Flavored gelatin contains carbohydrate in addition to the incomplete protein contained in unflavored gelatin. Some fruit-flavored gelatins have vitamin C added, about 8 mg. per ½ cup serving.

□ ½ cup prepared gelatin = 80 to 83 calories

Basic Preparation—Flavored gelatin dishes are molded and unmolded in the same way unflavored gelatin dishes are.

□ **To Dissolve**—Follow package directions. In general, 1 cup hot or boiling water is added to the flavored gelatin, the mixture is stirred until gelatin is completely dissolved, and then 1 cup cold water, juice, or other liquid is added.

To use for a molded form, reduce the cold water to ¾ cup for a 3-ounce package, 1½ cups for a 6-ounce package. Takes 3 to 6 hours chilling to become firm.

□ **To Set Quickly**—Dissolve contents in 1 cup hot or boiling water. Add 1 cup ice water. Pour into molds, then set into cracked ice and chill in refrigerator.

To set extra quickly, dissolve contents in 1 cup hot or boiling water. Add 8 to 12 ice cubes; stir for 3 minutes. When slightly thickened, remove ice and chill.

GELATIN COOK BOOK

APPETIZERS AND SOUPS

SEAFOOD COCKTAIL SALAD
1¾ cups tomato juice
1 envelope unflavored gelatin
1 teaspoon instant minced onion
½ bay leaf
2 tablespoons fresh lemon juice

½ teaspoon Worcestershire
1 tablespoon prepared horseradish
½ cup diced celery
2 pimientos, chopped
2 cups cooked shrimps, flaked crabmeat, or lobster (alone or in combination)
Salt and pepper to taste
Shredded lettuce
Mayonnaise

Put tomato juice in saucepan and sprinkle with gelatin. Add onion and bay leaf; heat, stirring, until gelatin dissolves. Remove bay leaf and add next 6 ingredients. Season. Pour into 6 individual molds and chill until firm. Unmold on lettuce. Serve with mayonnaise. Makes 6 servings.

SHERRY TOMATO BOUILLON
1 envelope unflavored gelatin
1 cup water
1 bouillon cube
1 cup tomato juice
⅓ cup sherry
1 tablespoon fresh lemon juice
Thinly sliced lemon
Chopped parsley

Soften gelatin in ½ cup water in saucepan. Add bouillon cube and heat, stirring, until cube is dissolved. Add remaining water and other ingredients except lemon and parsley. Pour into 8-inch square pan and chill until firm. Cut into squares and pile in soup cups. Top with lemon slices and parsley. Makes 4 servings.

JELLIED EGG SOUP

Put ¼ cup cold water in bowl and sprinkle with 1 envelope unflavored gelatin. Add 4 chicken bouillon cubes and 4 cups boiling water. Stir until cubes are dissolved. Beat 4 egg yolks slightly. Gradually beat in about 1 cup of the bouillon. Add remaining bouillon, cool, and chill until firm. Break up with fork and serve garnished with chopped chives. Makes 4 to 6 servings.

SALADS

MOLDED SALMON SALAD RING WITH CUCUMBERS IN SOUR CREAM
1 can (1 pound) pink salmon
1 envelope unflavored gelatin
2 egg yolks
¾ cup milk
2½ tablespoons fresh lemon juice
1 teaspoon salt
1 teaspoon powdered mustard
Paprika
2 tablespoons butter
1 cup dairy sour cream
Few sprigs of fresh dill, chopped
1 teaspoon seasoned salt
1 cucumber, peeled and thinly sliced
Watercress

Drain liquid from salmon into top part of small double boiler. Sprinkle with gelatin. Add next 5 ingredients and ¼ teaspoon paprika; beat with rotary beater. Add butter and put mixture over boiling water. Cook, stirring, until smooth and slightly thickened. Flake salmon, removing skin and bones if desired. Add to first mixture and pour into 1-quart ring mold. Chill until firm. Unmold and fill with next 4 ingredients, mixed. Sprinkle cucumber mixture with paprika. Garnish the mold with watercress. Makes 4 servings.

MOLDED TUNA AND AVOCADO SALAD
Avocado Layer:

- 1 envelope unflavored gelatin
- ¾ cup water
- 1 large avocado, peeled and mashed (1 cup)
- 2 tablespoons fresh lemon juice
- ½ cup dairy sour cream
- ½ cup mayonnaise
- 1 teaspoon salt
- ⅛ teaspoon hot pepper sauce

Tuna Layer:

- 1 envelope unflavored gelatin
- 1¼ cups water
- 3 tablespoons fresh lemon juice
- 1 teaspoon salt
- 1 can (7 ounces) tuna, drained and flaked
- 1 cup diced celery
- ⅓ cup diced pimiento
  Salad greens
  Avocado slices

To make avocado layer, soften gelatin in water. Stir over low heat until gelatin is dissolved. Chill until slightly thickened. Fold in remaining ingredients and pour into loaf pan (9 x 5 x 3 inches). Chill until almost firm. To make tuna layer, soften gelatin in ½ cup water. Stir over low heat until dissolved. Stir in ¾ cup water, the lemon juice, and salt. Chill until slightly thickened. Fold in next 3 ingredients and pour over avocado layer. Chill until firm. Unmold on greens and garnish with avocado. Makes 8 servings.

BASIC ASPIC

- 1 envelope unflavored gelatin
- ¼ cup cold water
- 1½ cups consommé

Soak gelatin in cold water for 5 minutes. Cook over low heat until gelatin is dissolved. Add dissolved gelatin to consommé and stir to blend thoroughly. Makes 1¾ cups.

BEEF IN ASPIC
Cut boiled beef or pot roast when cold into thin slices. Pour a thin layer of Basic Aspic onto the bottom of a mold; chill until partially set. Decorate with slices of egg, olives, pimiento, and thin carrot slices. Chill until firm. Top with slices of beef arranged in the original shape of the meat. Fill mold with remaining aspic. Chill until firm. Unmold and cut into slices. It may be necessary to

double or triple the above recipe depending on the shape and size of the mold and piece of meat.

SANDWICHES EN GELÉE
Prepare open-face sandwiches with pretty garnishes and chill until very cold. Prepare Basic Aspic as above and chill until cold and slightly thickened. Place sandwiches on a rack and spoon aspic over them, coating the sandwiches. The excess which drips down can be heated over low heat and reused after chilling. Chill sandwiches until aspic is firm. It may be necessary to give the sandwiches several coats of gelatin, until desired thickness is achieved.

LIVER, TOMATO, AND CREAM-CHEESE LOAF

- 1 envelope unflavored gelatin
- 2 cups tomato juice
- ½ teaspoon salt
- ½ teaspoon onion salt
- ½ teaspoon celery salt
- ¼ teaspoon crumbled dried basil
- 1 can (4½ ounces) liver pate
- 2 packages (3 ounces each) cream cheese, softened
- 2 teaspoons milk
- ¼ cup chopped pimiento-stuffed olives
  Salad greens

Soften gelatin in tomato juice in saucepan. Add next 4 ingredients and bring to boil, stirring. Pour half into 1-quart mold and chill until firm. Mash liver pâté until very soft and carefully spread on firm tomato mixture. Chill remaining mixture until slightly thickened and pour over liver pâté. Chill until firm. Beat cheese and milk until blended; add olives and spread on firm mixture. Chill for about 1 hour. Unmold on greens and slices. Makes 6 servings.

SPINACH SALAD MOLD WITH HAM

- 1 envelope unflavored gelatin
- 2 tablespoons sugar
- 1 teaspoon salt
- ⅛ teaspoon pepper
- 1¾ cups water
- 2 tablespoons vinegar
- 1 tablespoon fresh lemon juice
- ¼ cup chopped green onion
- 1 cup shredded raw spinach
- 1 cup diced celery
- ¼ cup shredded raw carrot
  Salad greens
  Diced cooked ham
  Mayonnaise
  Chopped parsley

In small saucepan mix gelatin, sugar, salt, and pepper. Add ½ cup water. Stir over low heat until gelatin is dissolved. Stir in 1¼ cups water, the vinegar, and lemon juice. Chill until slightly thickened. Fold in next 4 ingredients and pour into 6-cup ring mold. Chill until firm. Unmold on greens and fill center with ham. Top with a large spoonful of mayonnaise and garnish with parsley. Makes 4 servings.

TOMATO ASPIC

- 1¼ cups (one 10-ounce can) tomatoes
- ¼ teaspoon salt
- 1½ teaspoons minced onion
- 1 small celery stalk and few celery leaves
- 3 peppercorns
- 3 whole cloves
- 1½ teaspoons unflavored gelatin
- 2 tablespoons cold water
- 1½ teaspoons vinegar
- 1 teaspoon fresh lemon juice
  Lettuce

Combine first 6 ingredients in small saucepan. Simmer for 10 minutes; strain. Sprinkle gelatin on water; let stand for 5 minutes. Add to tomato liquid; stir until dissolved. Add vinegar and lemon juice. Pour into two ½-cup molds or custard cups. Chill until firm. Unmold on lettuce; serve with buttermik or yogurt dressing if desired. Makes 2 servings.

JELLIED POTATO SALAD

- 2½ cups diced hot cooked potato
- 2 teaspoons instant minced onion
- 2 tablespoons salad oil
- 1¾ teaspoons salt
  Dash of pepper
- 6 tablespoons vinegar
- 1 box (3 ounces) lemon-flavored gelatin
- 1¼ cups hot water
  Green pepper strips
- 2 tablespoons diced green pepper
- 1 cup diced celery
- ¼ cup sliced radishes
- ⅓ cup mayonnaise
  Salad greens
  Deviled eggs
  Sliced cucumbers
- 1 pimiento

Mix first 5 ingredients and 3 tablespoons vinegar; let stand for 25 minutes to marinate, stirring occasionally. Dissolve gelatin in hot water. Add remaining vinegar. To ⅔ cup of gelatin, add 3 tablespoons water. Pour into loaf pan (9 x 5 x 3 inches) and chill until slightly thickened. Arrange 6 pepper strips down length of pan. Chill until firm. Chill remaining gelatin until slightly thickened. Put in bowl of ice and water and whip with rotary beater until fluffy. Fold in potato mixture, diced green pepper, celery, radishes, and mayonnaise. Spread on firm gelatin and chill until firm. Unmold; garnish with greens, eggs, cucumbers, and pimiento in the shape of a rose. Makes 6 servings.

VEGETABLE SALAD

- 2 boxes (3 ounces each) lemon-flavored gelatin
- 1 teaspoon salt
- 2 cups boiling water
- ¾ cup cold water
  Dash of pepper
- ¼ cup vinegar
- 2 stuffed green olives, sliced
- 1 small tomato cut in wedges
  About 1 cup (one 8-ounce can) sliced carrots, drained
  About 2 cups (one 1-pound can) green Lima beans, drained
  Salad greens
  Mayonnaise

Dissolve gelatin and salt in boiling water. Add cold water, pepper, and vinegar. Pour a little into a 1½-quart mold and arrange olive slices; let set. Add tomato wedges and a little more gelatin; let set. Chill remaining gelatin until slightly thickened. Divide and fold carrots into one portion and pour into mold. Then fold Lima beans into other portion and pour into mold. Let stand overnight. Unmold on greens and serve with mayonnaise. Makes 6 to 8 servings.

PINEAPPLE CHEESE MOLD

2 boxes (3 ounces each) lime-flavored gelatin
2 cups boiling water
About 1 cup (one 9-ounce can) crushed pineapple, undrained
2 tablespoons prepared harseradish
⅔ cup evaporated milk, undiluted
1 cup mayonnaise
1 cup creamed cottage cheese
Salad greens

Dissolve gelatin in boiling water; cool. Add pineapple, horseradish, evaporated milk, and mayonnaise. Chill until slightly thickened. Fold in cottage cheese. Turn into 1½-quart mold. Chill until firm. Unmold on salad greens. Makes 8 servings.

ORANGE-PINEAPPLE SALAD

1 box (3 ounces) orange- or orange-pineapple-flavored gelatin
1 cup hot water
About 1 cup (8½ ounces) crushed pineapple, undrained
1 cup diced orange sections
About 1¼ cups (one 11-ounce can) mandrain oranges, drained
1 cup miniature marshmallows
1 cup dairy sour cream
2 tablespoons mayonnaise
2 tablespoons grated Cheddar cheese
Salad greens

Dissolve gelatin in hot water. Add pineapple and chill until slightly thickened. Fold in next 3 ingredients. Pour into pan (8 x 8 x 2 inches) and chill until firm. Mix sour cream and mayonnaise and spread on salad. Sprinkle with cheese. Serve on greens. Makes 6 to 8 servings.

PEAR AND BLUE-CHEESE SALAD

1 box (3 ounces) orange-flavored gelatin
1 cup hot water
1 cup cold water
1 tablespoon vinegar
1⅓ cups diced fresh or canned pears
1½ ounces (⅓ cup crumbled) blue cheese
1 tablespoon heavy cream
Salad greens
French dressing or mayonnaise

Dissolve gelatin in hot water. Add cold water and vinegar. Chill until slightly thickened. Fold pears into half of mixture. Turn into 1-quart mold or 6 individual molds. Chill until firm. Set remaining gelatin in larger bowl of ice and water and whip with rotary beater until fluffy and thick. Blend cheese with cream and beat into whipped gelatin. Turn onto firm gelatin. Chill until firm. Unmold on greens. Serve with French dressing or mayonnaise. Makes 6 servings.

FRUIT-COCKTAIL SALAD LOAF

1 envelope unflavored gelatin
About 3⅓ cups (one 1-pound, 13-ounce can) fruit cocktail
Syrup from fruit
1 package (3 ounces) cream cheese, softened
1 cup mayonnaise
1 box (3 ounces) cherry-, black-cherry-, or raspberry-flavored gelatin
Salad greens

Soften unflavored gelatin in ¼ cup cold water. Drain fruit, reserving syrup. Heat ¾ cup syrup, add gelatin, and stir until gelatin is dissolved; cool. Beat cheese until fluffy; blend in mayonnaise. Gradually beat in gelatin mixture. Dissolve flavored gelatin in 1 cup boiling water. Add 1 cup cold water or syrup and water. Chill until slightly thickened. Put half of fruit in loaf pan (9 x 5 x 3 inches), add 1 cup flavored gelatin, and chill until set. Pour in cheese mixture and chill until set. Top with remaining fruit and gelatin. Chill for several hours, or until firm. Unmold on greens and slice to serve. Makes 8 servings.

DEVILED-EGG SALAD

1 box (3 ounces) lemon-flavored gelatin
½ teaspoon salt
1 cup hot water
1 cup cold water
1 tablespoon vinegar
Dash of cayenne
4 eggs, deviled and chilled
¾ cup diced celery
⅓ cup chopped stuffed olives
Salad greens

Dissolve gelatin and salt in hot water. Add the cold water, vinegar, and cayenne. Pour some of mixture into loaf pan (9 x 5 x 3 inches) to depth of ¼ inch. Chill until almost firm. Chill remaining mixture until slightly thickened. Spread tops of egg halves with a small amount of gelatin. Chill until firm; then invert on firm gelatin layer. Fold celery and olives into remaining gelatin. Turn into loaf pan. Chill until firm. Unmold and serve on greens. Makes 4 servings.

DESSERTS

COEUR À LA CRÈME

1 envelope unflavored gelatin
¼ cup cold milk
1 pound creamed cottage cheese
2 packages (3 ounces each) cream cheese
1½ teaspoons vanilla extract
¾ cup heavy cream
½ cup sugar
Cherry-Pineapple Sauce

Soften gelatin in cold milk. Stir over low heat until gelatin is dissolved. Force cottage cheese through food mill or sieve or beat with electric mixer at high speed until fairly smooth. Beat in cream cheese, dissolved gelatin, and vanilla. Beat cream with sugar until stiff. Fold into first mixture. Pour into heart-shaped or other 5-cup mold and chill until firm. Unmold; serve with Cherry-Pineapple Sauce.

Cherry-Pineapple Sauce

Mix 1 cup (one 8-ounce can) crushed pineapple, ½ cup sliced maraschino cherries, and ¼ cup maraschino cherry liquid. Chill.

STRAWBERRY CHARLOTTE DESSERT

2 envelopes unflavored gelatin
¾ cup sugar
¼ teaspoon salt
4 eggs, separated
½ cup water
2 packages (10 ounces each) frozen sliced strawberries
2 tablespoons fresh lemon juice
2 teaspoons grated lemon rind
10 ladyfingers
1 cup heavy cream, whipped
Whipped cream
Fresh strawberries

In top part of double boiler mix gelatin, ¼ cup sugar, and the salt. Beat egg yolks with water and add to gelatin mixture. Add 1 package strawberries. Cook over boiling water, stirring, until gelatin is dissolved and berries thawed. Remove from water and add remaining strawberries and lemon juice and rind. Stir until berries are thawed. Chill, stirring occasionally, until mixture mounds when dropped from spoon. Split ladyfingers and stand around edge of 9-inch springform or loose-bottomed pan. Beat egg whites until stiff. Gradually beat in remaining sugar. Fold into gelatin mixture with whipped cream. Pour into pan and chill until firm. Remove from pan and garnish with more whipped cream and strawberries. Makes 8 to 10 servings.

PARTY FRUIT DESSERT

1 box (3 ounces) lime-flavored gelatin
2 cups boiling water
1 cup cold water
1 cup fine graham-cracker crumbs
¼ cup butter or margarine, melted
1 box (3 ounces) pineapple-flavored gelatin
¼ cup sugar
2 cups heavy cream, whipped
1 cup (one 8-ounce can) pineapple tidbits, drained
1 cup (one 8-ounce can) sliced peaches, drained
1 cup miniature marshmallows
10 maraschino cheeries, halved

Dissolve lime gelatin in 1 cup boiling water. Stir in ½ cup cold water. Pour into 8-inch square pan and chill until firm. Mix crumbs and butter. Press on bottom of 9-inch springform or loose-bottomed pan; chill. Mix pineapple gelatin and sugar and dissolve in 1 cup boiling water. Add ½ cup cold water and chill until slightly thickened. Cut firm lime gelatin into cubes. Fold cubes, whipped cream, and remaining ingre-

move sides of pan before serving. Makes 12 servings.

Note: Make this the day before you plan to use it.

JELLIED APPLESAUCE

Dissolve 1 box (3 ounces) black-raspberry-flavored gelatin, or use apple, orange, or lemon, in 1½ cups boiling water. Chill until slightly thickened. Fold in 1 cup sweetened applesauce and pour into 8-inch square pan. Chill until firm. Unmold and cut into cubes. Serve with soft custard or whipped cream. Makes 4 servings.

SHERRY JELLY

    1 box (3 ounces) lemon-flavored gelatin
    ⅔ cup boiling water
      Juice of 1 orange
      Juice of 1 lemon
    1 cup sherry
      Cream

Dissolve gelatin in boiling water. Add fruit juices and sherry. Pour into 4 individual molds and chill until firm. Unmold; serve with cream. Makes 4 servings.

FRUITED WINE GELATIN

    3 cups prepared fresh fruit
    2 boxes (3 ounces each) lemon-flavored gelatin
    2¼ cups boiling water
    ½ cup white wine
    ¾ cup heavy cream, whipped
    8 pecan halves

When preparing fruit, be sure to use some orange and grapefruit; leave a little juice on fruit to prevent discoloration; use any remaining juice instead of part of the water. (If fresh or frozen pineapple is used, bring to boil and drain.) Dissolve gelatin in boiling water; cool and add wine. Pour a thin layer of liquid gelatin mixture in bottom of each of 8 sherbet glasses. Chill until firm. Arrange some fruit on this, then pour on a little more of the liquid gelatin; do not cover completely. Chill until firm. Combine remaining drained fruit and gelatin; chill until syrupy and put on top of fruit. Chill until firm. Top each serving with a pecan. Makes 8 servings.

INDIVIDUAL PRUNE MOLDS

    1 box (3 ounces) orange- or lemon-flavored gelatin
    1 cup boiling water
    ½ cup cold water
    1 tablespoon grated lemon rind
    3 tablespoons fresh lemon juice
    ¼ cup sugar
    ¼ cup rum or 2 teaspoons rum flavoring
    1 cup diced pitted plumped dried prunes
    ¼ cup chopped California walnuts
    ¾ cup heavy cream, whipped

Dissolve gelatin in boiling water. Add next 5 ingredients. Chill until slightly thickened. Fold in remaining ingredients and pour into individual molds. Chill

Blueberry Fluff Pie, Fruited Wine Gelatin, and Sandwiches en Gelée

until firm; unmold in serving dishes. Makes 6 or 7 servings.

Note: To plump prunes, let prunes stand in water to cover for 2 hours.

JELLIED PEACH MELBA

- 1 box (3 ounces) raspberry-flavored gelatin
- 1 cup hot water
- 1 package (12 ounces) frozen raspberries
- 6 canned or fresh peach halves
- 1 pint vanilla ice cream

Dissolve gelatin in hot water. Add berries and stir gently until thawed. Chill until slightly thickened. Put a peach half, rounded side up, in bottom of each of 6 individual molds. Pour gelatin over peach halves and chill until firm. Unmold; top each with a scoop of ice cream. Makes 6 servings.

SPICED JELLY WITH RUM CREAM

- 4 cups hot strong coffee
- 2 whole cloves
- 1 cinnamon stick
- 2 envelopes unflavored gelatin
- ⅓ cup cold water
  Sugar (about 1 cup)
- ⅓ cup chopped nuts
- 1 tablespoon minced candied gingerroot
- 2 tablespoons rum
- 1 cup heavy cream, whipped

Simmer coffee and spices for 10 minutes; remove spices. Soften gelatin in water. Add coffee and ¾ cup sugar; stir until gelatin is dissolved. Chill until mixture begins to set. Add nuts and gingerroot. Pour mixture into individual molds and chill until set. Add 2 tablespoons sugar and rum to cream. Unmold jelly and serve with rum cream. Makes 6 servings.

CHOCOLATE MOUSSE

- 2 envelopes unflavored gelatin
- 1 cup sugar
- ¼ teaspoon salt
- 2½ cups milk
- 12 ounces (1 large package) semisweet chocolate pieces
- 2 teaspoons vanilla extract
- 2 cups heavy cream, whipped

In 2½-quart saucepan mix gelatin, sugar, and salt. Stir in milk and chocolate. Stir over medium heat until gelatin is dissolved and chocolate melted. Remove from heat and beat with rotary beater until chocolate is blended. Stir in vanilla. Chill in saucepan in bowl of ice and water, stirring occasionally, until slightly thickened. Fold in cream. Turn into 10-cup mold or 12 individual molds. Chill until firm. Unmold. Makes 12 servings.

SHERRY PARFAIT

- ¼ cup cold water
- 1 envelope unflavored gelatin
- ¼ cup boiling water
- ¾ cup confectioners' sugar
- ¾ cup sherry
  Dash of salt
- ¾ cup heavy cream, whipped

Put cold water in bowl and sprinkle with gelatin. Add boiling water and stir until gelatin is dissolved. Stir in sugar. Add sherry and salt. Chill until thickened but not firm. Fold in cream and pile in glasses. Chill until firm. Makes 4 to 6 servings.

FLUFFY FRUIT SQUARES

- 1 envelope unflavored gelatin
- ¼ cup cold water
- ½ cup boiling water
- ⅔ cup sugar
- ¼ cup fresh orange juice
- ¼ cup fresh lemon juice
- 3 egg whites
- ¼ teaspoon salt
- ⅔ cup fine graham-cracker crumbs
  Lemon Sauce

Sprinkle gelatin over cold water; let stand for 5 minutes. Add boiling water; stir until dissolved. Add sugar and fruit juices; stir until sugar is dissolved. Cool until mixture begins to thicken. Add unbeaten egg whites and salt; beat with rotary beater for 10 minutes, or until mixture is white and very fluffy. Pour into oiled, 8-inch square pan. Chill until firm. This can be made a day ahead. Just before serving, cut gelatin into 16 squares. Roll each square in graham-cracker crumbs. Put 2 squares in each serving dish; top with Lemon Sauce. Makes 8 servings.

Lemon Sauce

- 3 egg yolks
- ⅓ cup sugar
- 1 tablespoon grated lemon rind
- 2 tablespoons fresh lemon juice
- ⅓ cup heavy cream, whipped

Beat egg yolks; gradually add sugar, rind, and juice. Cook over boiling water until thickened, stirring constantly. Cool. Fold in cream.

CRÈME LOUISA

- 1 cup heavy cream
- ½ cup milk
- ½ cup sugar
  Dash of salt
- 1 envelope unflavored gelatin
- ¼ cup cold water
- 1 cup dairy sour cream
- ½ teaspoon almond flavoring or 2 tablespoons brandy or liqueur
  Crushed and sweetened strawberries, raspberries, blueberries, or red currants

Combine heavy cream, milk, sugar, and salt in saucepan and cook over low heat until sugar is dissolved. Remove from heat. Soften gelatin in cold water and stir into the cream mixture. When gelatin is dissolved, beat in the sour cream with a rotary beater; beat only until thoroughly blended and smooth. Blend in flavoring. Pour into lightly oiled 2-cup mold or individual molds. Chill until firm. Unmold and serve with crushed sweetened berries or mixed fruit. Makes 4 to 6 servings.

BLUEBERRY FLUFF PIE

- 1¼ cups fresh blueberries, washed
- 3 eggs
- ¼ teaspoon salt
- ½ cup sugar
- 1 teaspoon vanilla extract
- 1 envelope unflavored gelatin
- ½ cup cold water
- 1 cup heavy cream, whipped
- 1 deep 9-inch pie shell, baked
  Whipped cream for decorating

Crush berries slightly and set aside. Beat eggs with salt until thick. Gradually beat in sugar and add vanilla. Soften gelatin in cold water and dissolve over hot water; cool and stir into egg mixture. Fold in cream and chill until mixture begins to set. Fold in berries and fill shell. Chill until firm. Decorate with whipped cream. Makes 6 to 8 servings.

WATERMELON ICE

- 3 cups watermelon juice
- ½ cup sugar
- ⅛ teaspoon salt
- 1 envelope unflavored gelatin
  Juice of 1 lemon

Mix first three ingredients. Remove about ¼ cup to small saucepan. Sprinkle gelatin on juice in saucepan and let stand for 5 minutes. Dissolve over hot water or very low heat. Add with lemon juice to first mixture. Freeze in crank-type freezer. Makes about 1 quart.

Note: To make juice, force watermelon pulp through a food mill or sieve. To get 3 cups of juice, you will need about 4 pounds of watermelon.

PEPPERMINT FREEZE

- 1 envelope unflavored gelatin
- 2 cups milk
- ⅛ teaspoon salt
- ¾ cup crushed hard peppermint candy
- 2 eggs, slightly beaten
- 1 cup heavy cream, whipped
  Red food coloring
  Hot fudge or chocolate sauce (optional)

Turn refrigerator control to coldest setting. Sprinkle gelatin on cold milk in top part of double boiler; let stand for 5 minutes. Add salt and heat over boiling water. Add candy and stir until dissolved. Pour slowly into beaten eggs; return to double boiler and cook over simmering water, stirring constantly, until mixture coats a metal spoon. Chill well, but not until set. Fold in cream and enough red coloring to tint a delicate pink. Pour into refrigerator tray and partially freeze. Stir once and freeze until firm. Serve with hot fudge or chocolate sauce, if desired. Makes about 6 servings.

LEMON-LIME SHERBET

- 1 envelope unflavored gelatin
- 2 cups milk
- 2 cups light cream
- ¼ teaspoon salt
- ¼ cup sugar
- ¾ cup (1 six-ounce can) frozen lemon-and-limeade, undiluted

Turn refrigerator control to coldest setting. Sprinkle gelatin on ½ cup milk in small saucepan and let stand for 5 minutes. Dissolve over hot water or very low heat. Mix with remaining ingredients. Freeze in refrigerator trays until frozen 1 inch in from edge of tray. Turn into chilled bowl and beat with rotary beater until smooth but not melted. Freeze in trays. Makes 6 servings.

FROZEN LEMON CHEESECAKE
3 eggs, separated
⅔ cup sugar
¼ teaspoon salt
⅓ cup milk
1 envelope unflavored gelatin
⅓ cup cold water
12 ounces cream cheese
1 large lemon, juice and grated rind
⅔ cup heavy cream, whipped
Gingersnap Crumb Crust

Beat egg yolks with ⅓ cup of the sugar, the salt, and milk. Cook over hot water, stirring, until mixture coats spoon. Add gelatin softened in water, stir until dissolved, and cool. Beat cheese until light; add lemon juice and grated rind. Mix with custard. Make meringue with egg whites and remaining sugar. Fold with whipped cream into first mixture. Pour into 9-inch springform pan lined with Gingersnap Crumb Crust. Freeze. Makes 8 servings.

Gingersnap Crumb Crust
Mix 1 cup gingersnap crumbs with ¼ cup melted butter.

FROZEN ORANGE CREAM, DE LUXE
¾ cup (one 6-ounce can) frozen orange juice, thawed
1½ cups cold water
1 envelope unflavored gelatin
¾ cup sugar
⅛ teaspoon salt
½ cup Grand Marnier liqueur, Curaçao, or Triple Sec
2 cups heavy cream, whipped

Turn refrigerator control to coldest setting. Beat orange juice and water until blended. Put ¼ cup in small saucepan, sprinkle with gelatin, and let stand for 5 minutes. Dissolve gelatin over hot water or very low heat. Add to orange juice. Add sugar, salt, and liqueur. Then fold in cream. Pour into refrigerator trays and freeze, stirring once or twice. Makes about 8 servings.

TURKISH PASTE
2 envelopes unflavored gelatin
⅓ cup cold water
3 cups sugar
¼ cup boiling water
⅛ teaspoon salt
¼ cup fresh orange juice
Few drops each of red and yellow food coloring
Confectioners' sugar

Soften gelatin in cold water. Mix sugar, boiling water, and salt, bring to boil and boil for 5 minutes. Add gelatin and sim-

mer for 20 minutes. Remove from heat and add orange juice and coloring. Rinse a loaf pan (9 x 5 x 3 inches) with cold water. Pour in mixture. Let stand overnight. Cut in cubes with a warm knife and roll in confectioners' sugar. Makes about 1 pound.

GÉNOISE—A spongecake made with melted butter. It is a very fine-textured cake used as the basis for many elegant creations, such as *gâteaux*. A recipe for a *génoise* appears on page 781.

GERANIUM or PELARGONIUM—
There are more than 250 varieties of this popular perennial. *Geranos* was the Greek word for crane and some of the varieties of the plant are called cranesbill because the fruit or seedpod is shaped like a crane's bill.

Some types of geraniums take their names from the scent of their fragrant leaves which smell like other plants. The apple, lemon, honey, and nutmeg geraniums all have an entrancing scent. Perhaps the most popular is the rose geranium with leaves which smell, naturally, like spicy roses.

Geraniums originally came from South Africa and were not introduced into Europe until the 17th century. There is a Moslem legend that the geranium was at first a lowly mallow until Mohammed happened to hang his shirt to dry on it. When he took away his shirt the simple plant had been rewarded with brightly colored flowers and a fragrant aroma.

Geranium leaves are traditionally used to heal wounds made by any iron weapon. In Massachusetts some people believe that a geranium in the window will

keep flies away from the house. The leaves of the fragrant varieties, especially the rose geranium, are used for flavoring food.

The rose geranium is a shrubby plant with divided leaves and bunches of small pinkish flowers. It is not particularly hardy and should be grown in the sun and taken indoors before frost. The oil from rose-geranium leaves is commercially extracted for use in perfume and soap, either by itself or with essence of roses, but the enthuiast can make balms and sweet-smelling potpourris at home with the leaves. The leaves also make an attractive and unusual garnish. Small ones perch on a fruit cup or enhance cold tea, fruit drinks, lemonades, and wine cups. Hot drinks have a subtle rose flavor if a leaf is crushed in the bottom of a cup or glass before the liquid is poured. A few leaves placed in the bottom of a pan of baked apples, custards, puddings, or ice cream is a good idea. And geranium jam or jelly tastes as good as it sounds.

ROSE-GERANIUM JELLY
4 pounds ripe apples (to make 5 cups prepared juice)
6½ cups water
7½ cups sugar
½ bottle fruit pectin
Rose-geranium leaves

Remove blossom and stem ends from apples, and cut apples in small pieces. Do not peel or core. (With soft, very sweet apples, add 2 tablespoons fresh lemon juice.) Add the water, bring to boil and simmer, covered, for 10 minutes. Crush with masher and simmer, covered, for 5 minutes longer. Put in a large sieve lined with a double thickness of cheesecloth. Drain. Use 5 cups of the juice to make the jelly. (Use fruit pulp in sieve to make apple butter, if desired.) Put a geranium leaf in each of 12 hot sterilized medium jelly glasses. Mix juice and sugar in large saucepan. Put over high heat and bring to boil, stirring constantly. At once stir in pectin. Then bring to a *full rolling boil and boil hard for 1 minute,* stirring constantly. Remove from heat, skim off foam with metal spoon and pour quickly into glasses. Cover at once with ⅛ inch hot paraffin. Makes 12 medium glasses.

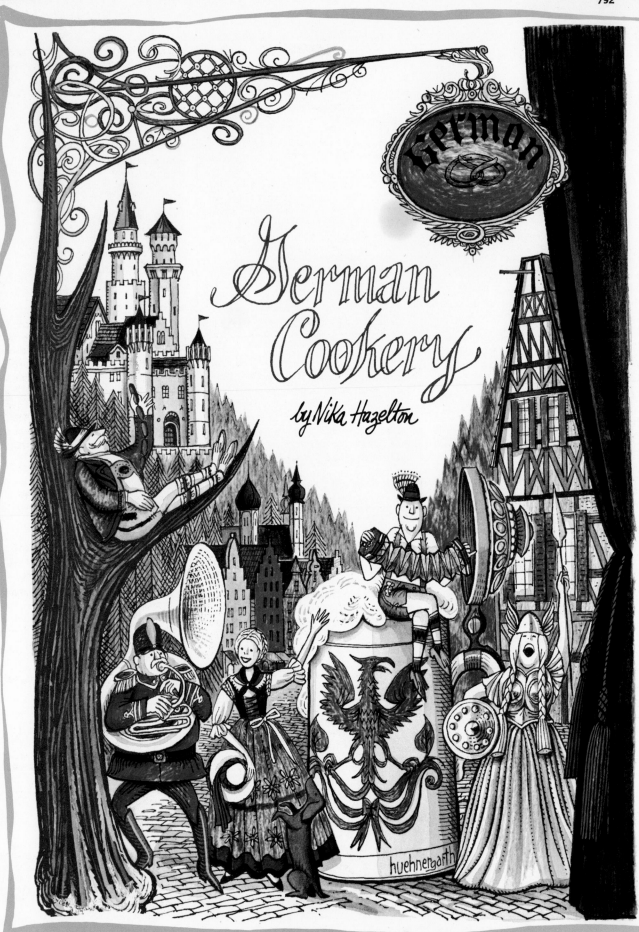

German Cookery

by Nika Hazelton

Germany is a country of many different regions, united by a common language and by a number of common traditions. The cooking of the country has a general character of its own; and it is rich in regional specialties.

The South Germans have different ideas about food than the North Germans, and the people of the Rhineland from those who live in the former German provinces of the East. Contributing to these regional preferences are the food resources and food habits of neighboring nations. The northern Germans, who are located near the Scandinavians, eat potatoes which grow well in their sandy soil. The southern Germans, with a ready supply of wheat, are dumpling eaters like the Austrians, Czechs, and Swiss who live nearby.

What unites the Germans is their predilection for savory, substantial food, suited to a climate that is, on the whole, cool and damp.

The most famous German specialties are the smoked pork and fine hams (such as the Westphalian ham) and the dozens of fresh or smoked sausages. The sight of a well-stocked German sausage store is never to be forgotten, especially at Christmastime when the artistically inclined *Schweinemetzger,* or pork butchers, build elaborate gingerbread-type houses with their wares.

Typical of German cooking are the sweet-sour combinations in main dishes (*sauerbraten* or "sour roast" is the best known), vegetables, salads, and sauces. In some cases, vinegar and sugar are combined; in others, fruits are cooked together with meats, vegetables, or legumes. The Germans rely heavily on fruit in their cooking and baking, witness the delicious *kuchen,* or cakes, with their fruit fillings. The country has lovely orchards, and in many parts fruit trees line the side of the country roads the way elms line ours. The fruits are traditionally dried for winter use.

A good deal of fish is eaten in Germany: fish which is caught in the lakes and streams and in the North Sea. The most distinguished German way of cooking fish is the "blue" method for carp and trout, which consists of a very brief dipping into hot fish stock or water. This gives the fish a bluish tinge.

Desserts play a prominent part in the German diet. Puddings, creams, cakes, and cookies are made in an infinite variety and they rank among the best in the world. Very often they are served with whipped cream.

SOUPS

LEBERKNÖDELSUPPE
(Liver Dumpling Soup)
- 1 pound beef liver
- 5 hard rolls
- 1 teaspoon salt
- 1 teaspoon crumbled dried marjoram
- 2 quarts chicken bouillon

Grind liver, removing all connecting tissue. Soak rolls in water, squeeze dry, and break up. Mix with liver, adding salt and marjoram. Form into large round balls and poach for 10 minutes in the lightly boiling bouillon. Makes 4 servings.

MARKKLÖSSCHEN
(Marrow Dumplings in Consommé)
- ⅔ cup beef marrow
- 4 slices of stale bread
- ¼ cup milk
- 2 eggs
- 2 tablespoons all-purpose flour
- Salt and pepper
- ⅛ teaspoon ground nutmeg

Scoop marrow from marrow bone with sharp pointed knife. Melt over low heat. Soak bread in milk and squeeze dry with hands. Combine all ingredients with salt and pepper to taste, and blend thoroughly. Drop dumplings by teaspoonfuls into simmering consommé. Cook until they float to the surface. Makes 4 to 6 servings.

FISH AND SHELLFISH

GEBRATENER HUMMER
(Fried Lobster)
Cut cooked fresh or frozen lobster or canned lobster into 1- to 2-inch pieces. Sprinkle with salt, pepper, and fresh lemon juice. Coat lobster pieces with fine white dry bread crumbs, dip into beaten egg yolk, and coat again with bread crumbs. Fry in deep fat (370°F. on a frying thermometer) until golden. Drain on absorbent paper. Serve with tartare sauce.

RHEIN LACHS VOM GRILL
(Broiled Salmon)
- 2 pounds salmon, center cut, in one piece
- Salt and pepper to taste
- Juice of 2 lemons
- ¼ cup olive oil
- 1 large onion, sliced

Wash and dry fish. Cut into slices 3 inches long and 1 inch wide. Sprinkle with salt, pepper, lemon juice, and olive oil. Top with onion slices. Refrigerate, covered, for 1 to 2 hours. Remove onion slices. Broil fish for approximately 5 to 8 minutes on each side. Turn only one time. Serve with plain boiled potatoes, cucumber salad, and mayonnaise. Makes 4 servings.

GEBACKENE SEEZUNGE
(Deep-Fried Sole)
- 2 pounds fillet of sole
- Salt and pepper to taste
- 3 eggs, beaten
- 6 tablespoons all-purpose flour
- 1½ cups (about) bread crumbs
- Fat for deep frying
- Lemon wedges
- Parsley

Wash fish and pat absolutely dry with paper towel. Cut into diagonal strips about 3 inches long, ¾ inch wide. Sprinkle with salt and pepper. Dip into beaten eggs and flour. Dip again into eggs and then into bread crumbs. Fry in hot deep fat (370°F. on frying thermometer) until browned on all sides. Drain on paper towel. Garnish with lemon wedges and parsley. Serve with potato salad and rémoulade sauce. Makes 3 to 4 servings.

MEAT AND POULTRY

SAUERBRATEN MIT SPÄTZLE
(Pot Roast with Dumplings)
- 5 pounds pot roast of beef (top, bottom, or eye of round)
- 4 cups each of water and wine vinegar
- 1 onion, coarsely chopped
- 2 bay leaves
- 10 peppercorns
- 5 whole cloves
- Rind of ½ lemon
- 1 tablespoon sugar
- 1 garlic clove
- 2 or 3 fresh pine twigs, about 5 inches long (if available)
- All-purpose flour
- Salt and pepper
- 2 tablespoons fat
- 1 onion, sliced
- 1 large carrot, sliced
- ¾ cup canned tomatoes
- 2 cups each of strained marinade and water
- Spätzle

Leberknödelsuppe ▲   **Tannenbaum Brot** ▼

Put meat in large bowl. Bring to boil water, vinegar, and next 7 ingredients. Cool and pour over meat; add pine twigs. Cover and put in refrigerator, turning meat once or twice a day. (If top or bottom round is´ used, it should marinate for 48 to 72 hours. For eye of the round, 24 to 40 hours is ample.) When ready, remove meat from the marinade; strain marinade and reserve. Rub meat with flour mixed with salt and pepper. Brown on all sides in hot fat, being sure not to pierce meat. Put meat on rack; add sliced onion, carrot, tomatoes, strained marinade, and water. Cover and simmer for 2½ hours, or until meat is tender. turning one or twice. Remove meat and thicken liquid with flour mixed with a little cold water. Simmer for a few minutes. Adjust seasoning if necessary. A little white wine or sour cream can be added to gravy, if desired. Serve with *Spätzle*. Makes 6 to 8 servings.

Spätzle
(Small Dumplings)
3 cups all-purpose flour
1 teaspoon salt
Dash each of ground nutmeg and
paprika
4 eggs, slightly beaten
¾ cup water
Boiling salted water

Sift flour with salt and spices. Add eggs and water. Beat batter until thick and smooth. Dampen the end of a small cutting board. Put on ¾ cup of the dough. With a spatula, smooth a small amount of the dough very thin. Cut off small strips of dough into a large kettle of boiling salted water. Dip spatula into water several times during cutting. If dough is too thin to hold together, add a little flour. Cook until tender, about 5 minutes. Lift out with a slotted spoon, drain, and place in serving dish. Continue with remaining dough, adding a little fresh boiling water to kettle each time. Serve with a little melted butter. Makes about 6 servings.

KALBSBRATEN
(Veal Roast)
One 5-pound leg or shoulder of veal
Salt and pepper
¼ cup butter or margarine
1 onion, thinly sliced
1 tomato (optional)

1 cup beef bouillon
2 tablespoons butter, melted
Green peas, carrots, and
cauliflowerets, cooked
Parsley sprigs

Sprinkle meat with salt and pepper. In heavy casserole or Dutch oven melt butter over high heat. Brown meat in it on all sides. Add onion, tomato (if desired), and beef bouillon. Lower heat as low as possible. Cook, covered for 1½ to 2 hours on top of the stove, or cook, covered, in preheated slow oven (300° F.) for about 2½ hours, or until meat is tender. Check occasionally; if necessary, add a little more hot bouillon, 1 or 2 tablespoons at a time. When meat is tender, some of the liquid should have evaporated. Brush melted butter over meat and return to oven for 15 minutes more. Remove meat to hot platter and slice. Make gravy in the usual manner. Spoon a little of the gravy over meat slices. Surround meat with mounds of buttered green peas, buttered carrots, and cauliflowerets, and garnish with parsley sprigs. Serve remaining gravy separately with boiled or roast potatoes. Makes approximately 12 servings.

FRANKFURTER RIPPCHEN
(Pot Roast of Smoked Loin of Pork)
2 pounds smoked loin of pork
1 onion, chopped
1 tomato, chopped
1 celery stalk, chopped
1 cup water
Salt and pepper

If necessary cut loin into several pieces to fit a deep pot. Put meat into pot with remaining ingredients. Simmer, covered, for 1½ hours. Add more water if necessary, but only just enough to prevent the meat from sticking. The cooking is really a steaming process. Serve with sauerkraut, mashed potatoes, and mustard. Makes 4 to 6 servings.

SCHWEINEKNIESTÜCKE MIT SAUERKRAUT UND KARTOFFELKLÖSSE
(Pigs' Knuckles, Sauerkraut, and Potato Dumplings)

Put 3 pounds pigs' knuckles, 2 pounds sauerkraut, and 6 cups water in kettle; cover; simmer for 3½ hours, or until meat is tender. Add 2 tablespoons caraway seeds and salt to taste. Serve with Kartoffelklösse. Makes 4 servings.

Kartoffelklösse
(Potato Dumplings)

8 medium potatoes
½ cup all-purpose flour
2 eggs, slightly beaten
1½ teaspoons salt
1 tablespoon minced onion
2 tablespoons butter
1 slice bread, cut into small cubes

Steam unpeeled potatoes until tender. Peel and force through a ricer onto platter. Let stand overnight, uncovered. Add flour, eggs, and salt; mix well. Brown onion in butter. Add bread cubes, and brown. Flatten a spoonful of potato mixture in your hand and put a few cubes of bread on dumpling. Roll into ball. Repeat until the mixture is used. Drop into large kettle of boiling salted water. Boil, uncovered, for 20 minutes, or until done. Drain and serve at once. Makes 8 to 10 dumplings.

HUHN IM BURGUNDER
(Chicken Cooked in Burgundy Wine)

5 tablespoons butter or margarine
3 slices of bacon, cut into matchstick size
1 medium onion, thinly sliced
1 broiling or frying chicken (2½ to 3 pounds), cut into pieces
1 tablespoon all-purpose flour
2 tablespoons brandy
2 cups Burgundy or other dry red wine
1 bay leaf
2 tablespoons chopped parsley
¼ teaspoon crumbled dried thyme
1 teaspoon salt
½ teaspoon pepper
⅛ teaspoon ground nutmeg
1 cup chopped fresh mushrooms, sautéed in butter

Melt ¼ cup butter over medium heat, stirring occasionally. Cook bacon and onion in it until soft and transparent. Remove bacon and onion with slotted spoon and reserve. Brown chicken on all sides in remaining fat. Sprinkle with flour. Add brandy, Burgundy, bay leaf, parsley, thyme, salt, pepper, and nutmeg. Cook, covered, in preheated moderate oven (350°F.) for 30 minutes, or until tender. Stir in reserved bacon and onion and the mushrooms. Return to oven and cook, covered, for another 5 to 10 minutes. Remove; stir remaining butter into the sauce. Serve with noodles or mashed potatoes. Makes 4 servings.

GEBRATENE ENTE
(Roast Stuffed Duck)
1 duck (4 to 5 pounds)
Salt
Stuffing:
3 cups crumbs of black pumpernickel
½ cup diced unpeeled apples
½ cup seedless raisins
½ cup diced pitted prunes
1 tablespoon sugar
2 teaspoons salt
2 teaspoons rum

Clean duck and remove excess fat. Rub outside and inside with salt. Combine all ingredients under Stuffing and stuff duck. Place breast side up in roasting pan. Roast in preheated moderate oven (350° F.) for 1½ to 2 hours, or until tender. Pour off excess fat as it drains from the duck into the roasting pan. Serve with stewed red cabbage, boiled potatoes, and a celery salad. Makes 3 to 4 servings.

VEGETABLES

SALZKARTOFFELN
(Boiled Potatoes)
Peel potatoes and cut them into halves or quarters. Place in cold water for 10 minutes; drain. This removes excess starch. Place in saucepan with just enough water to cover. Salt the water to taste. Bring to a boil and cook, covered, until tender; drain. Shake pan with potatoes over medium heat to allow all steam to escape. The potatoes must be dry and mealy. The ideal way of serving these potatoes is to line the serving dish with a napkin and place the potatoes on it. The napkin will absorb any remaining moisture.

ERBSENPUREE
(Purée of Dried Peas)
1 pound dried yellow or green peas
4 slices of bacon
1 medium onion, sliced thin

Soak peas in water overnight. Drain and cook in fresh salted water for 1½ to 2 hours until soft. Drain, reserving cooking liquid. Put through a food mill or whirl in the blender, adding enough of the water in which the peas were cooked to make purée of the consistency you like. Fry bacon crisp and drain it. Fry onion in the bacon fat. Crumble bacon

and sprinkle it and the onion over the purée. Makes 4 servings.

LEIPZIGER ALLERLEI
(Vegetable Medley)

1½ cups raw fresh peas
1 cup raw sliced carrots
1 cup 1-inch pieces of raw asparagus
1 kohlrabi, peeled and sliced
1 small cauliflower, broken into flowerets
3 tablespoons butter or margarine
1 cup water
Salt and sugar to taste
1½ teaspoons cornstarch
2 tablespoons cold water
1 tablespoon chopped parsley

Wash vegetables and drain thoroughly. Melt butter and sauté vegetables for 5 minutes. Add water, cover, and simmer until vegetables are tender. Season to taste with salt and sugar. Mix cornstarch with cold water and add gradually to hot vegetables. Stir over low heat until vegetables and juice are slightly thickened. Serve sprinkled with chopped parsley. Makes 4 to 6 servings.

Note: Vegetables may be steamed separately and then combined, with the vegetable juices thickened and used for a sauce.

KARTOFFELSALAT
(Potato Salad)

2 pounds potatoes
¼ cup bacon fat, melted
2 tablespoons vinegar
1 cup beef bouillon
1 small onion, chopped
Salt and pepper

Cook potatoes in boiling salted water until tender. Peel and slice. When slightly cooled, sprinkle with bacon fat and vinegar. Add beef bouillon, onion, and seasonings to taste. Mix gently and let stand for several hours at room temperature. This salad must not be chilled. Makes 6 servings.

BAYERISCHES KRAUT
(Bavarian Cabbage)

1 medium head red cabbage
1 tart apple
2 tablespoons butter or margarine
1 bay leaf
2 juniper berries
Salt and pepper
¼ cup dry white wine
2 tablespoons vinegar
1 teaspoon sugar

Wash and shred cabbage. Peel, core, and slice apple. Melt butter and add cabbage and apple, mixing well. Add bay leaf, juniper berries, and salt and pepper to taste. Cover and cook over low heat for about 10 minutes. Add wine, vinegar, and sugar and mix well. Cook for 30 minutes to 1 hour longer. Makes 4 to 6 servings.

SAUERKRAUTSALAT
(Sauerkraut Salad)

About 2 cups (one 16- to 17-ounce can) sauerkraut
3 tablespoons olive oil

Schweinekniestücke mit Sauerkraut und Kartoffelklösse

2 tart apples, peeled, cored, and grated
1 onion, chopped
1 teaspoon sugar
   Salt and pepper to taste

Rinse sauerkraut under cold water and drain well. Mix other ingredients, pour over sauerkraut, and toss well. Let stand for 30 minutes before serving. Makes 4 servings.

BREAD

TANNENBAUM BROT
(Christmas Tree Bread)
2 packages active dry or 2 cakes compressed yeast
¼ cup lukewarm water*
2 teaspoons salt
½ cup sugar
1½ cups milk, scalded and cooled
½ cup melted butter
2 eggs
6 cups sifted all-purpose flour, about
½ teaspoon each of ground nutmeg and cinnamon
½ cup each of raisins, cut-up candied cherries, and chopped nuts
   Confectioners' sugar

Sprinkle dry yeast or crumble cake yeast into warm water.* Use very warm water (105°F. to 115°F.) for dry yeast; use lukewarm water (80°F. to 90°F.) for compressed. Let stand for a few minutes, then stir until dissolved. Now add the salt, sugar, cooled milk, butter, eggs, and 4 cups of flour. Beat with a spoon until thoroughly mixed. Stir in remaining flour and the rest of the ingredients; by this time you will have to use your hands. Turn out on a lightly floured board and knead until smooth, about 5 minutes. Place in a greased bowl, cover, and let rise until doubled. Punch down and let rise again until doubled. These two rising times will take about 2½ hours in all. Now turn the dough out and shape it into 2 loaves. Place in greased loaf pans (9 x 5 x 3 inches) and let rise again until doubled. Bake in preheated moderate oven (350° F.) for about 45 minutes. Cool. Before serving sprinkle with confectioners' sugar. Makes 3 loaves.

Note: When making this bread, remember to start it in the morning, and give it plenty of rising time.

CAKES AND COOKIES

STOLLEN
(Christmas Fruitcake)
2 packages active dry yeast or 2 cakes compressed yeast
¼ cup lukewarm water*
1¾ cups milk, scalded and cooled
1 cup butter
1½ cups sugar
3 eggs

1 box (15 ounces) raisins
1 cup chopped walnuts
   Grated rind of 1 lemon
   Candied peel of 1 lemon, chopped (¼ cup)
   Candied peel of 2 oranges, chopped (¾ cup)
2 teaspoons salt
½ teaspoon ground nutmeg
7 to 8 cups sifted all-purpose flour (about)
   Confectioners' Sugar Frosting, page 751

Sprinkle dry yeast or crumble cake yeast into warm water. *Use very warm water (105°F. to 115°F.) for dry yeast; use lukewarm water (80°F. to 90°F.) for compressed. Let stand for a few minutes, then stir until dissolved. Add the other ingredients and enough of the flour to make a medium-firm dough. Let it rise until doubled, punch down, and let rise again. Form into long loaves and press along the center with a rolling pin to flatten down. Fold over like a pocketbook roll, making the bottom larger than the top. Set on greased cookie sheets to rise. Bake in preheated moderate oven (350°F.) for 45 minutes to 1 hour. When done, frost lightly with Confectioners'-Sugar Frosting. Makes 2 stollens.

BIENENSTICH
("Bee's Sting" Coffeecake)
½ pound farmer cheese
½ cup milk
½ cup cooking oil
½ cup sugar
⅛ teaspoon salt
3½ cups sifted all-purpose flour
2 teaspoons baking powder

Topping:
½ cup butter or margarine
1 cup sugar
1 teaspoon vanilla extract
2 tablespoons milk
1 cup slivered blanched almonds

Press farmer cheese through a sieve. Add milk, oil, sugar, and salt. Blend well. Sift flour with baking powder and beat it into the cheese mixture. Roll out dough on a lightly floured board to ¼-inch thickness and spread in a greased jelly-roll pan (15½ x 10½ x 1 inch). Melt butter and stir in remaining ingredients. Cook until mixture starts to bubble. Cool. Spread mixture evenly over the dough. Bake in preheated mod-

erate oven (350°F.) for about 20 minutes, or until cake is golden brown. Cut into squares or bars.

MANDELKRÄNZE
(Almond Wreaths)
1 cup butter
1 cup sugar
2 eggs
   Grated rind of 1 lemon
2 cups sifted all-purpose flour
1 cup blanched almonds, chopped

Topping:
1 egg white, unbeaten
2 tablespoons sugar
⅓ cup blanched almonds, chopped
1 teaspoon ground cinnamon

Cream butter; gradually beat in sugar. Add eggs, one at a time, beating well after each addition. Add grated lemon rind, flour, and 1 cup chopped blanched almonds. Chill. Roll out on lightly floured board; cut with 2½-inch doughnut cutter and put on greased cookie sheets. Brush with unbeaten egg white and sprinkle with a mixture of remaining sugar and almonds and the ground cinnamon. Bake in preheated hot oven (400°F.) for 8 minutes, or until lightly browned. Store airtight. Can be frozen. Makes 5 dozen.

ELISEN LEBKUCHEN
(Elisen Ginger Cookies)
2¼ cups sugar
4 eggs
   Grated rind and juice of 1 lemon
1 teaspoon each of ground nutmeg and cinnamon
½ teaspoon ground cloves
3½ cups finely ground almonds
4 ounces candied lemon peel, finely ground
1 cup sifted all-purpose flour
½ teaspoon baking powder
   Thin lemon frosting
   Colored sugar

With electric beater at medium speed, beat sugar with eggs, lemon rind, and lemon juice for 10 minutes. Blend in thoroughly nutmeg, cinnamon, cloves, almonds, and lemon peel. Sift in flour and baking powder. Mix thoroughly. The dough will be soft and sticky. Line 2 greased pans (1 x 7 x 11 inches) with unglazed heavy brown paper so that ends reach over about 2 inches on all sides. Divide dough between pans. Bake in

preheated slow oven (325°F.) for 40 minutes, or until golden on top and testing done. Do not overbake. Lift carefully out of pan and cool on rack. Frost with thin lemon frosting and decorate with colored sugar while warm. Let frosting harden. With sharp knife dipped into water, cut contents of each pan into 30 strips. Remove very carefully from paper by pushing wet spatula underneath each strip and pushing to the side. Makes about 5 dozen.

Note: These cookies are not neat; they will have ragged edges.

SPITZBUBEN
(Urchins)

⅔ cup soft butter or margarine
2 cups sifted all-purpose flour
¼ teaspoon salt
1 cup sugar
2 tablespoons heavy cream
½ teaspoon vanilla extract
½ cup nuts, ground fine
　Currant jelly
　Vanilla sugar

With hands, mix first 7 ingredients to form a smooth dough. Chill for several hours. Roll to ⅛-inch thickness and cut with floured scalloped 2-inch cutter or other fancy cutter. Bake in preheated moderate oven (375°F.) for about 12 minutes. Cool; put together in pairs with jelly. Sprinkle with vanilla sugar. Makes about 2 dozen.

KUCHEN

Kuchen means "cake" in German, but to millions of Americans, *kuchen*, or coffeecake, is the basis for a typical Sunday morning breakfast. *Kuchen* dough is not too sweet or rich; it is rather the foil for luscious toppings. "Thin dough and thick topping" make for perfect coffeecakes. The topping can be sugar and cinnamon, applied before or during the baking period; with or without sour cream, orange marmalade, or blueberries; it can be crumbly streusel, or streusel over a thick poppy-seed filling; it can be fruit: apples, peaches, plums, or cherries. *Kuchen* dough has many possibilities; it is also quick and easy to make. It's delicious!

Kuchen Dough

1 package active dry yeast or 1 cake compressed yeast
¼ cup warm water*
2 egg yolks
1 whole egg
¼ cup sugar
1 cup milk
½ cup butter
3 cups sifted all-purpose flour
1 teaspoon salt
¼ teaspoon ground mace
　Grated rind of ½ lemon

Sprinkle dry yeast or crumble cake yeast into warm water. *Use very warm water (105°F. to 115°F.) for dry yeast; use lukewarm water (80°F. to 90°F.) for compressed. Let stand for a few minutes, then stir until dissolved. Using an electric mixer, beat egg yolks and whole egg until thick and lemon colored; gradually beat in the sugar. Scald the milk and melt the butter in it; cool to lukewarm. Add 1 cup of flour and the yeast to the egg mixture; beat well. Add the milk, salt, mace, grated lemon rind, and remaining flour; beat for 5 minutes. Cover; let rise in a warm place until doubled in bulk. Pour into 2 buttered 9-inch layer-cake pans making the layer of dough only ½ inch thick. Let rise until doubled in bulk. Cover with topping. Bake in preheated moderate oven (350°F.) for 20 to 25 minutes. Makes 2 kuchen.

Cinnamon and Sugar Toppings for Kuchen

Spread the kuchen, before it goes into the oven, with melted butter; sprinkle liberally with cinnamon and sugar, using the proportion of 1 cup sugar and 1 tablespoon ground cinnamon. Bake for 15 minutes; remove from oven, drizzle with more butter and sprinkle with more sugar and cinnamon. Return to the oven for 5 more minutes.

■ **Interesting Variations**—Make depressions in the risen dough, using the handle of a wooden spoon. Fill with dairy sour cream, orange marmalade, or 3 or 4 large blueberries. Spread with melted butter; sprinkle with cinnamon and sugar. Bake as above.

Streusel Topping

Sift together ½ cup all-purpose flour and ½ cup sugar; add ½ cup ground almonds and 2 teaspoons ground cinnamon. Work in ½ cup butter until mixture is crumbly. Sprinkle over risen *kuchen* dough that has been brushed with butter. Bake as above.

Mohn Kuchen

Grind 1 cup poppy seeds and boil until thick with 1 cup milk, 2 tablespoons butter, grated rind of ½ lemon, ¼ cup sugar, and ¼ cup seedless raisins. Spread over risen *kuchen* dough that has been brushed with melted butter. Top with streusel. Bake as above.

Apple, Plum, or Peach Kuchen

Spread *kuchen* dough ½ inch thick in buttered pan. Pare, core, and quarter tart apples; or halve and stone blue Italian plums; or pare, stone, and quarter peaches. Arrange fruit in neat rows, pressing fruit lightly into dough. Sprinkle cakes made with apples or peaches with 2 tablespoons currants. Mix together ¾ cup sugar, 1 teaspoon ground cinnamon, and 2 tablespoons all-purpose flour; work in 2 tablespoons butter. Spread over fruit. Cover and let rise for 45 minutes. Bake in preheated moderate oven (350°F.) for 30 minutes.

Schnecken

Turn ½ recipe of *kuchen* dough on lightly floured board and pat to a triangle. Brush with melted butter and sprinkle with ¼ cup brown sugar, 1 teaspoon ground cinnamon, ½ cup chopped nuts, and ½ cup currants. Roll as for jelly roll. Cut into twelve 1-inch slices. Place in buttered pan. Cover and let rise until double in bulk. Brush with butter and sprinkle with sugar and cinnamon. Bake in preheated moderate oven (350°F.) for 25 minutes. Makes 12.

Walnut Rolls

Make a syrup of ¼ cup butter, ½ cup brown sugar, and 1 tablespoon water; boil for 1 minute. Pour into 12 buttered muffin tins. Place 3 or 4 walnut halves in each tin. Place slices, prepared as for Schnecken, on syrup in muffin tins. Cover and let rise until doubled in bulk. Bake in preheated moderate oven (350°F.) for 25 minutes. Remove from oven, invert on cookie sheet, and remove rolls. Serve caramel side up. Makes 12.

GHEE—This is the anglicized version of the Hindustani word *ghi,* which means "clarified butter" and is a basic ingredient in the cooking of India. Indian butter is made from buffalo's or cow's milk. To clarify it, the butter is heated until the milk solids are separated from the clear fat. Then it is strained through a cloth and poured into a container for storage. The reason for clarifying butter

in a hot climate (the Arabs do it, as well) is that it will keep without refrigeration for quite a long time, depending on the temperature.

───── 🎀 ─────

GHERKIN—These very small cucumbers grow to a length of about one to three inches. They are used to make either sweet or sour pickles. Gherkins are good condiments; they can be chopped into salads, sauces, stuffings, and fish dishes.

───── 🎀 ─────

GIBLETS—The gizzard, liver, and heart of any kind of poultry are called giblets. They are an inexpensive, good-quality source of protein and minerals. Poultry livers cook quickly, but the remaining giblets must be simmered in water to cover, with seasonings added, for about 1 hour, or until they are tender. They are then chopped and mixed with the cooked liver for rice and noodle dishes, dressings, pâtes, sandwich fillings, gravies, etc. The broth can be used for soup or gravies, or for cooking.

Availability and Purchasing Guide—Chicken giblets without the liver are available packaged. Livers are sold separately.

Select giblets with a fresh, firm appearance and no strong odor.

Storage—Store loosely wrapped in wax paper in coldest part of refrigerator. Use within 24 hours.

☐ Refrigerator shelf: 24 hours
☐ Refrigerator frozen-food compartment, prepared for freezing: 1 week
☐ Freezer, prepared for freezing: 2 to 3 months

Caloric Values—All the following caloric values are based on 3½ ounces:

☐ Giblets, chicken, raw = 135 calories
   goose, raw = 156 calories
   turkey, raw = 150 calories
☐ Liver, chicken, simmered = 165 calories
   goose, raw = 182 calories
   turkey, simmered = 174 calories

GIBLET PÂTÉ
½ pound chicken giblets including livers
  Salt and pepper to taste
¼ cup chopped celery
¼ cup chopped onion
¼ cup butter or margarine
1 tablespoon brandy

Remove livers from giblets. Cover remaining giblets with water and add salt, pepper, celery, and half of onion. Simmer, covered, for 1 hour, or until giblets are tender. Drain and reserve broth. Melt butter and sauté chicken livers with remaining onion until cooked through. Pass all the giblets with sautéed onions through coarse blade of a food chopper. Mash to form a smooth paste. Stir in brandy and add enough melted butter from the skillet or liquid drained from giblets to make a smooth spreadable paste. Chill until ready to serve. Serve on toast or crackers. Makes about 1 cup.

CHICKEN GIBLETS WITH RICE
1 pound chicken giblets including livers
½ cup chopped onions
¼ cup diced carrots
2 parsley sprigs
1½ teaspoons salt
½ cup butter or margarine
1⅓ cups uncooked rice
½ teaspoon crumbled dried oregano
½ teaspoon pepper

Place giblets except livers in a saucepan. Add ¼ cup onions, the carrots, parsley, and salt. Add water to cover. Cover and simmer for 1 hour, or until giblets are tender. Drain and reserve broth. Chop giblets and save with carrots. Add enough water to giblet broth to make 2½ cups. Melt butter and add remaining onions and livers. Sauté until onions are golden brown and livers are cooked through. Remove livers and set aside. Add rice, oregano, and pepper. Add giblet broth. Simmer, covered, stirring occasionally, until rice is tender, adding more water if necessary. Add livers, chopped giblets, and carrots. Add more salt and pepper if desired. Reheat until piping hot. Makes 4 to 6 servings.

GIBLET SANDWICH FILLING
1 cup ground cooked chicken giblets
¼ cup minced celery
1 pimiento, chopped
½ small onion, minced
⅓ cup mayonnaise or salad dressing
1 tablespoon chopped green pepper
⅓ cup minced sweet pickles
  Salt and pepper to taste

Combine all ingredients and mix well. Makes enough filling for 6 sandwiches.

MUSHROOM-GIBLET DRESSING FOR POULTRY
½ pound mushrooms, sliced
1 medium onion, sliced
½ cup chopped parsley
1 teaspoon crumbled dried marjoram
1 teaspoon crumbled dried sage
1 teaspoon salt
½ teaspoon pepper
¼ cup butter or margarine
  Chopped cooked giblets and neck meat from poultry
1 cup giblet broth
3 cups soft stale-bread crumbs

Cook mushrooms and onions with seasonings in butter for 5 minutes. Add remaining ingredients and mix well. Makes about 4 cups.

GIBLET GRAVY
Wash giblets from chicken or turkey. Cook neck, heart, and gizzard in boiling water to cover with a bay leaf, 1 onion, and a few celery leaves for about 2 hours. Add liver for last 20 minutes of cooking. Drain, reserving stock, Remove meat from neck; grind or chop with giblets.

To make gravy; pour dripping from roasting pan into bowl. Skim off fat and put ½ cup into saucepan. Blend in ½ cup all-purpose flour. Measure skimmed drippings and add enough stock and water to make 6 cups. Cook fat and flour until bubbly. Add liquid all at once and cook until thickened, stirring constantly. Add giblets and season mixture to taste. Makes about 6 cups.

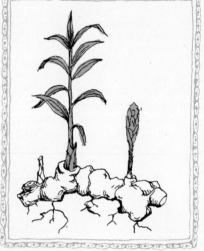

GINGER—Ginger is a spice obtained from the root of *Zingiber officinale,* an erect perennial plant that grows to a height of three feet, and has large brilliant yellowish flowers with purple lips, which are borne in a spike. Both the botanical and common name of the plant are from Sanskrit, the ancient classical language of India. There are several hundred varieties of ginger. We import it from Jamaica, India, Sierra Leone, and Nigeria.

The pungent smell of ginger comes from an aromatic oil, the peppery taste from a substance called "gingerin." The root, or rhizome, of the plant is the part that is prepared for use. The root branches into what is known as a "hand" and it is pale yellow in color on the outside and a greenish-yellow on the inside.

Ginger's original home was southeastern Asia, and it was used in India and China before the days of Rome. The Talmud mentions ginger many times. Marco Polo wrote of Chinese ginger plantations in the 13th century, and the Spaniards brought it to the New World in the 16th.

For a long time ginger was considered a medicine as well as a spice. It was said to cure the troubles of love and to prolong life. More importantly, ginger was used as a remedy against the plague; King Henry VIII of England suggested that it be taken with wine and herbs as a preventive against the dreaded disease that decimated Europe periodically. Ginger is still used in medicine as a digestive stimulant.

Ginger is used crystallized, preserved, or dried; whole, cracked, or ground to a powder. Crystallized and preserved gingerroot is looked upon as a confection and widely enjoyed.

To preserve gingerroot, juicy young roots are cleaned, peeled, and boiled in water until tender, and then boiled with a sugar syrup. Preserved or green gingerroot, in lovely blue and white china jars with domed lids, is a specialty of southern China, and dear to the eyes and palate of all who enjoy it.

Gingerroot is also dried and coated with sugar. It makes a delicious low-calorie candy or dessert.

Dried ground ginger is used as a spice, in soups, meat, and poultry dishes, in curries except fish curries, for pickling, and especially for baking gingerbread and flavoring many cakes. When applied with a light hand, it is also an excellent spice for fresh-fruit salads or compotes, and is used to make a comforting tea.

Finally, ginger is widely used for flavoring ginger ale, one of the most popular beverages.

GINGERED MELON

Peel, seed, and slice a ripe melon. Arrange melon in overlapping slices on platter. Sprinkle melon with sifted sugar and ¼ to 1 teaspoon ground ginger, depending on taste. Chill before serving.

GINGERED FLANK STEAK ORIENTALE

    1 large flank steak, about 1½ pounds
      All-purpose flour
1½ teaspoons ground ginger
    ¼ teaspoon pepper
    2 tablespoons cooking oil
    1 medium onion, chopped
    1 garlic clove, minced
    ½ teaspoon dried thyme
      Hot bouillon or water
      Salt
      Cooked rice

Pound flank steak with flour, ginger, and pepper. Cut steak into 3-inch strips. Heat oil in deep heavy skillet or Dutch oven. Brown steak strips in it on both sides. Add onion, garlic, thyme, and just enough hot bouillon to cover meat. Cook, covered, over low heat or in slow oven (325°F.) for 1½ to 2 hours, or until meat is tender. Check liquid; if necessary, add a little more hot bouillon, a little at a time, but never more than enough to cover. Add salt if necessary. Serve with hot rice. Makes 3 or 4 servings.

GINGER BEEF

    4 pounds beef for pot roast
    1 teaspoon ground turmeric
    2 teaspoons ground ginger
    2 teaspoons salt
    2 tablespoons fat
    2 onions, chopped
    2 garlic cloves, minced
    1 cup canned tomatoes
    1 cup beef bouillon
    2 dried red peppers, crushed

Rub meat with turmeric, ginger, and salt. Brown on all sides in fat in heavy kettle. Put meat on rack in kettle. Add remaining ingredients. Simmer, covered, over low heat for 3½ hours. Makes 6 servings.

GINGER WAFFLES

    1 package waffle mix
    ½ cup molasses
    1 teaspoon ground ginger

Prepare waffles according to directions on package, omitting ½ cup liquid. Add molasses and ginger. Make in hot waffle iron. Serve with sweetened fresh or canned peaches, ice cream, hard sauce, cream cheese, cottage cheese, or whipped cream. Makes 6 to 8 waffles.

GINGERED PEARS

    7 cups (two 1-pound, 13-ounce cans)
      pear halves
    1 cup firmly packed light brown sugar
1½ cups granulated sugar
      Grated rind and juice of 2 lemons
    1 tablespoon ground ginger
    ½ cup diced crystallized gingerroot
    ½ teaspoon ground cinnamon
    ¼ cup drained (one 4-ounce bottle)
      maraschino cherries

Drain pears. Combine 1 cup pear syrup with sugar, lemon rind, and juice. Add spices. Boil gently for 5 minutes. Add pears and cherries and cook until pears are heated through, about 10 minutes. Pack in hot sterilized jars; seal. Makes 3 pints.

CREAMY BANANA NUT PIE

    2 cups water
    ¼ cup fresh lemon juice
3½ cups sliced ripe bananas (4 medium)
    ½ cup sifted confectioners' sugar
    1 teaspoon ground ginger
    ¼ teaspoon salt
    1 envelope unflavored gelatin
    ¼ cup water
    1 cup heavy cream, whipped
    1 cup chopped pecans
    1 deep 9-inch pie shell, baked

Combine water and lemon juice. Add bananas, cover, and refrigerate for 1 hour. Mix next 3 ingredients. Soften gelatin in cold water; dissolve over hot water. Drain bananas and beat until almost smooth. Stir in sugar mixture and gelatin. Fold in cream and ¾ cup nuts. Pour into baked shell and sprinkle with remaining nuts. Chill until set. Makes 6 to 8 servings.

GINGER PUMPKIN PIE

1¾ cups canned pumpkin
    1 can (14 ounces) sweetened

      condensed milk
    2 eggs
    1 teaspoon each of ground cinnamon
      and ginger
    ½ teaspoon salt
    ¼ teaspoon ground nutmeg
    ⅛ teaspoon ground cloves
    ½ cup hot water
      Pastry for 1-crust 9-inch pie,
      unbaked

Put all ingredients except pastry into bowl and beat until blended. Pour into pastry-lined pie pan. Bake in preheated moderate oven (375°F.) for 45 to 50 minutes. Makes 6 to 8 servings.

CRISP GINGER COOKIES

    1 cup soft butter or margarine
    ½ cup granulated sugar
    ½ cup firmly packed light brown sugar
    ⅓ cup molasses
    ⅔ cups light corn syrup
4½ cups sifted all-purpose flour
    1 teaspoon each of baking soda, salt,
      ground ginger, and cinnamon
    ½ teaspoon ground cloves

Cream butter; add sugar; beat until light. Add molasses and corn syrup; mix well. Add sifted dry ingredients and knead until smooth. Chill until firm. Roll out on lightly floured board to less than ⅛ inch thickness. Cut with floured fancy cutter. Bake on a greased cookie sheet in preheated moderate oven, (350°F.) for about 8 minutes. Makes about 12 dozen. Store airtight.

GINGER CUTOUTS

    ½ cup molasses
    ½ cup sugar
    ½ cup soft butter or margarine
2¾ cups sifted all-purpose flour
    2 teaspoons ground ginger
    ½ teaspoon salt
    1 teaspoon baking soda
    ½ cup buttermilk

Mix first 3 ingredients well; add sifted dry ingredients alternately with buttermilk and mix until smooth. Chill for several hours. Roll out on floured board to about ¼-inch thickness. Cut with floured cutter. Place on ungreased cookie sheets. Bake in preheated moderate oven (375°F.) for about 15 minutes. Cool and decorate as desired. Makes 5 to 6 dozen.

GINGER DROP COOKIES

1½ cups sifted all-purpose flour
    ½ cup sugar
    1 teaspoon baking soda
    ½ teaspoon salt
1½ teaspoons ground ginger
    ½ cup instant or regular whole-wheat
      cereal, uncooked
    ½ cup soft shortening
    1 egg
    ½ cup molasses

Mix dry ingredients in bowl. Add remaining ingredients and beat until smooth. Drop by teaspoonfuls onto greased cookie sheets 2 inches apart. Bake in preheated moderate oven (350°F.) for 12 to 15 minutes, or until lightly browned. Re-

{ Pain d'Épice }

move from sheet at once. Makes about 4 dozen 2-inch cookies.

GINGER WAFERS
¾ cup butter or margarine
1 cup firmly packed light brown sugar
1 cup molasses
3⅔ cup sifted all-purpose flour
1 tablespoon ground ginger
½ teaspoon salt
1 teaspoon baking soda
2 eggs, beaten
Grated rind of 1 orange
Confectioners'-sugar frosting
Tiny multicolored candies

Bring butter, sugar, and molasses to a rolling boil; boil for 6 minutes. Remove from heat; cool slightly. Add sifted dry ingredients, eggs, and grated rind. Mix well; chill. Roll paper-thin and cut with 3-inch star cookie cutter; put on buttered cookies sheets. Bake in preheated moderate oven (375°F.) for 8 to 10 minutes. Frost and decorate with candies. Store airtight. Makes 6 dozen.

FRUIT SPICE ROLL
2 cups prepared biscuit mix
1 teaspoon ground ginger
Grated rind of ½ lemon
About ⅔ cup milk
2 cups chopped cooked dried fruit
2 teaspoons butter
½ cup firmly packed brown sugar
½ teaspoon ground nutmeg

Combine biscuit mix with ginger and lemon rind; add enough milk to make a dough just stiff enough to be rolled. Turn out on floured board and roll into a long rectangle about ¼ inch thick. Spread with fruit, dot with butter, and sprinkle with sugar and nutmeg. Roll up like jelly roll. Place on greased baking pan and bake in preheated very hot oven (450°F.) for 10 minutes. Then reduce heat to moderate (350°F.) and continue baking for about 30 minutes. Slice; serve hot with a lemon sauce, if desired. Makes 8 servings.

PRESERVED GINGER AND CREAM
Serve little dishes of chilled preserved gingerroot with either heavy cream or dairy sour cream on the side. The cream should be chilled and need not be sweetened. The contrast between the peppy gingerroot and the bland cream is delightful.

FLORIDA GINGERED ORANGE PEEL
Cover peel of 3 large oranges with cold water. Bring to boil and cook until tender, pouring off the water and adding fresh cold water several times. Drain peel and cut into thin strips with scissors. In saucepan mix 1 cup sugar and 2 teaspoons ground ginger. Add ½ cup water and cook until mixture threads (242°F. on a candy thermometer). Add peel and cook over low heat until syrup is absorbed. Roll each strip in ginger-flavored sugar. Cool and pack airtight. Makes about ½ pound.

Gingered Grapefruit Peel
Follow recipe above, using 1 large grapefruit.

GINGER TOMATO CONSERVE
1¼ pounds (1 quart) small yellow or red tomatoes
2¾ cups sugar
Grated rind of 1 lemon
1 tablespoon chopped candied gingerroot or 1 piece of whole dried gingerroot
1 teaspoon whole cloves
1 tablespoon fresh lemon juice

Core tomatoes and prick several times with fork. Heat tomatoes and sugar slowly with lemon rind, gingerroot, and cloves until sugar dissolves. Bring to boil and simmer, uncovered, for 20 minutes, or until thick. Add lemon juice and pour into 3 hot sterilized 6-ounce glasses. Seal with paraffin.
Note: Peeled and quartered larger red or yellow tomatoes can be substituted for the small tomatoes.

FRESH GINGERROOT PRESERVE
1 pound fresh gingerroot
2 cups sugar
Water
½ teaspoon cream of tartar

Peel gingerroots and cut into bite-size pieces. Soak peeled roots in cold water to cover for 1 hour. Drain and cover with fresh cold water. Bring to a boil and cook for 5 minutes. Drain, cover with fresh cold water, and boil again for 5 minutes, or until tender. Drain and reserve. Combine sugar and 1 cup of water and cook, uncovered, for 5 minutes, or until thick. Add gingerroot and cream of tartar. Bring to a boil and boil for 2 minutes. Place in sterilized jars, seal, and store in cool place. Makes three 6-ounce jars.
Note: Fresh gingerroot can be bought in Chinese and other oriental markets.

GINGER TEA
Stir ¼ teaspoon powdered ginger into 1 cup hot water. Add sugar to taste and lemon, if desired. Makes 1 serving.

GINGER ALE—A carbonated beverage flavored with ginger, sugar, capsicum, and other flavorings and colored with caramel. Ginger ale is also made with an artificial sweetener rather than with sugar.

In addition to its uses as a beverage and mixer, ginger ale can be used as a basting liquid, in aspics, and in gelatin molds. It gives an interesting, zestful flavor to foods.

Caloric Values
☐ 3½ ounces = 31 calories
☐ 3½ ounces, ginger ale, with artificial sweetener = less than 1 calorie

HAM SIMMERED IN GINGER ALE
In a large saucepan cover a smoked ham with hot ginger ale. Bring to a boil, lower heat, and simmer until ham is tender about 25 minutes per pound for ham up to 10 pounds and 20 minutes per pound for ham 10 to 15 pounds. Cool ham in ginger ale. Remove from ginger ale and skin. Cut into slices. "Tenderized" hams need not be soaked before cooking; however, smoked country hams should be soaked overnight before cooking.

GINGER-ALE GLAZE FOR BAKED HAM
Press ½ cup brown sugar through sieve onto scored ham; pat on evenly. Finish baking, basting several times with a little ginger ale.

ORANGE-GINGER-ALE MOLD
1 box (3 ounces) orange-flavored gelatin
1 cup hot water
1 bottle (7 ounces) ginger ale
¼ cup chopped nuts
¼ cup diced celery
1 cup drained diced sweetened fresh or frozen peaches
Salad greens
Peach slices

Dissolve gelatin in hot water. Add ginger ale. Chill until slightly thickened. Fold in nuts, celery, and diced peaches. Turn into 1-quart mold and chill until firm. Unmold on greens; garnish with peaches. Makes 6 servings.

GINGER-ALE FRUIT MOLD
1 box (3 ounces) lemon-flavored gelatin
2 cups ginger ale
2 cups diced fruit (orange, pear, banana, cherries, apple), drained
¼ cup chopped nuts
1 tablespoon chopped candied gingerroot
Salad greens
Mayonnaise

Dissolve gelatin in 1 cup hot ginger ale; cool. Add 1 cup cold ginger ale. Chill until partially set; then stir in fruit, nuts, and gingerroot. Pour into 1-quart mold. Chill until firm. Unmold on salad greens; serve with mayonnaise. Makes 4 servings.

GINGER-FRUIT FROST
1 pint orange sherbet
1 bottle (29 ounces) ginger ale, chilled
Peach slices
Fresh berries
Mint sprigs

Divide sherbet among 6 chilled tall glasses. Fill with ginger ale. Garnish with fruit and mint. Serve with straws and iced-tea spoons. Makes 6 servings.

PINEAPPLE-GINGER-ALE JELLY WITH PEACHES
2 boxes (3 ounces each) lemon-flavored gelatin
2 cups canned pineapple juice, heated
2 cups ginger ale
1 teaspoon unflavored gelatin
¼ cup cold water
2 tablespoons dried-milk crystals

1 tablespoon sugar
⅛ teaspoon almond extract
   Dash of salt
8 canned peach halves
   Candied gingerroot, orange peel,
   or cherries

Dissolve lemon-flavored gelatin in hot juice. Add ginger ale; pour into 1½-quart mold. Chill until firm. Meanwhile, sprinkle unflavored gelatin on cold water and let stand for 5 minutes. Dissolve over hot water. Cool slightly. Sprinkle dried-milk crystals over mixture; stir to blend. Chill until slightly thickened. Beat with rotary beater until mixture holds its shape. Blend in sugar, flavoring, and salt. Unmold gelatin on serving plate. Arrange peach halves around mold. Fill peaches with whipped mixture. Garnish with candied fruit. Makes 8 servings.

GINGER BUTTERMILK
To a chilled glass half full of cold buttermilk, add enough cold ginger ale to fill.

LEMONADE-MINT PUNCH
Mash ¼ cup mint jelly with fork. Add 1 can (6 ounces) frozen lemonade concentrate and mix well. Add ice cubes and 1 bottle (29 ounces) chilled ginger ale. Stir well and serve at once. Makes 4 tall glasses.

ORANGE-GINGER FIZZ
In a gallon vacuum jug, combine 3 cans (6 ounces each) frozen orange-juice concentrate and 1½ quarts water. Add 1 bottle (29 ounces) chilled ginger ale and fill with ice. Makes 3 quarts.

PATRIOT PUNCH
1 can (6 ounces) frozen lemonade
1 can (6 ounces) frozen orange juice
1 can (6 ounces) frozen pineapple
   juice
3 bottles (29 ounces each) ginger ale
2 packages cherry-flavored drink mix
3 quarts water

Freeze some ice in star molds to pretty up the punch bowl, or use plain cubes. Combine all ingredients, add ice, serve. Makes 25 servings, allowing two 4-ounce cups for each.

GINGER BEER
GINGER BEER—A clear effervescent beverage made of ginger, sugar, and water, and fermented by yeast. It has a stronger ginger flavor than ginger ale and is popular in the British Isles.

GINGERBREAD
GINGERBREAD—A flat, square, spicy bread-cake made with brown sugar or honey and molasses (or just molasses), leavened with baking powder and baking soda (or just baking soda), and heavily spiced with ground ginger and other spices. It is usually cut into squares and served warm, plain or with ice cream, hot applesauce, or whipped cream.

Gingerbread is one of the oldest of cakes, dating back to the Middle Ages. The original gingerbread was not a cake, but a solid bread of honey, spices, and flour. In the days when knighthood was in flower, and knights fought tournaments to please their ladies, gingerbread was one of the gifts the ladies bestowed upon them as a favor. The gingerbread gift looked like a piece of tooled and gilt leather, since it was decorated with cloves, with gold leaf, often in the shape of a fleur-de-lys.

The great fairs of Europe, which were the social events of the Middle Ages and later centuries, where rich and poor, old and young gathered, would not have been complete without gingerbread stalls. Neither would the holidays, for which gingerbread was baked in special molds that are now museum prizes; the six-foot gingerbread men and women of Belgium and Holland, baked for St. Nicholas Day, come to mind, along with the *pain d'épices,* the spice- or gingerbread of the French; the *lebkuchen* of the Germans Swiss, and Austrians; and the *panforte* of Italy. Many of them were not only elaborate and fanciful in shape, but also in decoration, painted with colored sugar and often gilded; hence the expression "the gilt on the gingerbread." Our own colonists were proud of their wood gingerbread molds and their gingerbreads, one of the favorite of Colonial and post-Colonial cakes. George Washington's mother made it at home and served it to famous visitors.

OLD COLONY GINGERBREAD
1 cup plus 2 tablespoons sifted
   all-purpose flour
1¼ teaspoons baking powder
¼ teaspoon baking soda
1 teaspoon ground ginger
¼ teaspoon ground nutmeg
¾ teaspoon ground cinnamon
⅛ teaspoon salt
⅓ cup butter and vegetable shortening
½ cup boiling water or coffee
⅓ cup firmly packed dark brown sugar
½ cup dark molasses
1 egg, well beaten
⅓ cup mincemeat (optional)

Sift dry ingredients together. Add shortenings to boiling water or coffee and stir until dissolved. Then add sugar and molasses. Combine with dry ingredients, adding egg and beating until batter is smooth. Fold in mincemeat. Pour batter into lightly buttered and floured 9-inch square pan. Bake in preheated moderate oven (350°F.) for 35 to 40 minutes. Cut into squares and serve warm or cool, plain or with Lemon Sauce.

Lemon Sauce
½ cup sugar
1 tablespoon cornstarch
¼ teaspoon salt
¼ cup cold water
¾ cup boiling water
3 tablespoons fresh lemon juice
1 teaspoon grated lemon rind
½ teaspoon vanilla extract
2 tablespoons butter

Combine sugar, cornstarch, and salt. Gradually stir in cold water. Gradually stir in boiling water and cook for 3 minutes, or until smooth, clear, and thickened slightly. Stir in remaining ingredients. Makes 1½ cups.

BUSY-DAY GINGERBREAD
½ cup lard
½ cup warm water
1 cup light molasses
2½ cups sifted all-purpose flour
¾ teaspoon salt
1 teaspoon each of baking soda and
   ground ginger
½ teaspoon ground cinnamon
¼ teaspoon each of ground cloves and
   nutmeg

Melt lard in large saucepan. Remove from heat; add water and molasses. Sift together remaining ingredients and add to first mixture, beating until well blended. Pour into 9-inch square pan that has been lightly greased and dusted with flour. Bake in preheated moderate oven (350°F.) for 25 minutes. Makes 1 loaf.

HONEY GINGERBREAD
1 cup sugar
½ teaspoon each of ground cinnamon,
   cloves, and mace
1 teaspoon ground ginger
3 eggs, beaten
1 cup honey
1 cup dairy sour cream
4 cups sifted all-purpose flour
2 teaspoons baking soda
½ teaspoon salt

Sift together sugar and spices. Beat together sugar and eggs. Beat honey and sour cream into egg mixture. Sift together flour, baking soda, and salt. Gradually stir into batter. Bake in a greased and floured pan (9 x 13 inches) in preheated moderate oven (350°F.) for 25 to 30 minutes. Makes 1 loaf.

PAIN D'ÉPICE
(Spiced Bread)
1¼ cups boiling water
1 teaspoon aniseed
1 cup honey
1¼ cups sugar
½ teaspoon baking soda
¼ cup rum
4 cups sifted all-purpose flour
2½ teaspoons baking powder
1 teaspoon cinnamon
½ teaspoon ginger
¼ teaspoon salt
¼ cup chopped candied citron
¼ cup chopped candied orange peel
½ teaspoon grated orange rind
¼ cup chopped almonds

Bring water to boil with aniseed. Add honey and sugar, and stir until dissolved. Remove from heat, and stir in soda and rum. Strain; add slowly to the flour sifted with baking powder, spices, and salt. Beat until smooth. Add fruit and nuts. Pour into buttered loaf pan (9 x 5 x 3 inches), and bake in preheated moderate oven (350°F.) for 1 hour or until done.

BLUEBERRY GINGERBREAD

½ cup butter or margarine
½ cup firmly packed dark brown sugar
1 cup dark molasses
1 egg
2½ cups sifted all-purpose flour
1 teaspoon baking soda
1 teaspoon each of ground ginger and cinnamon
½ teaspoon ground cloves
½ teaspoon salt
1¼ cups fresh blueberries, washed
1 cup hot water
Lemon Sauce (see page 804)

Cream butter; add sugar and molasses; beat until light. Add egg and beat well. Sift dry ingredients and use a small amount to coat blueberries. Add remainder alternately with hot water to first mixture, beating until smooth. Fold in floured berries. Bake in greased baking pan (13 x 9 x 3 inches) in preheated moderate oven (350°F.) for about 35 minutes. Serve with Lemon Sauce. Makes 9 servings.

CREAM-CHEESE TOPPING FOR GINGERBREAD

Cream each 3-ounce package cream cheese with 3 tablespoons milk, 1 tablespoon sugar, and grated rind ½ lemon. Spoon over gingerbread; sprinkle with nuts. Makes about ½ cup topping.

GLACÉ—In American culinary language this French word refers to a coating of sugar or sugar syrup used on fruits, cakes, and breads. The sugar syrup is cooked to a hard-crack stage, or until a small amount of syrup dropped into cold water separates into hard and brittle shreds (300° to 310°F. on a candy thermometer).

The term is most often used for fruits, such as cherries, pineapple, orange, lemon, or citrus peel, apricots, and angelica. Sometimes they have been glacéed with sugar so that they are dry; at other times they have been coated with a sticky sugar syrup to keep them moist.

In French culinary language, *glacé* (or *glacéed*) means either frozen or glazed. In the latter case, the glazing need not necessarily be sweet, but may be done with butter, sauce, or gelatin or, of course, with sugar.

GLACÉ NUT PATTIES

3 cups nutmeats
2 cups granulated sugar
1 cup firmly packed light brown sugar
½ cup light corn syrup
½ cup water
¼ teaspoon salt
¼ cup butter

Break half of nuts into small pieces; leave the rest whole. Spread out in tins to heat in slow oven. Combine white and brown sugars, syrup, and water in saucepan; cook, stirring constantly, until sugar is dissolved. Continue cooking to the crack stage (300°F.), or until a little tried in cold water is brittle. Use very low heat toward the end of cooking to prevent darkening of syrup; stir only enough to prevent scorching. When done, remove from heat. Add salt, butter, and warm nuts; stir only enough to mix; do not scrape sides of pan. Spoon candy out in small amounts onto a buttered enamel tabletop. When candy is cold, tap table lightly to help loosen patties; remove with spatula. Keep in closely covered tin box. Makes about 3 dozen, depending on size.

ORANGE SLICES, GLACÉES

Combine 1 cup granulated sugar and ½ cup water in large heavy skillet. Heat, stirring, until sugar is dissolved. Add 12 seedless-orange slices, ¼ inch thick, arranging them so they lie flat. Bring to boil. Remove from heat and cool. Tip skillet occasionally to cover fruit with syrup, or spoon syrup over fruit. Repeat boiling and cooling process 6 or 7 times, or until all syrup has been absorbed. Remove slices and put on rack. Let stand overnight. Combine ½ cup confectioners' sugar and ¼ cup water in a small saucepan. Heat enough to dissolve sugar. *Do not boil.* Cut orange slices into halves and dip into warm syrup. Drain and return to rack to cool and dry. Store airtight in cool dry place. Makes 2 dozen pieces.

ORANGES GLACÉES

10 large navel oranges
4½ cups sugar
6 cups water
Few drops of red food coloring or grenadine syrup

Trim peel from oranges with a sharp knife and cut into tiny strips. Drop peel into boiling water and boil for 2 minutes. Drain. Repeat boiling and draining twice with fresh boiling water to remove the bitterness from the peel. Reserve peel. Remove all inner white skin from oranges. Cut 8 of the oranges into halves crosswise; remove seeds, if any. Cut remaining oranges into sections and cover bottom of serving dish. Put orange halves in dish, cut side down. Boil sugar and water for 10 minutes. Add food coloring or grenadine until syrup is clear red. Pour syrup over oranges. Let stand for 15 minutes. Drain off syrup and boil again for 15 minutes. Pour syrup over oranges and add reserved peel. Refrigerate at least 8 hours before serving. Makes 8 servings.

PINEAPPLE CHUNKS, GLACÉES

Drain 2½ cups (one 1-pound, 4-ounce can) pineapple chunks. Put chunks in saucepan; add 2 tablespoons butter or margarine and 2 or 3 tablespoons each of bottled barbecue sauce or ketchup and brown sugar. Cook, stirring frequently, for 15 minutes, or until glazed. Serve hot with sausages, hash, frankfurters, or chops. Makes 4 servings.

GLAZE—A glaze is a smooth glossy surface. In cookery, "to glaze" means to cover food with a mixture, often liquid, which hardens, becomes glossy, and gives an attractive finish to either hot or cold dishes. Glazing is an art practiced by all conscientious chefs who feel that an unglazed dish lacks distinction.

Hot meats and vegetables are glazed with either stock, sugar, syrup, or fruit juices thickened to a syrupy consistency. Cold foods are usually glazed with aspic, flavored gelatin, fortified mayonnaise, or white sauce. Desserts are glazed with sugar, syrup, fruit sauces, or jams and preserves. Cakes are glazed with mixtures similar to frostings, but thinner.

CAKE GLAZES

CARAMEL GLAZE

Combine ¾ cup sugar and 1 teaspoon fresh lemon juice in a skillet. Heat over low heat until sugar melts and turns golden brown. Remove from heat immediately, and spoon or drizzle over pastries. Makes enough glaze for 12 cupcakes.

CLEAR, VERY THIN GLAZE

Cook 2 tablespoons water, 2½ tablespoons corn syrup, 1 teaspoon flavoring, and 2 cups confectioners' sugar over boiling water in double boiler until hot. Pour, while still hot, over cake so that it barely covers cake. Makes enough glaze for one 9-inch fruit or applesauce cake.

CHOCOLATE GLAZE

2 squares (2 ounces) semisweet or unsweetened chocolate
¼ cup butter or margarine
3 tablespoons milk
2 cups sifted confectioners' sugar
⅛ teaspoon salt
½ teaspoon vanilla extract

Melt chocolate in top part of double boiler over hot water. Blend in butter and milk and remove from heat. Add remaining ingredients and blend until smooth. If necessary, thin with a few drops of cream. Spread on top of cake, allowing glaze to run down sides. Makes enough glaze for a 9-inch or 10-inch tube cake.

ORANGE-LEMON GLAZE

1¼ cups sifted confectioners' sugar
Grated rind of 1 orange
Grated rind of ½ lemon
2 tablespoons fresh orange juice
1 teaspoon fresh lemon juice

Combine sugar, rinds, and juices. Stir until well blended. Spread over top and sides of cake. Let stand to set before cutting cake. Makes enough glaze to cover top and sides of one 8-inch cake.

RUM GLAZE

1¼ cups sugar
⅓ cup white corn syrup
½ cup plus 2 tablespoons water
½ cup rum

Combine all ingredients except rum in a saucepan. Cook over low heat until sugar is dissolved. Cover and let cook over low heat for 5 minutes. Raise heat and boil for 5 minutes. Remove from heat and add rum. Spoon over cakes, usually babas, and allow to soak into the cake. Makes enough glaze for one 9-inch cake or 12 individual babas.

VANILLA GLAZE

Combine 2 cups sifted confectioners' sugar and ⅛ teaspoon salt in bowl. Add 3 to 4 tablespoons hot cream and beat until smooth. Add ½ teaspoon vanilla extract. Spread on top of cake, allowing glaze to run down sides. Makes enough glaze for a 9-inch or 10-inch tube cake.

PIE-CRUST GLAZES

Before baking, brush the upper crust of a two-crust pie with one of the following:

■ Slightly beaten egg or egg white
■ Cream or evaporated milk
■ Melted butter, margarine, or shortening
■ A little sugar sprinkled on top of any of the above adds sparkle.

GNOCCHI—*Gnocco,* the plural is *gnocchi,* is the Italian word for dumpling.

Italian *gnocchi* are small and delicate. They are made from potatoes, farina, or flour, and sometimes with eggs; they are cooked in fast-boiling, salted water and served with a sauce or with butter and grated Parmesan cheese.

The Italians do not know many kinds of *gnocchi.* For starch, they eat pasta rather than dumplings, whereas the dumpling-eating nations, such as Austria, Czechoslovakia, and Germany, use dumplings the way the Italians use pasta.

GNOCCHI PARMESAN

½ cup milk
½ cup water
½ cup butter or margarine
¼ teaspoon salt
1⅓ cups unsifted all-purpose flour
5 eggs
Boiling salted water
Cheese Sauce
½ cup grated Parmesan cheese
Paprika

Heat liquids and butter to boiling. Add salt and flour all at once and stir vigorously until mixture leaves sides of saucepan and forms a ball. Remove from heat and add eggs, one at a time, beating well after each addition. Drop mixture by half teaspoonfuls into boiling salted water. When balls come to the surface, remove to a bowl of cold water. Drain well and mix with Cheese Sauce. Put in a shallow baking dish and sprinkle with cheese and paprika. Bake in preheated moderate oven (375°F.) for about 30 minutes. Makes 4 servings.

Cheese Sauce

Add ¼ cup grated Parmesan cheese, a dash of hot pepper sauce, and a dash of onion salt to 1 cup hot seasoned medium white sauce. Also good on croquettes or rice. Makes about 1 cup.

GNOCCHI DI PATATE ALLA PIEMONTESE

3 medium potatoes
4 cups all-purpose flour
2 eggs
Salt
Tomato Sauce
1 cup ricotta or mashed cream cheese

Boil potatoes in their jackets; peel; mash with a fork. Add flour, eggs, and salt to taste. Dough should be well mixed and fairly moist. Roll into sticks about ½ inch in diameter. Cut each stick into pieces about ½ inch long and press flat. (The traditional way is to press the pieces with tines of a fork on the outside and with the thumb on the inside.) Boil in a pan of salted water for about 15 minutes. When the *gnocchi* are done, the edges become translucent. Drain thoroughly in a colander. Meanwhile, prepare the Tomato Sauce. Add dry *gnocchi* to the sauce. Stir in ricotta and cook for 15 minutes longer. Makes 6 to 8 servings.

Tomato Sauce

¼ cup olive oil
3 small onions, sliced
3 garlic cloves, minced
About 2½ cups (1-pound, 4-ounce can) tomatoes
Salt and pepper
Few grains of cayenne

Heat oil; add onions; fry until light yellow. Add garlic; continue frying until well done. Press tomatoes through a colander and add to onion-garlic mixture. Continue cooking slowly for about 20 minutes. Add seasonings. Makes about 2 cups.

GNOCCHI ROMANA

1½ cups milk
1½ cups water
1½ teaspoons salt
1 cup farina
½ cup butter or margarine
2 eggs
2 cups grated Parmesan or Swiss cheese
½ pound ham slices, quartered

Combine liquids and bring to boil. Add salt. Gradually stir in farina, avoiding lumps. Cook over medium heat, stirring, until very thick. Remove from heat. Beat in ¼ cup butter, the eggs, and ½ cup cheese. Spread ¼ inch thick on a shallow platter or cookie sheet. Chill until firm. Cut into small rounds or squares and place in a greased shallow baking dish so they overlap, alternating with ham. Melt ¼ cup butter and pour over top. Sprinkle with 1½ cups cheese. Bake in preheated moderate oven (350° F.) for 30 minutes, or until golden. Makes 4 to 6 servings.

GOOSE—The goose is a waterfowl, first cousin to the duck and the swan; all these birds belong to the Anatidae family. There are wild geese and domesticated ones and different varieties of each kind. Geese are smaller than swans, with longer legs, a shorter neck, and a larger head. The male goose is called a gander; the young goose, a gosling. Male and female geese have the same kind of plumage, which is rather unusual in the world of birds where the males are generally far more attractively plumed than the females.

Wild geese are resourceful and brave with an intelligence above that of other birds. They are long-lived; some birds are as old as forty years. Geese fly in a V formation to cut down air resistance and are well known in almost all parts of the United States, where their honking appearance announces spring or fall. Their flesh is rather tough and fishy in taste, since wild geese live largely on fish.

Domesticated geese are also resourceful, with much strength in their wings. Their disposition leaves much to be desired as many a farm child who has been nipped by a goose knows. On the other hand, their family life is close and wholly admirable. Geese pair for life. They build their nests on the ground and the parents guard their young faithfully against intruders. Their flesh is tenderer and milder than that of their wild cousins.

Geese have been bred since antiquity, and they play an extremely important part in the folklore of many different countries, including Siberia (where some of the northern natives worshipped a goose god), China, India, ancient Egypt, Rome, Germany, and the Slavic and Scandinavian countries. Tales of the goose that laid golden eggs, until its foolish and avaricious owner killed it, occur all over the world.

The geese were sacred to the Romans; a legend tells how in 390 B.C. a flock of cackling geese warned the sleeping Roman senators that their enemies, the Gauls, were about to raid the city. The Chinese raised geese as long as 3,000 years ago, and it was their custom to give a pair of geese as a wedding present to symbolize faithfulness. The Hindu held the wild goose in high respect; the great god Brahma is shown riding on a magnificent gander, symbol of freedom through spiritual purity.

The goose was, and is, a standard barnyard fowl in England and in continental Europe. No self-respecting farmer's wife would be without a flock to prepare for holiday eating and later to stuff her beds with their feathers. As goose featherbeds and pillows were essential to men's comfort for many centuries, so goose quills were essential to writing for almost as long. Goose grease was used for medicine, as a skin ointment for man and beast, and to soften and polish leather.

Rendered goose fat is a popular spread in central and northern Europe.

Geese are the traditional Christmas birds of many European countries, especially Austria, Germany, Czechoslovakia, Hungary, England, and the Scandinavian countries. In England, geese were used as payment of rent to landlords, and they still are a feature of Michaelmas Day (September 29) when "one goose fit for a lord's dinner" may still be part of a tenant farmer's rent due on that day. The Germans have but one complaint to make of the goose: one bird is too much for one man to eat yet not enough to feed two.

In America, various Indian tribes performed goose dances at the time of the migrations of the wild geese. As a table bird, the goose has never enjoyed the great popularity it has in Europe. Roast goose deserves to grace our tables more often. Since geese are fat, it is essential to cook out as much fat as possible. The fat should be poured from the pan as it accumulates during roasting. Geese are best stuffed with a tart stuffing to counteract their natural richness.

Availability and Purchasing Guide— Young domestic geese or goslings are available in markets in the early fall with the heaviest concentration in November and December. Look for fresh geese with a good layer of fat and soft, clean, and unbruised skin. A pliable upper bill is an indication of a young bird. Ready-to-cook weight of fresh geese, young and mature, is 4 to over 14 pounds. Frozen geese are available all year around, weighing 5 to 8 pounds. They are packaged with the giblets in the cavity.

Storage—Fresh goose should be loosely covered and kept in the coldest part of the refrigerator. Plan to use it within 2 to 3 days. Wrap giblets separately and use as soon as possible. Frozen goose, wrapped in moisture- and vapor-proof paper and sealed, may be kept at 0°F. or lower for several months. Wild goose should be plucked and eviscerated before freezing. Once thawed, goose should be cooked like fresh goose. Cooked goose is perishable and must be refrigerated as soon as possible.

☐ Refrigerator shelf, raw: 2 to 3 days

☐ Refrigerator shelf, cooked and covered: 4 to 5 days

☐ Refrigerator frozen-food compart-
ment, raw or cooked, prepared for freezing: 2 to 3 weeks

☐ Freezer, prepared for freezing, raw or cooked: 6 months

Nutritive Food Values—Goose is an excellent source of protein and a fair source of iron. It is higher in fat than duck and therefore higher in calories.

☐ 3½ ounces, roasted = 426 calories

Basic Preparation—Rinse goose in clear hot running water, inside and out; pat dry. If goose is frozen, allow 2 to 3 days for thawing in the refrigerator, or place packaged bird under cool running water for 1 to 3 hours until it is pliable. Trim away excess fat.

☐ **To Roast Domestic Goose**—Place trussed goose, breast side up, on rack in shallow open roasting pan. Do not brush with fat. Prick the breast skin of the goose in several places to allow fat to drain away. Rub goose inside and out with cut lemon halves to crisp skin, and rub inside and out with salt and pepper. Roast in preheated slow oven (325°F.).

☐ **To Stuff**—Sprinkle cavity with salt. Prepare dressing and spoon lightly into cavity just before roasting. Truss bird.

☐ **To Freeze**—Wash thoroughly. Pat dry. Wrap closely in moisture- vapor-proof material, excluding as much air as possible. Seal tightly and freeze. Frozen storage life is short (6 months) since high fat content causes rancidity. Do not stuff before freezing.

☐ **To Prepare Wild Goose**—If to be used at once, wild geese should be bled and eviscerated as soon as possible. Remove crop. Rub dry inside and out with a clean dry cloth or dry grass. When removing entrails, handle gall bladder carefully to avoid breakage. Pluck feathers and singe pin feathers. Plucking can be done best dry, by pulling out feathers, starting at the base of the neck, and singeing them down with a small flame. Or birds can be plucked by dipping into water heated to a temperature of 165°F. to 175°F. until feathers loosen. After plucking, remove head and feet. Hang carcasses singly and protect against dirt and insects until cool. Hang for 4 to 8 days. If refrigeration is not available, do not eviscerate birds until after hanging. Young birds spoil more quickly than older ones. To remove any fishy taste, soak geese in milk overnight before using.

TIMETABLE FOR ROASTING STUFFED, CHILLED DOMESTIC GOOSE

READY-TO-COOK WEIGHT	AMOUNT OF STUFFING	APPROXIMATE TOTAL TIME AT 525°F.
4 to 8 pounds	¾ to 1½ quarts	2¾ to 3½ hours
8 to 14 pounds	1½ to 2½ quarts	3½ to 5 hours

☐ **To Roast Wild Goose**—Sprinkle a 6- to 8-pound young goose inside and out with juice of 1 lemon, salt, and pepper. Fill body cavity with preferred dressing, truss bird and put, breast side up, on rack in shallow open roasting pan. Cover breast with bacon slices and cheesecloth soaked in melted bacon fat. Roast in preheated slow oven (325°F.) for 2 to 3 hours, or until tender. If age of goose is uncertain, add 1 cup water to pan and cover for last hour of roasting. Makes 6 to 8 servings.

THREE DRESSINGS FOR GOOSE

APPLE-PRUNE DRESSING

Combine 6 cups chopped unpeeled tart apples and ½ pound prunes, pitted. Makes enough for a 10-pound bird.

SAUERKRAUT DRESSING

Mix 6 cups drained sauerkraut and 2 teaspoons caraway seed. Makes enough for a 10-pound bird.

GREEN-VEGETABLE DRESSING

    2 cups watercress or spinach
      Several parsley sprigs
    1 large carrot
    1 small green pepper
    3 large celery stalks
    3 tablespoons butter or margarine
 1⅓ cups soda-cracker crumbs
    1 egg
    2 teaspoons poultry seasoning
  ¼ cup milk

Wash and drain vegetables and force through food chopper, using medium blade. Sauté vegetables in the butter for 10 minutes, stirring occasionally. Mix with crumbs, egg, seasoning, and milk. Makes enough for a 10-pound goose.

SLICED GOOSE IN SPANISH SAUCE

    2 tablespoons each minced celery and carrot
    1 tablespoon minced onion
  ¼ cup butter or margarine
  ¼ cup all-purpose flour
 1⅓ cups goose or chicken broth
  ½ cup canned tomatoes
  ⅛ teaspoon monosodium glutamate
      Seasoned salt and pepper
    3 cups sliced cooked goose

Cook celery, carrot, and onion in butter for 2 or 3 minutes. Blend in flour. Stir in broth and tomatoes and cook, stirring, until thickened. Add monosodium glutamate and seasoned salt and pepper to taste. Add goose and heat. Makes 4 servings.

SPICY SLICED GOOSE IN GRAVY

    4 cups sliced cooked goose
    2 tablespoons fresh lemon juice
    1 tablespoon steak sauce
    2 cups goose gravy
  ½ cup pitted ripe olives, sliced
  ¼ cup dry sherry
      Buttered hot toast points

Combine first 4 ingredients, and simmer for 15 to 20 minutes. Add olives and

sherry, heat well and serve on toast points. Makes 6 servings.

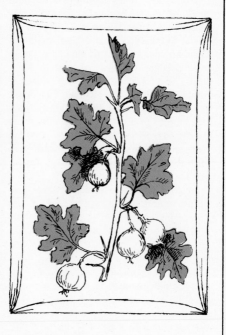

GOOSEBERRY—This round juicy berry, a first cousin of the fresh currant, belongs to the *Ribes* family. It grows on a bush. The flavor is tart, yet sweet when the berries are fully ripened. Gooseberries can grow as large as one inch in diameter and one and a half inches in length. There are a number of varieties: red, green, white, or yellow, and smooth or hairy. Gooseberries require cool weather to flourish. They are native to Europe and Asia and also to America, and have been cultivated since the beginning of the 17th century.

Gooseberries are widely used in the northern countries of Europe. In English home cooking, gooseberries are prized in tarts and jams, canned, or as a sauce. The varieties used for cooking are the smaller, tarter ones.

The great yellow and red gooseberries of the kitchen garden, bursting with sweet juices, are best eaten out of hand. They are the symbol of a perfect English summer day, filled with drowsy sunshine, the buzz of the bees, and the scents of flowers and fruit mingling in the still air.

Availability and Purchasing Guide—Fresh gooseberries are available from April through August in very limited quantities. Canned gooseberries are available.

Fresh berries should be firm.

Storage

☐ Fresh, room temperature: 1 or 2 days
☐ Fresh, refrigerator shelf, in moisture-proof wrapping: 1 or 2 days
☐ Fresh, refrigerator frozen-food com-

partment, prepared for freezing: 2 months
☐ Fresh, freezer, prepared for freezing: 1½ years

Caloric Values

☐ 3½ ounces, raw = 39 calories
☐ 3½ ounces, canned, heavy syrup = 90 calories

Home Freezing—Use firm, fully ripe berries. Wash and drain well. Pour unsweetened berries into freezer containers allowing ½-inch headspace.

☐ **To Freeze, Dry Sugar Pack**—Fill leakproof freezing containers with gooseberries: Use 1 pound sugar to 4 pounds berries, adding berries and sugar alternately until the container is filled, allowing ½-inch headspace at the top for expansion. Seal, freeze immediately, and store at 0°F. or below.

STEWED GOOSEBERRIES

    1 quart gooseberries
 1½ cups water
 1½ cups sugar

Wash berries, and remove blossoms and stems. Discard any soft berries. Bring water and sugar to boil, and simmer for 5 minutes. Add berries and simmer for 10 to 15 minutes, stirring occasionally. Makes 6 servings.

GOOSEBERRY DUMPLINGS

    2 cups gooseberries
 1¼ cups sugar
    2 cups water
  ½ teaspoon grated lemon rind
      Dumpling Batter
      Cream

Combine berries, sugar, water, and lemon rind in deep medium skillet. Cook slowly for 5 minutes. Drop Dumpling Batter by tablespoonfuls to make 6 dumplings on top of fruit. Cover and cook gently for 20 minutes. Serve these with cream for dessert. Makes 6 servings.

Dumpling Batter

    1 cup sifted cake flour
    2 tablespoons sugar
    1 teaspoon baking powder
  ¼ teaspoon salt
    1 tablespoon melted butter
  ¼ cup milk

Sift dry ingredients together. Add butter and milk. Mix only until flour is moistened.

GOOSEBERRY SAUCE

    2 cups gooseberries
    1 cup water
      Handful of spinach or sorrel leaves, chopped (optional)
    1 tablespoon butter
  ⅛ teaspoon grated nutmeg
      Sugar to taste

Cook gooseberries and water together until berries are soft. Add spinach leaves and cook for 3 minutes longer. Drain and reserve juice. Rub berries and spinach through a food mill or a fine sieve. Return to saucepan and combine with juice. The purée should be of the consistency of a thin batter. If too liquid, boil over high heat until right consistency is achieved by evaporation. Add butter, nutmeg, and sugar to taste. Simmer for 2 to 3 minutes, stirring constantly. (If no spinach is used, add a few drops of green food coloring for right color.) Makes about 1½ cups.

Note: A good side dish for fish, especially mackerel, and for goose, duck, and roast pork.

CANADIAN SPICED GOOSEBERRIES
4 cans (1 pound each) gooseberries
2 cups firmly packed light brown sugar
½ cup cider vinegar
¼ teaspoon salt
¼ teaspoon each of ground allspice, cinnamon, and cloves

Combine first 4 ingredients in a 3-quart saucepan. Mix well. Cook over medium heat for 30 to 40 minutes, or until thickened, stirring frequently. Add spices about 10 minutes before cooking time is up. Pack in hot sterilized jars. Seal at once. If desired, store in a covered container in the refrigerator and serve as needed. Makes four ½-pint jars.

Note: This is a fine tart relish for meat and fowl.

GOOSEBERRY JAM
2 quarts gooseberries (4 cups prepared)
6 cups sugar
½ bottle fruit pectin

Remove blossom and stem ends from gooseberries. Force berries through food chopper, using medium blade. Measure 4 cups into very large saucepan. Add sugar and mix well. Put over high heat, bring to a *full rolling boil and boil hard for 1 minute,* stirring constantly. Remove from heat, and at once stir in pectin. Skim off foam with metal spoon. Then stir and skim by turns for 5 minutes to cool slightly and to prevent floating fruit. Ladle into hot sterilized glasses. Cover at once with ⅛ inch hot paraffin. Makes 10 medium glasses.

GOULASH—This is the national meat dish of Hungary and a popular one all over the world. It is a thick stew that always contains meat, onions, and sweet or hot paprika. The meat is usually beef or veal, but there are other goulash dishes which incorporate three kinds of meat. Tomatoes, vegetables, potatoes, and even sauerkraut are often part of a goulash.

The correct Hungarian spelling of the word is *gulyás.* It means "herdsman's stew" and probably originated from the wandering Hungarian herdsmen's habit of cooking one-dish meals in a pot over the campfire.

Goulash has been adopted in all of central Europe as native food. Czechs, Yugoslavs, Germans, and Austrians make it and include the paprika. As with all folk dishes, feelings about the proportion of ingredients vary. The true Hungarian goulash, however, is hotter and uses more onions than other varieties.

Goulash, apart from being excellent food, is a most practical dish. It is thrifty, easy to make, and can be reheated with great success. Goulash is a popular party dish and a good solution for winter buffet parties or summer outdoor entertaining.

BEEF GOULASH
2 pounds boneless beef chuck
1 teaspoon salt
¼ teaspoon pepper
1 teaspoon each of seasoned salt and paprika
¼ cup all-purpose flour
2 tablespoons fat
2 cups water
1 tablespoon Worcestershire
1 garlic clove, minced
1 teaspoon powdered mustard
1 bay leaf
1 teaspoon caraway seeds
1 tablespoon vinegar

Cut beef in 1-inch cubes. Mix next 5 ingredients. Dredge beef with the mixture and brown on all sides in hot fat. Put in 2-quart casserole. Sprinkle with remaining flour, if any. Add remaining ingredients. Simmer, covered, over lowest possible heat for 2 hours, or until meat is tender. Makes 6 servings.

PORK GOULASH
1½ pounds lean pork
2 tablespoons lard
1 medium onion, diced
½ green pepper, diced
½ cup tomato juice
Salt to taste
2 teaspoons paprika
2 tablespoons all-purpose flour
¼ cup water

Cut pork into 1½-inch cubes. Melt lard and sauté onion and pepper in it until soft. Add pork, tomato juice, salt, and paprika. Cover and simmer for 1½ hours, adding more water if necessary. Make a paste of flour and water; gradually add some of the juice from goulash, stirring constantly. Return to pot and cook until thickened. Makes 6 servings.

VEAL GOULASH
2-inch cube salt pork, diced
2 pounds boneless veal shoulder, cut in 1-inch cubes
1 medium onion, chopped
2 teaspoons sweet Hungarian-style paprika

1 tablespoon vinegar
Salt
½ cup stock or water
¼ cup tomato sauce
¼ cup dairy sour cream

Cook salt pork in kettle until golden brown. Remove pork. Brown meat on all sides in fat remaining in kettle. Add onion, and cook for about 5 minutes longer. Add paprika, vinegar, 1 teaspoon salt, stock, and tomato sauce. Cover and simmer for 1½ hours, or until tender, adding a little more stock or water, if necessary to prevent drying out. Just before serving, stir in browned pork and sour cream. Add additional salt to taste. Makes 6 servings.

MEAT AND POTATO GOULASH
2 pounds boneless beef chuck
2 tablespoons fat
2 cups thinly sliced onions
2 teaspoons paprika
1½ teaspoons salt
Water
About 2 cups (1-pound can) whole potatoes, drained
1 package (10 ounces) frozen peas

Cut meat into pieces about 1½ inches square. Heat fat, add meat and onions, and sprinkle with paprika and salt. Brown slightly and cook, uncovered, stirring occasionally, for about 20 minutes. Add 1 cup water. Cover and cook slowly for 2 hours, until meat is very tender, adding more water if necessary. Add potatoes and peas and let simmer for about 5 minutes longer. Makes 4 servings.

GOULASH WITH NOODLES
6 pounds pork loin (rib end)
6 cups thinly sliced onions
Salt
Paprika
Hot cooked noodles

Remove meat from bones and cut into bite-size pieces. Put bones in kettle and cover with water. Simmer for about 20 minutes. Drain, reserving liquid; there should be at least 2 cups. Meanwhile, brown meat in a heavy kettle, using a small amount of fat if necessary. Add onions and cook for 5 minutes. Sprinkle with salt and paprika to taste. Add the 2 cups liquid, cover, and simmer for 1 hour, or until meat is tender, adding more liquid if necessary. Serve on noodles. Makes 8 servings.

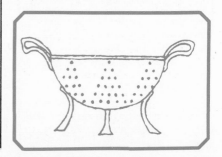

GOURMAND, GOURMET—These are two words taken directly from the French which characterize a person by his eating habits. A gourmand is a hearty, sometimes greedy, eater who delights in luxurious food. A gourmet is a connoisseur who knows and appreciates fine food and wine.

━━━━━ ✒ ━━━━━

GRANITÉ—This is an ice made from fruit syrup and frozen without stirring. It is slightly granular in consistency, accounting for its name, which means "granulated" in French. *Granités* are served in sherbet glasses.

LEMON GRANITÉ

2 cups sugar
4 cups water
¾ cup fresh lemon juice
3 teaspoons grated lemon rind
Dash of salt

Combine sugar and water; bring to boil and simmer for 5 minutes. Cool, and add remaining ingredients. Put in refrigerator trays, and freeze until firm and granular. Makes 1½ quarts.

━━━━━ ✒ ━━━━━

GRAPE—Botanically speaking, the grape is the berry of any vine of the *Vitaceae* family, which has leaves with tendril-bearing stems and sweet-smelling flowers that grow in clusters as do the fruits. Grapes grow wild in many temperate zones of Europe, Africa, Asia, and America; there are thousands of varieties. The cultivated species include varieties grown for wine making, for sweet juices, for the production of raisins, and for the table.

The European, or wine, grape (*Vitis vinefera*) is one of the oldest of all cultivated plants and is found in all temperate zones. The Egyptians grew them 6,000 years ago, the Greeks prized them greatly, and the Romans planted them in their far-flung empire. The Bible mentions grapes and wine in both the Old and New Testaments. Through the ages painters have given us brilliant grape portraits and poets have sung their praise.

As wine, grapes have inspired man and also served him ill when he abused them. As fruit, they are one of the loveliest to see and tastiest to eat. As a crop, they have added beauty to the landscape. Well-tended vineyards on terraced hillsides in California, France, Italy, Greece, and other grape-growing countries are indeed a joyful, peaceful sight.

The European grape, source of most wine grapes, is a plant that must be protected against various fungus and insect pests. One insect, phylloxera or the root louse, almost wiped out the entire French grape-growing industry. Since grapes are propagated by grafting, the industry was saved by introducing native American grape stocks which are much hardier, and grafting European grapes on them. To balance this debt, the extensive California grape-growing industry is based upon the varieties native to Europe.

One of the best-known native American grapes is the northern fox grape, from which come hybrids such as the Concord grape and the Muscadine, which grows in the Atlantic and Gulf states. This grape is parent of the famous Scuppernong.

The European grape was first introduced into this country by Lord Baltimore in 1616. It never flourished in the eastern part of the United States because of its susceptibility to cold and pests, but it came into its own in California's vast vineyards. Other varieties of grapes are extensively grown in New York, Michigan, and Ohio.

Availability—Most fresh table grapes available in food stores are grown primarily in California. They include the following varieties:

Almeria—Medium-large; greenish-white, thick, tough skin; dry and firm; normally seeded; neutral flavor. Available from September to November.

Cardinal—Large, dark red, slightly tough skin; firm pulp; few seeds; slightly pungent, sweet flavor. It is the result of a cross between the Ribier and Tokay, and is available from June to August.

Emperor—Large, elongated; light red and reddish-purple thin skins; normally seeded; neutral flavor. Available from November to May.

Olivette Blanche—Elongated, "ladyfinger"-shape; green delicate skin; a few seeds; pungent, sweet flavor. Available from June to August.

Red Malaga—Large spherical shape; pink to reddish-purple with crisp hard skin; normally seeded; neutral flavor. Available July to October.

Ribier—Very large, round; jet black, tough skin; meaty; normally seeded; medium-sweet flavor. Available July to February.

Thompson Seedless—Medium-size, elongated; greenish-white, tender thin skin; firm; always seedless; neutral flavor. Available June to November.

Tokay or Flame Tokay—Large, oval; bright red, thick tough skin; normally seeded; neutral flavor. Available August to January.

White Malaga—Large; greenish-white to yellow, thick tough skin; normally seeded; neutral flavor. Available September to November.

Some of the table grapes grown in the eastern part of the United States are available in local food stores. (They are easily crushed and are not generally shipped long distances.) They include the following varieties:

Catawba—Medium-size oval; purple-red, slip-skin; seeded; sweet intense flavor. Available September to November.

Concord—Medium-size; blue-black, slip-skin; seeded; mild flavor. Available September to October. In addition to its use as a table grape, the Concord is also used for making juice and jelly.

Delaware—Small; light-red, tender skin; juicy; seeded; sweet flavor. Available August to September.

Niagara—Large, round to egg-shape; amber to white, slip-skin; seeded; juicy; sweet flavor. Available September to October.

Whole grapes are available canned, in water or sugar packs, and are also included in fruit cocktails. Grape juice, canned and bottled, sweetened and unsweetened, is available. Vitamin C is sometimes added. Grape juice in combination with other fruit juices is available. Concentrated frozen grape juice is available.

Grape jams, jellies, conserves, and preserves, usually packaged in glass containers, are available.

Purchasing Guide—Select grapes that are fresh, plump, well formed, and firmly attached to the stems. Look for high color for the variety. Dark grapes should be free of green tinges; light grapes are best with an amber coloring. Fully ripe grapes are soft and tender. Avoid bunches with dry, brittle stems. A few shriveled or unripened grapes do not affect the flavor of the bunch, but avoid bunches in which the general appearance is shriveled, sticky, or dull.

Storage—Sort grapes and store in refrigerator in covered container or perforated plastic bags.

☐ Fresh, refrigerator shelf: 2 or 3 days
☐ Canned, kitchen shelf, unopened: 1 year
☐ Canned, refrigerator shelf, opened and covered: 4 to 5 days
☐ Frozen juice, refrigerator frozen-food compartment: 3 weeks
☐ Frozen juice, freezer: 1 year
☐ Jams, jellies: kitchen shelf, unopened: 1 year
☐ Jams, jellies: refrigerator shelf, opened and covered: 4 to 5 weeks

Nutritive Food Values—Fresh grapes contain small amounts of vitamins and minerals.

☐ 3½ ounces = about 68 calories
☐ Juice, 3½ ounces = 66 calories

Basic Preparation—Wash grapes. Drain. Chill. Seedless grapes are used whole; cut other grapes into halves and remove seeds.

□ **To Frost**—Beat egg white until frothy. Brush on grapes. Sprinkle with sugar. Let stand until dry.

FRESH GRAPE AND AVOCADO COCKTAIL
    2 cups fresh green seedless grapes
      or seeded grape halves
    1 cup diced (1 medium) ripe avocado
  ¼ cup French dressing
      Head lettuce
      Fresh parsley

Combine grapes, avocado, and French dressing. Chill for 30 minutes. Line 6 sherbet glasses with lettuce. Place ½ cup of the grape and avocado mixture in each glass. Garnish with fresh parsley. Makes 6 servings.

FILLET OF SOLE VÉRONIQUE
1½ pounds fillet of sole
    3 tablespoons butter or margarine
    1 teaspoon instant minced onion
      Salt
  ⅔ cup dry white wine
    1 tablespoon all-purpose flour
  ½ cup heavy cream
      Pepper
    1 cup seedless green grapes

Put fish in skillet with 1 tablespoon butter, onion, ¼ teaspoon salt, and wine. Cut a piece of brown paper the same size as skillet and make ½-inch hole in center. Butter paper and cover fish. Top with skillet lid, bring to boil, and simmer for 10 minutes, or until fish is done. Remove fish to a broilerproof platter. Cook liquid down until about ⅓ cup remains. Melt 2 tablespoons butter and blend in flour; add liquid and cream and cook, stirring, until thickened. Season to taste. Cook grapes for 3 or 4 minutes in boiling water to cover. Drain and put around fish. Cover with sauce. Put under broiler; brown lightly. Makes 4 servings.

GRAPE-TURKEY SALAD
    2 cups diced cooked turkey
    1 cup sliced celery
  ¼ cup French dressing
    2 cups seedless grapes
      Salt and pepper
      Salad greens
  ½ cup cooked salad dressing
  ⅓ cup dairy sour cream
  ¼ cup toasted slivered almonds

Marinate turkey and celery in French dressing for 1 hour. Add grapes and season to taste with salt and pepper. Arrange on greens. Mix salad dressing with sour cream. Add to salad; garnish with almonds. Makes 4 servings.

FRESH GRAPE AND CHICKEN MOLD
    2 envelopes unflavored gelatin
  ½ cup cold water
1½ cups hot chicken bouillon
  ⅓ cup sugar
  ¼ teaspoon salt
  ¼ cup fresh lemon juice
    2 cups whole seedless green grapes
      or seeded grape halves
    2 cups diced cold cooked chicken
    1 cup mayonnaise

Soften gelatin in cold water. Stir in chicken bouillon, sugar, salt, and lemon juice. Chill until the mixture is about as thick as fresh egg whites. Fold in grapes, chicken, and mayonnaise. Rinse a 2-quart mold in cold water. Fill with gelatin mixture. Chill until firm and ready to serve. Unmold onto a serving plate. Garnish with fresh grapes and mint leaves. Makes 8 to 10 servings.

FRESH GRAPE AND PLUM SALAD
    3 cups green seedless grapes
    3 cups sliced fresh Italian plums
    2 tablespoons French dressing
      Head lettuce
      Mayonnaise

Combine grapes, plums, and French dressing. Let stand for 1 hour or more. Serve on lettuce with mayonnaise. Makes 4 to 6 servings.

GRAPE AND CHEESE SALAD
Wash and stem ¾ pound Ribier or Tokay grapes. Split grapes halfway through and remove seeds. Combine 1 package (3 ounces) cream cheese with 1 tablespoon heavy cream and put a dab of mixture on each grape. Put grapes on salad greens and serve with French dressing. Makes 4 servings.

CONCORD GRAPE PIE
    7 cups stemmed Concord grapes
    3 tablespoons cornstarch
1½ cups sugar
  ¼ teaspoon salt
      Grated rind of 1 orange
      Pastry for 2-crust 9-inch pie, unbaked

Wash grapes and slip skins from pulp. Reserve skins. Heat pulp to boiling and rub through a coarse sieve to remove seeds. Add remaining ingredients except pastry to pulp and cook over low heat, stirring constantly, until thickened. Add skins. Cool. Line a 9-inch pie pan with pastry. Pour in filling. Top with a lattice made of strips of remaining pastry. Bake in preheated very hot oven (450°F.) for 10 minutes. Reduce heat to moderate (350°F.) and bake for 25 minutes longer. Cool pie before serving. Makes 6 to 8 servings.

ORANGE-GLAZED GRAPE TARTS
    3 tablespoons cornstarch
  ½ cup sugar
      Pinch of salt
1½ cups fresh orange juice
    2 cups seeded or seedless grapes
      Six 3-inch tart shells, baked

Mix cornstarch, sugar, and salt in saucepan; stir in orange juice. Cook until thick, stirring constantly, about 5 minutes. Add a little red food coloring if desired; cool. Shortly before serving put grapes in tart shells; cover with glaze. Garnish with whipped cream if desired. Makes 6 servings.

GRAPES IN WHITE-WINE GELATIN
    1 package (3 ounces) lemon-flavored gelatin
    1 cup boiling water
    1 cup dry white wine
    1 cup seedless grapes
      Mint sprigs
    1 egg white
      Grape clusters
      Sugar

Dissolve gelatin in water; cool. Add wine; chill until partially thickened. Fold in grapes. Pour into 1-quart mold rinsed with cold water; chill until set. Turn out on platter and garnish with mint sprigs and frosted grapes. To frost grapes, beat egg white until frothy. Dip small clusters of grapes into beaten white and roll in granulated sugar to coat lightly. Chill. Makes 4 servings.

BLUEBERRY-GRAPE MOLD
    2 envelopes unflavored gelatin
      Water
    1 can (6 ounces) frozen grape-lemon punch concentrate
  ⅛ teaspoon salt
    1 cup dairy sour cream
    1 can (14 ounces) blueberries, drained
  ½ cup sliced almonds

Soften gelatin in ½ cup cold water; dissolve over hot water. Dilute punch with 3 cans water. Add gelatin and salt. Blend 1½ cups gelatin mixture with sour cream. Pour into 2-quart loaf pan and chill until firm. Add berries and nuts to remaining gelatin; chill until slightly thickened. Spoon over firm layer and chill until firm. Unmold and slice. Makes 8 servings.

FRESH-GRAPE AND LEMON-ICE CUP
    3 cups fresh green seedless grapes or seeded grape halves
  ¾ cup fresh orange juice
    6 scoops lemon ice or sherbet

Place ½ cup grapes in each of 6 sherbet glasses. Pour over each 2 tablespoons orange juice. Top with lemon sherbet. Serve as appetizer or dessert course. Makes 6 servings.

OLD-FASHIONED GRAPE JELLY
Wash 3 pounds Concord grapes and remove from stems. Put in kettle and crush well. Do not add water. Heat to boiling and simmer for 20 minutes. Strain juice through flannel jelly bag into large bowl. Do not squeeze bag. Chill juice. Measure juice by dipping it from bowl into large kettle. Do not use sediment at bottom of bowl. Bring juice to full rolling boil. Add sugar, about 2½ cups, using 5 parts sugar to 4 of juice by measure. Remove from heat and stir until sugar is dissolved. Pour into hot sterilized jelly glasses and seal at once with paraffin. Makes four 6-ounce glasses.

GRAPE CONSERVE

4 pounds Concord grapes
½ cup water
Grated rind and juice of 1 orange
Grated rind and juice of 1 lemon
¼ teaspoon salt
1½ cups seeded raisins
4 cups sugar
1 cup chopped walnuts or pecans

Wash grapes, drain, and stem. Slip skins from pulp and reserve. Heat pulp to boiling and rub through coarse sieve to remove seeds. Add water, grated orange and lemon rind, salt, and raisins. Cook for 15 minutes. Add orange and lemon juice and grape skins; heat to boiling. Add sugar and cook until conserve is thick, stirring frequently to prevent burning. Add nuts during last few minutes of cooking. Pour into hot sterilized jelly glasses and seal with paraffin. Makes twelve 6-ounce glasses.

GRAPE APPLES

In saucepan bring to boil 1 cup grape juice, dash of salt, and ⅔ cup sugar; boil for 5 minutes. Peel and core 6 medium tart apples. Put in saucepan with grape mixture. Cover and simmer for 10 to 15 minutes, or until tender, basting occasionally with some of the syrup in pan. Serve warm or chilled with whipped or heavy cream. Makes 6 servings.

GRAPEFRUIT—This important member of the citrus family, also called "pomelo," is large and round with a rind colored from pale yellow to bronze, a juicy pulp which may be yellowish-white or pink, and a slightly bitter flavor. Grapefruit can weigh from two to twelve pounds and have a diameter of four to six inches. They grow in clusters (hence the name) on trees some twenty to forty feet high, in Florida, Texas, Arizona, and California. Whether grapefruit are a fruit by themselves or a hybrid is a moot point. Some authorities say that their ancestor was the shaddock, native to India and imported into the West Indies; others say that the grapefruit is a hybrid of the sweet orange.

Grapefruit are wholly American. They were quite unknown in the citrus-growing countries of Europe such as Spain, Italy, and Greece until they were introduced from America. To this day, millions of orange-eating Europeans have never seen or heard of a grapefruit.

Availability—Fresh grapefruit are available throughout the year, but are most plentiful from October through June. There are four market types:

Burgundy—Large size; thin skin with red flush; deep pink flesh; some seeds; sweet flavor. November to May
Duncan—Large size; smooth thin skin of pale yellow which may be tinged with green or russet; yellowish-white flesh; seeds; excellent flavor. October to June
Marsh—Medium size; pale yellow, thin skin; yellowish-white flesh; seedless; tart flavor. October to June
Thompson Pink (Marsh Pink)—Small to medium; light yellow, smooth skin; pink flesh; seedless; juicy with tart flavor. January to May

Grapefruit segments are also available canned in syrup and water packs, with or without artificial sweetener.

Grapefruit segments are also available frozen, usually in a sweetened pack.

Grapefruit juice is available fresh in quart containers. It is also available canned and frozen (concentrated), sweetened and unsweetened. Canned grapefruit juice is available combined with orange and other fruit juices. Grapefruit crystals are also available. One pound of crystals yields about one gallon of reconstituted grapefruit juice.

Purchasing Guide—They may be purchased individually, by the dozen, and sometimes by the pound. Varieties are usually not marked, other than seeded or seedless, and pink- or white-fleshed. Look for well-shaped fruit that is firm but springy and heavy for its size. The color of the rind may be yellow, tinged with pink or russet. Russeting does not affect the quality of the fruit. Because the fruits ripen at different times on a tree, chlorophyll produced for new blooms may color fruit that is already ripe, and grapefruit may be tinged with green. The quality of the fruit is not affected. Minor surface skin blemishes affect appearance rather than flavor. Avoid fruit with softened or pointed ends and a puffy appearance.

Storage—Avoid extreme temperatures in storing fresh grapefruit. It may be kept for a day or two at moderate room temperature. Refrigerate to avoid drying and wrinkling.

☐ Fresh, kitchen shelf, uncut: 1 or 2 days
☐ Fresh, refrigerator shelf, uncut: 1 to 4 months
☐ Fresh juice, refrigerator shelf: 1 or 2 days
☐ Canned, kitchen shelf: 1 year
☐ Canned, refrigerator shelf, opened and covered: 5 days
☐ Frozen, refrigerator frozen-food compartment: 5 days
☐ Frozen, or fresh, prepared for freezing, freezer: 1 year

Nutritive Food Values—Grapefruit is a good source of vitamin C and is also low in calories. Fresh grapefruit or juice should be used as soon as possible as long storage or exposure to air decreases vitamin C content.

☐ Fresh, 3½ ounces = 41 calories
☐ Canned, 3½ ounces segments and liquid, water pack = 30 calories
☐ Canned and frozen, 3½ ounces segments and liquid, sugar pack = 70 calories
☐ Fresh juice, 3½ ounces = 39 calories
☐ Canned juice, and frozen juice diluted with 3 parts water, 3½ ounces, unsweetened = 41 calories
☐ Canned juice, 3½ ounces, sweetened = 53 calories
☐ Frozen juice, 3½ ounces, sweetened, diluted with 3 parts water = 47 calories
☐ Canned grapefruit and orange juice, 3½ ounces, unsweetened = 43 calories
☐ Canned grapefruit and orange juice, 3½ ounces, sweetened = 50 calories

Basic Preparation

☐ To Serve Halved—Cut washed and chilled grapefruit into halves; use small diagonal cuts to make a fluted half, if desired. Remove seeds and cut around sections to loosen. Sweeten, if desired, with sugar, maple sugar, brown sugar, honey, or jelly. Serve at once.
☐ To Peel and Section—Cut thin slice from top; remove peel and membrane in strips from top to bottom, or round and round in a spiral. Cut along each dividing membrane and lift out sections. Peel and section over a bowl to save the juice. Sweeten, if desired.
☐ To Squeeze—Leave them at room temperature to make them easier to squeeze.
☐ To Broil—Sprinkle each half with brown sugar or honey; dot with butter. Broil or bake in hot oven (450°F.) until sugar or honey melts and surface is slightly browned.
☐ To Freeze—Use firm fruit. With a sharp knife peel and section, removing all rind, membranes, and seeds. Pack sec-

tions in containers and cover with a syrup made by cooking 4 cups water with 6 cups sugar. Add ½ teaspoon ascorbic acid to every 4 cups syrup. Pack, allowing ½-inch headspace. Seal.

FRESH-GRAPEFRUIT AND CRAB SALAD

    2 cups cold cooked crabmeat
    1 cup diced celery
    1 teaspoon salt
    ⅛ teaspoon pepper
    ⅓ cup mayonnaise
 1½ cups diced fresh grapefruit
      sections, drained
      Head lettuce
      Fresh grapefruit sections for garnish

Combine first 5 ingredients. Add grapefruit sections and toss lightly. Serve on a bed of lettuce. Garnish with fresh grapefruit sections. Makes 6 servings.

BAKED FISH WITH FRESH-GRAPEFRUIT STUFFING

    2- pound whole bass, bluefish, or other
      baking fish
      Salt and pepper
    ¼ cup finely chopped celery
    1 tablespoon finely chopped onion
    3 tablespoons butter or margarine
    2 cups toasted bread cubes, measured
      after toasting
    ½ cup fresh grapefruit sections
    ¼ teaspoon grated grapefruit rind
    1 teaspoon chopped fresh parsley
    ¼ teaspoon crumbled dried thyme
    3 slices of bacon
   12 fresh grapefruit sections

Wash fish, wipe dry, and remove bones for easier stuffing and eating. (Split fish open and lay out flat. Beginning at tail, with a sharp pointed knife loosen flesh close to bone along one side. Turn; loosen flesh on other side. Then remove backbone, being careful not to cut through the skin. Pick out small bones.) Rub inside with salt and pepper. Sauté celery and onion in 2 tablespoons butter. Blend in next 5 ingredients and ¼ teaspoon salt and ⅛ teaspoon pepper. Spoon into body cavity of fish. Close openings with skewers. Place in a buttered baking pan. Cut three gashes over the top to prevent splitting. Insert a slice of bacon in each. Bake in preheated moderate oven (350° F.) for 1 hour. Remove from oven and arrange 5 or 6 grapefruit sections over top. Brush with remaining butter. Place under broiler for a few minutes to brown top. Garnish with remaining grapefruit. Makes 4 servings.

FRESH-GRAPEFRUIT AND SALMON SALAD

    2 cups fresh grapefruit sections
    1 cup diced celery
    ¼ cup diced green pepper
    1 tablespoon fresh lemon juice
    ½ teaspoon salt
    ⅛ teaspoon pepper
      One 7¾-ounce can salmon
    ¼ cup mayonnaise
      Lettuce
      Fresh grapefruit sections
      Pimiento strips

Combine first 6 ingredients. Drain and flake salmon, and add to mixture with mayonnaise. Toss lightly. Serve on lettuce. Garnish with fresh grapefruit sections and pimiento strips. Makes 6 servings.

BAKED HAM WITH GRAPEFRUIT

      One 2-pound ham slice, cut 1 inch
      thick
    3 tablespoons brown sugar
    1 tablespoon ketchup
    ½ teaspoon powdered mustard
    2 grapefruit, peeled and sectioned

Place ham slice in a shallow baking dish. Mix together sugar, ketchup, and mustard. Spread over top of ham. Arrange grapefruit sections over the top. Bake in preheated moderate oven (350°F.) for 35 to 45 minutes, or until ham is thoroughly cooked. Makes 4 servings.

MOLDED FRESH-GRAPEFRUIT AND APPLE SALAD

    2 envelopes unflavored gelatin
    1 cup fresh grapefruit juice
    ⅓ cup fresh lemon juice
    ½ cup sugar
    2 cups hot water
    ⅛ teaspoon salt
    2 cups fresh grapefruit sections
    1 cup diced fresh apples
      Fresh apple slices

Soften gelatin in grapefruit juice. Add lemon juice, sugar, hot water, and salt. Mix well. Chill until mixture is about as thick as fresh egg whites. Fold in grapefruit sections and diced apples. Rinse a 5-cup mold with cold water. Fill with gelatin mixture. Chill until firm and ready to serve. Turn out onto a serving plate. Garnish with apple slices. Makes 8 servings.

JELLIED GRAPEFRUIT SALAD

    2 envelopes unflavored gelatin
    ½ cup cold water
    2 large or 3 medium grapefruits
    ½ cup honey
      Dash of salt
    ¾ cup sauterne
    ⅓ cup fresh lemon juice
      Salad greens
      French dressing

Sprinkle gelatin on cold water to soften. Peel grapefruits and remove segments, reserving all juice. Add enough water to juice to make 2 cups; heat to boiling. Pour over gelatin and stir until dissolved. Add next 4 ingredients and mix well. Chill until mixture begins to thicken. Fold in grapefruit segments. Pour into 2-quart mold and chill until firm. Unmold on salad greens. Serve with French dressing. Makes 6 servings.

FRESH-GRAPEFRUIT SALAD DRESSING

    1 teaspoon salt
    ½ teaspoon celery seeds
    ½ teaspoon paprika
    ⅛ teaspoon white pepper
    1 teaspoon chopped onion
    1 garlic clove, minced

    2 tablespoons sugar
    1 cup salad oil
    ½ cup fresh lemon juice
    ⅔ cup fresh grapefruit segments,
      broken into pieces, and juice

Combine first 8 ingredients and let stand for 1 hour. Add remaining ingredients and beat mixture with a rotary beater. Serve over mild-flavored salad greens or over fruit salad. Makes about 2 cups.

GRAPEFRUIT BAKED ALASKA

    2 grapefruits
    1 pint hard ice cream (vanilla,
      chocolate, or strawberry)
    3 egg whites
    ¼ teaspoon cream of tartar
    6 tablespoons sugar

Cut grapefruits into halves. Carefully scoop out pulp and reserve segments. Chill segments and shells. Place 4 drained grapefruit segments in each half. Fill shells to within ¼-inch of top with hard ice cream. (It is possible to shape small scoops of ice cream and freeze them until time to serve. Place hard balls of ice cream in shells.) Beat egg whites with cream of tartar until stiff but not dry. Gradually beat in sugar until mixture is stiff and glossy. Spread meringue over ice cream and edge of shells, making sure tops are completely covered. Brown quickly in preheated very hot oven (450°F.). Serve at once. Makes 4 servings.

AVOCADO-GRAPEFRUIT DESSERT

Halve unpeeled avocados and remove seeds. Sprinkle with lemon juice and fill with grapefruit segments. Serve with honey French dressing and a garnish of mint.

HONEYED GRAPEFRUIT

    2 grapefruits
    ¼ cup honey
    4 strawberries

Cut grapefruits into halves, remove any seeds, and cut around each section with a sharp knife. Remove core. Put 1 tablespoon honey and 1 strawberry in each half. Keep in refrigerator until serving time. Makes 4 servings.

PICKLED GRAPEFRUIT RIND

Select 5 or 6 thick-skinned grapefruits without blemishes. Wash in warm soapy water and rinse well. With a sharp knife cut rind-deep sections, starting at either stem or blossom end and terminating at opposite end. The middle of the sections should be about 1¾ inches wide. Carefully peel off one section at a time. Remove any white membrane and cut sections crosswise into 2 or 3 pieces of uniform size.

  Place cut-up peel in a kettle; cover with cold water; put on lid and boil for a few minutes. Discard water; replace with fresh water and boil again. Repeat 2 or

3 times. Finally, boil peel, well covered with water, until it is tender. Test by biting into a piece. Drain well; transfer to a smaller kettle and cover with hot Pickle-Preserve Syrup. Boil for 10 minutes; remove from heat and let stand in syrup overnight. Drain off syrup; reheat syrup to boiling point and pour again over rind. Pack rind in hot sterilized jars. Cover with hot syrup, remove bubbles, and seal according to manufacturer's directions. Boil gently in water bath for 10 minutes. This is exceptionally good served with a starchy casserole or roast meat. Makes about six ½-pint jars.

Pickle-Preserve Syrup
2 tablespoons cracked cinnamon
1 rounded tablespoon pickling spices
4 cups sugar
2 cups cider vinegar
1 cup water

Tie spices loosely in a thin white cloth. Boil with other ingredients for 5 minutes. Then remove the spice sack and use syrup as directed above. Syrup will be light colored if spices are removed at once. Makes about 3 cups.

GRATE, TO—In cookery the term means to reduce a hard food into smaller pieces by rubbing against a rough or indented surface. The resulting pieces may be very fine and dustlike or coarse. It depends on the size of the grater used. Spices, hard cheeses, lemon and orange peel, onions, cabbage, carrots, and potatoes are grated for use in cooking. Grating brings out the flavor of such foods as spices and fruit peels, and it also makes food easier to mix with other foods, for example, when mixing grated cheese and spaghetti.

There are hand graters, wired graters, and mechanical graters. They come with fine to coarse meshes. Some are round and can be placed over a bowl; some are square and stand on the table; some are oblong and can be placed over a loaf pan; some are made of crimped wire or plastic. Some are very small for grating nutmeg or peel and others are rotary graters which are turned by a handle.There are small rotary graters which are used for grating nuts finely.

GRATIN, GRATINATE—*Gratin* is the French word for a dish which has been gratinated: that is, it has acquired a crisp golden-brown crust after having been exposed to high heat; *gratin* is also the word used to describe the crust itself. Generally, a covering of buttered crumbs or grated cheese is used to gratinate a dish.

GRAVY—Gravy is a sauce that utilizes the fat, meat drippings, and juices of the meat or poultry with which it is to be served. It also contains a thickening agent, such as flour, cornstarch, potato starch, or gingersnaps, and a liquid, such as water, broth, bouillon, milk, or sweet or sour cream.

Gravy can be brown, red, or whitish, depending on whether the starch in it has been browned, on the color of the pan juices, and on the kind of liquid used. The color should conform to the nature of the gravy. It should be well seasoned, thoroughly cooked, smooth, and of the consistency of light or heavy cream.

Gravy differs from *jus,* the French word for "juice," which in culinary language means the juices that drip from the meat. Gravy is thickened whereas *jus* is either served as is or diluted with a little bouillon or water and brought to a boil in the pan, which has been scraped. It is what we generally refer to as "natural gravy."

Gravy is a time-hallowed dish, for it makes the flavor of a little meat go a very long way with such inexpensive and plentiful foods as potatoes, rice, pasta, dumplings, and stuffings. Gravy is part and parcel of English and North American cooking, and of central European, German, and Scandinavian cuisines. The reputation of many a cook has been made on her gravy.

HINTS FOR MAKING GRAVY

■ For those who experience difficulty in making gravy, it may be helpful to know that the same rules and precautions for any kind of starch cookery must be observed. The tiny grains of starch from flour, cornstarch, or other thickeners swell and burst when liquid is added and the mixture is heated. To prevent the tiny particles from forming large unpleasant lumps, the starch particles must be separated and kept apart, first by mixing them with a fat or a cold liquid, then, after more liquid is added and the mixture is heated, by rapid complete stirring. The stirring must continue until the starch particles swell, then burst, thus thickening the mixture. After that, the cooking is continued for flavor, with occasional stirring, until the starch is completely cooked and no raw starch appearance or taste remains.

In the event that lumps do form, pour gravy through a strainer and discard lumps. If preferred, beat vigorously with a rotary or electric beater or whirl in blender until smooth. Reheat before serving.

■ The new instant-type flour is an easy gravy maker. It may be used to make pan gravy or flour-paste gravy or mixed with

any cold liquid without the addition of fat.

■ Canned gravy and packaged gravy mixes are available. Among these convenience items are brown, chicken, mushroom, and beef.

■ There are two basic types of gravy: Pan gravy and flour-paste gravy. Pan gravy is preferred when cooking the dish has resulted in a high proportion of fat in relation to the liquid, as is the case with country-fried steak or fried chicken. Flour-paste gravy is used to thicken meat or poultry drippings when the cooking has resulted in a fairly high proportion of liquid to fat, with braised meats and pot roasts, for example, or with stews and fricassees.

■ Gravy does not have to be plain. Here are a few of the items which may be added during the cooking:

- Chopped or grated onion
- Onion, celery, or garlic salt
- Worcestershire or other meat sauces
- Powdered or prepared mustard
- Monosodium glutamate, plain or flavored
- Pickle juice
- Herbs
- Cooked or canned mushrooms
- Finely shredded carrot or celery
- Finely chopped cooked poultry giblets (for fried or roasted poultry)
- Paprika
- Curry powder
- Canned cream soups, such as mushroom or chicken
- Soup mixes, diluted according to directions

PAN GRAVY
Make the gravy in the pan in which the meat or poultry was roasted, baked, or fried. The cooked meat is taken from the pan, excess fat is poured or skimmed off, leaving the desired amount of fat and all the browned drippings resulting from cooking the meat or poultry. It is important to scrape all the particles from the bottom of the pan to give the gravy a deep brown color and a more robust flavor. If the color of the finished gravy is pale, bottled gravy coloring can be added until desired color is obtained. To prepare, use these measures:

Thin Gravy
1 tablespoon flour
1 tablespoon fat
Drippings
1 cup liquid*
Salt and pepper to taste

Medium-Thick Gravy
2 tablespoons flour
2 tablespoons fat
Drippings
1 cup liquid
Salt and pepper to taste

(*The liquid may be pan juice, stock, water, water in which vegetables were cooked, milk, tomato juice, bouillon, or consommé.)

Place the pan or roaster over low heat; quickly stir in flour, combining well with the fat and drippings. Then remove pan from heat; stir in about half of the liquid; combine completely. Return pan to heat; pour in rest of liquid slowly, stirring constantly. Continue to cook until creamy and thickened, stirring occasionally, for at least 3 minutes. Stir in salt and pepper. **Note:** To prepare pan juice, if that is the liquid to be used, drain off all fat drippings. Reserve. Add a small amount of water to the pan and heat over low heat, stirring to remove all particles from bottom of pan. Strain to remove all lumps after juices have simmered for 2 or 3 minutes.

FLOUR-PASTE GRAVY

Add 1 part flour to 2 parts cold water, milk, or broth. Beat until completely smooth, using a fork. Or use a metal or plastic shaker sold for combining flour or other starch with cold liquid. Stir paste slowly into the hot meat liquid, a small amount at a time, and combine well. Cook and stir for at least 3 minutes.

CREAM OR MILK GIBLET GRAVY FOR POULTRY

2 tablespoons fat drippings
2 tablespoons flour
1 cup light cream or milk, or ½ cup stock or pan juices and ½ cup light cream or milk
Chopped cooked giblets
Salt and pepper to taste

Heat drippings and stir in flour; cook over low heat until it is browned, but not burned. Gradually stir in cream, stirring constantly, until gravy is thickened. Add giblets and stir. Season with salt and pepper. Makes 1¼ cups.

RED-EYE GRAVY FOR HAM

After fried ham has been removed from a skillet, for each pound of ham quickly add ½ cup cold water or strong black coffee to pan drippings. Bring to a boil and stir well. Blend well and spoon over fried ham.

GREASE—The word covers any animal fat, usually pork, beef, or lamb, that is rendered. It also refers to spreading a pan thinly with fat (greasing the pan) to keep foods from sticking during cooking or baking.

Greek Cookery
by Louise Shattuck

The Greek people are home lovers and have strong family ties. Although they are a devout people, they love a party and frequently entertain in their homes. Food is an important part of their celebrations and religious holidays.

Orthodox Greeks do not eat meat on Fridays or during Lent, and the most devout observe Holy Week by eliminating from their diet foods taken from anything living, which includes dairy products and seafoods. So it is no wonder that their Easter feast is lavish. It begins with *mageritsa* (a soup made of the heart, lungs, and liver of a baby spring lamb), which is traditionally served after the midnight Resurrection service. Then the lamb is roasted for the Easter feast. Traditionally, it is cooked in an open pit, but today, especially in this country, it is more convenient for the housewife to have it roasted in one of the large ovens in a commercial bakery.

Colored eggs are also a part of their Easter festivities, but instead of coloring the eggs many colors, the Greeks dye them all a deep red to signify the blood of Christ, and embed them in the sweet bread which they bake for the occasion.

Special breads are also served on other religious holidays. Christmas breads are usually decorated with nuts. *Vasilopitta,* a New Year's bread served to guests on the stroke of midnight, is baked with a coin inside to bring prosperity to the finder during the coming year. The bread is cut with great ceremony, the first slice being for the house, the next for the father, the third slice for the mother, the fourth for the eldest child, and so on.

Greek cooking is neither oily nor hotly seasoned as some people who are not familiar with it believe, but some flavors and seasonings are typical of Greek foods. Olive oil is used extensively, even in pastries, in Greece. However, Americanized Greeks usually prefer to use butter in pastry baking and save their olive oil for meats, casseroles, vegetables, and salads. Mint and oregano are two herbs frequently used with meats and vegetables. Cinnamon, too, often flavors meat dishes as well as pastries and puddings.

Because sheep and goats flourish in the rocky hills of Greece, lamb is the meat most often used in making Greek dishes and cheese made from goats' milk is a staple food.

The Greeks are fond of broiled steak and lamb chops. To give them a Grecian flavor, broil chops or your favorite cut of beefsteak to the desired doneness, then sprinkle with crushed oregano and lemon juice. Liver, panfried or broiled, may be seasoned similarly.

The three kinds of Greek cheese most often used and most easily obtainable in specialty food stores are feta, kaseri, and kefaloteri.

Feta cheese is a soft, salty white cheese made of goats' milk; firmer than cottage cheese or ricotta, it is similar in flavor, though much saltier. It crumbles easily and is frequently added to salads or served with meals. It is also the cheese most often used in salads and in hot dishes, combined with meat, cheese, eggs, or *phyllo*.

Kaseri cheese is creamy in color and similar to Cheddar in texture and flavor, though not as runny when melted.

Kefaloteri cheese is also creamy in color. It is a hard cheese, very much like Parmesan, which can be used as a substitute for kefaloteri.

In the rural areas of Greece, many backyards contain a few chickens and a beehive, so eggs and chicken appear often on Greek tables. All kinds of fish and shellfish are plentiful and popular, too.

The Greeks are not fond of sauces; you will seldom find a sauce served with a typical Greek dish unless it consists of the juices in which the food was cooked. Nor will you find these juices thickened with either flour or cornstarch. Lemons and eggs being readily available, the gravies are thickened with a combination of beaten egg and lemon juice, giving the dish a piquant flavor and foamy consistency which are typically Greek.

Eggplant is popular with Greeks and used in many ways—stuffed, baked, combined with other vegetables, meat, or eggs, or used in salads. The summer varieties of squash are favorite vegetables, too. Beans, both dried and fresh, and tomatoes appear again and again in Greek recipes. Here we use cabbage leaves to wrap meat mixtures for steaming, as they do in Greece, where the plentiful grapevines also provide leaves for the purpose.

Pasta is as popular in Greece as in other Mediterranean countries, and rice is a staple, too.

Greek soups are hearty fare and usually served as a meal in themselves, perhaps with a salad and with fruit for dessert. A typical Greek salad, combining fresh and cooked vegetables, fish, and cheese is also a meal in itself, served with wonderful crusty bread, for lunch.

The pastries, rich and flaky and often soaked in a honey syrup, for which the Greeks are so justly famous, are reserved for between-meal snacks to be served to guests with the strong, sweet, foamy coffee which the Greeks adopted from the Turks—said to be the only thing about the long Turkish occupation which met with the Greeks' approval!

GREEK COOKERY

Greek cooking is a richly varied cuisine
of subtle flavors and seasonings

SOUPS

AVGOLEMONO SOUPA
(Egg-Lemon Soup)
2 quarts chicken bouillon
¾ cup manestra*
Salt and pepper
Juice of 1 lemon
2 eggs, beaten

Bring bouillon to a boil. Add manestra and simmer for 15 to 20 minutes, or until tender. Season with salt and pepper. Add lemon juice to beaten eggs. Slowly stir some of the hot soup into egg yolks. Stir egg-yolk mixture into soup. Remove from heat. Let stand, covered, for 5 minutes to thicken. Serve at once. Do not reheat. Makes 6 servings.

* **Note:** Manestra is a pasta about the size of cantaloupe seeds. Spaghetti broken into very short lengths may be substituted.

MAGERITSA
(Easter Soup)
Heart, lungs, and ½ liver of a
  spring lamb
¼ cup butter
1 medium onion, finely chopped
1 cup green onions, finely chopped
½ cup minced parsley
2 tablespoons fresh dill, finely chopped,
  or 1 tablespoon dried dill
4 cups water
Salt and pepper
Juice of 1½ lemons
3 eggs, beaten

Wash and trim membrance from heart, lungs, and liver. Cover with water and simmer for 15 minutes. Cool. Chop meat into pieces the size of grains of rice. Strain broth. Sauté meat in butter until browned. Add onions, parsley, dill, water, and the broth in which meat was cooked. Add salt and pepper to taste. Simmer for 2 hours. Add lemon juice to eggs. Slowly stir some of the hot soup into egg yolks. Stir egg-yolk mixture into soup. Remove from heat. Let stand, covered, for 5 minutes to thicken. Serve at once. Do not reheat. Makes 4 servings.

Note: Lamb kidneys may be substituted for the lungs.

FAKI SOUPA
(Lentil Soup)
2 quarts beef or chicken bouillon
1 cup lentils
Salt and pepper
1 large onion, finely chopped
1 celery stalk, finely chopped
1 medium carrot, finely chopped
1 garlic clove, minced, or put through
  garlic press
¼ cup olive oil
½ cup tomato sauce
Vinegar (optional)

Simmer lentils in bouillon with salt and pepper to taste for 1 hour. Add remaining ingredients. Continue to cook for 30 minutes, or until vegetables are tender.

If desired, 1 teaspoon vinegar may be added to each bowl of soup as it is served. Makes 6 servings.

SEAFOOD

GARIDES SALTSA TOMATE
(Shrimps with Spicy Tomato Sauce)
2 pounds large shrimps
1 teaspoon salt
1 bay leaf
Saltsa Tomate

Cover shrimps with boiling water. Add salt and bay leaf and simmer for 12 minutes. Cool by rinsing in cold water. Peel and remove black veins. Add to Saltsa Tomate and heat. May be served over rice or pasta. Makes 4 servings.

Saltsa Tomate
(Tomato Sauce)
¼ cup butter
2 tablespoons olive oil
1 large onion, finely chopped
1 garlic clove, minced or put through
  garlic press
One 6-ounce can tomato paste
  diluted with 1 can water
2 tablespoons white-wine vinegar
1 tablespoon brown sugar
½ teaspoon dried basil
Salt and pepper to taste

Sauté onion in butter and olive oil until golden brown. Add rest of ingredients and simmer, uncovered, for 30 minutes.

KTENIA ME RYZI
(Scallops with Rice)
1 large onion, finely chopped
¼ cup butter
2 pounds scallops
1 cup uncooked rice
2 tablespoons olive oil
Water
1½ teaspoons salt
Parsley

Sauté onion in butter until golden. Wash scallops and add. Simmer for 15 minutes, turning occasionally. Brown rice in olive oil until golden and place in a 2-quart casserole. Drain juice from scallops and add water to make 2½ cups. Add salt and pour over rice. Bake, covered, in preheated hot oven (400°F.) for 20 minutes. Stir in scallops and onion and bake for 10 minutes longer. Sprinkle with chopped parsley. Makes 6 to 8 servings.

ACHIVADES PILAFI
(Clam Pilaf)
1 medium onion, finely chopped
2 tablespoons butter
2 tablespoons olive oil
Two 7-ounce cans tiny whole baby
  clams or equal amount of fresh
  clams
Water
1½ cups canned tomatoes
1 cup uncooked rice
½ teaspoon dried oregano
Salt and pepper to taste

Sauté onion in butter and olive oil until golden brown. Drain clams and add

enough water to make 1½ cups liquid. Combine all ingredients. Simmer, covered, for 25 minutes, or until rice is tender. Makes 6 servings.

MEAT AND CHEESE

MOUSSAKA
*In Greek and English,
this baked meat custard is always
known under the same name*

1½ pounds potatoes
Fat for deep frying
2 medium onions, finely chopped
¼ cup olive oil
1 pound ground lean beef
2 garlic cloves, minced or put through
  garlic press
One 8-ounce can tomato sauce
1 teaspoon ground cinnamon
Salt and pepper
2 eggs
1 cup milk
⅓ cup grated kefaloteri cheese

Peel potatoes and cut into ¼-inch slices. Deep fry in hot fat until golden brown and drain. Arrange half of potatoes in an even layer on the bottom of a pan (7 x 11 inches). Sauté onions in olive oil until soft. Set aside. In oil remaining in pan cook beef, stirring with a fork, until redness disappears. Add onions, garlic, tomato sauce, cinnamon, and salt and pepper to taste. Pour over potatoes. Arrange remaining potato slices over meat. Beat eggs and add milk. Pour mixture over meat and potatoes. Sprinkle with cheese. Bake in preheated moderate oven (350°F.) for 45 minutes. Cut into squares to serve. Makes 4 servings.

Note: Zucchini or eggplant may be substituted for potatoes. Fry the vegetables in a small amount of oil rather than deep fry them.

SFOUGATO
(Meat Custard)
2 medium onions, finely chopped
1½ pounds zucchini squash, finely diced
½ cup butter
1 pound ground beef
1 tablespoon minced parsley
8 eggs, beaten
2 cups milk
Salt and pepper

Sauté onion and squash in butter for about 15 minutes, or until vegetables are soft, stirring frequently. Set aside. In butter remaining in pan cook beef, stirring with a fork, until redness disappears. Beat eggs; add milk, vegetables, beef, parsley, and salt and pepper to taste. Place in a 2½-quart baking dish. Bake in preheated moderate oven (350°F.) for 45 to 60 minutes, or until firm. Makes 4 to 6 servings.

GEMISTI MELITZANA
(Stuffed Eggplant)
4 medium eggplants
Salt and pepper

2 medium onions, finely chopped
½ cup olive oil
2 pounds ground beef
1 tablespoon minced parsley
1 teaspoon dried mint leaves, crumbled
3½ cups (one 1-pound, 12-ounce can) tomatoes

Wash eggplants. Cut off stems and cut each eggplant into halves lengthwise. Scoop out pulp, leaving a shell about ½ inch thick. Sprinkle shell with salt and pepper. Chop pulp and sauté with onions in olive oil for about 15 minutes, or until soft, stirring frequently. Set aside. Cook beef in oil remaining in pan, stirring with a fork, until redness disappears. Mix vegetables and beef with parsley, mint, and tomatoes which have been broken up with a fork. Add salt and pepper to taste. Arrange eggplant in a baking pan and fill with meat and vegetable mixture. Pour any remaining mixture into pan around eggplant. Cover; bake in preheated moderate oven (350°F.) for 45 minutes. Makes 8 servings.

DOLMATHES
(Stuffed Grape Leaves)

1 pound ground lean beef
1 egg, beaten
1 medium onion, finely chopped
½ cup raw rice
¼ cup chopped parsley
1 teaspoon chopped fresh mint leaves or ½ teaspoon dried mint
2 tablespoons olive oil
1¾ cups water
Salt and pepper
Grape or cabbage leaves
1½ cups undiluted canned beef bouillon
Avgolemono Sauce

Mix beef with egg. Add onion, rice, parsley, mint, olive oil, and ¼ cup water. Season to taste with salt and pepper. If using fresh grape leaves or cabbage, soak in hot water for 5 minutes to soften. (Remove core of cabbage and soak whole head so that leaves may be peeled off without breaking.) If using canned grape leaves, rinse in warm water.

Place a spoonful of meat mixture on a leaf. Be sure the shiny side is down if using grape leaves. Roll, folding ends in as you go to seal mixture in. Place folded side down in a saucepan, making more than 1 layer if necessary. Add bouillon and remaining water. Cover and simmer for 45 minutes. Serve with Avgolemono Sauce. Makes 4 to 6 servings.

Avgolemono Sauce
(Egg-Lemon Sauce)

2 eggs
Juice of 1 lemon

Beat eggs and add lemon juice. Slowly add some of the hot broth to egg yolks while continuing to beat. Stir egg-yolk mixture into remaining broth. Remove from heat. Cover and let stand for 5 minutes to thicken. Serve at once. Do not reheat.

Note: This sauce is always made from the liquid in which meats or vegetables have been cooked, thickened with beaten egg and fresh lemon juice. The mixture is also used to thicken soups.

GIOUVARLAKIA AVGOLEMONO
(Meatballs with Egg-Lemon Sauce)

1 pound ground lean beef
½ medium onion, finely chopped
1 tablespoon minced parsley
1 teaspoon minced fresh mint leaves or ½ teaspoon dried mint
2 tablespoons raw rice
Salt and pepper
1½ cups beef bouillon
1 cup water
2 egg yolks
Juice of 1 lemon

Mix beef, onion, parsley, mint and rice. Season with salt and pepper to taste and add ¼ cup of bouillon. Mix well and form into small balls, about the size of a walnut. Bring the remaining bouillon and the water to a boil and drop meatballs into it. Simmer for 25 minutes. Beat eggs and add lemon juice. Slowly add some of the hot broth to egg yolks while continuing to beat. Stir egg-yolk mixture into remaining broth. Remove from heat. Cover and let stand for 5 minutes to thicken. Serve at once. Do not reheat. Makes 4 to 6 servings.

PSITA PAIDAKIA
(Baked Lamb Chops)

6 lean loin lamb chops
2 tablespoons butter
Salt and pepper
½ cup water
One 8-ounce can tomato sauce
¼ cup ketchup
1 tablespoon Worcestershire
¼ teaspoon garlic salt
½ teaspoon dried oregano

Brown lamb chops in butter and place in a casserole. Sprinkle with salt and pepper. Pour water into pan and stir to loosen drippings. Add rest of ingredients and pour over chops. Cover and bake in preheated moderate oven (350°F.) for 1 hour. Serve with pilaf. (After the fat has been skimmed from the sauce, it can be used on the pilaf.) Makes 3 servings.

VRASTO ARNI ME MANESTRA
(Lamb Stew with Manestra)

2 pounds lean stewing lamb
¼ cup butter
2 medium onions, finely chopped
1 bay leaf

Juice of ½ lemon
Salt and pepper to taste
2 cups manestra (see Note on page 818)

Brown lamb in butter. Add remaining ingredients except manestra and enough water to cover. Simmer for 2 hours. Cook manestra in boiling salted water for 20 minutes, or until tender. Rinse and drain well. Fry in butter until golden brown, turning occasionally with a spatula. Serve the stew over the manestra. Thicken the gravy with a mixture of flour and water if desired. Makes 4 servings.

VRASTO ARNI ME FAVA
(Stewed Lamb and Fava Beans)

2 cups dried fava beans or large Lima beans
1 large onion, chopped
Olive oil
1 garlic clove, minced
2 pounds lean stewing lamb
3½ cups (one 1-pound, 12-ounce can) tomatoes
1 teaspoon dried mint leaves, crumbled
Salt and pepper to taste
Chopped parsley

Soak beans overnight in water. Simmer beans for 1 hour. Drain. Sauté onion in olive oil until golden. Remove onion and brown meat well. Combine all ingredients except parsley in saucepan. Cover and simmer for 2 hours, or until meat and beans are tender. Sprinkle with chopped parsley. Serve in bowls. Makes 6 servings.

TIROPITTA
(Cheese Pie)

30 sheets of phyllo (to fit pan 8-inches square or 7 x 11 inches) (see page 822)
1 cup butter, melted
4 eggs
2 cups (about ½ pound) feta cheese, crumbled or grated
2 cups (about 1 pound) cottage cheese (small curd)
2 tablespoons milk
Salt

Brush a baking pan with melted butter. Lay 10 sheets of *phyllo* on bottom of pan, brushing each sheet with melted butter as it is placed in the pan.

Beat eggs until thick and foamy. Add cheeses and beat well. Add 2 tablespoons of the melted butter and the milk. Add salt if needed. Beat again. Spread half of mixture over *phyllo* in pan. Top with another 10 sheets of *phyllo*, brushing butter on each sheet. Repeat. Trim any excess pastry from edge. Bake in preheated moderate oven (350°F.) for 1¼ hours. Cut into squares or triangles and serve warm. Makes 16 pieces.

POULTRY

KOTTA PILAFI
(Chicken Pilaf)

6 chicken breasts (about 3 pounds)
¼ cup butter
1 medium onion, fiinely chopped
1½ cups canned tomatoes
2 cups water
1 teaspoon ground cinnamon
 Salt and pepper
1 cup raw rice

Sauté chicken breasts in butter until golden brown. Add onion, tomatoes, water, cinnamon, and salt and pepper to taste. Cover and simmer for 30 minutes. Add rice and stir to mix evenly. Cover and simmer for an additional 20 minutes, or until rice is tender, adding more water if necessary. Serve with a bowl of cold dairy sour cream, to be spooned over the hot pilaf. Makes 6 servings.

GEMISTI KOTTA
(Baked Chicken)

1 lemon
1 roasting chicken (3 to 3½ pounds)
 Salt and pepper
½ teaspoon ground oregano
¼ cup butter
1 celery stalk, sliced
½ cup boiling water

Grate lemon peel and reserve. Cut lemon into halves and rub outside of chicken with cut sides. Squeeze lemon and reserve juice. Sprinkle chicken inside and out with salt, pepper, and oregano. Place lemon peel and sliced celery in chicken. In skillet brown chicken lightly in butter. Remove chicken to casserole. Pour off remaining butter and reserve. Pour boiling water into skillet in which chicken was browned. Scrape chicken bits from bottom of skillet. Pour pan juices over chicken in casserole. Add lemon juice. Bake, uncovered, in preheated slow oven (300°F.) for 1½ hours. Baste occasionally with butter in which chicken was browned. Serve with Pilaf and Giblet Sauce, page 822. Makes 4 servings.

Gemisti Melitzana

Avgolemono Soupa
Kolokythia Krokettes

Dolmathes
Tiropitta

VEGETABLES

VRASTA FASOLAKIA FRESKA
(Stewed Green Beans)

1 small onion, finely chopped
¼ cup butter
1 pound green beans
1 garlic clove, minced or put through garlic press
1 teaspoon fresh mint leaves, minced, or ½ teaspoon dried mint
1 tablespoon minced parsley
1 teaspoon fennel seeds
½ cup tomato sauce
¼ cup water
Salt and pepper to taste

Sauté onion in butter until golden brown. Wash and trim beans. Cut beans into 2-inch lengths. Add to onions and sauté, stirring constantly, until beans have turned a bright green. Add remaining ingredients and simmer for 30 minutes, or until beans are tender. Makes 4 to 6 servings.

SPANAKORYZO
(Spinach and Rice)

1 cup uncooked rice
1 medium onion, finely chopped
⅓ cup olive oil
2 cups boiling water
1½ teaspoons salt
1 pound fresh spinach

Sauté rice and onion in olive oil, stirring occasionally, for 15 minutes. Add boiling water and salt. Simmer, covered, for 10 minutes. Meanwhile, wash spinach and cut into ½-inch lengths with scissors. Add to rice and mix thoroughly. Cover and continue to simmer, stirring occasionally, for 15 minutes longer. Makes 4 servings.

KOLOKYTHIA KROKETTES
(Zucchini Pancakes)

3 medium zucchini, grated (3 cups)
1 teaspoon salt
3 eggs
1 cup grated feta cheese
1½ teaspoons fresh mint leaves, minced, or ¾ teaspoon dried mint
3 tablespoons all-purpose flour
Pepper
Butter

Mix zucchini with salt and let stand for 1 hour. Squeeze moisture from zucchini. Beat eggs. Add zucchini, cheese, mint, flour, and pepper to taste. Fry in butter, 1 tablespoon at a time, turning to brown both sides. Makes about 18 pancakes.

SELINO AVGOLEMONO
(Celery with Egg-Lemon Sauce)

1 large onion, finely chopped
¼ cup butter
1 bunch of celery (about 2 pounds)
2 cups chicken bouillon
Salt and pepper
2 egg yolks
Juice of 1 lemon

Sauté onion in butter until golden brown. Wash celery, remove strings and tops, and cut stalks into 2-inch lengths. Add to onion with bouillon and salt and pepper to taste; simmer for 30 minutes. Beat egg yolks and add lemon juice. Slowly stir some of the hot broth into egg yolks. Stir egg-yolk mixture into remaining broth. Remove from heat. Cover and let stand for 5 minutes to thicken. Serve at once. Do not reheat. Makes 4 servings.

PILAFI
(Pilaf)

1 cup uncooked rice
¼ cup butter
2½ cups chicken bouillon
1 teaspoon salt

Brown rice in butter until golden brown. Add bouillon and salt and stir. Cover and simmer gently for 15 to 20 minutes, or until liquid is absorbed. Delicious with a spoonful of cold dairy sour cream served on each portion. Makes 4 servings.

SALADS

SALATA
(Salad)

A typical Greek salad is similar to our green salad with the addition of cubes of feta cheese, black Greek olives, beets, and either anchovies or sardines, with a sprinkling of oregano. There is no hard-and-fast rule governing ingredients. In addition to a variety of greens, all or any of the following might be included with the above:

Celery, finely diced
Tomato wedges
Thinly sliced cucumber
Green-pepper rings
Green or dried onion slices
Radishes, sliced or diced
Avocado slices
Potatoes, cooked and cubed or sliced

The dressing is simple: 2 parts olive oil to 1 part white-wine vinegar or lemon juice are combined and seasoned with salt and pepper. The dressing is poured over the salad and tossed just before serving.

AGOURONTOMATOSALATA
(Tomato and Cucumber Salad)

3 large tomatoes
1 large cucumber
2 green onions
1 teaspoon dried oregano
2 tablespoons olive oil
Juice of ½ lemon
Salt and pepper to taste

Peel tomatoes and cut into wedges. Wash cucumber and score skin with tines of a fork. Cut into thin slices. Slice onions, using some of the green tops. Combine vegetables with oregano in a salad bowl. Mix together olive oil, lemon, juice, and salt and pepper and pour over salad, tossing to mix. Makes 4 to 6 servings.

MELITZANOSALATA
(Eggplant Salad)

1 large eggplant
1 garlic clove
¼ cup olive oil
Salt and pepper
1 tomato, diced
2 tablespoons minced parsley
1 tablespoon grated onion
1 teaspoon dried oregano, crumbled
2 tablespoons white-wine vinegar
Salt and pepper

Bake eggplant in preheated moderate oven (350°F.) for 1 hour. Cool, peel, and dice. Rub a salad bowl with cut garlic clove. Discard garlic. Put olive oil and salt and pepper in the bowl. Combine eggplant, tomato, parsley, onion, and oregano in the bowl. Pour vinegar over vegetables and mix thoroughly. Season with salt and pepper to taste. Chill before serving. Makes 3 or 4 servings.

SAUCES

SKORDALIA
(Garlic Sauce)

1 small potato
3 garlic cloves, minced
1 teaspoon salt
1 cup olive oil
⅓ cup vinegar

Peel potato and boil until tender. Put through a ricer or sieve. Measure ½ cup potato and place in a bowl; mix in garlic and salt. Gradually add olive oil and vinegar alternately while beating with a spoon. Chill. Serve with meat or fish. Makes about 1¼ cups.

SIKOTAKIA SALTSA
(Giblet Sauce)

Heart, liver, and gizzard of 1 chicken
1½ cups boiling water
Salt and pepper to taste
1 medium onion, finely chopped
2 tablespoons butter
2 tablespoons all-purpose flour
1 garlic clove, minced or put through garlic press
¼ cup tomato paste

Simmer heart, liver, and gizzard in boiling water with salt and pepper until tender. Drain and reserve liquid. Chop meat fine. Sauté onion in butter until golden. Blend in flour and gradually add liquid in which giblets were cooked, stirring until smooth. Cook, stirring constantly, until thickened. Add garlic, tomato paste, and giblets. Serve hot over pilaf. Makes 4 servings.

BREADS

PHYLLO OR FILO

This paper-thin pastry is used for making meat, vegetable, cheese, and egg dishes as well as sweet pastries, for which the

Greeks are so well known. It can be purchased in 1-pound packages in some specialty food stores or in Greek, Italian, Austrian, or German food stores. If you prefer to make your own, follow the directions carefully and you will find it is not difficult to make.

Hints on Handling Phyllo

Do not use a moist mixture, such as cheese, custard, meat, or vegetable filling, with dry sheets of *phyllo*. It is better to use moist *phyllo* with moist fillings.

Do not use dry *phyllo* in any recipe in which the *phyllo* is rolled or folded.

If dry *phyllo* is too hard to handle, it can be sprinkled with water or brushed with water to make it more pliable.

Because the sheets of moist *phyllo* dry quickly, keep all but the sheet you are working on covered with a towel. Do not unwrap *phyllo* until you have filling prepared and are ready to use it.

Phyllo freezes satisfactorily and will keep frozen for several months. Keep the package sealed while frozen. Thaw at room temperature when ready to use.

HOMEMADE PHYLLO
2⅔ cups sifted all-purpose flour
1 teaspoon salt
½ cup lukewarm water
2 tablespoons salad oil

Sift flour and salt into a bowl. Gradually add water, stirring to make a stiff dough. Turn onto a pastry board. Place the oil in a bowl and spread a little of it on the palms of your hands. Knead the dough with a folding-and-turning motion, adding more oil to your hands when dough begins to stick. Continue until you have a smooth, elastic ball of dough and the oil is nearly all used. Then roll the ball of dough in the remaining oil to cover all sides, place a clean cloth over the bowl, and allow the dough to rest for 2 hours or more in a warm place away from drafts. A barely warm oven is satisfactory.

Separate ¼ of the dough and roll to ¼-inch thickness on a pastry board rubbed with cornstarch. Cover with a clean cloth and let it rest for 10 minutes. Cover a table (cardtable or larger) with a smooth cloth and carefully lift dough onto it. Put your hands under the dough, palms down, and gently stretch and pull the dough with the backs of your hands, working your way around the table, until the dough is as thin as tissue paper. Do not worry if it hangs down around the edges of the table, or if some holes appear, especially around the edges. Cut off the thicker edge and save the scraps.

The *phyllo* is now ready to be cut into pieces with scissors if you wish to use it moist. If you prefer dry *phyllo*, allow it to stand until dry, about 10 minutes, then cut into desired sizes.

The scraps of dough can be put into a moist bowl and kneaded and rolled again.

VASILOPITTA
(Sweet Bread)
1 package active dry yeast or 1 cake compressed yeast*
2 tablespoons water*
⅔ cup milk, scalded
1 teaspoon sugar
2¾ to 3¼ cups sifted all-purpose flour
½ cup sugar
3 eggs, beaten
¼ teaspoon each of ground cinnamon, nutmeg, and cloves
¼ cup butter, melted
Sesame seeds
Blanched almond halves

Dissolve yeast in the water. *Use very warm water (105° to 115°F.) for dry yeast; use lukewarm water (80° to 90°F.) for compressed. Scald milk and cool to lukewarm. Combine yeast, milk, and 1 teaspoon sugar in a large bowl. Sift in ½ cup of the flour. Stir until flour is dampened. Cover bowl with a clean cloth, and set in a warm place for 1 hour.

Add remaining flour, ½ cup sugar, 2 of the eggs, and spices to melted butter and stir into dough. Put on a floured pastry board and knead until smooth and elastic. Place in an oiled bowl, turning dough to cover all sides with oil. Cover with a cloth and let rise in a warm place until doubled, about 1½ hours.

Divide dough into thirds and roll each part into a strip about 18 inches long. Braid loosely on a greased cookie sheet. Cover with a cloth and let rise until doubled, about 1 hour. Brush with remaining beaten egg and sprinkle with sesame seeds. Arrange blanched almond halves in a decorative pattern on top. Bake in preheated moderate oven (375° F.) for 25 to 30 minutes.

DESSERTS AND PASTRIES

BAKLAVA
(Filled Pastry)
30 sheets of phyllo (8 x 8 inches) (see page 822)
1 cup butter, melted
1 cup finely chopped or ground walnuts
½ cup finely chopped or ground blanched almonds
2 tablespoons sugar
1 teaspoon ground cinnamon
½ teaspoon ground nutmeg
⅛ teaspoon ground cloves
Lemon-Honey Syrup

Butter the bottom of an 8-inch square baking pan. Lay 10 sheets of *phyllo* in pan, brushing each sheet with melted butter. Mix nuts with sugar and spices and sprinkle half of this over *phyllo*. Drizzle with melted butter. Lay on another 10 sheets of *phyllo,* brushing each with butter. Repeat with another layer of nut mixture and remaining *phyllo*. Cut, without cutting through bottom layer, into diamond-shaped pieces. Bake in preheated moderate oven (350°F.) for 1 hour. Finish cutting and allow Baklava to cool. Pour warm Lemon-Honey Syrup over. Makes about 20 diamonds.

Lemon-Honey Syrup
Boil 1 cup sugar, 1 cup water, and ½ lemon for 15 minutes. Remove lemon and add 2 tablespoons honey. Stir.

GALOTOBOUREKO
(Farina Pastries)
4 cups milk
1 cup farina or cream of wheat
½ teaspoon salt
6 eggs, beaten
¾ cup sugar
6 tablespoons butter
1 teaspoon vanilla extract
½ teaspoon ground cinnamon
24 sheets of phyllo (12 x 15 inches) (see page 822)
¾ cup butter, melted
Honey Syrup

Heat milk; slowly add farina, stirring constantly. Add salt and boil, continuing to stir, for 5 minutes. Beat eggs until light and gradually beat in sugar. Fold into farina mixture and continue to cook, stirring constantly, for 3 minutes more. Add 6 tablespoons butter and stir until absorbed. Remove from heat, add vanilla and cinnamon, and cool while you prepare pastry. Stir occasionally.

Brush a baking pan (12 x 15 inches) with melted butter and lay in 12 sheets of *phyllo,* brushing each with melted butter. Spread farina mixture over pastry and cover with remaining *phyllo,* brushing each sheet with melted butter. Pour any remaining butter over top. Trim any uneven edges of pastry with scissors and cut through the top layer of pastry in 2-inch squares. Bake in preheated moderate oven (350°F.) for 45 minutes. When *Galotoboureko* is lukewarm, cut through custard layer and bottom pastry, following the cuts made before baking. Pour lukewarm Honey Syrup over *Galotoboureko* and cool before serving.

Honey Syrup
1 cup water
1 cup sugar
¼ cup honey

Combine water, sugar, and honey and boil for 10 minutes. Cool slightly.

PURA
(Nut Pastries)
¾ cup finely chopped or ground walnuts
½ cup finely chopped or ground
    blanched almonds
1 teaspoon sugar
¼ teaspoon ground cinnamon
⅛ teaspoon ground nutmeg
20 sheets phyllo (12 x 15 inches)
    (see page 822)
1 cup butter, melted
    Cinnamon-Honey Syrup

Mix together nuts, sugar, and spices. Brush half of a sheet of *phyllo* with melted butter, fold other half over, and brush with butter so that you have a piece of *phyllo* 7½ x 12 inches. Sprinkle with 1 tablespoon of nut mixture. Beginning at one end, roll *phyllo* as you would a jelly roll. Cut into halves, making 2 rolls approximately 3¼ inches in length. Place on greased cookie sheet with smooth side of pastry up and brush with melted butter. Bake in preheated moderate oven (350°F.) for 20 minutes, or until golden brown. While hot, dip into warm Cinnamon-Honey Syrup and drain. Makes 40.

Cinnamon-Honey Syrup
1 cup sugar
⅔ cup water
¼ cup honey
    Small cinnamon stick
1 teaspoon fresh lemon juice

Mix all ingredients together and simmer for 30 minutes. Cook only until light brown.

HALVA
(Nut Confection)
½ cup butter
⅔ cup sugar
2 eggs
1 cup farina
½ teaspoon ground cinnamon
½ cup ground almonds
    Syrup

Cream butter; add sugar gradually, creaming well after each addition. Beat in eggs, one at a time. Gradually fold in farina, cinnamon, and almonds. Place in a greased 8-inch square cake pan, and bake in preheated moderate oven (350°F.) for 35 minutes. Cool for 15 minutes; then pour Syrup over. Cool and cut into squares or diamonds. Makes 16 pieces.

Syrup
1 cup honey
½ cup water

Simmer together for 10 minutes.

KAFES
(Greek Coffee)
2 cups water
6 lumps sugar
6 heaping teaspoons finely ground
    coffee

Boil water and sugar in heavy pot, stir in coffee. When boiling, remove from heat; skim off foam; reserve. Bring again to boil and skim. Repeat once more. Remove from heat; add 1 tablespoon cold water. Put a little foam in each demitasse cup and pour in coffee. Makes 6 cups.

GREENGAGE—A fine quality dessert plum, round in shape and greenish-yellow in color. The flesh is juicy and sweet, yet it has a tang. The stone is small and round and the flesh clings to it.

Greengages, provided they are tree ripened, have more flavor than all other plums. Greengages do not ripen well after picking. They are highly regarded in Europe and the United States although they are not as popular in our country as are the blue and purple plum varieties.

The fruit was named after Sir William Gage, an Englishman who imported the plum from France in the latter part of the 18th century. France is the country where greengages reach a height of flavor seldom found elsewhere. The French name for the plum is Reine Claude, in honor of Queen Claude, wife of the French king Francis I (1515-1547). She was a modest retiring queen with little public flair, a far cry from the brilliant and worldly Catherine de Medici, who was to marry her son and later become queen. During Claude's and Francis' reign there were many hearty banquets, as the king's appetite was prodigious. But the ladies of the court did not usually share the culinary festivities, for the task of chewing was so great that the "movement of the jaws deformed the contours of their faces and detracted from the ethereal appeal of their beauty."

Availability—The peak season for fresh plums is July and August. Greengages are also available canned, in water and heavy syrup packs.

Purchasing Guide—Select plums that are fresh in appearance, plump and full-colored. Fruit with firm flesh that yields slightly when gently pressed is best. Avoid hard, cracked, shriveled, or softened fruit. Buy in amounts which can be used within a week.

Storage—Fruit should be covered and refrigerated.
☐ Canned, kitchen shelf: 1 year
☐ Fresh, refrigerator shelf: 3 to 7 days
☐ Fresh, refrigerator shelf, cooked and covered: 4 to 5 days
☐ Canned, refrigerator shell, opened and covered: 4 to 5 days

Caloric Values
☐ Fresh, 3½ ounces = 75 calories
☐ Canned, 3½ ounces, water pack = 33 calories
☐ Canned, 3½ ounces, heavy syrup = 70 calories

Basic Preparation—Wash thoroughly before serving.
☐ **To Stew**—Prick skins. Add water to half cover. Simmer, covered, until tender, about 20 minutes. Stir in sugar to preferred taste. Continue cooking, uncovered, for about 5 minutes longer.

FRESH GREENGAGE PLUM BETTY
2 cups coarse soft bread crumbs
4 cups thickly sliced ripe greengage plums
½ cup chopped nuts
¾ cup sugar
¼ cup butter or margarine
    Cream

Arrange crumbs, plums, and nuts in layers in preheated electric skillet or baking pan of table oven, beginning and ending with crumbs; sprinkle each layer with sugar. Dot with butter; bake at moderate heat for about 15 minutes. Serve warm with cream slightly sweetened and flavored with cinnamon. Makes 4 to 6 servings.

GREENS—The term covers any wild or cultivated green herbage which is eaten raw or cooked.

In the days when fresh green vegetables were not available all year round, a "mess of greens" in the spring meant a health tonic. The monotony of the old winter diets brought on a longing and a need for fresh green foodstuffs for well-being. Hence the pleasure in the "mess of greens" freshly picked in field or meadow.

Greens are usually classified in two ways: those eaten raw, as in salads; and those cooked and served as a vegetable dish, with or without meat. The latter are a basic part of rural Southern cooking, which features them with ham or pork.

The most commonly used salad greens are lettuce, endive, escarole, chicory, and watercress. Among the greens to cook are beet tops, collards, dandelion, mustard, spinach, kale, Swiss chard, turnip tops.

Many wild plants are favored in season as cooked greens: fiddlehead ferns, lamb's quarter, burdock, sour dock, mustard, milkweed, dandelion, poke stalks, etc. They should be picked when young and tender and eaten as soon as possible after picking.

Availability—Most of the greens used raw are available year round, although they are slightly more widespread during the spring and summer months. With the exception of Swiss chard, the fresh greens most often cooked are more widely available during the spring, fall, and winter. Swiss chard is most plentiful in the summer months.

Spinach, kale, collards, and mustard greens are available canned and frozen.

Purchasing Guide—Look for young, green, tender leaves, free of excess dirt. Avoid dry, yellow leaves or leaves that may be flabby or wilted. The presence of seed stems in almost any greens indicates age and toughness.

Storage—Trim and remove any discolored leaves. Wash thoroughly in running water. Drain and blot dry with paper towels. Store in the refrigerator in the vegetable compartment or in a pliofilm bag.

☐ Refrigerator shelf, wrapped: 3 to 8 days
☐ Refrigerator frozen-food compartment, cooked and covered: 2 to 3 months
☐ Freezer, cooked and prepared for freezing: 1 year
Do not freeze raw greens.

Nutritive Food Values—Green leafy vegetables are the best sources of vitamin A, which is apparently formed in the leaf and is associated with a bright green or yellow color. Green leafy vegetables are important sources of minerals and vitamins, especially iron, calcium, and riboflavin, and they are very low in calories.

Raw greens, as a source of ascorbic acid, compare favorably with citrus fruits.
Basic Preparation—Wash all greens well to remove sand and wilted leaves.
☐ **To Prepare Raw Greens**—Trim, rinse, and drain greens. Place in a colander lightly covered with wax paper to crisp until ready to prepare salad. Toss salad with dressing just before serving.
☐ **To Prepare Cooked Greens**—Add as little water as possible. Add salt. Cook greens until tender. Drain, using liquid to prepare a sauce, or serve liquid in soups since it is rich in vitamins and minerals and should not be wasted.

CALIFORNIA CHEF'S SALAD
½ head each of lettuce and romaine
½ bunch of watercress
1 small bunch of chicory
2 tomatoes, peeled, seeded, and diced
2 cooked chicken breasts, diced
6 strips of crisp bacon, crumbled
1 avocado, diced
3 hard-cooked eggs, diced
2 tablespoons chopped chives
½ cup finely crumbled Roquefort
¾ cup Italian-type dressing

Cut greens quite fine and put in large salad bowl. Add remaining ingredients and toss well. Makes 8 servings.

MIXED GREEN SALAD
Any combination of greens can be used but choose two or more, such as romaine, Boston lettuce, and watercress. Wash greens carefully to remove any grit and dry gently on a clean absorbent towel. Spread out on a fresh towel, roll up very loosely and put in refrigerator until ready to make salad. Just before serving, break greens in bite-size pieces and put in a salad bowl. Add French dressing made with 3 or 4 parts oil to 1 part mild vinegar or lemon juice. Season with salt and pepper to taste, and toss lightly with a fork and spoon until greens are well coated with the dressing. Serve at once.

BLACK-BUTTER SAUCE FOR COOKED GREENS
Heat butter in skillet until well browned. Add fresh lemon juice or wine vinegar to taste, and pour over hot cooked greens.

PANNED GARDEN GREENS
Cook 2 quarts finely chopped beet or turnip tops, cabbage, escarole, romaine, lettuce, spinach, chard, or mustard greens quickly in 2 tablespoons bacon fat or butter in large heavy saucepan for 3 to 5 minutes, stirring constantly. Season to taste. Makes 4 servings.

SOUTHERN PORK AND GREENS
Cook ¼ to ½ pound salt pork in 1½ to 2 quarts water for about 1 hour, or until tender. Place turnip or other greens in pot and cook for 30 more minutes. Drain and save the liquid; this is the famous "potlikker." Chop greens. Season with salt and pepper to taste. Slice pork and place on chopped greens. Pour potlikker over pork and greens. Serve hot.

FRIED MUSTARD GREENS
Cook greens in as little water as possible until tender. Drain. Fry in bacon fat or salt-pork drippings. Season to taste with salt and pepper.
Note: Other greens may also be used.

GRENADINE—This is a brilliant scarlet, non-alcoholic French syrup made with the juice of pomegranates. The taste is sweet and distinctive. Grenadine is used as a cocktail or punch ingredient, as a soft drink when diluted with water or soda, and as a sweetening and flavoring agent for fruits and desserts.

Grenadine is a highly favored fruit syrup in France. With water, it is the standard treat for children taken to a café by their elders. The sight of scrubbed, combed, and starched little French boys and girls, sitting upright and silent for hours in a café of the French provinces, as the aftermath of *la promenade du dimanche,* the Sunday family walk, is one not easily forgotten.

Grenadine can be added to milk, iced tea, milk shakes, sodas, lemonades, and fruit punches as a flavoring. It can be used as a sweetener and sauce for ice cream, yogurt, fruit cups and salads, vanilla and tapioca puddings. When used as a sauce, grenadine should be diluted. Bottled grenadine is available in food stores.

GRIDDLE CAKE—This is a thin round cake made from a batter and cooked on a griddle. Griddle cakes can be made with practically any kind of flour or meal and any liquid, though sweet or sour milk are preferred.

One of the secrets of successful griddle cakes lies in beating the batter only until it is just smooth, since overbeating makes the cakes tough. The batter should not be held unused for too long. The griddle should be heated slowly, so that the heat will be evenly distributed. Whether it is greased (but only very lightly) or not greased depends on the cook's opinion. If an ungreased griddle is used, it should be rubbed clean with a cloth bag filled with salt after each batch of cakes is made. To test the griddle for heat, sprinkle a few drops of water on it. If the drops dance, the heat is right, but if the drops explode, the griddle is too hot.

Cooking on a griddle is an old form of cookery which developed in many countries where cooking was simple and fuel scarce. In America such cooking is associated with pioneer life. Griddle cakes provided a hot bread when circumstances did not permit setting up a bake oven or taking the time to use one.

A basic food, griddle cakes have as much appeal now as they did in the past. They are very compelling when stacked up, with butter in between the cakes, drenched with maple syrup, molasses, honey, or any other liquid sweetening custom provides or the heart desires.

RHODE ISLAND GRIDDLE CAKES
1 cup sour milk or buttermilk
½ teaspoon baking soda

1 cup soft bread crumbs
1 egg, beaten
1 tablespoon sugar
About ¼ cup unsifted all-purpose
flour

Combine sour milk and baking soda. Pour over bread crumbs. Let stand until crumbs are very soft. Beat in egg, sugar, and enough flour to make a batter that can be dropped from a spoon. Bake on slightly greased griddle. Turn cakes carefully since they are somewhat fragile. Makes about twelve 4-inch cakes.

MAPLE BUCKWHEAT CAKES

½ cup maple sugar, crumbled
1 egg, beaten
1 cup dairy sour cream
½ cup water
1 cup buckwheat flour
1 teaspoon baking soda
½ teaspoon baking powder
½ teaspoon salt

Beat together maple sugar, egg, sour cream, and water until mixture is smooth. Sift together buckwheat flour, soda, baking powder, and salt. Combine mixture and beat quickly until smooth. Batter will be very thick. Drop by spoonful onto hot griddle. Leave space between cakes since they spread in cooking. Makes about sixteen 4-inch cakes.

CORNMEAL GRIDDLE CAKES

½ cup cornmeal
1½ cups cold water
1¼ cups sour milk or buttermilk
2 cups milk
⅓ cup sugar
1 teaspoon salt
1 teaspoon baking powder
¾ teaspoon baking soda
1 egg, well beaten
2 tablespoons butter or margarine

Add meal to cold water, bring to boil, and cook for 5 minutes. Turn into bowl; add all the milk and remaining dry ingredients, mixed and sifted, then egg and butter. Cook on lightly greased griddle. Makes about 24 griddle cakes.

OATMEAL GRIDDLE CAKES

2 cups milk
2 cups quick-cooking rolled oats
⅓ cup sifted all-purpose flour
2½ teaspoons baking powder
1 teaspoon salt
2 tablespoons sugar
2 eggs, separated
½ cup melted fat or cooking oil

Heat milk and pour over oats; cool. Sift dry ingredients. Beat egg yolks and add to oat mixture. Add fat and stir in dry ingredients. Beat egg whites until stiff and fold into first mixture. Drop by spoonful onto hot greased griddle and spread with pancake turner. When surface is bubbly, turn and brown on other side. Serve with syrup or honey. Makes 4 servings.

APPLE-WALNUT GRIDDLE CAKES

2 cups sifted all-purpose flour
1 teaspoon baking soda

Breakfast favorite: a stack of griddle cakes

½ teaspoon salt
2 tablespoons sugar
2 eggs, beaten
2 cups buttermilk
2 tablespoons salad oil
1½ cups very finely chopped peeled apples
½ cup chopped walnuts
Maple syrup

Sift flour, soda, salt, and sugar. Mix egg, buttermilk, and oil. Add liquid ingredients to dry ingredients all at once. Stir until smooth. Fold in apples and nuts. Spoon batter onto hot greased griddle. Brown on one side, turn and brown on the other side. Serve with syrup. Makes about 20.

GRILL

GRILL—"To grill" means to cook by direct heat by (1) broiling in an oven; (2) cooking over a gas flame, briquets, charcoal, or heated stones, either indoors or out; (3) cooking on a griddle or grill, either electric or non-electric. Meats of many kinds, sandwiches, and vegetables lend themselves to this kind of cooking.

In American culinary language the term is synonymous with "to broil," but in England, people use the words "to grill" since broiling is a term unknown to them.

The term "mixed grill" is used to describe certain foods cooked in this manner. A mixed grill may consist of a combination of meat, fish, or poultry with vegetables and sometimes fruit: for example, lamb chops, bacon, kidney, tomato, and mushrooms cooked simultaneously and served together.

As a noun the word grill refers to the utensil or piece of equipment on which food is grilled, such as an hibachi, a barbecue grill, rotisserie, brazier, camp stove, or stationary barbecue pit.

The Fabulous Mixed Grill

For 4 servings:

Cut stems from 4 large mushrooms and reserve stems for other use. Wipe mushrooms with damp cloth and put, rounded side down, on rack on broiler pan. Put 4 small link sausages and 4 slices of bacon on rack with mushrooms. Wash 4 lamb kidneys; split and remove fat and membrane with scissors. Arrange, split side up, on rack. Melt ¼ cup butter or margarine in small saucepan and brush some on kidneys and mushrooms. Broil under medium heat about 4 inches from heat, turning foods as they brown and brushing kidneys and mushrooms again with butter. (The bacon and mushrooms will be ready first. Kidneys need 6 to 8 minutes on each side, and sausages will be done at about the same time.) Sprinkle a little onion salt on mushrooms, salt and pepper on kidneys.

As foods are done, remove with tongs to a cake rack on a cookie sheet with sides; add 4 slices of bread, toasted and cut into halves diagonally. Put in a warm place. (If you have no toaster, brown the bread under broiler later after removing chops.)

To keep food warm while chops are broiling: If you have an oven which is separate from the broiler, set it at low temperature, and put kidneys, etc., in it. If the broiler is in the top of the oven, put rack of cooked foods below broiler pan while chops are broiling. If your broiler is underneath your oven, put rack of foods in oven for a few minutes after turning off broiler. If you have 2 broilers, all foods can be broiled at the same time.

Arrange 8 small rib lamb chops on broiler rack and broil under medium heat, 4 inches below the heat, for 7 or 8 minutes on each side. When chops are turned, put 4 scored tomato halves on rack with chops. Brush with butter. When chops and tomatoes are done, season.

GRIND

GRIND—To grind is to crush food into small pieces by passing it through a grinder. A grinder may be mechanical or electrical and can grind foods into particles from coarse all the way to fine, depending on the blade used. Dry foods, cheese, meats, fruits, coffee beans, vegetables, nuts, etc., cooked or raw, can all be ground into uniform particles.

As a noun, grind is used in reference to coffee to describe the degree to which the beans have been crushed.

GRITS, GROATS

GRITS, GROATS—Both words refer to hulled and coarsely ground cereal grains and both have the meaning of "fragment" or "part." Grits are smaller than groats, more finely ground, usually from corn, but also from buckwheat, rye, oats, or rice. Grits ground from corn are known as hominy grits.

Groats are most often ground from buckwheat, oats, barley, and wheat, as well as corn. Cracked wheat is another name for wheat groats or grits. Buckwheat groats are the most commonly used. They are also called *kasha*, a Russian word, and are a staple of Russia's diet.

Grits and groats are very old foods and, with the exception of those made from corn, which is a native American grain, typical of the folk foods of Europe. In Germany, England, Scandinavia, and the Slavic countries, people lived on grits and groats for centuries. Their health was maintained by the use of these unrefined and most nutritious cereals. All these countries have favorite recipes which resemble each other and are on the hearty side. They boiled groats in water or milk; ate them in soup, as mush, or made into a pudding; for breakfast, lunch, and supper; and fed them, well cooked, to infants and invalids. Grits and groats bring to mind the days of the past, when each peasant or farmer ground his own cereals or brought them to the village mill to be ground.

Today, with a lighter diet and more highly refined foods, grits and groats have gone out of fashion with the exception of hominy grits in the southern states. However, many grits and groats can be bought in food stores or health-food stores or at local mills specializing in old-fashioned cereals.

KASHA IN CHICKEN SOUP
1 egg, beaten
1 cup brown buckwheat groats
1 teaspoon salt
¼ cup butter or margarine
2 cups water
3 to 4 cups hot chicken soup

Mix egg, groats, and salt. Melt butter in skillet. Stir in groat mixture and the water; bring to boil. Cook, tightly covered, over low heat for 15 minutes. Spoon into hot soup. Makes 4 servings.

HOMINY GRITS
1 cup hominy grits
4 cups boiling water
1 teaspoon salt
1 tablespoon butter

Pour grits into boiling water and stir until mixture boils. Add salt, cover and simmer for 1 hour, stirring frequently. When ready to serve, add butter and beat well. Serve as a vegetable with butter or gravy, or as cereal with milk. Makes 4 to 6 servings.

PORK CHOPS AND GRITS
4 thick pork chops
Salt and pepper to taste
Fat for browning
2 medium onions, chopped
2 cups oat, wheat, or rye grits or groats
3 cups bouillon, heated to boiling

Season chops and brown on both sides in fat. Remove chops, and brown onions slightly. Put 1 cup grits into casserole. Add chops, onions, and top with second cup of grits. Add bouillon, cover, and bake in preheated slow oven (300°F.) for 1¼ hours. Makes 4 servings.

GROUPER—Groupers are salt-water fish which live in warm waters, at the bottom of the sea, and in rocky nooks and crevices. They resemble sea bass. Groupers are found from Virginia in the United States to Brazil and they are an important food fish in Florida, the Gulf States, and the West Indies. Some California rockfish are also called groupers.

Groupers can grow to a great size, about forty to fifty pounds. They are wily fish and endowed with the gift of camouflage: they take on the color of their surroundings. Down in the coral or seaweed they sprout stripes; up on the top of the water, they blend in with the color of the sea.

Groupers can be cooked like sea bass or red snapper. The fillets are excellent when broiled or stuffed and baked.

Availability—Groupers are available year round. Market sizes range from 3 to 15 pounds. Small groupers are marketed as whole fish; larger groupers are filleted.

Caloric Value

☐ 3½ ounces, raw = 87 calories

BAKED GROUPER

Clean and wash a 5-pound grouper. Put in buttered shallow baking dish or roasting pan. Dot with butter and sprinkle with salt and pepper. Bake in preheated hot oven (400°F.) for 45 minutes, or until fish flakes easily with a fork. Baste fish occasionally with melted butter during the baking. Serve hot with lemon wedges and a garnish of parsley. Makes 6 servings.

GROUSE—There are many varieties of this plump game bird of the northern hemisphere. Grouse are related to the pheasant family.

Grouse are usually some fifteen inches tall, the size of a small chicken, and weigh from one to two pounds. Their feathers are brown. The meat is dark and rich and is best broiled or roasted. Depending on size, one bird will make one or two servings.

The foremost American grouse is the Ruffed Grouse, which takes its name from the ruffs of feathers on each side of its head. The Prairie Chicken, which resembles a hen, is another kind of grouse; others are the Sage Grouse, the Dusky Grouse, and the Black Grouse.

Grouse have adapted themselves to living in varied conditions, both here and in Europe. Several kinds of ptarmigan, one of the grouse family and especially delicious, live as far north as Spitsbergen in the vicinity of the North Pole, or at high altitudes in the Rocky Mountains.

Grouse is highly thought of by the British, and the Scotch Grouse, simply called grouse in England, is said to be finer than other grouse.

ROAST GROUSE WITH ORANGE SLICES

    4 grouse
      Salt and pepper
      Four ¼-inch orange slices, peeled and seeded
    4 slices of bacon
    ¼ cup butter or margarine, melted
      Grated peel of 1 orange
    2 tablespoons fresh orange juice
    1 teaspoon fresh lemon juice
    ¼ cup chopped parsley

Rub grouse inside and out with salt and pepper. Place 1 orange slice and 1 bacon slice on the breast of each bird. Fasten with string. Place grouse breast upward in roasting pan. Roast in preheated moderate oven (350°F.) for 20 to 45 minutes, depending on age of bird. Combine melted butter, orange peel, and fruit juices. Baste birds frequently with mixture. Place on serving platter and remove strings. Sprinkle with parsley. Serve with roasted orange and bacon slices, corn pudding, and a green vegetable. Makes 4 servings.
Note: Grouse is usually served rare, with the flesh a pale pink.

GRUEL—An old-fashioned dish made from a cereal boiled with water to the consistency of a thin porridge. It can be flavored with sugar, honey, wine, butter, salt, or lemon peel, and eaten plain or with milk.

Gruels are the forebears of our modern cereal and pasta dishes. They were the staple food of the people of Europe for many centuries before the potato was introduced to Europe in 1580 by the Spanish explorers who had discovered it in the New World.

In Scandinavia, thick or thin gruels were the mainstay of rural populations until canned foods, and later frozen foods, and modern methods of food distribution made a more varied diet possible.

OATMEAL GRUEL

    3 tablespoons oatmeal
    ⅛ teaspoon salt
    ½ tablespoon sugar
    1 cup boiling water
    1 cup milk
    1 teaspoon butter (optional)
    ⅛ teaspoon ground nutmeg (optional)

Combine oatmeal, salt, and sugar in top part of double boiler. Pour boiling water over mixture and blend. Cook over boiling water for 30 minutes, stirring frequently. Strain through a fine sieve. Add milk. Bring to just below boiling point. Stir in butter and nutmeg. Makes about 2 cups.

GRUNION—A small, salt-water fish, somewhat similar to the smelt. The grunion is found in the waters off the California coast. Grunions belong to the silversides (any small fish related to the gray mullets), which have silvery stripes along each side of the body. Their taste is delicate and flavorful.

Grunions are fish of predictable habits. They come up to the beaches at spawning time and deposit their eggs in holes which they dig. The running of the grunions can be forecast and people gather on the beaches for the event, to catch the grunions in nets or scoops.

Grunions are cooked like any other small fish; boiled, sautéed, or deep fried.

GUAVA—The guava is a tropical fruit which belongs to the Myrtle family. There are many varieties of guavas, usually oval in shape, with fruits from the size of a walnut to that of an apple. The plant varies in size according to the climate in which it is grown and may be a shrub or a fair-size tree. The guava has a thin skin and its flesh can be yellow or red; it is very aromatic, sweet, and juicy and has a high vitamin content. It is eaten fresh, or used for jellies, jams, and preserves.

Availability and Purchasing Guide—Fresh guava is available all year round in localities in which it is grown. Some guava is being shipped to more distant markets. When buying fresh guava, choose firm fruit on the verge of softening, but not spotting.

Whole guava and guava jelly, preserves, butter, paste, sauce, and juice are available canned.

Storage—Ripen at room temperature. If they are to be eaten raw, they must be very ripe.

☐ Fresh, refrigerator shelf: 1 to 3 days
☐ Canned, kitchen shelf: 6 to 12 months
☐ Canned, whole, juice, and sauce, refrigerator shelf, opened and covered: 3 to 4 days
☐ Canned, butter, jelly, and preserves,

refrigerator shelf, opened and covered: 4 to 5 weeks

Nutritive Food Values—Guavas are an excellent source of vitamins A and C.
☐ 3½ ounces, raw = 65 calories

Basic Preparation—Wash fruit, and remove blossom end. Remove skin carefully since most of the nutrients lie close to the surface; cut in slices.

MELON COCKTAIL WITH GUAVA JELLY
Cut equal portions of watermelon, cantaloupe, and honeydew into squares, diamonds, and spheres. Dribble over fruit a half-and-half mixture of melted guava jelly and fresh lemon juice.

GUAVA FRUIT SALAD
Use equal quantities of oranges, grapefruit, and pineapple (either canned or fresh); toss in a generous number of tiny cubes of guava paste. Serve with a dressing of half-and-half whipped cream and mayonnaise.

GUAVA-CHEESE PIE
1 cup guava paste
½ cup heavy cream
3 eggs
1 pound cottage cheese
1 tablespoon fresh lemon juice
  Pinch of salt
  Dash of ground mace
  One 9-inch graham-cracker-crumb crust

Chop the guava paste into small cubes and heat in the cream over the lowest possible heat until only partially melted, so tiny blobs of paste are left. Beat the eggs well; add to the cottage cheese, which has been put through a coarse sieve. Quickly mix with paste-cream mixture, lemon juice, and salt. Pour into crumb crust; sprinkle with mace. Bake in preheated moderate oven (350°F.) for 45 minutes. Makes 6 to 8 servings.

GUAVA YAMS WITH BAKED HAM
Peel and slice yams as if for French frying, but make pieces twice as big. Boil until about half done; drain, put in a baking dish and dot thickly with small amount of guava jelly and butter. Finish cooking in the oven.

GUAVA-PECAN PIE
1 cup guava jelly
2 tablespoons butter
½ cup water
2 tablespoons fresh lemon juice
3 eggs, separated
  Pinch of salt
  Pastry for 1-crust 9-inch pie, unbaked
1 cup pecans

Melt jelly and butter in water; let cool until lukewarm. Add lemon juice. Beat in egg yolks, one at a time; fold in stiffly beaten salted whites. Turn into pastry-lined pie pan. Sprinkle pecans over pie filling. Bake in preheated slow oven (300°F.) for 50 minutes. Makes 6 to 8 servings.

GUAVA JELLY
Cut underripe guavas into quarters. Cover with water and simmer until they are tender, about 10 minutes. Let juice drip through a jelly bag or several thicknesses of cheesecloth. Do not press juice through or jelly will have a bitter flavor. Measure juice and add 1 cup sugar for each cup of juice. Bring mixture to a boil; add 1 teaspoon lime juice, if desired, for every cup of juice. Cook until the mixture sheets from a spoon (when 2 drops come together and fall as 1). Cook 4 cups at a time and pour into hot sterilized glasses. Seal and store.

GUINEA FOWL—This small fowl, originally wild, has been domesticated and is now raised chiefly for food. It was introduced to Europe from the region of Guinea in West Africa. The female bird is called guinea hen and is better eating than the male. Guinea fowl are attractive birds. Usually their plumage is dark, gray-lavender with light dots. Some guinea fowl are pearl-colored or white. The head and upper neck are bare, but certain varieties have a feathered crest. The most striking guinea fowl comes from East Africa; it has bright blue feathers and a vividly colored neck.

The Greeks and Romans raised guinea hens and enjoyed eating them. They were unknown to the rest of Europe until the Portuguese brought them back from their West African explorations in the 16th century.

The habits of guinea fowl are not always admirable. They are gregarious and polygamous. They make a lot of noise and they lay their eggs in a casual and haphazard manner on the ground; they resist regimentation. Unless their wings are clipped they can fly higher than most domesticated birds.

The taste of guinea fowl is slightly and pleasantly gamy. It can be prepared in any way chicken and other small birds are cooked, but the meat is drier and must be treated accordingly.

Availability and Purchasing Guide—Fresh guinea hens are available from October to March. Guinea squabs and chicks are available from late summer to early autumn. Guinea hen, ready-to-cook, is also available frozen.
  Squab—¾ to 1¼ pounds
  Chick—1½ to 2¼ pounds
  Young Guinea Hen (under 1 year)— 2 to 4 pounds
  Mature Guinea Hen—2 to 4 pounds

Storage—Loosen any tight transparent film packaging and place immediately in the coldest part of the refrigerator. If bird is not purchased ready-to-cook, it should be eviscerated and plucked before refrigeration.
☐ Refrigerator shelf, raw: 2 days
☐ Refrigerator shelf, cooked and covered: 1 to 2 days
☐ Refrigerator frozen-food compartment, prepared for freezing, raw: 1 week
☐ Freezer, prepared for freezing, raw: 6 to 7 months
☐ Freezer, prepared for freezing, cooked, without gravy: 1 month
  Do not refreeze once thawed. Use within 2 days of thawing.

Nutritive Food Values—Guinea hen is high in protein.
☐ 3½ ounces, raw = 156 calories

Basic Preparation—If not purchased ready-to-cook, eviscerate and pluck. Before cooking, rinse in cold water. Drain and pat dry. If frozen, thaw in refrigerator: allow 12 to 24 hours. Or place in a pan under cold running water; allow ½ to 1 hour.

Guinea hen is prepared much as is chicken of the same age and size. However, slightly more time must be allowed for cooking. Squab, chick, and young guinea hen can be roasted, fried, or broiled. Mature guinea hen should be cooked with moist heat, either braised or stewed.
☐ **To Eviscerate**—Bleed, then remove crop. Rub dry inside and out with a clean dry cloth. When removing entrails, handle gall bladder carefully to avoid breakage.
☐ **To Pluck**—Pluck dry by pulling out feathers, starting at the base of the neck, and singeing them down with a small flame. Or pluck by dipping in water heated to 165°F. to 175°F. until feathers loosen.
☐ **To Broil**—Allow 35 to 45 minutes for a 1½-pound bird.
☐ **To Roast**—Place bird, breast side down, in roasting pan and put strips of bacon or salt pork on top. Roast in preheated moderate oven (350°F.) and allow 35 to 45 minutes per pound. Baste with melted fat or pan drippings.
☐ **To Freeze**—Eviscerate and pluck, if necessary. Do not stuff before freezing. Truss to make body as compact as possible. Wrap tightly in moisture- vapor-proof material. Seal.

GUMBO

ROAST GUINEA HEN WITH WILD-RICE STUFFING

2 guinea hens
1 cup wild rice
1 large onion, chopped
½ cup chopped celery with leaves
  Melted butter or margarine
2 cups chicken broth
½ cup chopped nuts
1 can (3 ounces) chopped mushrooms, drained
  Poultry seasoning, salt, and pepper

Wash guinea hens and pat dry. Cook rice, onion, and celery in ¼ cup butter for 5 minutes. Add broth and bring to boil. Cover and simmer for 30 minutes, or until liquid is absorbed and rice is tender. Add nuts, mushrooms, poultry seasoning, and salt and pepper to taste. Stuff guinea hens and truss. Put, breast down, on rack in roasting pan and brush with butter. Bake in preheated moderate oven (350° F.) for 1 hour. Turn breast side up, and brush again with butter. Roast for 1 hour longer, or until tender. Makes 4 to 6 servings.

FRIED GUINEA BREASTS

4 breasts of guinea chick
  Salt and pepper to taste
  Butter
¼ pound mushrooms, sliced
2 tablespoons sherry
1 cup heavy cream
  Brown rice, cooked

Season guinea breasts with salt and pepper, and sauté in butter until tender and golden brown, 20 to 30 minutes. Sauté mushrooms in 1 tablespoon butter, add sherry and cream, and heat. Serve guinea breasts on rice topped with mushroom sauce. Makes 4 servings.

———— 🐚 ————

GUMBO—A gumbo is a well-seasoned Creole dish which takes its name from a corruption of the African Bantu word for okra. It may be thickened with okra or with filé powder. The consistency of a gumbo is between that of soup and stew. It is usually served over boiled rice. Gumbos can be made with seafood, poultry, meat, especially salt pork or ham, and with vegetables. The name qualifies the gumbo: chicken gumbo, shrimp gumbo, turkey gumbo, etc.

Gumbos are a native American dish, born of the meeting of French, Spanish, and African cookery in old New Orleans' kitchens. They are a delicious example of what can be done with simple ingredients.

TURKEY, DUCK, OR CHICKEN GUMBO

  Bones and trimmings from roast poultry
2 tablespoons bacon or other fat
2 tablespoons flour
3 medium onions, chopped
1 medium green pepper, chopped
1 cup sliced celery
1 bay leaf
1 teaspoon Worcestershire
1 to 1½ cups diced cooked poultry

2½ cups (1-pound, 4-ounce can) okra
1 pint oysters, if desired
  Salt and pepper

Break bones after meat has been removed. Add 2 quarts water. Cover; bring to boil and simmer for 3 hours in large heavy kettle. Meanwhile, melt fat in skillet; stir in flour; cook slowly until lightly browned. Add onions, green pepper, and celery; cook for 5 minutes. Remove meat from bones; discard bones. Add meat, sautéed vegetables, bay leaf, and Worcestershire to broth; bring to boil, stirring constantly. Cover and simmer for about 1 hour. Add poultry, okra, and oysters. Season with salt and pepper to taste. Simmer until edges of oysters begin to curl. Makes about 1½ quarts.

Note: Two pounds chicken necks, backs, and giblets can be substituted for bones and meat.

CAJUN CRAB GUMBO

2 packages (10 ounces each) frozen okra, thawed
2 tablespoons margarine
2 tablespoons all-purpose flour
1 large onion, chopped
2⅓ cups (one 1-pound, 3-ounce can) tomatoes
1 bay leaf, crushed
2 tablespoons chopped parsley
¼ teaspoon ground thyme
⅛ teaspoon cayenne
1 garlic clove, minced
1½ pounds crabmeat, lump preferred
8 cups boiling water
1 teaspoon salt
3 cups boiled rice

Slice okra into ½-inch pieces. Melt margarine in bottom of heavy kettle. Blend in flour, add okra, onions, tomatoes with the juice, bay leaf, parsley, thyme, cayenne, garlic, and crabmeat. Simmer slowly for 10 minutes, stirring often to keep okra from scorching. Add water and salt. Simmer, covered, for 1 hour. Uncover and simmer until of the consistency of thick soup. Stir often. Put a scoop of rice in each of 6 large soup bowls or plates and ladle soup over it. Makes 6 servings.
Note: Eat with buttered French bread and a tossed salad, beverage, and fruit dessert for a complete meal.

———— 🐚 ————

GUMDROP—This is a colorful, soft candy made of sugar and water with flavoring and coloring added. Gum arabic gives it a chewy gelatinous texture. Gumdrops are made commercially in the shape of drops, rings, bars, fingers, fruit slices, or molded into a variety of other shapes, and covered with sugar crystals.

Gumdrops can be used to decorate cakes and puddings in an effortless merry way that will delight children.

Caloric Value

☐ 3½ ounces = 347 calories

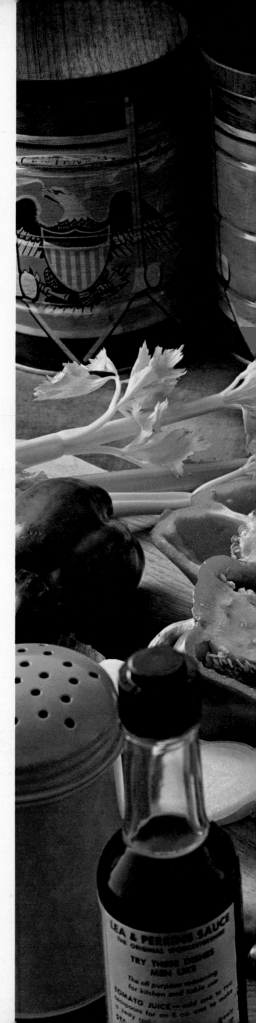

100 Menus
to help you plan
more varied meals
for your family with
the recipes in this volume

*Recipes for all starred dishes found in this volume.

BREAKFASTS

Tomato Juice on the Rocks
Country-Style Frankfurters*
Hominy Grits*
Spitzbuben (Urchins)*

Baked Apples
Fried Ham
Red-Eye Gravy*
Loggers' Flapjacks*
Melted Butter
Maple Syrup

Apple Juice with Lemon
Fish Fry Mullet and
Hush Puppies*
Broiled Tomato Halves

Grapefruit Sections with
Cranberry Juice
Finnan Haddie
in Cream Sauce*
French-Fried Potatoes
Toast

Fresh Fruit Wedges with
Orange Juice*
Crisp Sausage Links
Ginger Waffles*
Corn Syrup

Tangerine Juice
Oatmeal Gruel*
Brown Sugar   Cream
Toasted English Muffins
Bacon Curls

Melon Balls with
Citrus Fruit Juice*
Ocean Perch Fritters*
Ketchup
Bien enstich
("Bee's Sting") Coffeecake*

Broiled Peach Halves
Sausage Patties
Maple Buckwheat Cakes*
Whipped Butter
Maple Syrup

LUNCH OR SUPPER

Double Fruit Cup*
Gnocchi Romana*
Walnut Rolls*

Vegetable Juice
Baked Ham with
Grapefruit*
Scrambled Eggs
Hot Biscuits
Honey Butter

Molded Fresh Grapefruit
and Apple Salad*
Pissaladière*
Old-Fashioned Chocolate
Fudge*
Iced Tea

Ham Mousse*
Cheese-Stuffed Apple
Salad* with Fresh
Orange French
Dressing*
Popovers   Butter
Ginger Marmalade

Meat Fritters*
Agourotomatosalata (Tomato
and Cucumber Salad)*
Vasilopita (Sweet Bread)*
Kafes (Greek Coffee)*

Liver, Tomato and
Cream-Cheese Loaf*
Melba Toast
Melitzanosalata
(Eggplant Salad)*
Ogmenapuuro (Apple Porridge)*

Bourride (Fish Stew)*
Celery, Carrot and Green
Pepper Sticks
Tangerine Frappé*
Hirvensarvet (Antler
Cookies)*

Sliced Swiss Cheese
Potatoes and Dab*
Coleslaw
Cranberry Applesauce

Frankfurter Tetrazzini*
Fresh Grape and Plum Salad*
Espresso

Molded Tuna
and Avocado Salad*
Toasted Cheese Sandwiches
on Rye Bread
Fondant-Dipped Almonds*

Marklösschen
(Marrow Dumplings
in Consommé)*
Salata (Greek Salad)*
Crackers
Pura (Nut Pastries)*

Italian Garlic Soup*
Deviled Egg Salad*
Seeded Bread Sticks
Apple Flan*

Quiche Lorraine*
Orange Ginger-Ale Mold*
with Fresh-Grapefruit
Salad Dressing*
Crisp Rye Wafers

Hamburgers on Toasted Buns
Sauerkrautsalat
(Sauerkraut Salad)*
Gingered Melon*

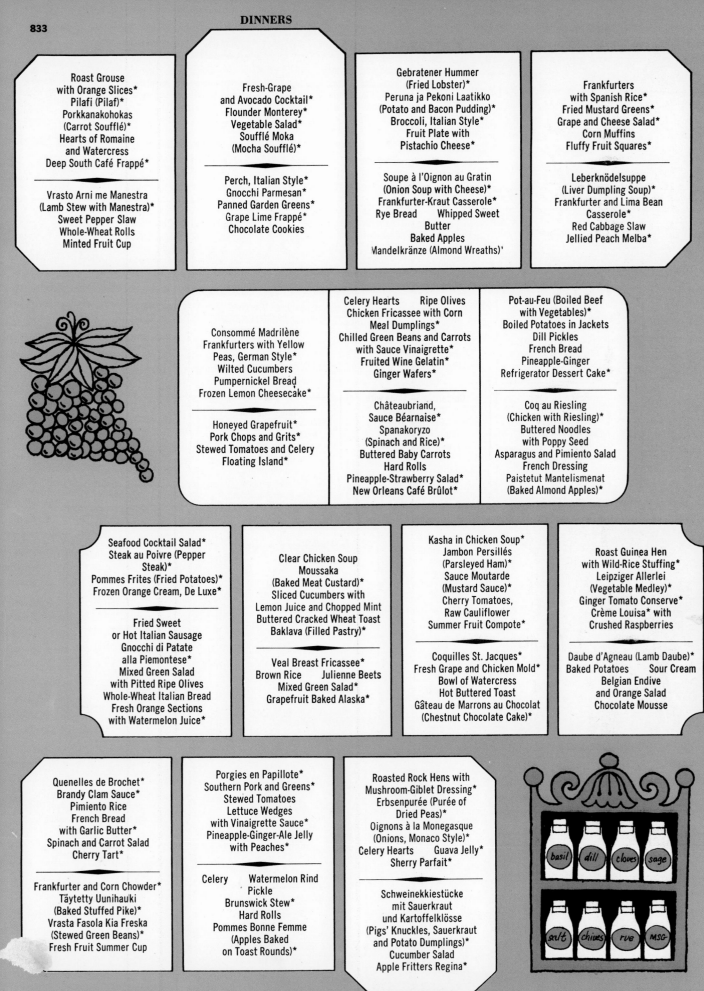

Roast Grouse
with Orange Slices*
Pilafi (Pilaf)*
Porkkanakohokas
(Carrot Soufflé)*
Hearts of Romaine
and Watercress
Deep South Café Frappé*

Vrasto Arni me Manestra
(Lamb Stew with Manestra)*
Sweet Pepper Slaw
Whole-Wheat Rolls
Minted Fruit Cup

Fresh-Grape
and Avocado Cocktail*
Flounder Monterey*
Vegetable Salad*
Soufflé Moka
(Mocha Soufflé)*

Perch, Italian Style*
Gnocchi Parmesan*
Panned Garden Greens*
Grape Lime Frappé*
Chocolate Cookies

Gebratener Hummer
(Fried Lobster)*
Peruna ja Pekoni Laatikko
(Potato and Bacon Pudding)*
Broccoli, Italian Style*
Fruit Plate with
Pistachio Cheese*

Soupe à l'Oignon au Gratin
(Onion Soup with Cheese)*
Frankfurter-Kraut Casserole*
Rye Bread   Whipped Sweet
Butter
Baked Apples
Mandelkränze (Almond Wreaths)'

Frankfurters
with Spanish Rice*
Fried Mustard Greens*
Grape and Cheese Salad*
Corn Muffins
Fluffy Fruit Squares*

Leberknödelsuppe
(Liver Dumpling Soup)*
Frankfurter and Lima Bean
Casserole*
Red Cabbage Slaw
Jellied Peach Melba*

Consommé Madrilène
Frankfurters with Yellow
Peas, German Style*
Wilted Cucumbers
Pumpernickel Bread
Frozen Lemon Cheesecake*

Honeyed Grapefruit*
Pork Chops and Grits*
Stewed Tomatoes and Celery
Floating Island*

Celery Hearts   Ripe Olives
Chicken Fricassee with Corn
Meal Dumplings*
Chilled Green Beans and Carrots
with Sauce Vinaigrette*
Fruited Wine Gelatin*
Ginger Wafers*

Châteaubriand,
Sauce Béarnaise*
Spanakoryzo
(Spinach and Rice)*
Buttered Baby Carrots
Hard Rolls
Pineapple-Strawberry Salad*
New Orleans Café Brûlot*

Pot-au-Feu (Boiled Beef
with Vegetables)*
Boiled Potatoes in Jackets
Dill Pickles
French Bread
Pineapple-Ginger
Refrigerator Dessert Cake*

Coq au Riesling
(Chicken with Riesling)*
Buttered Noodles
with Poppy Seed
Asparagus and Pimiento Salad
French Dressing
Paistetut Mantelismenat
(Baked Almond Apples)*

Seafood Cocktail Salad*
Steak au Poivre (Pepper
Steak)*
Pommes Frites (Fried Potatoes)*
Frozen Orange Cream, De Luxe*

Fried Sweet
or Hot Italian Sausage
Gnocchi di Patate
alla Piemontese*
Mixed Green Salad
with Pitted Ripe Olives
Whole-Wheat Italian Bread
Fresh Orange Sections
with Watermelon Juice*

Clear Chicken Soup
Moussaka
(Baked Meat Custard)*
Sliced Cucumbers with
Lemon Juice and Chopped Mint
Buttered Cracked Wheat Toast
Baklava (Filled Pastry)*

Veal Breast Fricassee*
Brown Rice   Julienne Beets
Mixed Green Salad*
Grapefruit Baked Alaska*

Kasha in Chicken Soup*
Jambon Persillés
(Parsleyed Ham)*
Sauce Moutarde
(Mustard Sauce)*
Cherry Tomatoes,
Raw Cauliflower
Summer Fruit Compote*

Coquilles St. Jacques*
Fresh Grape and Chicken Mold*
Bowl of Watercress
Hot Buttered Toast
Gâteau de Marrons au Chocolat
(Chestnut Chocolate Cake)*

Roast Guinea Hen
with Wild-Rice Stuffing*
Leipziger Allerlei
(Vegetable Medley)*
Ginger Tomato Conserve*
Crème Louisa* with
Crushed Raspberries

Daube d'Agneau (Lamb Daube)*
Baked Potatoes   Sour Cream
Belgian Endive
and Orange Salad
Chocolate Mousse

Quenelles de Brochet*
Brandy Clam Sauce*
Pimiento Rice
French Bread
with Garlic Butter*
Spinach and Carrot Salad
Cherry Tart*

Frankfurter and Corn Chowder*
Täytetty Uunihauki
(Baked Stuffed Pike)*
Vrasta Fasola Kia Freska
(Stewed Green Beans)*
Fresh Fruit Summer Cup

Porgies en Papillote*
Southern Pork and Greens*
Stewed Tomatoes
Lettuce Wedges
with Vinaigrette Sauce*
Pineapple-Ginger-Ale Jelly
with Peaches*

Celery   Watermelon Rind
Pickle
Brunswick Stew*
Hard Rolls
Pommes Bonne Femme
(Apples Baked
on Toast Rounds)*

Roasted Rock Hens with
Mushroom-Giblet Dressing*
Erbsenpurée (Purée of
Dried Peas)*
Oignons à la Monegasque
(Onions, Monaco Style)*
Celery Hearts   Guava Jelly*
Sherry Parfait*

Schweinekkiestücke
mit Sauerkraut
und Kartoffelklösse
(Pigs' Knuckles, Sauerkraut
and Potato Dumplings)*
Cucumber Salad
Apple Fritters Regina*

basil   dill   cloves   sage

salt   chives   rye   MSG

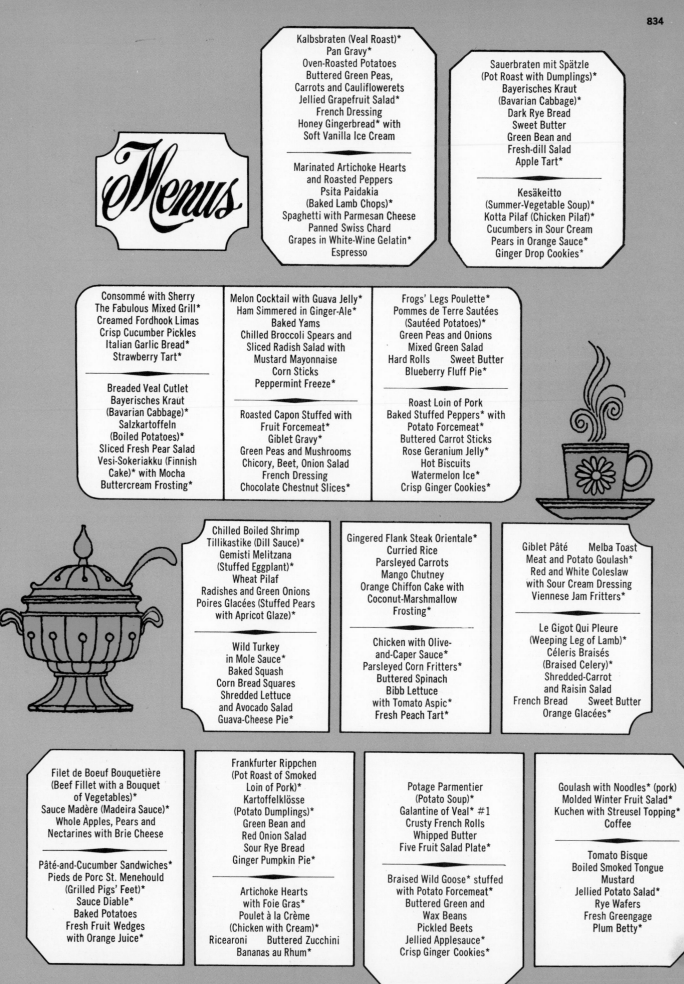

Menus

Kalbsbraten (Veal Roast)*
Pan Gravy*
Oven-Roasted Potatoes
Buttered Green Peas,
Carrots and Cauliflowerets
Jellied Grapefruit Salad*
French Dressing
Honey Gingerbread* with
Soft Vanilla Ice Cream

———

Marinated Artichoke Hearts
and Roasted Peppers
Psita Paidakia
(Baked Lamb Chops)*
Spaghetti with Parmesan Cheese
Panned Swiss Chard
Grapes in White-Wine Gelatin*
Espresso

Sauerbraten mit Spätzle
(Pot Roast with Dumplings)*
Bayerisches Kraut
(Bavarian Cabbage)*
Dark Rye Bread
Sweet Butter
Green Bean and
Fresh-dill Salad
Apple Tart*

———

Kesäkeitto
(Summer-Vegetable Soup)*
Kotta Pilaf (Chicken Pilaf)*
Cucumbers in Sour Cream
Pears in Orange Sauce*
Ginger Drop Cookies*

Consommé with Sherry
The Fabulous Mixed Grill*
Creamed Fordhook Limas
Crisp Cucumber Pickles
Italian Garlic Bread*
Strawberry Tart*

———

Breaded Veal Cutlet
Bayerisches Kraut
(Bavarian Cabbage)*
Salzkartoffeln
(Boiled Potatoes)*
Sliced Fresh Pear Salad
Vesi-Sokeriakku (Finnish
Cake)* with Mocha
Buttercream Frosting*

Melon Cocktail with Guava Jelly*
Ham Simmered in Ginger-Ale*
Baked Yams
Chilled Broccoli Spears and
Sliced Radish Salad with
Mustard Mayonnaise
Corn Sticks
Peppermint Freeze*

———

Roasted Capon Stuffed with
Fruit Forcemeat*
Giblet Gravy*
Green Peas and Mushrooms
Chicory, Beet, Onion Salad
French Dressing
Chocolate Chestnut Slices*

Frogs' Legs Poulette*
Pommes de Terre Sautées
(Sautéed Potatoes)*
Green Peas and Onions
Mixed Green Salad
Hard Rolls   Sweet Butter
Blueberry Fluff Pie*

———

Roast Loin of Pork
Baked Stuffed Peppers* with
Potato Forcemeat*
Buttered Carrot Sticks
Rose Geranium Jelly*
Hot Biscuits
Watermelon Ice*
Crisp Ginger Cookies*

Chilled Boiled Shrimp
Tillikastike (Dill Sauce)*
Gemisti Melitzana
(Stuffed Eggplant)*
Wheat Pilaf
Radishes and Green Onions
Poires Glacées (Stuffed Pears
with Apricot Glaze)*

———

Wild Turkey
in Mole Sauce*
Baked Squash
Corn Bread Squares
Shredded Lettuce
and Avocado Salad
Guava-Cheese Pie*

Gingered Flank Steak Orientale*
Curried Rice
Parsleyed Carrots
Mango Chutney
Orange Chiffon Cake with
Coconut-Marshmallow
Frosting*

———

Chicken with Olive-
and-Caper Sauce*
Parsleyed Corn Fritters*
Buttered Spinach
Bibb Lettuce
with Tomato Aspic*
Fresh Peach Tart*

Giblet Pâté   Melba Toast
Meat and Potato Goulash*
Red and White Coleslaw
with Sour Cream Dressing
Viennese Jam Fritters*

———

Le Gigot Qui Pleure
(Weeping Leg of Lamb)*
Céleris Braisés
(Braised Celery)*
Shredded-Carrot
and Raisin Salad
French Bread   Sweet Butter
Orange Glacées*

Filet de Boeuf Bouquetière
(Beef Fillet with a Bouquet
of Vegetables)*
Sauce Madère (Madeira Sauce)*
Whole Apples, Pears and
Nectarines with Brie Cheese

———

Pâté-and-Cucumber Sandwiches*
Pieds de Porc St. Menehould
(Grilled Pigs' Feet)*
Sauce Diable*
Baked Potatoes
Fresh Fruit Wedges
with Orange Juice*

Frankfurter Rippchen
(Pot Roast of Smoked
Loin of Pork)*
Kartoffelklösse
(Potato Dumplings)*
Green Bean and
Red Onion Salad
Sour Rye Bread
Ginger Pumpkin Pie*

———

Artichoke Hearts
with Foie Gras*
Poulet à la Crème
(Chicken with Cream)*
Ricearoni   Buttered Zucchini
Bananas au Rhum*

Potage Parmentier
(Potato Soup)*
Galantine of Veal* #1
Crusty French Rolls
Whipped Butter
Five Fruit Salad Plate*

———

Braised Wild Goose* stuffed
with Potato Forcemeat*
Buttered Green and
Wax Beans
Pickled Beets
Jellied Applesauce*
Crisp Ginger Cookies*

Goulash with Noodles* (pork)
Molded Winter Fruit Salad*
Kuchen with Streusel Topping*
Coffee

———

Tomato Bisque
Boiled Smoked Tongue
Mustard
Jellied Potato Salad*
Rye Wafers
Fresh Greengage
Plum Betty*

Avgolemono Soupa
(Egg-Lemon Soup)*
Vrasto Arni me Fava
(Stewed Lamb and Fava Beans)*
Sesame Seed Wafers
Lettuce, Olive, Anchovy Salad
Galotoboureko
(Farina Pastries)*
Kafes (Greek Coffee)*

Canards aux Navets
(Ducklings with Turnips)*
Wild Rice
Gooseberry Sauce*
Waldorf Salad
Baba au Rhum (Rum Cake)*

Garbure Basque (Ham, Sausage,
and Bean Soup
with Vegetables)*
Seeded Hard Rolls   Butter
Flan de Piña (Pineapple
Caramel Custard)*
Ginger Cutouts*

Barbecued Turkey
Kartoffelsalat
(Potato Salad)*
Sliced Tomatoes, Cucumbers,
and Green Peppers
Buttered Brown and Serve
Dinner Rolls
Fresh Fruit Medley*

Clam Juice Cocktail
Quiche de Langouste
(Lobster Pie)*
Tomatoes Stuffed with
Marinated Cucumbers
on Watercress
Blackberry Flummery*
Sugar Cookies

Celery   Pickles
Cajun Crab Gumbo* Rice
Sourdough Bread   Butter
Guava Pecan Pie*

Potage au Cresson
(Watercress Soup)*
Garlic Ginger Shrimps*
Chinese Cabbage, Watercress,
and Fresh Pineapple Salad
Corn Chips
Sherry Jelly*
Coconut Cookies

Chicken Stew with Dumplings*
Buttered Mixed Vegetables
Romaine Hearts and
Cherry Tomatoes
Old Alabama Fruitcake
à la Mode*

Liha ja Perunamureke
(Sliced Beef and Potato Loaf)*
Cabbage and Apple Salad
Rye Rolls   Butter
Coffee Ice Cream
Ginger Cutouts*

Faki Soupa (Lentil Soup)*
Giouvarlaka Avgolemono
(Meatballs with
Egg-Lemon Sauce)*
Pilaf*
Celery   Greek Olives
Pickled Peppers
Peach, Plum, and
Apricot Medley*

Broiled Salmon with Herbs*
Kolokythia Krokettes
(Zucchini Pancakes)*
Corn on the Cob
Garlic Butter*
Ginger-Ale Fruit Mold*

Steak Bordelaise*
Moelle Pochée
(Poached Marrow)*
Duchess Potatoes
Green Peas with Mushrooms
Endive, Mandarin Orange,
and Onion Salad
French Dressing
Crêpes Suzette*

Ktenia me Ryzi
(Scallops with Rice)*
Spinach Salad Mold with Ham*
Corn Muffins
Fresh-Grape and
Lemon-Ice Cup*

Sherry Tomato Bouillon*
Pan-Fried Trout with
Anchovy Fillets*
Creamed Cauliflower
Gâteau Praliné*

Ginger Beef*
Mashed Yellow Turnips
Asparagus
Escarole Salad
Blue Cheese Dressing
Vienna Bread
Concord Grape Pie*

Gemisti Kotta (Baked Chicken)*
Rice or Wheat Pilaf
Giblet Gravy*
Cucumbers in Yogurt with
Fresh Mint
Orange-glazed Grape Tarts*

Pâté de Foie Gras in Aspic*
Huhn im Burgunder (Chicken
Cooked in Burgundy Wine)*
Mashed Parsnips
Italian Green Beans
French Bread
Berry Charlotte*

Baked Scrod Paprika*
Achivades Pilafi (Clam Pilaf)*
Wilted Dandelion
or Spinach Salad
Corn Relish
Gooseberry Fool*
Brownies

Chicken Giblets with Rice*
California Chef's Salad*
Assorted Crisp Breads
Butter
Spiced Jelly with Rum Cream*

Veal Goulash*
Green Noodles
Buttered Cut Asparagus
Radishes and Carrot Sticks
Stewed Rhubarb
Elisen Lebkuchen
(Elisen Ginger Cookies)*

Clear Green Turtle Soup
Terrine de Porc, Veau, et
Jambon (Pork and Veal
Pâté with Ham)*
Italian Bread   Whipped Butter
White Asparagus, Romaine
and Cherry Tomato Salad
Swiss Classic*

Beef Goulash*
Noodles with Sour Cream
Brussels Sprouts
Pascal-Celery Slaw
Apple, Plum or Peach Kuchen*

Broiled Chopped
Top Sirloin Steak
Paistetut Sienet
(Fried Mushrooms)*
Mexican Corn
Mixed Green Salad*
Scandinavian Fruit Pudding*

Pan Broiled Shoulder Lamb
Chops with Rosemary
Parsleyed New Potatoes and
Green Peas
Leaf Lettuce, Radish and
Green Onion Salad
Creamy Banana Nut Pie*

Chicken Florentine*
Salade de Tomates
(Tomato Salad)*
Seeded Hard Rolls
Grape Apples*   Whipped Cream

Poulet à l'Estragon (Roast
Chicken with Tarragon)*
Pommes de Terre Sautées
(Sautéed Potatoes)*
Hearts of Lettuce, Peas,
and Pimiento Salad
Tartes aux Fruits avec Crème
Patissière (Fruit Tarts
with Pastry Cream)*

*Recipes for all starred dishes found in this volume.

GENERAL INFORMATION

The Ingredients and Measurements Used in Recipes

All recipes in this book have been tested in the Woman's Day Kitchens with standard American measuring cups (8 ounces = 16 tablespoons), measuring spoons (1 tablespoon = 3 teaspoons), and other standard kitchen equipment. All measurements are level. Liquids are measured in standard 8-ounce glass measuring cups, at eye level.

All sugar is granulated white sugar unless otherwise specified.

All flours, cake and all-purpose, are sifted before measuring unless otherwise specified. No self-rising flour is used.

All baking powder is double-acting baking powder.

All brown sugar is firmly packed when measured.

All confectioners' sugar is sifted before measuring.

All pepper is ground black pepper unless otherwise specified.

Fats and shortening are measured at room temperature, packed firmly into measuring cup and leveled with a straight knife. They are scraped out with a rubber spatula.

Salted butter or margarine, packed in ¼-pound sticks, is used unless otherwise specified. 1 stick = ½ cup = 8 tablespoons = ¼ pound.

1 tall can evaporated milk (14½ ounces) contains 1⅔ cups undiluted evaporated milk. Unsweetened condensed milk is an entirely different product, and cannot be used interchangeably with evaporated milk.

⅓ to ½ teaspoon dried herbs can be substituted for each tablespoon fresh herbs. Crumble herbs before using to release flavor.

Before starting to cook or to bake, read the recipes carefully. Assemble all ingredients and equipment. Follow recipe exactly. Do not increase or decrease recipe unless you are a skilled enough cook to recognize what adjustments must be made as to ingredients, pan sizes, and/or cooking time.

Cooking Temperatures and Times

Cooking temperatures and times are approximate for meat. They depend not only on the weight and kind of meat, but also on its shape, temperature, and its bone and fat contents. A meat thermometer was used in testing.

Cooking times for meats are as recommended by the National Live Stock and Meat Board, 36 Wabash Avenue, Chicago, Illinois 60603.

Oven Temperatures

TEMPERATURES (Degree F.)	TERM
250 to 275	VERY SLOW
300 to 325	SLOW
350 to 375	MODERATE
400 to 425	HOT
450 to 475	VERY HOT
500 to 525	EXTREMELY HOT

Important—Preheat oven for 10 to 15 minutes before placing food in it. Many a cake has been spoiled by being placed in a barely heated oven. Baking times are based on the assumption that the oven is already at the stated temperature.

Check the oven temperature control frequently, especially if baking times vary from those given in recipes. (This can be done with a portable oven thermometer.) If a control is consistently off, call your public utility. They should be able to reset the oven temperature control.

Caloric Values

The caloric values, where mentioned, for each food are based on 100 grams, about 3½ ounces edible portion, as mentioned in Composition of Foods, Agriculture Handbook No. 8, Agricultural Service of the United States Department of Agriculture, Washington, D. C., revised December 1963.